SPIRITS OF SALTS

a working guide to old photographic processes

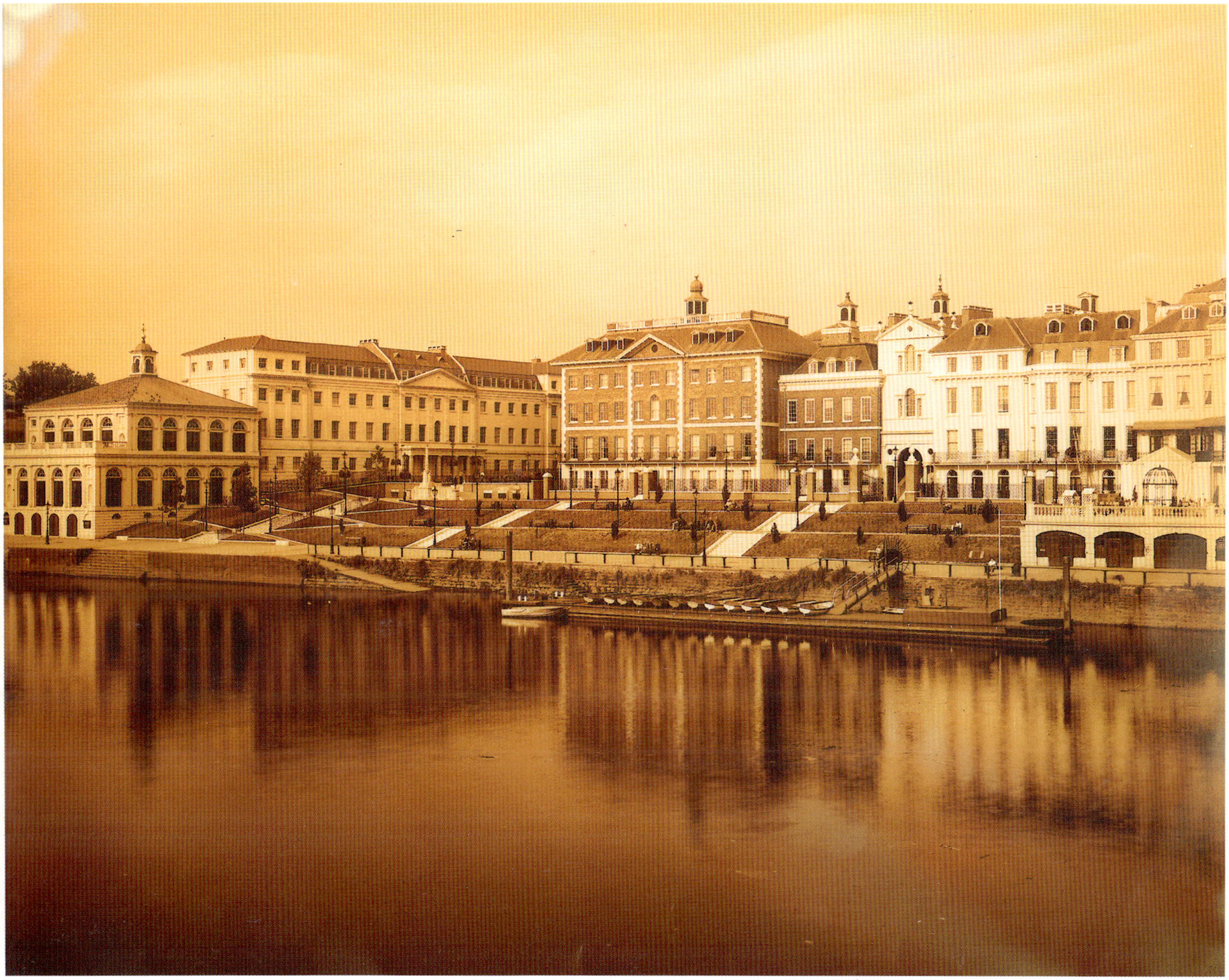

Randall Webb & Martin Reed

Argentum

First published 1999 by Argentum, an imprint of
Aurum Press Ltd, 25 Bedford Avenue, London, WC1B 3AT.

A catalogue record for this book is available
from the British Library.

ISBN 1-902538-05-6

Design by Martin Reed & Randall Webb
Layout by Martin Reed @ Silverprint
Origination - Graphic Ideas, London, N1
Printed in Singapore by Imago

Acknowledgements

It is impossible to complete a project such as this without calling upon the support, the expertise and, occasionally, the wisdom of a large number of friends and colleagues. This one is certainly no exception. So, in no particular order, we would like to go some way towards repaying these favours with a thank you.

Included in a long list are: our families, especially Janice, Howard, Pilar and Nigel for all their advice and encouragement; all those who generously allowed us to reproduce their images; students past and present; Silverprint for the use of its production facilities; all the staff at Silverprint; and all the members of the 120 Group for their continual encouragement.

There are several individuals who gave us specific and invaluable advice.
They are: Michael Maunder, Mike Ware, Mike Shorter, Amanda Lane, Gerard Anniere, Peter Strachan, Terry Greaves and at the RPS in Bath, Debbie Ireland.

Thanks also to Joanne Kaar, the paper maker from Thurso, who allowed us to photograph her paper making course on Orkney.

And a special thank you to a small, select group from colleges, universities and museums in London and the south of England. They are Andy Malone at Canterbury, Clair Williams at Portsmouth, Graham Murrell at St. Martin's, Jill Wilkinson at the Julia Margaret Cameron Trust, and Andrew Ashmore and Maureen Marron at the Museum of the Moving Image.

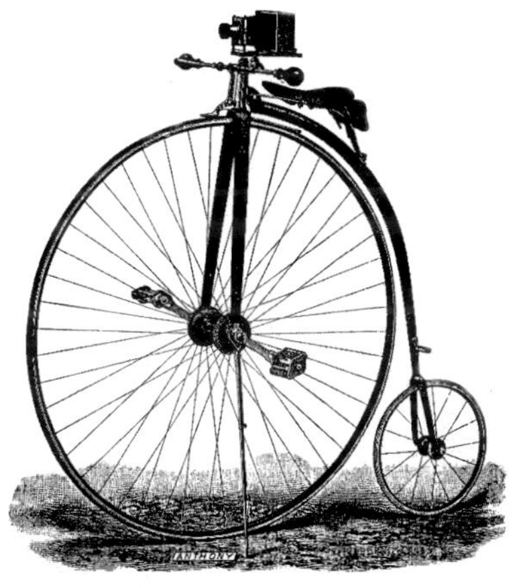

CONTENTS

1 Using the manual
page 7

2 Historical notes
page 11

3 Old vs. current processes
page 13

4 Equipment
page 15

5 Papers
page 19

6 Chemicals
page 27

7 Coating techniques
page 33

8 Exposing the print
page 37

9 Making contact negatives
page 39

10 Salt printing
page 47

11 Albumen printing
page 57

12 Printing-out paper
page 61

13 Van Dyke prints & Kallitypes
page 63

14 Cyanotype
page 71

15 Pellet prints
page 79

16 Platinum & palladium printing
page 81

17 Bromoil
page 89

18 Bromoil transfer
page 97

19 Oil printing
page 99

20 Carbon printing

page 101

21 Gum printing

page 109

22 Casein printing

page 115

23 Photo mechanical printingg

page 117

24 Photo etching

page 119

25 Photo gravure

page 125

26 Photo silkscreen printing

page 133

27 Cliche Verre

page 139

28 Bleach-etch

page 143

29 Solvent transfer

page 145

30 Printing on other materials

page 147

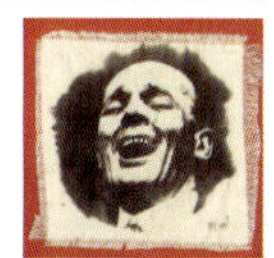

31 Combination printing

page 151

32 Presentation & editions

page 153

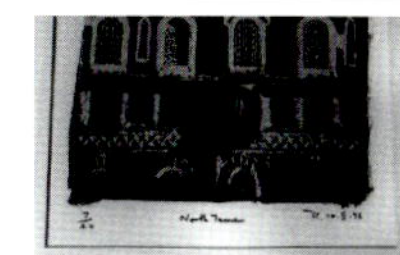

33 Resources

page 155

34 Index

page 160

Using the manual 1

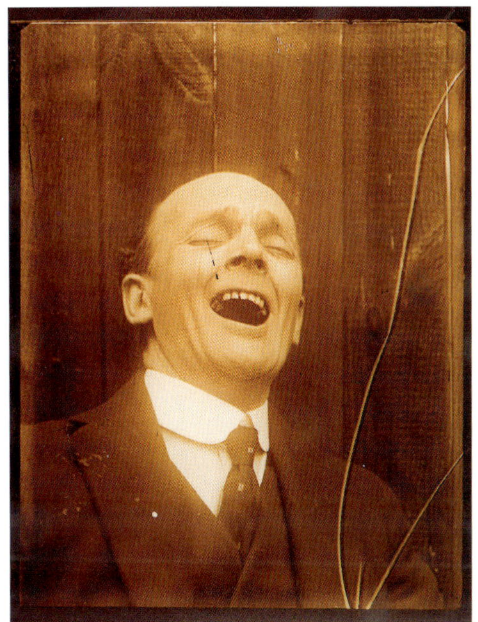

Cousin Cyril. Glass plate negative from 1916 on modern printing out paper.

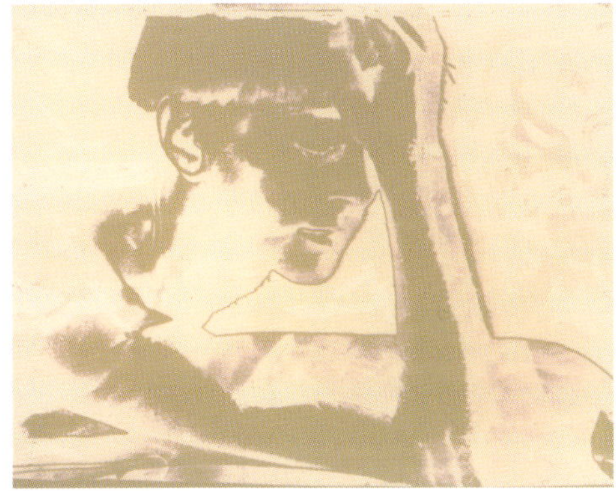

Modern sabattier and bas-relief negative, printed out on resin coated Multigrade paper. Fixed but not developed. It is not normally recognised that most modern silver gelatin papers will print out either in the sun or by UV lamp. The colours are dependent on the particular paper used. See also the printed out image overleaf.

This manual has been written for one simple reason. It satisfies an unfulfilled need. We felt that there was a demand for a simple darkroom manual giving a comprehensive survey of the history, theory and practice of all the ways of putting photographic images on paper, as well as on other surfaces such as fabric, ceramics, wood, metal and glass. It should contain reference only to those processes that are able to be done by the average competent photographer or printmaker. It should also avoid those processes that are either unsafe, impractical or for which materials are no longer available and which are of academic interest only. It should (if such a thing is possible) bridge the gap between an illustrated 'coffee table' book for the general reader and a textbook for the specialised reader to dip into for specific reference.

It comes from teaching photographers and students of every age from seven to seventy, from teaching in primary schools, museums, photographic colleges and art schools; from conducting workshops all round the country; from giving demonstrations in draughty church halls on wet winter evenings. It also arises from the accumulated experience of selling the materials for alternative photographic printing to students of all kinds, anxious to unravel the mysteries of early printing techniques. From this experience we have attempted to make some reasoned assumptions about our readers, what they are likely to require from a textbook such as this and if possible, the uses to which they may put their newly acquired knowledge. Having identified a number of possible categories of readership, we hope to supply the information they need as succinctly as we can.

Many of our readers will be students, wanting to expand the range of their techniques or to find new ways of presenting their course projects. There will be teachers who may not have had the time or the opportunity to attend workshops, or to carry out the lengthy research necessary to teach the basics of alternative processing. There may be professional photographers looking for new ways to present their work to prospective clients. Or serious amateur photographers with a desire to cross the creative divide between conventional photography and that of the artist printmaker. Similarly, there are many printmakers who have a need to use camera-based images in their own hand-drawn or hand-painted work. We hope they find plenty to interest them.

Collectors of old prints and photographs who may not wish to practise any of the methods in the manual may find it a useful source of information on their particular area of interest. For example, they may have heard about cyanotypes but it would be much more useful if they knew how they were made. Whatever their reasons are for reading this manual we hope they find something useful or entertaining. This applies to all those experts who will no doubt find great pleasure in looking for the mistakes or pointing out that we have given the wrong formula! A work such as this cannot be, however, represented, as the equivalent of some

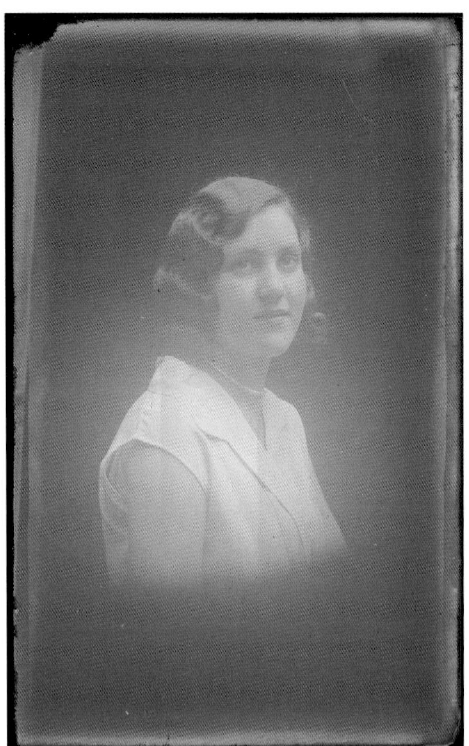

Glass plate negative from a photographers studio in Clapham, about 1935. Printed out in sunlight on modern Ilford Galerie grade 3 photographic paper. Unprocessed, and therefore unstable, so must be viewed by low artificial light. Many enlarging papers will print-out in this way, particularly warmer tone papers, and there are some specifically designed for printing-out and will give the strongest image density. Covered in [12 . Printing-out paper].

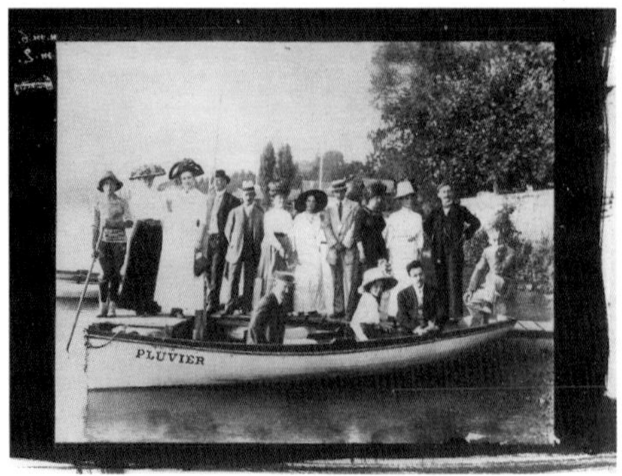

Modern cyanotype print from glass plate negative, dating from the start of the 20'th century. Fabriano 100% cotton paper.

form of magic bullet. What we hope it will do is to help brush away many of the myths that have grown up around the subject.

It is an account of the development of photographic printing technology from the earliest days of the art and craft of the process, and an attempt to de-mystify what has always been a straightforward means of producing images mechanically, using the action of light on a few basic substances such as silver and iron.

It would be comforting to imagine that art and alchemy have combined in some magical way to produce this phenomenon that we know as photography. Sadly, as in the case of most great inventions this is not how it happened. The truth is more mundane, with a number of inventors and craftsmen blundering on, in the hope of improving on the previous ways of presenting a true two-dimensional image of the world around them. Their motives have often been commercial rather than scientific or artistic.

There are countless books on early photographic processes, and the contemporary records vary from the precise to the downright vague. Many of the materials, products and terminologies used are no longer available - how many people now would recognise muriatic acid if they saw it? There is a profusion of recent books on the most popular processes such as platinum and gum printing, which tend to cover only one process in great detail and reflect the authors' own specialist interests. Thus it is possible that an author who has spent a long time investigating, say, kallitype or platinum, may be less than comfortable with photo silkscreen or bromoil transfer. In this manual we tend to live dangerously by describing the complete range!

A more pressing problem for the reader of these publications is one of readability. A writer who produces a book on one subject only, usually has to fill it with a lot of words and even more spurious detail. These latest accounts range from the obvious home spun variety - take a teaspoonful of potassium dichromate and make a saturated solution - to the self-consciously academic doctoral thesis. Most photographers in our experience assume that chemicals come in bottles marked Ilford or Kodak and have instructions on the side for mixing. It is highly unlikely that the average photographer or darkroom worker would have any need for the following gem of information:

$$FE_2\ (C_2O_4)_3\ \text{UV light / Time} > FE\ (C_2O_4).$$

This is part of the description of the platinum process and only comprehensible to a chemist. It is more effective and not in the least bit patronising to describe silver printing-out processes in simple terms. Thus we can say, without too much head-scratching, that silver nitrate, when exposed to ultra violet light, reverts back to microscopically small particles of dark metallic silver to produce an image. Finding your way through a treatise on chemistry or a lengthy piece of historical research can be daunting. Translating this into practical terms can be even worse.

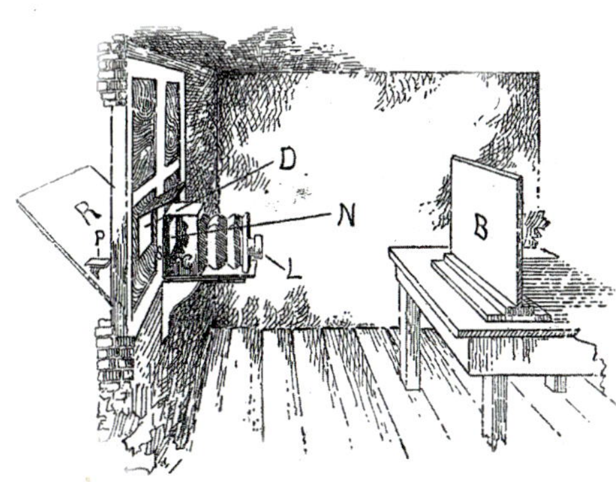

An early daylight enlarger.

Re-creating defunct or obsolete processes quite often needs recourse to currently available substitutes in terms of chemicals and other materials. This is not unreasonable. All the processes described in this manual are, wherever possible, the genuine articles as practised in their original form and can be managed in a darkroom, classroom, studio, or on a kitchen table and are the result of practical experience.

In producing this work, we have used as our watchwords clarity, directness, accessibility, and above all, simplicity. The text has been used to give the reader the impression of being talked through a classroom demonstration at the same time trying to anticipate any difficulties or uncertainties by frequent cross references to other relevant sections. Much of what you do will be somewhat unfamiliar, and we suggest you make a thorough study of the contents of the early chapters on negatives, coating, exposing, paper etc. There are two things you should always bear in mind;

Don't be put off by the chemistry. Chemicals, if used sensibly, are not dangerous and we do not intend to confuse you with chemical science.

Remember that for many processes the sun is the best form of ultra-violet light.

For most of the method sections in the manual we have maintained a standard format;

1 The introduction which contains a brief historical overview of the process. The reading lists will give you access to much more historical and technical background if you need it.

2 Advantages and disadvantages. This will give you some idea of the technical and aesthetic possibilities of each process and how they compare with conventional photographic printing.

3 The shopping lists may appear to be slightly superfluous, but they are in fact derived from bitter experience. If you turn up to run a workshop and have forgotten the silver nitrate, you feel like the plumber's mate who has left the spanners behind.

4 The advice on the sort of negative you will need should be used in conjunction with the earlier chapter on making negatives, whether you intend to judge them by inspection or by using a densitometer.

5 On the question of the choice of paper most suited to the particular process you intend to use, we have made suggestions in the form of a quick reference table. Once you are familiar with a process we suggest you experiment with other papers which may give you an unusual or more pleasing result.

Remember that you are dealing with a somewhat crude early technology. It is not an exact science. Even temperamental media such as platinum and palladium will work on out of the way papers. They may not look like Ilford fibre-based Multigrade, but they could be an artistic breakthrough. If you want your images to look like C41 prints then perhaps you should send them to Boots.

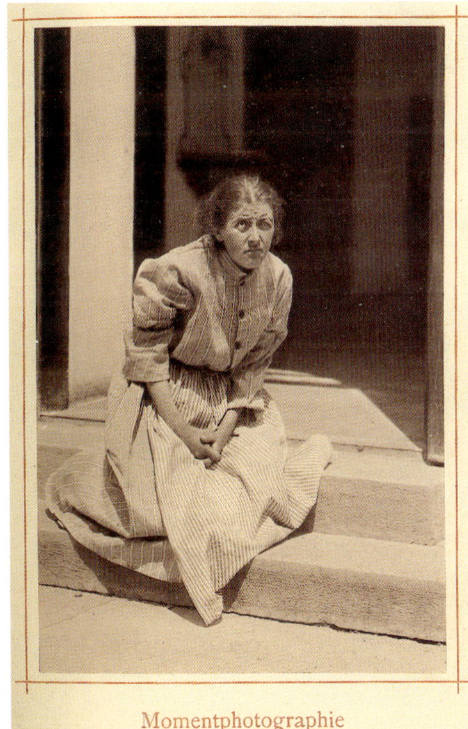

Momentphotographie. Illustration from Eders Yearbook, 1890, collotype of original POP print. Collotype is now practised by only a handful of people in the world. It occupies a place somewhere between bromoil and gravure. An inked up reticulated gelatin matrix on glass or film is printed in a proofing press.

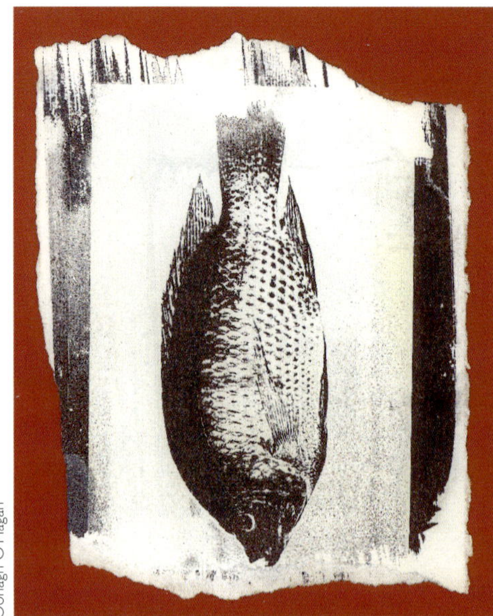
Oonagh O'Hagan

Cyanotype. First attempt at using this process by a non-photographer. Image copied onto acetate as negative in a photocopier.

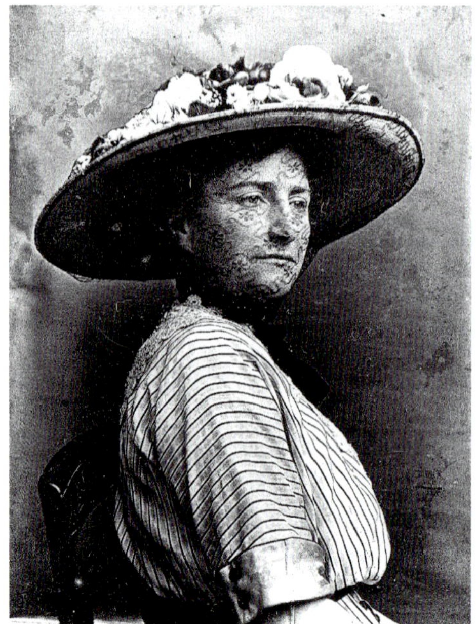
High contrast positive made in contact with glass plate negative. From original negative dated 1916.

6 We are assuming a basic knowledge of standard darkroom techniques, ie use of conventional photographic papers, enlarging and wet processing. If you need to brush up in this area there are a few suggested texts in the bibliography.

7 The method sections are obviously the longest sections and are as self contained as possible, We have tried to anticipate any problems you may encounter and have cross referenced to the earlier chapters when we think it may be necessary. There is frequent cross-referencing to other chapters, and we have used the convention [(chap. no **.** (chap name)], eg [12 **.** Kallitype].

8 One other word of advice. Don't try to start the whole experience by picking the most difficult process. Start with the simplest and progress to the harder ones. The skills acquired from the easy methods will be very useful at a later stage. Cyanotypes are the traditional grounding for newcomers to old processes. They are cheap, easy and require few chemicals or equipment. Also, the chemicals you use double up for other processes.

We hope this manual contains enough to satisfy the needs of both photographers, who are notoriously conservative, as well as the devotees of the avant-garde and wild experimentation.

Finally, a few words on the illustrations. Although many of the processes date from the last century, we have tried where possible to avoid the 19'th century aesthetic, especially in terms of style and subject matter. It is very easy to be seduced into producing some form of pastiche of the work of the turn of the century high pictorialists and forget we are at the end of the 20'th century and not the 19'th. We have also tried not to overload the pages with too many old favourites.

The pictures come from various sources. Our guest contributors are all established photographers and print makers with a firm commitment to the use of alternative processes in a modern context. The other images are a selection of work by the author which could be safely described as experiments on paper.

The 'how-to-hold-a-brush' photographs were taken purposely for this manual and include hands and fingers generously donated by a few friends in the interest of science or art.

All the black and white line drawings have been culled from long out of date catalogues as a tribute to that vast, anonymous army of engravers who provided illustrations for the printed page before the advent of half tone reproductions.

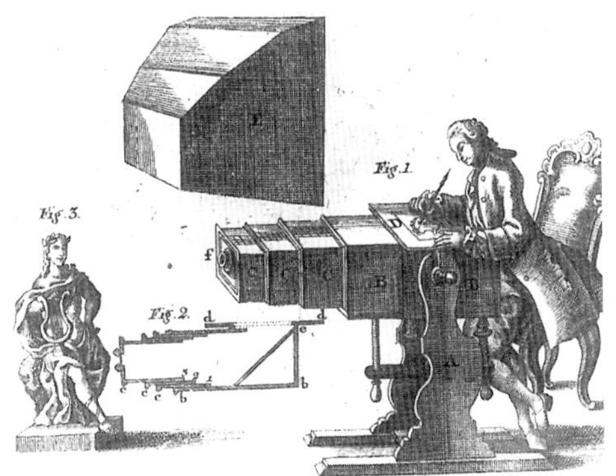

An early device used by artists to obtain an accurate rendering of scenes from nature by means of tracing an image projected onto paper.

At the beginning of the nineteenth century, the primitive technology required to make photographs as we now know them was already in place. All it needed was to bring the various component parts together to make the whole process possible.

Artists had been using the camera obscura and the camera lucida to project images on to a flat plane via a simple lens. The Italian painter Canaletto used this principle to enhance the perspectives of his paintings of Venice.

It was also known that certain compounds of silver darkened when exposed for a period of time to sunlight. What in fact happened was that they reverted back to microscopically small particles of metallic silver. All that was needed was to find a way of bringing these together in order to fix a projected image on to readily available material. And, incidentally, to find a word to describe this new science.

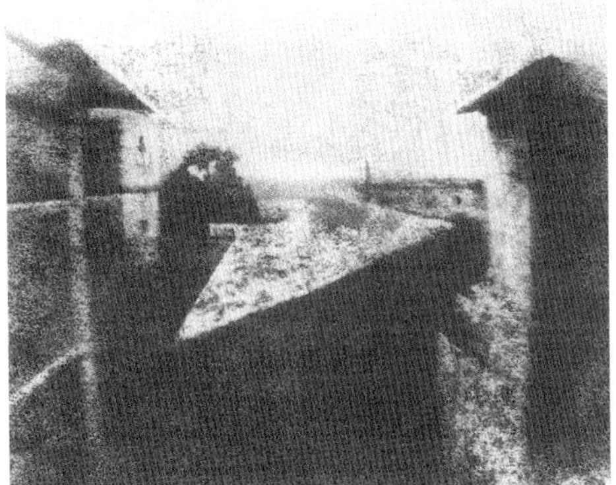

The first photographic image made in a camera by Niephore Niepce, using a zinc plate coated with bitumen of Judea.

For a painter the obvious choice of material on which to present this image would have been a piece of primed canvas. As it happened this was never considered an avenue worth pursuing although very early experiments had been made with leather as a potential medium. An artist using watercolours or pencil drawings would have been more inclined to favour paper. At the time the only means of reproducing images on paper was by engraving a copper plate or a wooden block or by etching a steel or zinc plate with acid and, having rubbed them with ink, pass them in contact with a sheet of paper through a heavy roller press to transfer the ink from the plate or block onto the paper. Thus the only alternative choice of a medium for the photographic process was a copper or zinc plate. The decision as to which method to use was crucial to the evolution of photography. The two main protagonists in what later became at times a bitter struggle to dominate a potentially unlimited commercial market were the French and the British. The French put all their efforts into working with metal plates. Niepce used a pewter plate coated with a substance known to lithographers as Bitumen of Judea, whereas Daguerre preferred to experiment with a copper plate coated with silver. Both of these produced a negative which, when turned at a certain angle to the light would appear as a positive.

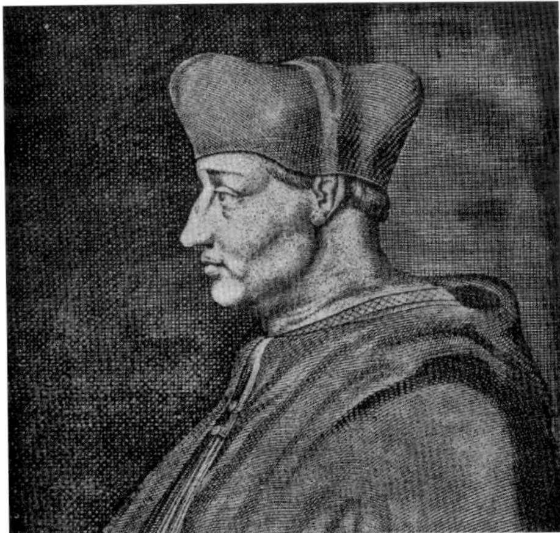

Niephore Niepce - etched plate. This image predates the work of Daguerre and Fox Talbot. It was made by contact printing an etching on paper onto a metal plate coated with bitumen.

The advantage of this method was its relatively 'instant' quality. In a very short time you could have a real picture of yourself or your family without the expense and the tedium of a sitting for a painter. Daguerre took his new invention to America where it became an immediate success. However, its limitations were serious enough to render the French process obsolete within less than twenty years after its introduction. The great disadvantage of Daguerre's images was that they were 'one-offs' and could not be reproduced in large numbers as etchings or engravings could be. They were small and enclosed for protection in an elaborate gilt and leather case, more suitable for standing on a mantel shelf than for hanging in a frame on a wall. Their production involved at one stage holding them

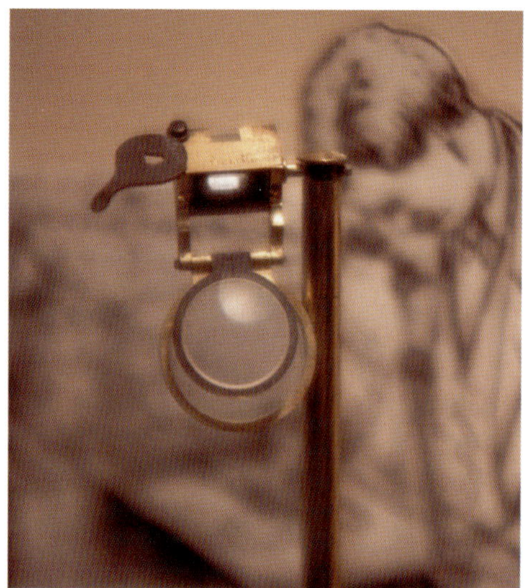

The prism and lenses of the camera lucida, which enabled an artist to trace an accurate drawing of a scene onto paper. This was the alternative to the more common camera obscura.

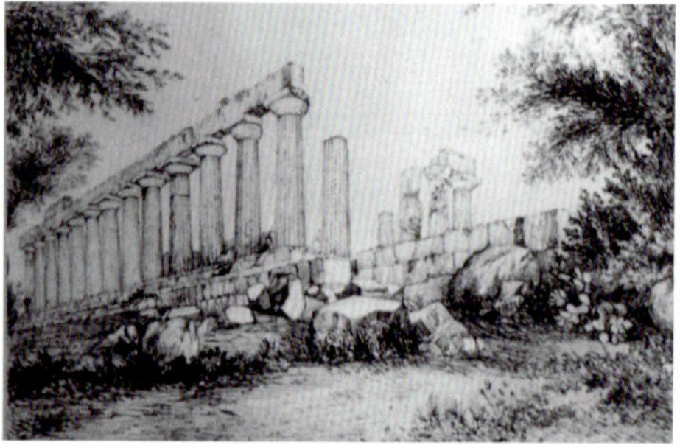

Drawing by Wollaston using the camera lucida. It was his failure to make drawings with this instrument that encouraged Fox Talbot to investigate production of photographic images.

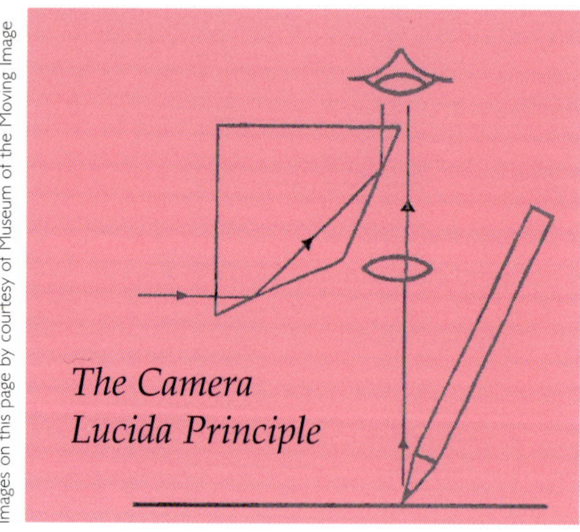

Diagram of the optical principle of camera lucida.

Images on this page by courtesy of Museum of the Moving Image

over mercury vapour which in the primitive conditions of the time was a very hazardous procedure. It is still as dangerous now, which is why there is no chapter in this manual entitled 'Making a Daguerreotype'.

At this point Fox Talbot entered the arena. An indifferent draughtsman and water-colourist, his main concern was to fix an image mechanically onto paper. His invention of the Calotype and the salt print gave us the negative positive process which became the the basis of photographic printing which is still used today. In fact there has been relatively little radical change in silver printing methods since his time. Salt prints were modified to produce albumen prints, which were common currency for much of the nineteenth century. Silver bromide printing took over from albumen, and with an increase in printing speed it was possible to make enlargements by projection in an enlarger. Finally, in the middle of the 20'th century, resin coated and variable contrast papers were introduced. The real technical advances were made in the field of negative making. Paper negatives gave way to wet glass plates, which were followed by dry plates, followed by flexible roll films and cine films for miniature cameras. Finally colour slides and colour negatives completed the picture.

Most of the alternative methods described in this manual were introduced for a variety of reasons. Some were developed as commercial alternatives to the predominant albumen print, or for greater permanence (carbon and platinum). Some appeared as a result of the various 'art' movements at the turn of the century (gum and bromoil). And some were brought in to satisfy the demand for photographs to be reproduced on the printed page (photo etching and photogravure) to replace the hand engraved plates taken from photographs which filled the pages of magazines, newspapers and books.

In the 1930's onwards there was a demand for sharp clear pictures, spearheaded by movements such as the f64 group, and the needs of documentary workers and photojournalists. The older processes became the domain of the salons and art exhibitors. A revival of early processes took place in the late 1960's as the result of work done in the University College of Los Angeles where well known names such as Todd Walker, Darryl Curran, Robert Fichter, Vida Freeman and Robert Heinicken used these processes to produce images in a 'contemporary' style. Eventually platinum and palladium became a regular feature of the work of Irving Penn, George Tice, Robert Mapplethorpe and Dick Arentz. All of these have exhibited over the last few years in the UK. It is interesting to note that few British artists of international stature have exhibited using alternative processes. A few exceptions have been Linda McCartney, (cyanotypes and kallitypes), and David Bailey, (platinum). One or two well known colour photographers have had their work printed by means of a four colour carbon process using a plastic based transfer material to achieve greater permanence than that offered by Ilfochrome or similar. Most of the other practioners have tended to be teachers and students from photographic schools around the country. Not withstanding this, there is still a strong revival which continues to grow.

Old vs. current processes 3

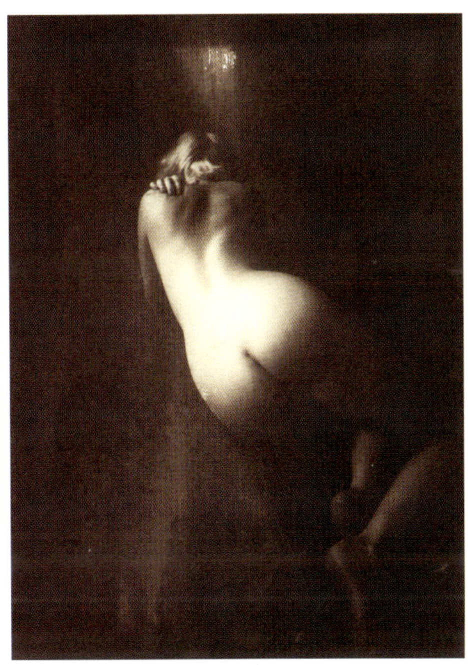

Contact print from 8x10" negative on modern chloro-bromide fibre base paper, selenium toned.

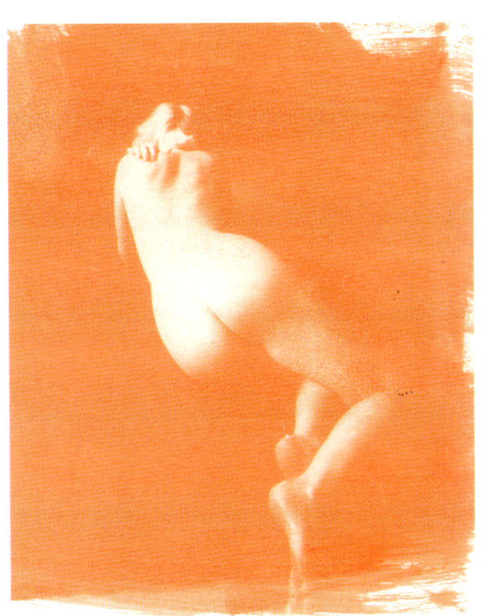

Gum print, single coating, from the same negative.

Now that you have read so far and may have already dipped into one or two of the chapters on the various methods, it would not be unreasonable to ask yourself if this is what you really want to be doing. Or more philosophically, why are you here. A number of explanations come to mind. You may just be a nostalgia freak. You may feel a need to present a completely new way of presenting your work to prospective clients. You may have seen an example of say a bromoil or a platinum print in a book or an exhibition, and would like to know more about the processes. You may have attended an old process workshop and have become hooked on the idea, but don't know where to find the necessary information. You might even know someone who has made a gum print but who has forgotten how they did it. You may be a photographer who has also worked with other forms of printmaking such as etching or silk screen printing and wants to be able to combine pure print making with photographic images. You may be a painter or etcher or embroiderer who wants to incorporate photographic images into other media. You may want to experiment with the idea of printing photographs on materials other than photographic paper such as cloth, T-shirts or wood. You may have considered the possibility that platinum is more exotic than standard photographic paper, and that you could make more money selling your images via old processes. On a grander scale you may feel that you have reached the point where you need to explore the current fashion for crossing the boundaries between pure photography and art printing. Or you may be just curious.

Whatever your reasons, it is worth looking at the possibilities offered by historical and alternative processes. But there is one important consideration that should always be borne in mind. If you have a third rate image, it is unlikely that you are going to improve it by messing it about by way of alternative processes. The best you can get is a manipulated version of a poor quality original. Having said that, there is of course, the possibility that you may have some images that in themselves may not make a prize winning entry for the Royal Photographic Society, but which may, if used as part of a larger montage or combination print, have a validity which would otherwise not have been apparent.

The crux of the matter is that when you have become familiar with old processes, the only factor that determines your output of images is your skill and your creative imagination. As one famous American photographer said, **'there ain't no rules'**. Visually and imaginatively that is. What you may have to face is a decision that you may never have realised you would have to make; are you going to be a print maker who uses camera originated images to work in a mixed media environment, or are you going to remain as a photographer who may venture into a strange world of print-making in the hope that something interesting will turn up? It could be an interesting decision.

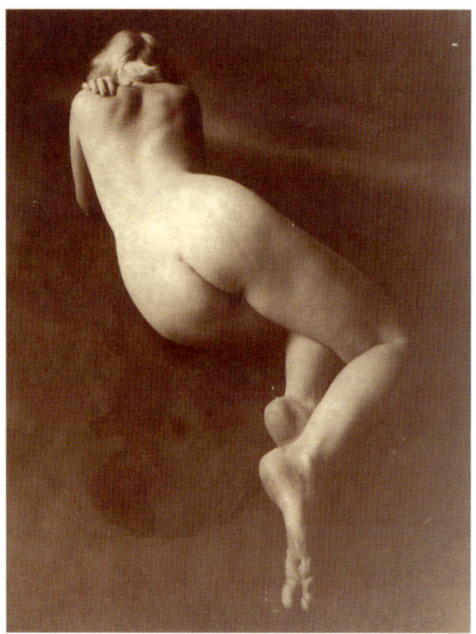

Salt print from the same negative.

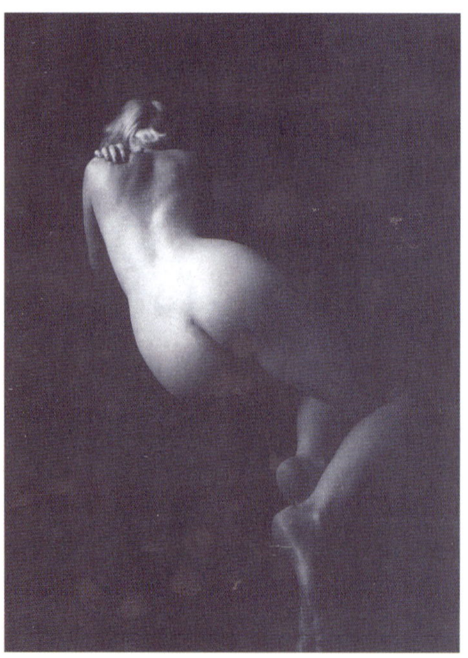

Cyanotype print from the same negative.

Present day conventional printing, both colour and black & white, is the culmination of 170 years of technological development, and it is unlikely that it will improve very much apart from some fine adjustments in various technical aspects. Even with the advent of digital imaging which has already taken over many of the functions of silver based photography, the fact remains that it still needs the presence out there of someone with a camera stuck to his or her face to take the original picture. Even modern Japanese wizardry is unlikely to find substitutes for that. In addition, there will still be a huge demand from individuals and galleries for original images to hang on the wall, not forgetting advertising agents and magazine and book publishers to fill their pages. The one real advantage of using old processes is the facility vastly to enlarge the boundaries of your creative output. A brief survey of present day photography shows a tendency on the part of exhibitors, in camera clubs at all levels and in the professional organisations, to produce work which possesses a depressing degree of creative and visual constipation. Playing about with the colour dials on your enlarger or dabbling with polaroid and infra-red film may not be enough. Nor will pressing the Van Gogh button on your Photoshop programme give you all the answers.

Conventional printing has many obvious merits. The materials are of very high quality and consistency. The use of different papers, developers, base colours, variable contrasts and toners all give rise to a complexity of effects which may not have existed in earlier times. The results are quick. easy and cheap to achieve. They can be made in a darkroom with modern technology under controlled conditions, with a good chance of consistent repetition. From both a technical and aesthetic point of view it is possible to produce a depth of black much greater than with any other process, as well as the potential for manipulating the tonalities of the image. A quick check with a reflection densitometer will confirm this.

Conversely, the possibilities opened up by the use of old processes may convince you that these are in themselves a far greater gain in visual terms which outweigh the immediate advantages of conventional methods. The prospect of printing on hand made paper or cloth, wood, ceramics and glass, to make photos using printers ink or coloured gelatin, to make composite pictures or constructions and installations, prints measured in feet rather than inches, and photographic images that are far removed from anything you have ever imagined before, may persuade you that old processes are really what you wanted to do but had never been able to ask! We repeat, without apology, 'there ain't no rules, and the only limits are those of your own imagination'.

Equipment you will need 4

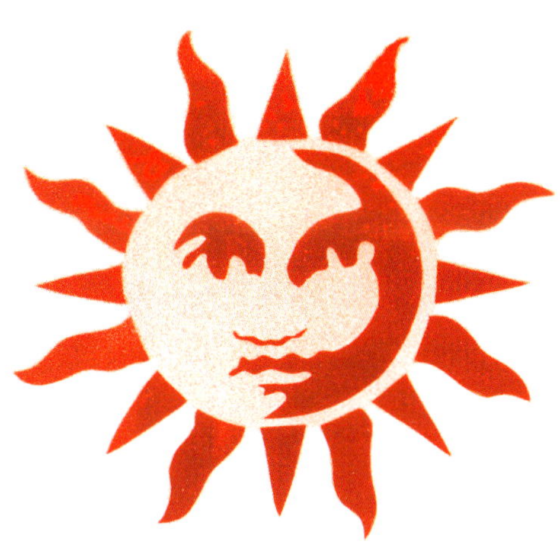

The mention of equipment in a manual on photography computers or hi-fi, usually provides the temptation for the reader to go out and indulge in an orgy of shopping. If you are going to work with old processes you don't really immediately need to acquire a densitometer, a mercury vapour lamp and an expensive printing frame. They may look good on your darkroom shelf but the fact of owning them does not automatically guarantee better results. The best pictures are quite often produced from a couple of dishes, a sink, a few brushes from the DIY shop and a piece of glass. If you eventually get round to etching or gravure you will need access to an etching press, a print studio and some other bits and pieces. You may of course be an equipment freak. In that case buy all you feel you need. Assuming that you are already involved in photography, you will have a camera and probably a simple darkroom with an enlarger and the basic tools for making black and white enlargements. This is all you will need to make the large contact negatives used in most of the old processes. Bear in mind that you are likely to use orthochromatic film (insensitive to red light) so a **red** safelight will be essential. If you're working to a budget, a photographic red bulb (about £5.00) is the minimum.

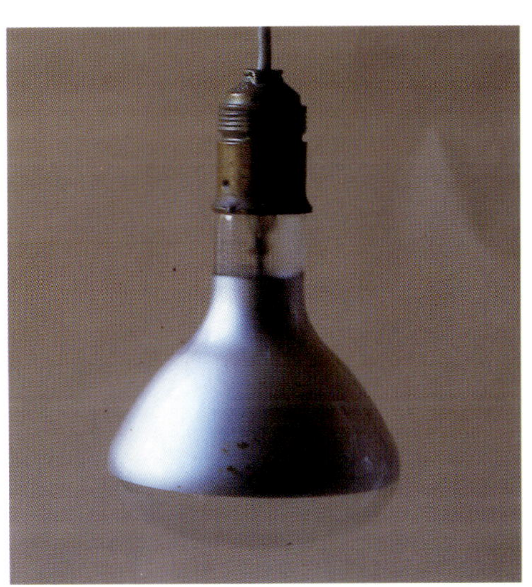

The cheapest form of ultra-violet light is the sun, or you can use a sun-ray lamp.

UV light sources

Rule No. 1: Make sure you don't look directly at any UV light source, especially the sun!

The majority of alternative processes are quite insensitive to visible light, and need the higher energy provided by ultra-violet rays. For the basic printing out processes sunlight is the most historically authentic source of ultra violet light. It is also cheap and readily available! You simply place your printing frame containing the negative and sensitised paper outdoors and wait for it to expose to the correct depth of tone. Unfortunately, daylight varies according to season, time of day, geographical location and cloud cover. The greatest advantage of using sunlight is that you can lie in the garden on a summer afternoon exposing your print and pretend that you are working.

Some processes such as gum, carbon and photo-etching need a more stable light source. In these cases you will need some form of lamp. For many years the cheapest lamps have been sun lamps which screw into a standard ES holder and plug into the mains. These are now hard to find, as it is very difficult to write safety instructions for a product which is used for the express purpose of burning your skin. The alternative is to use an industrial UV lamp. Osram make a lamp called Vitalux, sold mainly for hardening the photo resists on printed circuits. These can be screwed into a brass and ceramic holder and plugged straight into the mains. They cost about £30 and last for over 1000 hours burning. They consume 300 watts and are available from most electrical wholesalers (see list of suppliers). Reasonable results can be obtained from fluorescent lighting tubes or

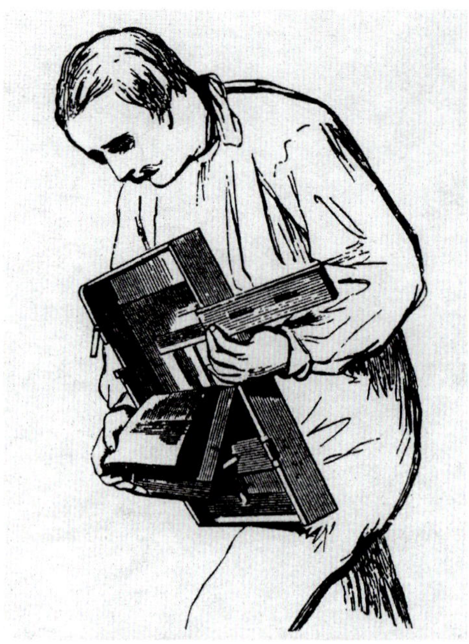

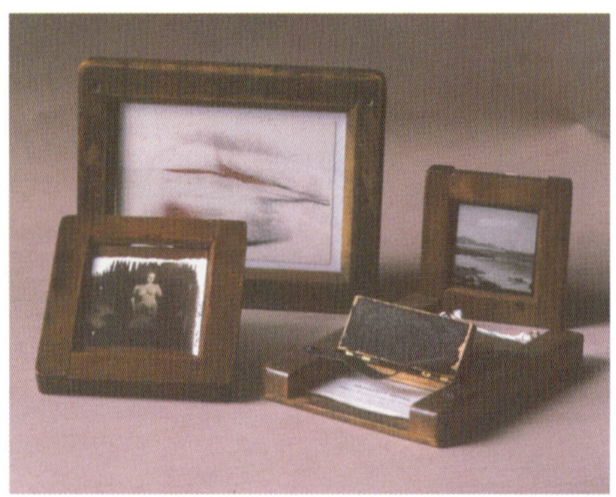

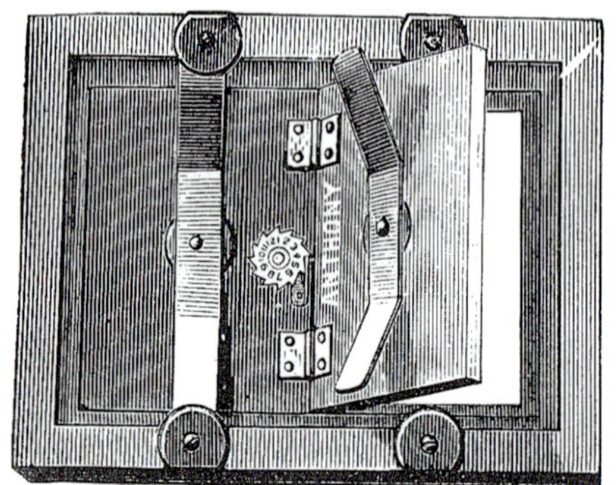

There are many variations possible in the design of on the traditional hinged back printing frame, the sole proviso is that it is possible to open and inspect the print without disturbing the registration.

studio photofloods. The former are quite slow but emit little heat whilst the latter run very hot and don't last very long. You could try using a sun bed, but avoid the temptation to lie on the bed in your swim suit with the print. You could get very red. Argos, the chain store, supply a small sun lamp on a stand which has a low wattage. It is fairly slow but quite safe to use, and costs about £50. All the other UV light sources are more expensive and far less portable.

Here is a selection.

1 Mercury vapour lamps. These are screw-in lamps similar to the Vitalux but need a choke and a ballast wired permanently into the circuit. The complete package costs well over £100 but for anyone who needs a custom-made set-up built into a bench or light tight housing they are ideal.

2 The Americans favour a system using a row of 12 inch long UV tubes set in a home-made exposing box. The box has a glass top with a hinged lid to keep the sandwich of paper and negative a few inches from the lamps. The light source puts out little heat and is very controllable. You need to be a reasonable carpenter and amateur electrician to construct one, but given these basic skills it is not that difficult to make. Occasionally on the second hand market one can find a ready made exposing box complete with UV tubes and a built in vacuum pump. This obviates the need for a printing frame. The writer uses one of these which was bought second hand for about £80, and which exposes a kallitype in about 5 minutes. The maximum negative size is about 10 x 12".

3 If you have access to an art school or evening institute with a print making department, you may be able to use their exposing box which is normally used for exposing silk screen film or etching plates. This box is a large floor-standing machine with several mercury vapour lamps, a timer and a shutter to cut out the direct rays of UV light while you are loading it. Of all the types of artificial light this is the fastest and the most effective.

Contact Frames

The next item you will need is a device for holding the sensitised paper and negative together in close contact to make the exposure. This can be anything from a sheet of glass, a sheet of plywood and four bulldog clips, to an expensive hand made wooden printing frame with a hinged back. In no particular order here are some suggestions.

1 Take a sheet of fairly thick plywood or MDF board 2 or 3 inches larger all round than the largest size of paper you are likely to use. Remember that you may want to make a small image on a large sheet of paper. You will also need a piece of clean, blemish-free glass. Plate glass is better than picture glass. Make sure all sides of the glass are milled to save cutting yourself. Four large bulldog clips, one on each side, will hold the sandwich together in close contact. Small frames of this sort are more effective than huge ones.

2 A slightly more sophisticated version of this is a picture frame, preferably of the clip frame variety. Make sure you can take it apart easily to check the progress of the exposure.

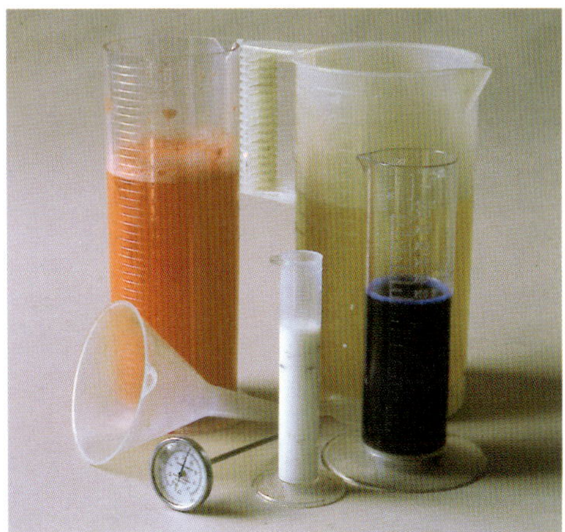

You cannot have too many measures.

3 An original 19'th century printing frame or a modern version of it. These can sometimes be picked up for very little money from junk shops or car boot sales. As nineteenth century glass plates tended to be no larger than about 5 x 7" you will obviously have to conform to nineteenth century sizes. (See illustrations for details of printing frames). The modern versions of these are much larger - up to 20 x 16" and correspondingly more expensive.

Liquid measures

You will need several graduated jars for measuring liquids. These should preferably be calibrated in millilitres. At least one small one holding no more than 45 ml, and two or three standard jars holding up to 1 litre. For larger quantities you can use plastic jugs from hardware stores. (Make sure they measure in millilitres - not pints or cupfuls).

Syringes are cheap and accurate for measuring small volumes, and are obtainable from 1ml, (which will measure down to 0.1ml), to sizes as large as 50ml. Make sure they don't come with needles.

A plastic funnel for pouring liquids back into the bottle.

A set of brown glass bottles with plastic screw tops for storing solutions. Sizes - 100 ml, 250 ml, 500 ml and 1 litre. Many pharmacies will supply waste bottles free. Wash them thoroughly as they have probably held cough mixture on draught.

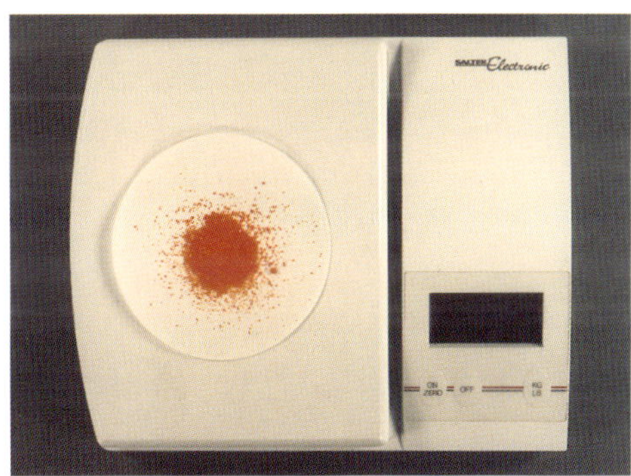

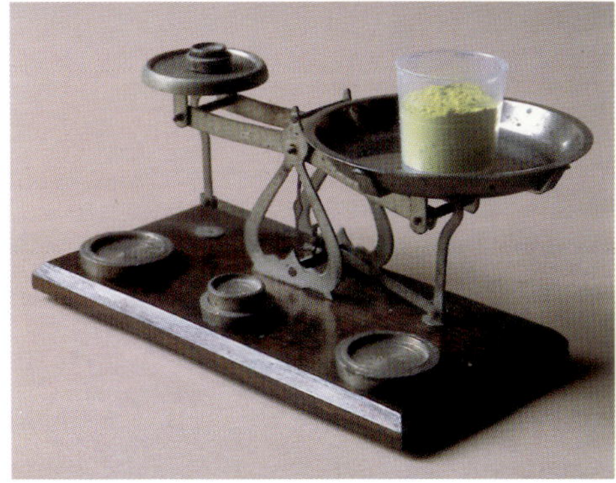

The traditional pan balance, using separate weights. These are getting more difficult to find. A simple electronic machine is usually the first choice. The Salter machine illustrated above is sold by kitchenware suppliers at about £25.

Scales

Working with old processes entails the use of raw chemicals. Very few solutions come ready mixed. It is possible to go to your local pharmacy to have your chemicals weighed. This is known in America as custom scaling, but on the whole it is better to acquire your own scales. The only exception is when you work with platinum or palladium where you may have to weigh out 0.6 of a gram or thereabouts. There is a small chemical balance on the market which will measure amounts down to about one gram. The alternative is a small electric kitchen scale with a digital read out which will go down to about 2 grams. These can be bought from mail order kitchen suppliers. The writer uses a small letter balance obtained from a camera club jumble sale 12 years ago for £1.50.

Dishes

You can never have too many dishes. Use the standard plastic ones with ridged bottoms and always buy ones slightly larger than the paper size you intend to use, but not too large, as you will waste money filling them with solutions you may not need. The heavy duty range made by Paterson are ideal. If you intend to work with platinum or palladium it is preferable, but not absolutely necessary, to buy four dishes of the required size to use specifically for that purpose. This will avoid contaminating them with silver, dichromate, hypo, biscuit crumbs or whatever.

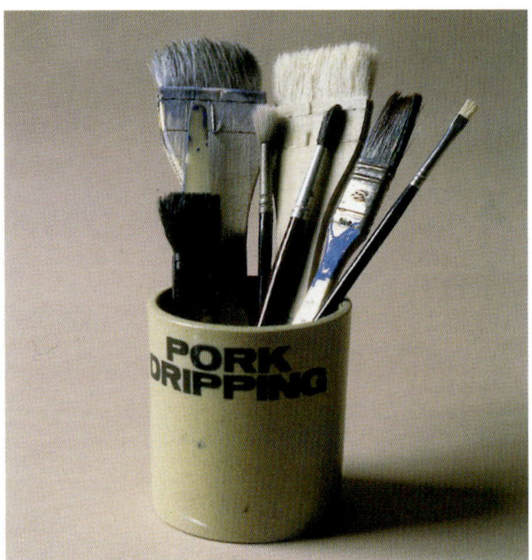

This looks very pretty, but water eventually goes into the stock of the brush and ruins it.

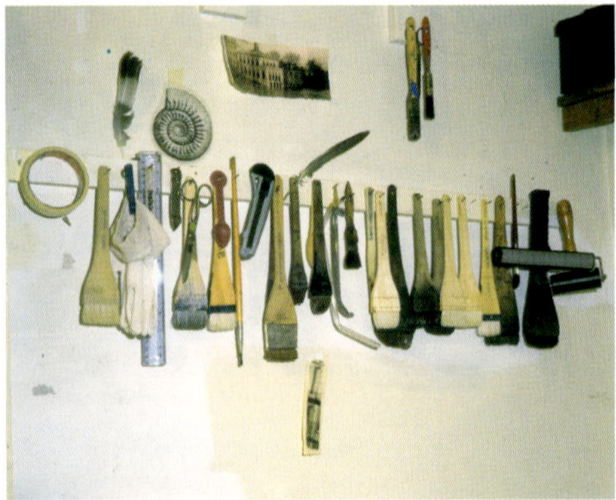
Not a very elegant solution, but effective.

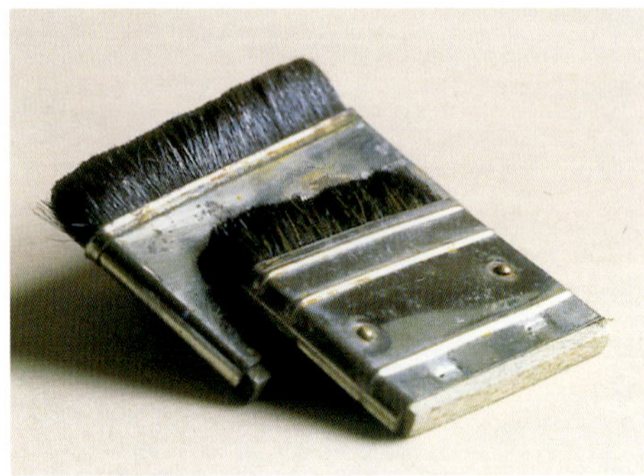
These are known as flat decorators sables, and are very useful for coating gum prints. Available from art shops and specialist decorators.

Brushes

Equip yourself with a generous supply of brushes. The best ones to buy are the flat wooden handled 'hake' brushes from any good art supplier. They have the advantage of not containing a metal ferrule which could react with some of the chemicals you brush onto your paper. They come in various widths, but measuring one to two inches wide will be suitable for most purposes. Reserve one for each process to avoid cross-contamination. Write the appropriate process on the handle with a felt tip pen, drill a small hole in it, and hang all the brushes on nails hammered into your darkroom or studio wall. When you come to experiment with bromoil you will need at least half a dozen brushes especially for this process only. Do not be seduced by earlier writers on the subject into buying exotic brushes such as polecat fitches and the like. They are extremely expensive and not really necessary. All you need will be a couple of cheap shaving brushes from Boots, and a packet of paint brushes of various sizes from your local DIY store.

The alternative coating method is by means of a tubular glass rod. See [7 . Coating]. If you intend to use the glass rod method you will also need a packet of plastic syringes holding up to 5 ml for measuring the solution in drops. They can be purchased from your local pharmacy very cheaply.

Miscellaneous Items

A dial or electronic **thermometer**. Don't use glass ones, they never last very long. And especially, although they are difficult to obtain nowadays, don't use a mercury thermometer. The hazards from spilt mercury are considerable.
Chemical stirring rod - plastic preferably.
Roll of translucent **Scotch tape**.
Roll of **masking tape** - the photographer's friend.
Roll of **red litho tape**.
Hair drier or small **fan heater**.
A set of **plastic print tongs**.
Two or three plastic **palette knives**.
A pair of **scissors**.
A **scalpel**.
Small plastic **washing line** and a supply of plastic **clothes pegs**.
A few **china saucers** or tea plates.
An old but clean car **windscreen wiper** for squeegeeing prints. (This tip comes from Ansel Adams as a matter of interest).
A sheet of **perspex** or formica coated hardboard for squeegeeing your prints on.
Filter papers for filtering solutions. Try using unbleached coffee filters.
Labels and a **felt tip pen** for marking the contents of your containers.
A roll of **cotton wool**.
Plastic sheets and **old newspapers** for protecting your work surfaces.
A bottle of frequent handwash **soap** and a reasonably clean **towel**.

Papers for old processes 5

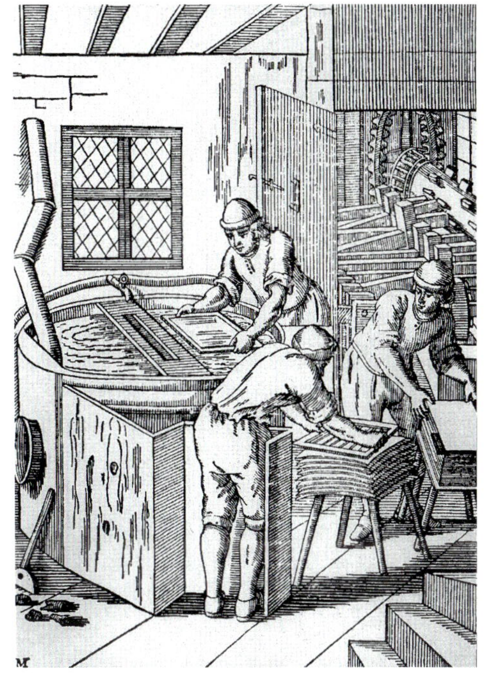

An example of an early paper mill in action. See overleaf for the equivalent in a workshop environment.

Hand-made paper from Northern Thailand viewed on a lightbox. It is made from a tree which sheds its bark annually, and so is one of the few environmentally correct papers. Needs gelatin size for wet processing.

Paper is a beautiful material, especially the sort we use in alternative printing. If you want to make old process work a really satisfying experience then you must learn to appreciate the qualities of paper in all its forms. The feel of good paper is exciting - from the velvet smoothness of hot pressed Fabriano, to the roughness of hand made Indian papers, and the soft absorbency of etching paper. When you hold up a sheet by the corner and shake it, it rattles like stage thunder in a Christmas pantomime. This is far removed from the world of grade three glossy or resin coated semi-matt used by conventional photographic printers. It is not difficult to make your own paper, but as the nineteenth century photographers bought theirs ready made from the shop there appears to be no reason why we at the end of the twentieth century shouldn't follow their example. It needs a lot of practice to produce a hand made paper of a quality suitable for most of the processes described in this manual. Photo-etching is probably the only one that lends itself to printing on the fairly primitive papers that newcomers to paper making usually produce.

When you do go to the artists' suppliers to buy your paper you will be faced with an array of sizes, textures, finishes, thicknesses and manufacturers names far in excess of anything you have ever met in a photographic suppliers. We suggest you spare some time making yourself familiar with the terminology of the art paper business, otherwise you will be at some disadvantage when you start ordering your paper from the shop. Being confronted with a barrage of obscure terms such as 'Whatman tub sized Not pressed double elephant 200 gram' can be daunting. Here is the basic vocabulary to enable you to bluff your way through the paper jungle.

First, it is worth spending a little time looking at how paper is made. There are three basic methods of paper manufacture.

1 Hand made.

2 Mould made.

3 Machine made.

Hand-made paper

Hand made paper is as its title suggests and the technique has changed little since it was first invented nearly two thousand years ago. The basic ingredient for all paper making is pulp. This is made by beating vegetable fibres - usually wood, cotton or linen - in water in order to separate the fibres. The final mix of about 10 per cent fibre to 90 per cent water is placed in a large tub or vat ready for use. At its simplest level it is possible to make a perfectly adequate pulp by mixing cotton or linen rags with water in a kitchen blender. However, for commercial paper making more sophisticated machinery is used to produce a mixture of more consistent quality.

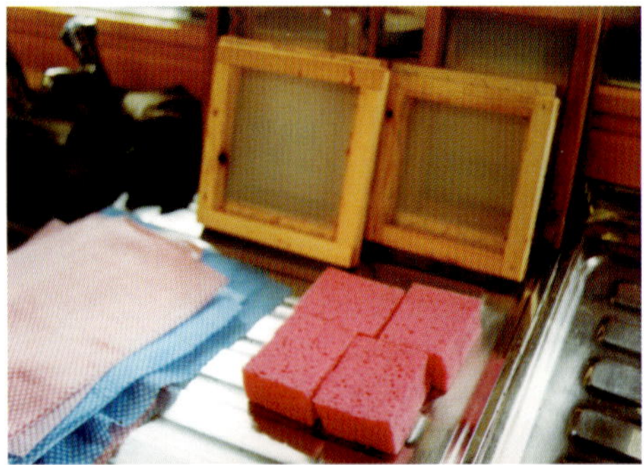

Materials for home-made paper making, sponges, moulds, deckles, J-cloths.

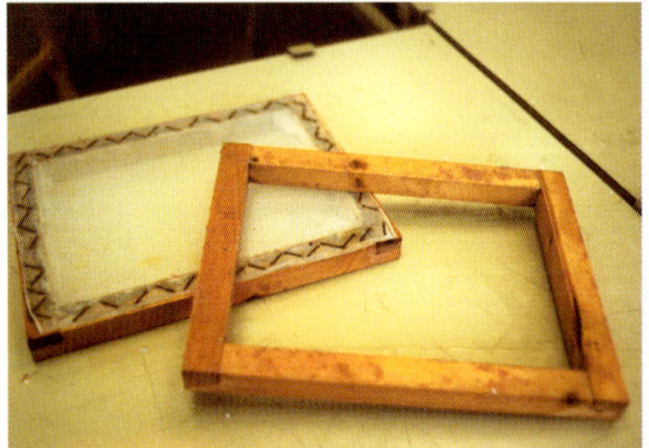

Mould on left, deckle on right.

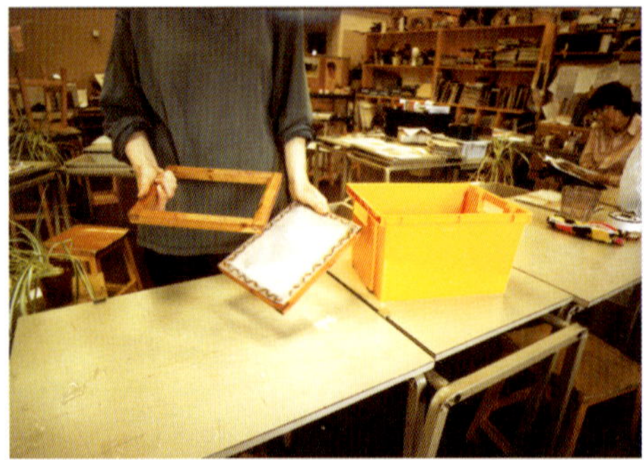

Placing the deckle on the mould.

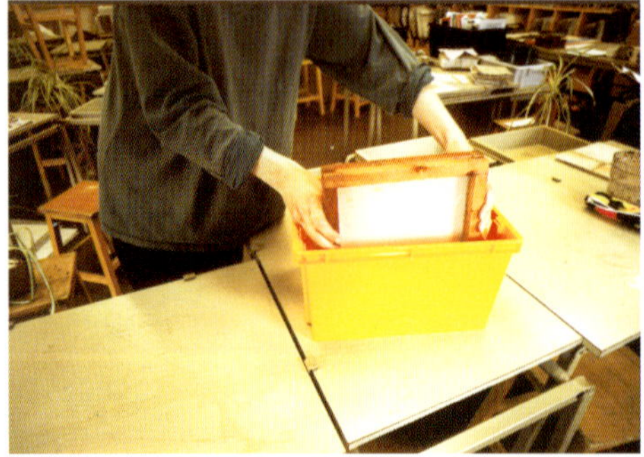

Immersing deckle and mould in tub of pulp made from recycled office stationary dyed with vegetable dye.

Forming pulp into a sheet of paper is done with the use of a fairly primitive apparatus called a mould and deckle. The mould is a fine wire mesh attached to a rectangular wooden frame slightly larger than the sheet of paper that is to be made. The deckle is another frame like a picture frame without glass or backing which fits over the mould, giving a raised edge around all four sides. The deckle frame is removable. The two are fitted together and dipped into the pulp. They are then held under the surface horizontally and then lifted out. As it is lifted out the pulp lies on the top of the mould, held at the edges by the raised rim of the deckle. The mould is shaken to and fro to make an even layer of pulp on top of the mould. The excess water immediately starts to drain through the mesh of the mould, leaving what is effectively a sheet of very soggy paper, known as 'waterleaf'. The deckle frame is now removed leaving a ragged edge all round the four sides of the paper sheet. These ragged edges are known as deckle edges. It is here that the skill of the paper maker comes into play, as the time taken to dip and shake the mould takes only a few seconds, during which a consistent thickness of paper must be achieved for sheet after sheet.

The sheet of waterleaf is then transferred onto a piece of felt blanket - an operation known as 'couching'. This is then covered with another sheet of felt. A stack or 'post' of alternate layers of newly made paper and felt is built up, and when a sufficient number of sheets have been made, the stack is placed in a press and the remaining water is squeezed out. The sheets of paper are then peeled from the sheets of felt and left to dry. It is fortunate for paper makers that although the fibres of the paper bind together to make the sheets of paper, they do not adhere to the felt and can be easily separated from it.

That's very briefly how paper has been made since its invention by Tsai Lun in China in AD 105. Paper making in Europe dates from about AD 1036 when it was introduced in Cordoba in Spain. One of the most popular papers at present is from the Fabriano mill in Italy which was founded in the 13th century. Some of the most readily available hand made papers are Fabriano Roma, Fabriano Umbria, Twin Rocker hand made, Two Rivers water colour, Wookey Hole hand made, and Barcham Green. This latter is no longer produced but can be found in certain specialist shops in the most unlikely places, where it is treated like fine wine and sold very sparingly.

These are all European or American papers, but there are of course other areas of the world that have been producing paper centuries before the European mills. The most notable are Japan, Nepal and India. Not all of them are suitable for wet processing as they are light weight and very delicate. The Japanese papers are more fitted to dry printing such as etching, silk screen and bromoil transfer. The obvious answer here is to experiment at a later stage after you have acquired a facility of using mould or machine made papers. (See the paper compatibility table.)

Advantages of using hand made papers.

1 Each sheet is a 'one-off' and subtly different from any other.

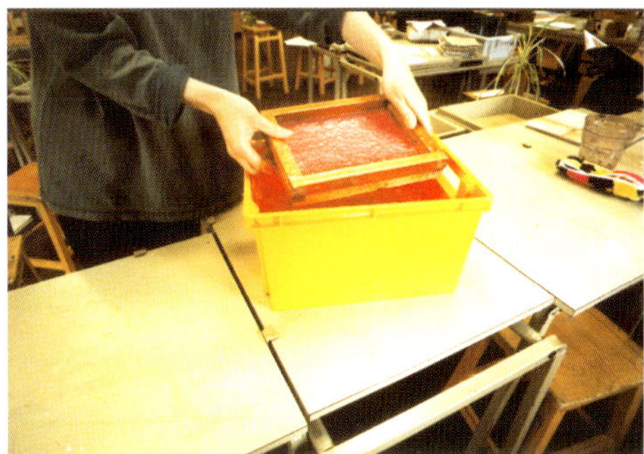

Removing mould and deckle from tub and allowing to drain.

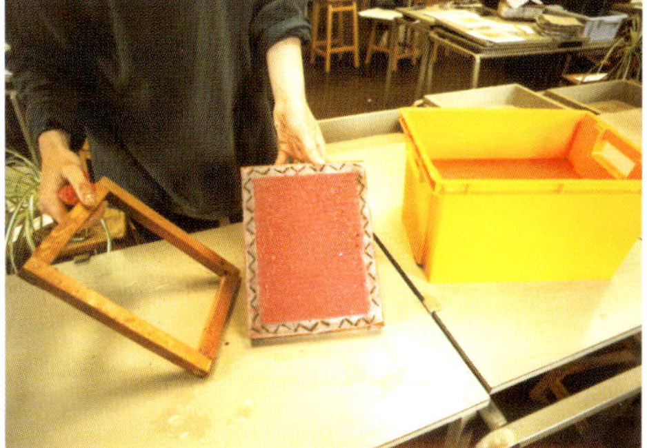

Removing the deckle revealing a sheet of wet pulp.

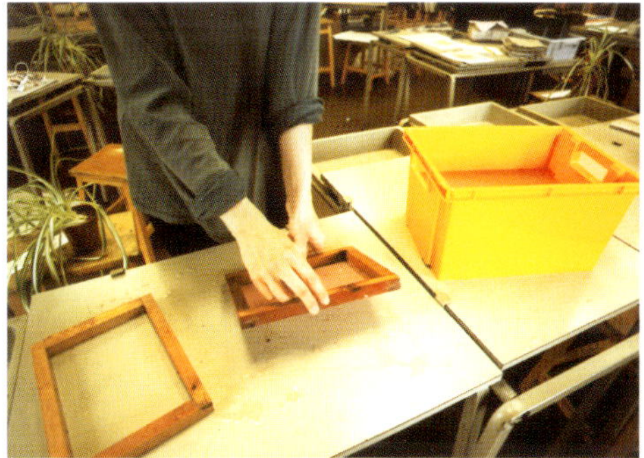

Couching, ot transferring the paper from the mould to a flat surface, in this case covered by a J-cloth.

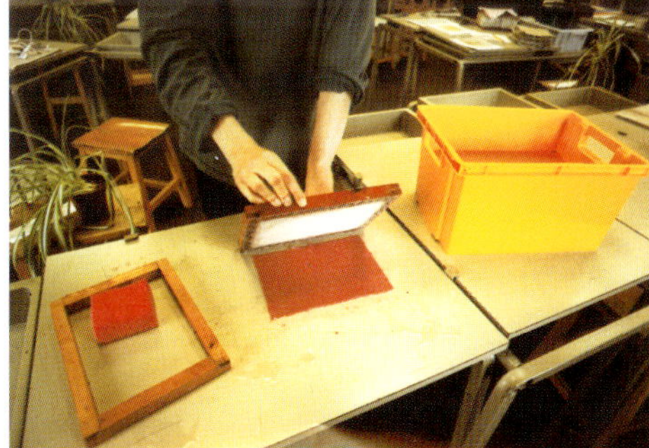

The excess water is sponged from the top of the mould, which is then lifted off the paper.

2 You have the satisfaction of working with a hand crafted material.

3 Each sheet has its own unique deckle edge on all four sides.

4 The qualities of the paper have their individual colour, surface and 'feel'.

5 Hand-made papers have a high degree of permanence.

Mould made paper

There may be some cause for confusion here. Mould made paper is not made with a mould, but with a revolving cylindrical drum. Having resolved that small problem, we can safely assume that a large proportion of your alternative print making will be done on mould made paper.

The wide variety of makes, colours textures and finishes will guarantee that mould made paper will feature prominently in your stock of papers. Mould made paper bridges the gap between hand made and machine made paper. It is, in fact, a mechanised version of hand made. Here, briefly, is an account of its manufacture.

A cylinder covered around its circumference with fine mesh is partially submerged in a vat of pulp. The cylinder is then made to revolve and as it revolves a layer of pulp is pulled onto the mesh by a vacuum action, making a sheet of paper which in this case becomes a continuous sheet, as it is taken off the cylinder and passed between two rollers which squeeze out the surplus water. These rollers are covered with felt which impart their own texture on the paper as it passes between them. Thus the surface textures of the rollers are responsible for the final appearance of the paper. The final drying stage of mould made paper is accomplished by passing the continuous web of paper between steam heated rollers. When dry the paper is cut into individual sheets ready for use. The one major difference that distinguishes hand made from mould made is the provision of deckle edges. Whereas hand made sheets have a deckle on all four sides, the continuous long sheets of mould made have a deckle only on two sides, the other two sides being cut as straight edges with a mechanical guillotine. It is possible to obtain mould made paper with four deckle edges but these are produced artificially. As there are a bewildering array of mould made papers on the market, we will list here a few of the best known brands. Please see later sections on the characteristics of these products.

1 Arches - made in France.

2 RKB. R. K. Burt is a London paper distributor and commissions paper from various mills in Europe.

3 Bockingford.

4 Saunders.

5 Somerset.

6 Fabriano.

7 Hahnemuhle - made in Germany.

8 Rives BFK, made by the same mill as Arches.

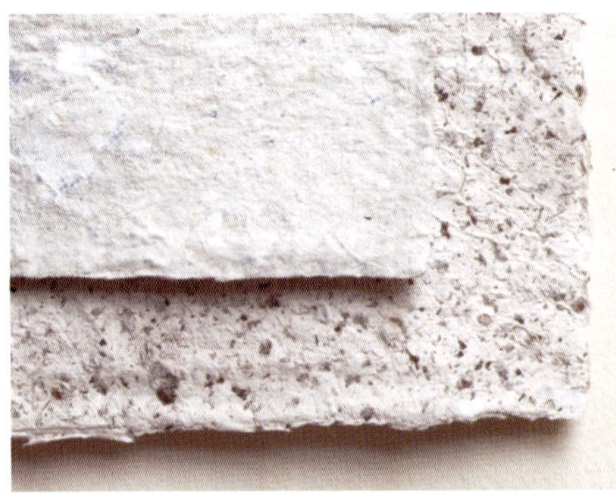

Close-up of home-made hand-made paper. This is again from recycled office stationary, and is not sized.

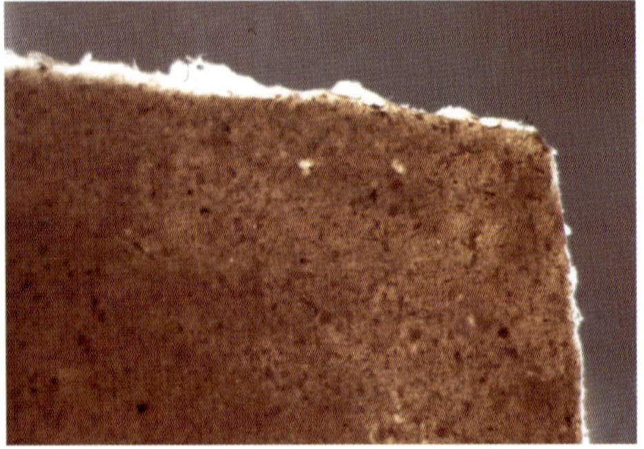

Close-up of hand-made paper from Nepal, of which the main ingredient is banana leaf fibres. Note the deckle edge and the irregular corner.

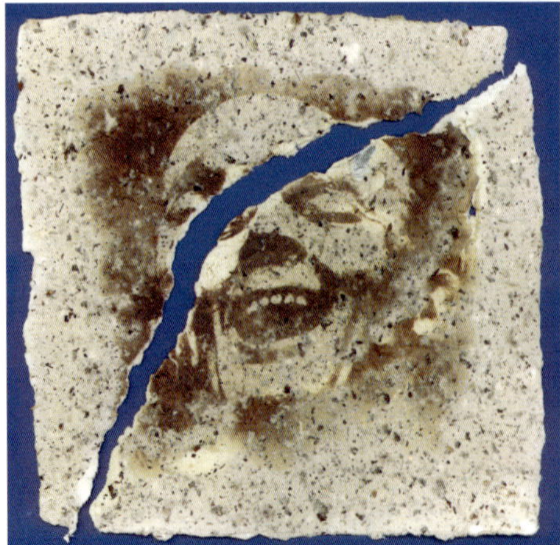

Unsuccessful attempt to make Van Dyke print on unsized paper! Note the sensitiser has vanished into the surface of the paper and the paper has broken in half during fixing and washing.

9 Whatman - this mill is over 250 years old and its paper was used by Fox Talbot in his early experiments with salt printing.

The advantages of using mould made papers:

1 They are on the whole less expensive than hand made.

2 They are more consistent in quality - or perhaps we should say they are less liable to inconsistency.

3 There is a vast range from which to choose in terms of surface, colour, absorbency and size. It is obviously easier to make larger sheets on a machine than by hand in a mould and deckle process.

Machine made papers

These represent the cheaper end of the market and are less likely to be of much interest to alternative printmakers, except for proofing and practising before committing ones best negatives to the more expensive mould or hand made papers. Machine made papers tend to be made from wood pulp or chemically treated pulp, and are used for newsprint, wrapping, packaging and office stationery. For our purposes, cartridge paper is the most likely to be used. Much machine made paper, because it is made from wood pulp is less archivally secure than the cotton and linen papers made by the other two processes. Libraries around the world are finding that books printed on cheap machine made paper dating from the end of the nineteenth century are now deteriorating rapidly. There is some dispute among paper conservators as to the best methods of transferring these onto microfilm or computer related storage systems. An interestingquestion is, will computer discs last as long as 2000 year old Japanese paper?

As far as the methods of making machine made paper are concerned, suffice it to say the machine it is made on is usually about the size of a football pitch and it spews out hundreds of yards of paper which is subsequently wound into enormous rolls and carted off in a large truck to be cut up into usable sizes. In practical terms it is unlikely that you will be producing your masterpieces for the Tate Gallery on machine made paper. Nevertheless there are many occasions when it can be used as a perfectly reasonable substitute for the higher quality and more expensive papers.

Here is another small fact to cause some confusion. Some machine made paper is described as 'wood free'. This is not strictly true. It is made from wood, but this has been chemically treated in the pulping process to remove some of the nastier wood components.

This is a short list of the better grades of machine made paper. Remember that many of the large manufacturers produce pads of drawing paper known simply as 'cartridge'. They are all very good for drawing on.

1 Atlantis Heritage Woodfree - very good quality.

2 Canford Cover paper - made in over 50 colours by Daler.

3 Canson Mi-teintes - similar to Canford but with more subtle colour tints, (as the name suggests).

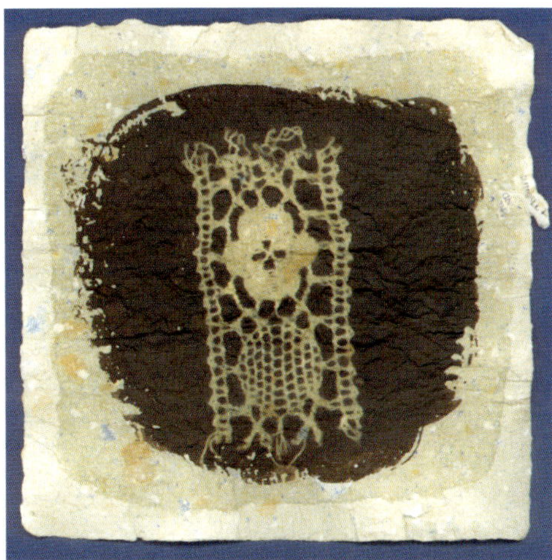

Photogram using Van Dyke process on home-made paper that has been brushed with gelatin size. Note the different quality from the unsized version.

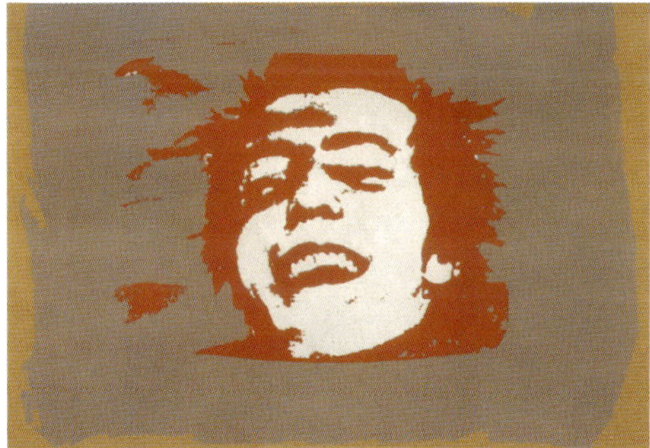

Silkscreen printed on brown wrapping paper.

Watermark of Fabriano Roma hand-made paper. When you buy this you will note it has four deckle edges which indicates that it is hand-made.

4 Cotman.

5 Fabriano 2.

6 Fabriano 4.

7 Georgian Watercolour - a good substitute for mould made paper.

8 Kent Edition.

9 Schoelleshammer - German made, good for gum printing for reasons best known to itself, but probably because of its hard sizing.

10 Strathmore.

There are a several low grade machine made papers which you will come across regularly. Among them are:

Newsprint
Don't print on this as it goes yellow in a few weeks and disintegrates in water. Useful under good paper in a printing press, [23 . Photo Etching].

Blotting paper
Very soft and absorbent. Use it for blotting!

Kraft or brown wrapping paper
Some people have been known to print silk screens on it in extreme circumstances. Use it for wrapping.

Here now are the main characteristics of paper which you know when you decide to print or to order from the paper supplier.

1 Makers name and brand name - eg Saunders, Waterford.

2 Its purpose - eg etching or watercolour.

3 Its fibre content - eg 100% cotton, wood fibre, etc.

4 How it was made - eg hand made, machine made etc.

5 Number of deckle edges per sheet.

6 Watermark. This is either the maker's logo in one corner of the sheet or the maker's name on the lower edge of the paper. It can best be seen by holding the paper up to the light, when it shows slightly more translucent than the rest of the paper. The most common watermark that we see every day is the one on a banknote which shows a picture of the Queen's head laid into the paper. The watermark on our paper also appears as being embossed on the surface of the sheet. It is sometimes regarded as 'artistic' to include the watermark on the edge of the print. However, if you don't want it to show you can tear it off, or cover it with the window matt when you mount the print. Make sure you print with the watermark showing the right way round!

7 Colour - eg white, cream, grey etc.

8 Special properties.

Sizing
This has nothing to with the dimensions but with the water resistance built in to the paper at the time of manufacture. Gelatin was the traditional sizing agent but other materials such as starch or a synthetic called Aquapel are also used. Papers are described as either 'tub sized' or 'internally sized'. Tub sizing is done by placing the paper in a tub of size

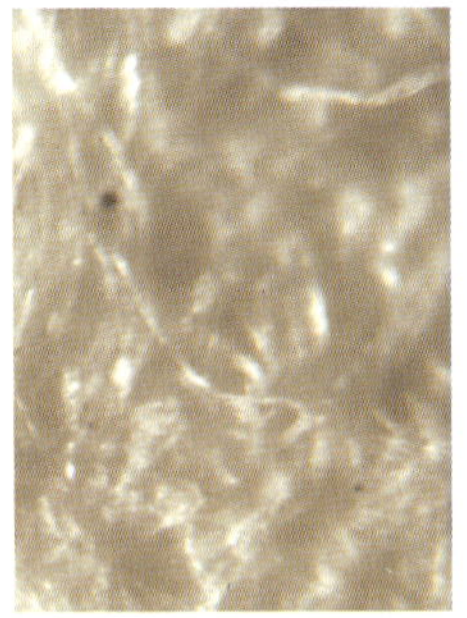

Fabriano

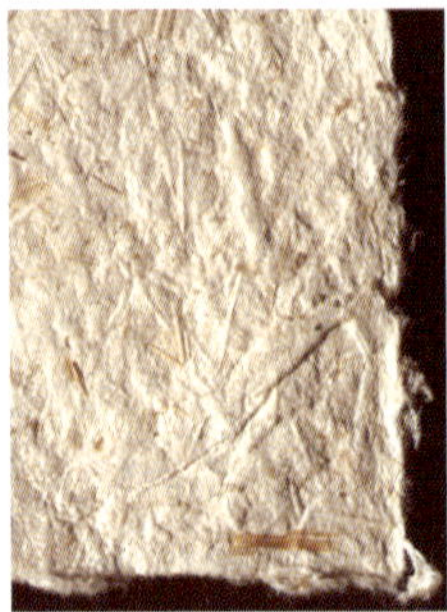
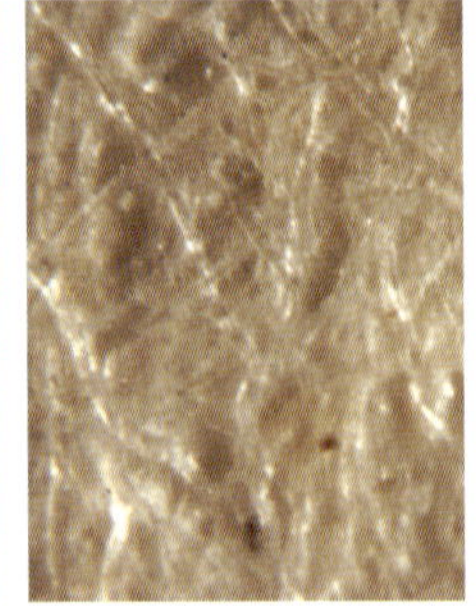

Banana fibre.

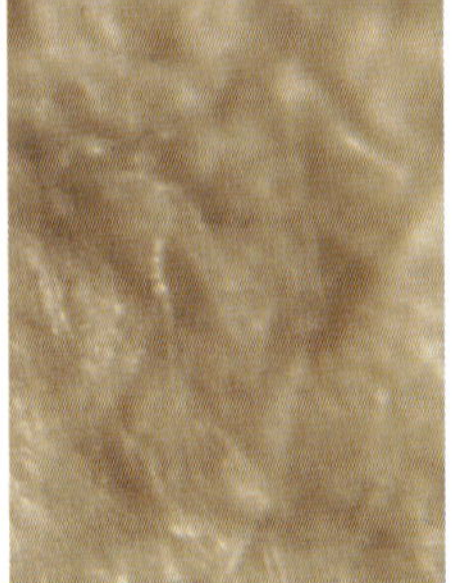

Arches cream

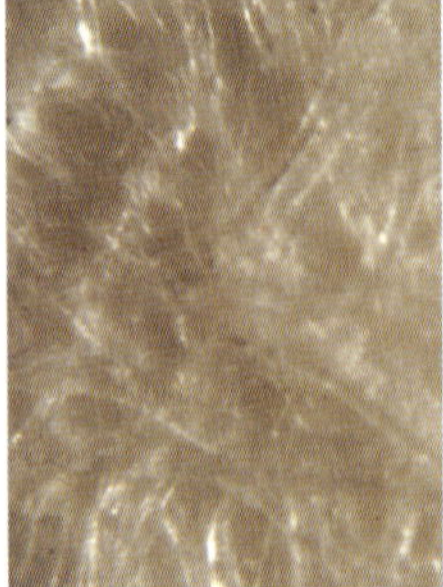

Hot pressed

Close-up pictures and photomicrographs showing the surface and fibre composition of various hand and mould made papers.

after it has been made and dried, followed by re-drying it. Internally sized paper has sizing agent added to the pulp before it is made into paper. The main fact to remember is that the more size the paper contains, the less your sensitiser will sink into the paper when you brush it on. Paper that contains no sizing is called 'waterleaf' and is similar to blotting paper. The only uses you may have for it will probably be for etching and gravure. You can of course size your own paper, [10 . Salt printing].

'Acid free' & buffering

Acid in connection with paper is bad news, and points to poor quality paper in the first place. The breakdown of the paper structure produces an acid condition and the paper is reduced in permanence and strength, as well as turning yellow. Avoid buying prints from 'artists', who for reasons of economy print on cheap cartridge paper. Acidity also builds up in paper due to airborne pollutants, including exhaust fumes and ozone from photocopiers etc. For this reason many high quality papers and boards are labelled 'buffered', meaning that they have an added mildly alkaline agent which neutralises any acid present, maintaining a safe neutral. Buffered papers and boards are excellent for all applications in this book, with one exception. It has been found that prints produced with iron processes, including platinum, palladium and kallitype prefer a completely neutral environment, and a number of papers have been specially formulated with this in mind, notably Arches Platine and Buxton.

9 Weight. The weight of a sheet of paper indicates its thickness expressed in **gsm** or grams per square metre. You will most likely use paper at about 150 - 200 gsm. The lower the number the thinner the paper and the higher the thicker.

10 The surface finish. This is expressed as Rough, HP (hot-pressed) or NOT. The surface texture is determined by the final pressing before it is dried during manufacture. Rough finish has a distinct coarse texture. Most hand made paper is rough. Some Indian papers look as though they have been pressed between sheets of old sacking. Hot pressing between heated rollers gives the paper a smooth sheen on the surface. 'Not' surface indicates that it has been passed through cold rollers or NOT hot-pressed. The smoothness falls between rough and hot pressed.

11 Dimensions. All these papers come in fairly large sizes and will need to be cut down to a usable dimension. The average size will be in the region of 50 cms x 75 cms. These measurements are sometimes in the old imperial name system. A classic one is Elephant (68.06 cms x 50.08 cms.) or Double Elephant (68.06 cms x 101.16 cms).

Finally, when using these papers it is considered rather naff to cut them with a scalpel or guillotine. Maintain the torn edge look by folding the sheet in half and then re-fold it back and forth to break the fibres. Now tear it along the fold carefully or while it is still folded run a blunt knife or pallette knife along the line of the fold. If you want to simulate a deckle edge paint the line of the fold with clean water on a brush and when it is well moistened tear it carefully. Paper is one of the vital parts of your print. Treat it with respect, use the best quality you can, and don't forget to experiment with as many different types as you can afford.

√ Suitable

👎 Not suitable

? Experiment

	Arches Ingres	Arches Platine	Arches Cream	Moulin du Verger	Two Rivers	Indian rag & fibre	Khadi	Arches 88	Rives Velin	Strathmore	Kent Edition	Whatman	Somerset	Hannemuhle Etching	Saunders Waterford	BFK Rives	Arches Aquarelle	Canford Cover	Cranes	Buxton	Bockingford	Fabriano 5	Fabriano 100%	Fabriano Roma
Salt & albumen	?	√	√	√	√	?	?	👎	√	√	?	√	√	👎	√	√	√	👎	√	√	√	√	√	√
Kallitype & Van Dyke	√	√	√	√	√	√	√	👎	√	√	√	√	√	👎	√	√	√	👎	√	√	√	√	√	√
Cyanotype	√	√	√	√	√	√	√	👎	√	√	√	√	√	👎	√	√	√	√	√	√	√	√	√	√
Platinum & palladium	👎	√	?	?	√	?	?	👎	√	?	?	√	√	👎	√	√	√	👎	√	√	√	√	√	√
Oil prints	√	√	√	√	√	√	√	👎	√	√	√	√	√	?	√	√	√	👎	√	√	√	√	√	?
Bromoil transfer	√	√	√	√	√	?	?	√	√	√	√	√	√	√	√	√	√	?	√	√	√	√	√	√
Carbon prints	√	👎	√	√	√	👎	👎	👎	√	√	√	√	√	👎	√	√	√	👎	√	√	√	√	√	👎
Gum prints	👎	👎	👎	√	√	?	?	👎	√	√	√	√	√	👎	√	√	√	√	?	√	√	√	√	√
Casein prints	👎	👎	👎	√	√	?	?	👎	√	√	√	√	√	👎	√	√	√	√	?	√	√	√	√	√
Photo etching	√	👎	√	√	√	?	?	√	√	√	√	√	√	√	√	√	√	√	√	√	√	√	√	√
Gravure	√	👎	√	√	√	?	?	√	√	√	√	√	√	√	√	√	√	√	√	√	√	√	√	√
Silk screen	√	👎	👎	√	√	?	?	👎	√	√	√	√	√	👎	√	√	√	√	√	√	√	√	√	√
Solvent transfer	√	√	√	√	√	√	√	👎	√	√	√	√	√	👎	√	√	√	√	√	√	√	√	√	√
Cliche Verre	√	√	√	√	√	√	√	👎	√	√	√	√	√	👎	√	√	√	√	√	√	√	√	√	√

This chart offers guidelines - at worst it will stop you wasting paper, at best allow you to experiment in a reasonably orderly way.

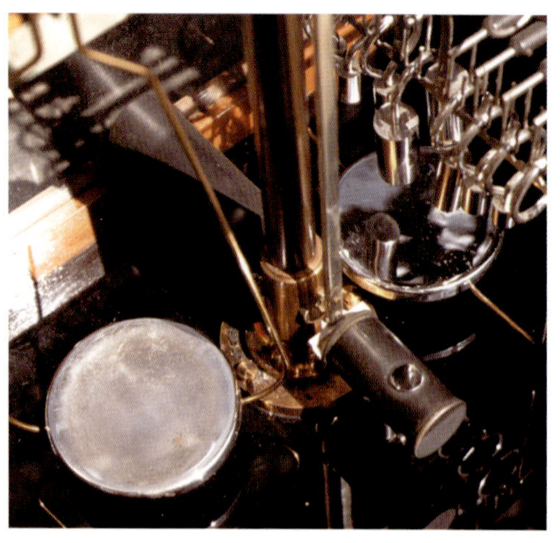

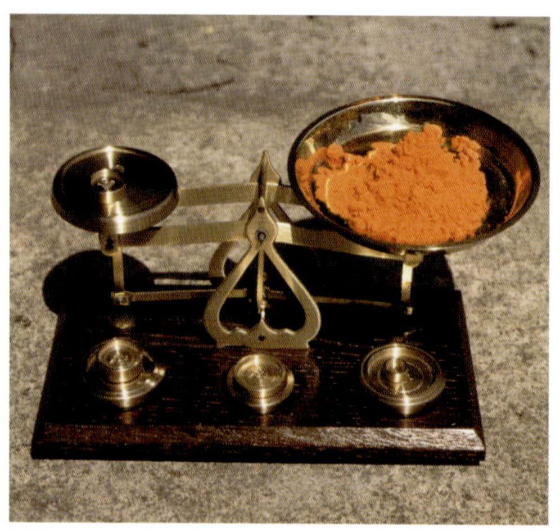

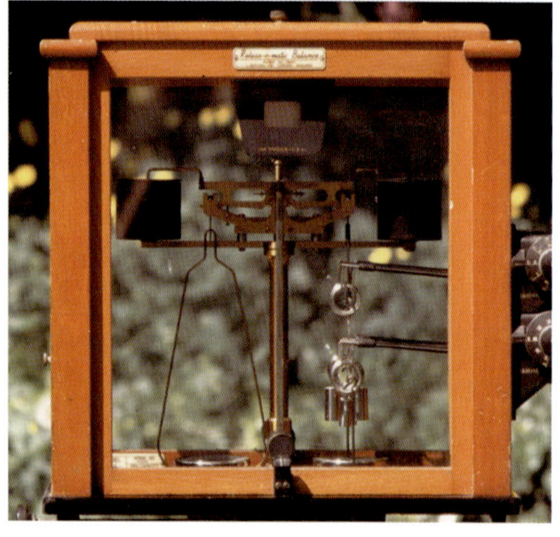

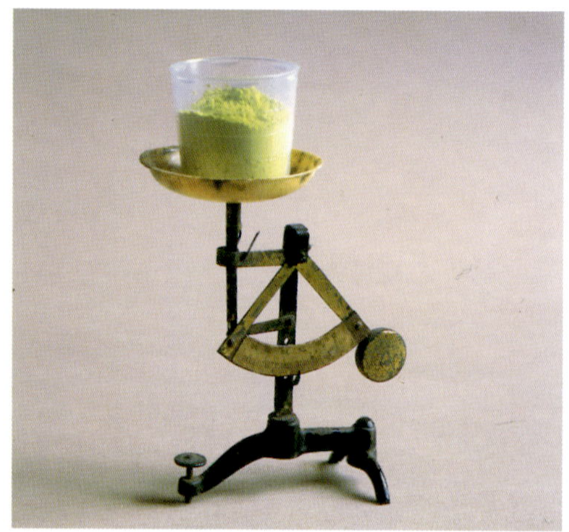

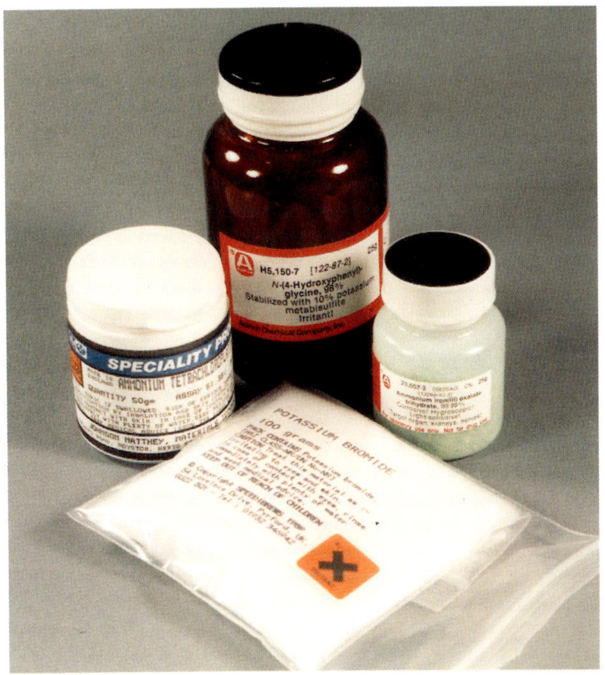

PLEASE READ THIS SECTION CAREFULLY

If you think that photographic chemicals come in bottles marked Ilford or Kodak, you may have to come to terms with a little basic chemistry when you start to explore old processes. Developers, stop baths and fixers come ready mixed with detailed instructions for dilution and use. Even the more complicated toners, reducers and bleaches are used straight from the bottle. Although they are very convenient to use, they are very expensive compared with the raw chemicals. This manual is not a learned treatise on chemistry and you will not need to memorise complicated formulae. All you will need to know is which chemicals are used for the different processes and what sort of reactions are likely to occur. Some of the chemicals you will need to use are toxic, ie poisonous. Some are irritating to the skin, and some are corrosive (they burn). However, if they are used according to the instruction guide in this manual, and sensible precautions added to a little common sense are observed when dealing with them, then they are no more dangerous than the chemicals already in your darkroom, your garage, or in the cupboard under the kitchen sink. If you treat chemicals with care and respect they can do you no harm.

Here is a list of do's and don'ts. Make sure you stick to a few simple rules. On the other hand, there is no need to dress up in a space suit for protection as this could inhibit your enjoyment of the processes and make working somewhat difficult.

DO use all chemicals according to the instructions. Don't be tempted to experiment. If you do, you may get an unexpected result, which could be dangerous. Leave the fancy stuff to research chemists.

DON'T leave chemicals within the reach of children, pets or inquisitive adults. Store them on a high shelf or in a locked cupboard.

DON'T use chemicals near food or drink, or where food is likely to be prepared.

DO avoid the temptation to eat, drink, or smoke in the place where you are working with chemicals.

Potassium dichromate in solution looks suspiciously like orange juice, and silver nitrate in solution much like flat tonic water. Some early books on photography describe the taste of some quite toxic chemicals. The mortality rate amongst photographers was higher in those days. Don't taste any chemical to find out what it is! Don't store chemical mixtures or raw chemicals in containers if either are used for food and drink, or which could be mistaken for such. Most pharmacies will give or sell you screw top brown bottles of various sizes which are obviously what they appear to be. Containers for dry chemicals can be bought from most chemical suppliers. If you use old jam jars, make sure they have been thoroughly washed and dried, the labels completely removed and new labels with large lettering describing the contents fixed firmly on the side.

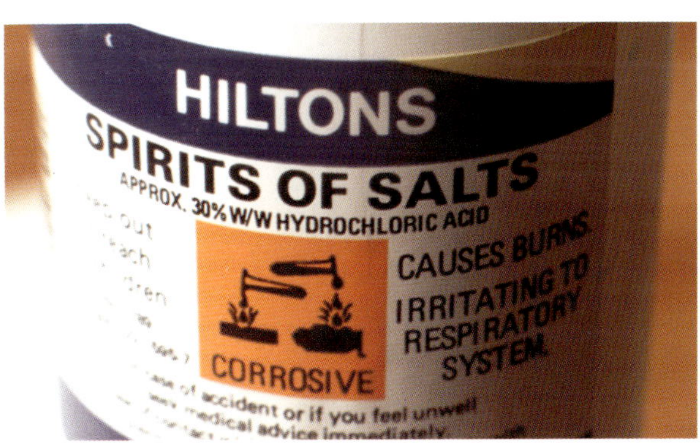

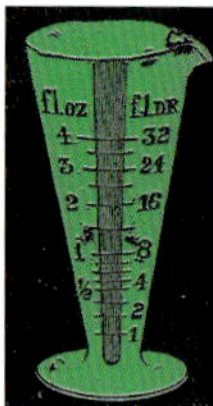

Mixing chemicals

When you first start working with old processes you will need a few simple basic ingredients. As you get farther into the various methods you will need a greater range, and slightly more sophisticated chemicals. At first do not order your chemicals in large quantities. A line of 1 kilo jars in line on a shelf may look impressive to the casual visitor, but they take up essential space and tie up your cash unnecessarily. Look at the relevant formula and then compare it with the amounts quoted in the suppliers catalogue. If the formula needs 10 gm and this particular chemical is supplied in 25 gm and 100 gm lots, then buy 25 gm to start and so on. Most books which deal with photographic chemistry appear to be written by chemists. Many of these experts seem to become paranoid about accuracy of measurement. They often forget that the average photographer knows little or nothing about atomic weights, pH, and the difference between ferric and ferrous, and consequently omit any real explanations about the effects the various substances have on each other. For most of the processes in this manual, precise and meticulous measurement of the materials is not absolutely essential. (Chemists please note - do not write or send faxes to us on this subject!)

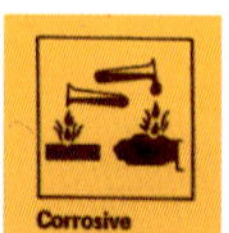

Hazard labels.

Mandatory now on all chemicals bought through normal supply channels. Though very necessary, they tend to make many raw chemicals seem more worrying to deal with than they are in reality. The listing on the following pages shows the hazard symbol for the more toxic chemicals. Assume all others to be irritant.

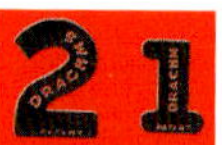

Labelling

Make sure all containers are clearly labelled. Any container which has chemicals in it but has no label should be disposed of safely. (Don't just pour them down the sink, take them to your local municipal disposal facility.) Use either self adhesive labels and waterproof felt tip pens, or self adhesive printed 'Dymo tape'. The label should show:

1 The name of the chemical in full, (as in this manual). 'F', 'Ferri' or 'Silver' is not enough.
2 Whether it is 'stock' or working strength.
3 The degree of dilution needed to make the working solution, i.e 1:9, 1:4 etc. Make sure you use a system which enables you remember which is water and which is chemical. Eg, 1:9 usually means one part chemical to nine parts of water.
4 The date on which it was made up.
5 Any other instructions that may be necessary, eg use 1:7 etc.

Make sure you use the correct amount, (see mixing chemicals). Make sure you clean all your utensils as soon as you have used them. This includes jugs, measures, stirring rods, scales and all working surfaces. If you spill any dry or liquid matter, wipe it up thoroughly at once. If you feel the need to wear goggles, rubber gloves or breathing masks, then do so. Wash your hands regularly with soap and hot water and keep an old nail brush handy. (Caustic soda granules under the finger nails are painful).
Always have plenty of paper towels handy in the working place.

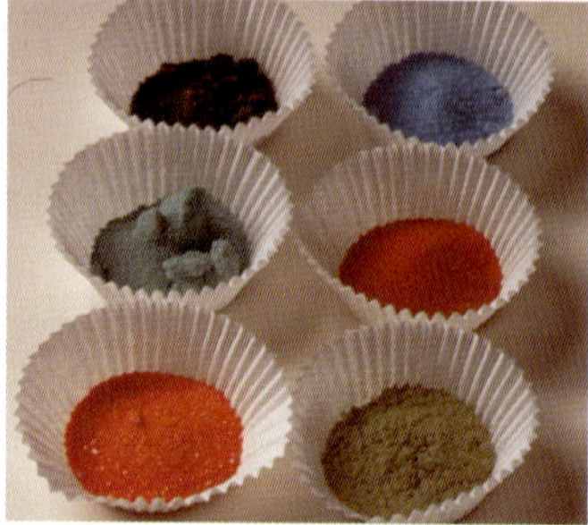

At the risk of labouring the point, keep chemicals out of the kitchen, and be meticulous in labelling them.

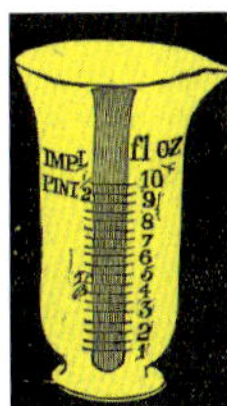

List of basic utensils for mixing chemicals

1 Small chemical balance. Alternatively you can use a small kitchen scales from a hardware store or a mail order supplier. Ideally the scale should measure down to 1 or 2 grams in 1 gram divisions. If you need very small amounts, such as 0.3 of gram, then you may find that your local chemist will help you out with measuring it. (This is known in the USA as custom scaling). However, assuming that your local chemist is of the non-helpful variety, see 'percentage solutions' below.

2 You will have done quite a bit of stirring by the time you get through the processes in this manual, so it is worth getting a proper stirring rod. Don't use a piece of glass rod, thermometer, or a desert spoon. Buy a stainless steel or plastic rod designed for the job.

3 A number of graduated measuring jugs. Plastic ones last longer than glass. You will need one that measures up to 600ml or 1 litre, and one that will take 2 litres. For the medium size, cheap plastic kitchen jugs will be adequate, provided they measure in millilitres - translating from ounces is a waste of time. There is no formula in this manual which needs a heat proof Pyrex jug, so don't bother buying one.

4 A plastic funnel for pouring liquids back into bottles.

5 A packet of filter papers for filtering liquid mixtures. Unbleached coffee filters work very well. (Make sure that you keep them in the darkroom for photographic use only).

6 A few small plastic spoons for ladling dry chemicals out of the jar.

7 Distilled water or purified water. Buy it from your chemist in 5 or 2.5 litre containers. They are much cheaper pro-rata than smaller bottles. If the formula says distilled water, it is for a good reason. If it doesn't, then use tap water. In the event of having a lot of distilled water left over, you can put it to good use by giving your films a final wash in it before hanging them up to dry.

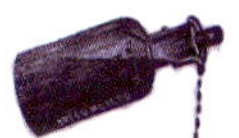

Mixing procedures

Always measure your water first and then stir in your chemical - whether it be liquid or dry. Using warm water will speed up dissolving considerably, but it should not be necessary to use it hotter than 30° C. The best method is to take slightly less water than is needed, mix in your chemical, and then finally add water to make the required amount. For example, to make 1 litre of solution containing 80 grams of powder, take 800 ml of water, add the 80 grams of powder and when it is dissolved, top it up with water to make 1 litre. For a given recipe, mix it in the order in which the ingredients are given, ensuring that each component is completely mixed before adding the next. Do not use any metallic mixing vessels or stirrers, except stainless steel.

When mixing acids (acetic, nitric, sulphuric etc.) make sure you add acid to water. If you pour water onto acid (**particularly** sulphuric) it is liable to spit, boil, and splatter over you and your clothes, and can cause nasty burns.

Using percentage solutions

A very simple way of measuring small amounts of chemical, using the principle that it is much easier to measure small volumes than small weights.

Using 10% solution is the most straightforward - take 10 grams of the chemical you are going to use and dissolve it in slightly less than 100ml of water. After it is dissolved, top the volume up to 100ml. You now know that 10ml of this solution contains 1 gram of the chemical. If a formula calls for 0.3 grams, 3ml can easily be measured with a syringe.

This manual will always give a formula stating a specific quantity of water to a specific amount of chemical, but many books on the subject refer to percentage solutions weight by volume. For example, to make a 10% solution weight by volume or w.v. - as it is usually known - take 100ml water and add 10 grams of chemical. For larger quantities at the same percentage ratio then 500 ml to 50 grams of chemical, or 1 litre to 100 grams of chemical would be mixed.

Some chemical terms used in the text

Anhydrous
Non crystalline powder chemicals that contain no water in their structure (water of crystallisation). If there is a crystalline alternative, a greater weight of it will be required fulfill the same function. Most recently published recipes will specify the anhydrous form.

Chemical
Really short for 'chemical compound', a combination of two, often more, elements giving a substance with distinct physical and chemical properties. A particular compound, however it has been made, will always contain the same elements in a fixed ratio.

Concentration
The amount of a chemical dissolved in a liquid can be expressed in a number of ways, but in the photographic work we are dealing with here will generally be grams of solid dissolved in a litre of water. In the case of liquids it will be millilitres per litre.

Deliquescent
A chemical which absorbs moisture from the air until it liquefies. Hygroscopic is another term for the same effect.

pH scale
Take it on faith that water is made up from equal numbers of hydrogen (H+) and hydroxyl (OH-) ions, and is chemically 'neutral'. Excess hydrogen ions in solution produces an acid condition, while if the balance is towards excess hydroxyl ions the solution is alkaline. This is measured on a scale from 1 to 14, 1 being the most acidic, 14 the most alkaline, and 7 being neutral.

Quality of chemicals
When ordering directly, or through a dealer, from one of the large chemical wholesalers there may be several choices of purity, and the higher the purity the more the price rises. Very pure **Analar** (analytical reagent quality) and **Aristar** (highest purity) are an unnecessary expense and usually not required for photographic work. Usually **GPR** (general purpose reagent) quality is adequate, and the slightly lower purity **Technical** grade should cause no problems.

Reduction & oxidation
Shifts of electrons between chemical compounds, reduction and oxidation always occur simultaneously. In the case of photographic development on exposed film, the latent image acts as a place where the developing agent (the reducing agent) transfers electrons to silver ions (the oxidising agent) to form the silver image.

Solution
Liquid in which mixtures of substances co-exist in even dispersion. In the case of a photo. processing solution the solvent, (almost always water) contains solute, which will be one or more chemical ingredients. A saturated solution contains the maximum dissolved amount of a chemical, for a particular temperature.

Stock solution
Concentrated long-life form of a liquid chemical or initial mixing strength of a powdered chemical, which can be diluted down with water to form a 'working solution'. This usually takes the form 1 plus X, 1 always being the concentrated chemical, and the larger number being the volume of water to use. So a dilution of 1 plus 3 for a developer, starting with 200ml developer stock solution will need 3 x 200ml water in which to dilute the concentrate.

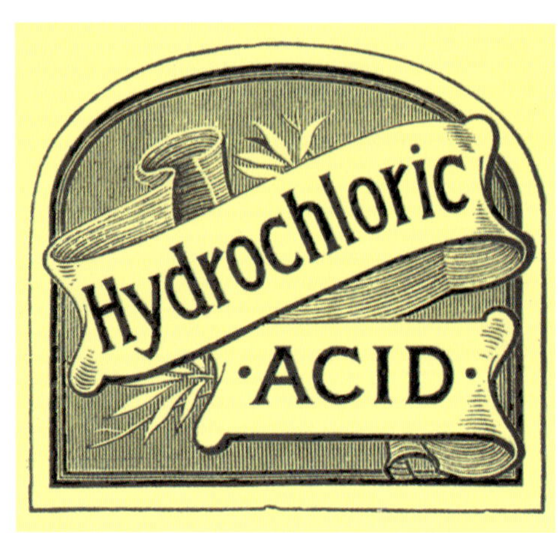

Chemicals used in this manual and how much to buy.

There are a number of basic chemicals which are common to the processes described here. These are the ones you should buy first and should always have on your shelf. They are all stocked by the chemical suppliers listed at the back of the book, and we give with each description the amount that would be practicable to buy when you first start using old processes.

Sodium chloride

Common salt. Buy 100 grams of the photographic quality or a packet of sea salt at the supermarket. Sea salt is purer than ordinary table salt, which contains a significant level of magnesium chloride.

Sodium thiosulphate

'Hypo'. Buy 500 grams You tend to use a lot of it. Get the powdered, or anhydrous form in preference to crystals.

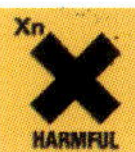

Potassium ferricyanide

Despite the name, it is not a serious poison like its close relative potassium cyanide, which is **not** used in any of these processes. It is a bright red powder. Buy 200gm. Apart from its use in the various iron processes, it is also used to bleach conventional black and white prints before sepia toning.

Potassium dichromate

Potassium bichromate is the older name; they are the same substance. For the rest of the text, apart from referring to the process by its established name 'gum bichromate', we will use the correct 'dichromate' term for the chemical. Buy 100gm. It is a bright orange powder very similar in appearance to potassium ferricyanide. Don't mix them up. It is poisonous so take care. It can also cause skin rashes, so don't slop your hands about in it. Some books state ammonium dichromate in their formulae. As well as being explosive if misused, it is really not any better than the potassium form.

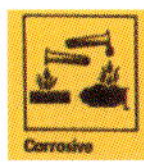

Silver nitrate

Small white granules, poisonous and highly corrosive - take care. Buy 10 or 25 gm. Take care when removing from the container, as the granules spill very easily. It stains anything it touches dark brown - especially fingers. Silver nitrate was once used for curing warts, but nobody has ever proved that it works! It reacts with salts in tap water and will go slightly milky, so should always be used with distilled water.

Ferric ammonium citrate

This can also be expressed as **ammonium ferric citrate**. A fine lime-green powder, or granules. The granular form is like volcanic dust, and just as good, although solutions are likely to need filtering. For photographic work. Avoid the brown variety, as it is not very effective. Buy 100gm. Make sure you keep it in an airtight container as it absorbs water from the air quickly and can end up as a solid blob at the bottom of the jar. As well as being used for old processes, it is a very cheap ingredient for making up blue toner.

Gelatin

If possible, buy the photographic quality which is higher 'bloom' (stronger) than the sort you buy in the supermarket for making jelly. However, either will do. Buy 50 to 100 gm.

Less common chemicals

These are used in only one or two processes and should not be bought until you are ready to work with the process of which they form a part.

Ammonium citrate

Fine white powder, intechangeable for most purposes with potassium citrate.

Ammonium chloride

Fine white crystals, usually goes solid quickly as it absorbs moisture from the air - don't worry if it is in a lump when you obtain it.

Citric acid

Mild acid, apart from use in these recipes can be used at about 3% as an odourless stopbath.

Copper chloride

Proper name cupric chloride, or copper (II) chloride, dark green crystals, poisonous.

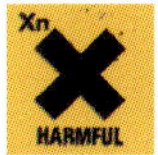

Copper sulphate

Proper name copper (II) sulphate or cupric sulphate. Bright blue crystals, but highly poisonous.

EDTA

Stands for ethylenediaminetetra-acetic acid, there are numerous variations, but the most commonly called for are the di-sodium and tetra-sodium forms.

Ferric chloride
Used in photogravure etching. Highly corrosive and one of the filthiest chemicals you are ever likely to encounter in alternative photography. Needs very careful handling.

Ferric oxalate
Sensitiser chemical used in the platinum / palladium process, best obtained from the platinum specialist Bostick & Sullivan.

Gold chloride
Can be obtained in one gram glass phials, although the best way to buy it is in a pre-dissolved form, which may be a 1 or 2% solution. Ready-made gold toners are more expensive, but more convenient.

Hypo clearing agent
It comes in different manufacturers' packages, and is a mixture of salts which speed up the washing of prints. The best known (and best value) is Kodak Hypo Clearing Agent, which comes as a powder in foil sachets. Others come as liquid, including Ilford Galerie Washaid and Tetenal Lavaquick.

Oxalic acid
Component of the traditional platinum process. Fine white crystals, highly poisonous.

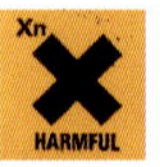

Palladium chloride & platinum chloride
Used in the platinum / palladium process, best source is the USA company 'Bostick & Sullivan.

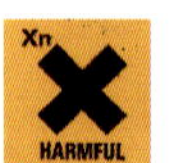

Phosphoric acid
Ortho-phosphoric acid is the usual form, and the powder is generally the cheapest.

Potassium bromide
Fine white crystals.

Potassium citrate
White granular powder.

Potassium ferrocyanide
Easy to mix up with the more commonly used ferricyanide, although visually they are different; ferrocyanide takes the form of light yellow crystals

Potassium metabisulphite
Fine white powder, solid and solutions emit pungent sulphur dioxide, use good ventilation when mixing.

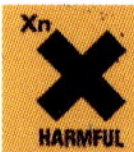

Potassium oxalate
Component of platinum / palladium process. Fine white powder, poisonous by ingestion.

Rochelle salt
The proper chemical name is potassium sodium tartrate.

Sodium tetraborate
Commonly known as **borax**, fine white mildly alkaline powder.

Sodium tetrachloroplatinite
Expensive component of the platinum / palladium process, best obtained from specialist platinum source Bostick & Sullivan.

Sodium carbonate
Usually in anhydrous form, as fine white powder. Moderately powerful alkali.

Tartaric acid
Mild acid, coming as a fine white powder.

Liquid chemicals

These are mainly strong acids and as they are not used at full strength there is no need to buy them this way. Get the 10% version and dilute them according to the formulae.

Nitric acid
Highly corrosive in concentrate. See [26 . Photo etching] for details.

Sulphuric acid
Highly corrosive in concentrate, buy in 10% form.

Hydrochloric acid
Highly corrosive in concentrate, buy in 10% form.

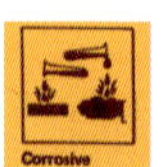

Acetic acid
Very pungent vinegar smell. Sometimes 'glacial' is specified; this is virtually 100% concentration, but freezes at 16° C, so the acid is normally sold at 80% strength. Corrosive, the concentrate causes severe burns.

Hydrogen peroxide
Buy this in a small bottle (250ml) from your local chemist. It doesn't last very long in the bottle, so only buy small quantities.

Coating the paper 7

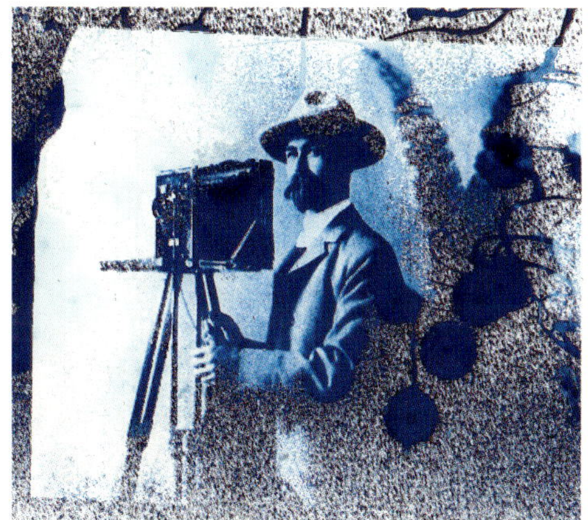

Wild experimental coating. Cyanotype sprayed, dropped with dropper from height of 3', and allowed to run on the page.

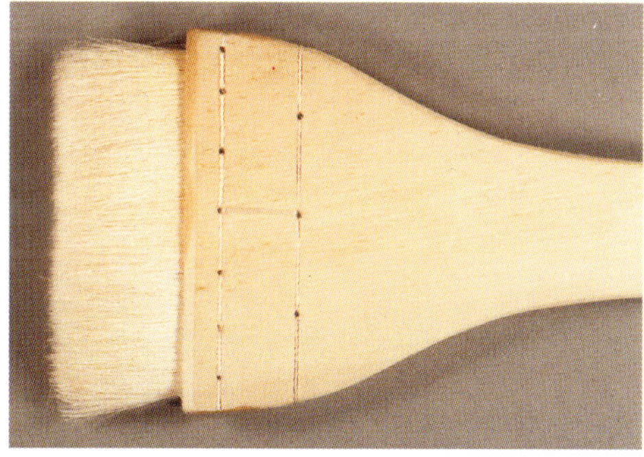

Hake or Jiaban brush, one of the most useful, if you can only afford one type get this one. Note the way it is constructed without using a metal ferrule.

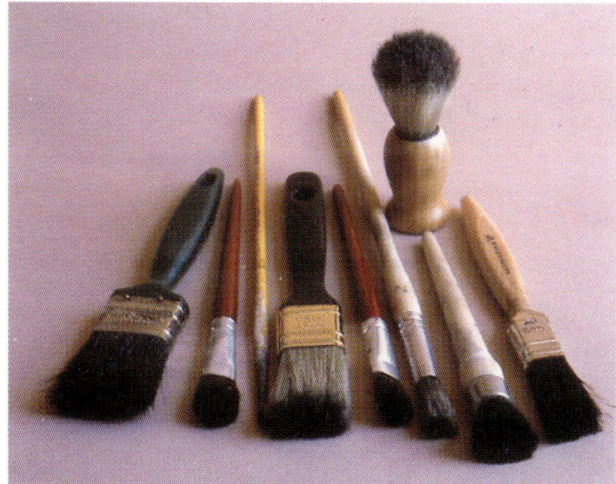

Selection of brushes, including shaving brush bromoil narrow fitches, and common DIY types.

Of all the aspects of alternative printmaking, the least familiar is the hand coating of the light sensitive sensitiser onto plain drawing paper. The nearest most photographers will have been to this operation is if they have used liquid emulsion. This involves applying to the paper a thin layer of gelatin containing silver bromide. This has to be done in orange safelight conditions. Exposure is the same as when using conventional paper, using an enlarger, and processing manually.

A large proportion of the sensitisers used in this manual have the appearance of no more than coloured water - usually yellow or orange, regardless of the final colour of the print. You may find it difficult to comprehend how a piece of drawing or cartridge paper stained with yellow liquid could possibly produce the rich chocolate brown of a kallitype or the cool grey tone of a platinum print. The answer is simple. The action of light on the various metallic salts, in conjunction with the appropriate chemistry reduces them to microscopically small particles of metal, which lodge in the fibres of the paper. In modern photographic papers, the salts of silver are suspended in a layer of gelatin coated onto paper by the manufacturer. In some cases, as in R.C. papers, this gelatin is itself coated onto an intermediate layer of poly-ethylene. Although modern papers are made in glossy, lustre or matt surfaces, none of them can really compare with the smooth velvety sheen of hand-coated prints.

Hand-coating paper is relatively simple and can be achieved successfully with a little practice. There are three basic methods and a fair number of variations.

1 Brushing the sensitiser onto the paper.

2 Coating using a cylindrical glass rod to spread the sensitiser.

3 Floating the paper face down in a dish of the liquid sensitiser.

Hand-coating paper lies somewhere between applying a watercolour wash and painting your living room wall with emulsion paint. Both have to be even and without streaks. Practice coating your paper with water to which has been mixed a little water colour pigment or writing ink, or even coffee (the colour at this stage is irrelevant).

Brushing

Take a piece of plain white drawing paper about 10 x 8" and attach it to a flat piece of hardboard either with a drawing pin at each corner or a strip of masking tape along each edge. Make sure the paper is flat and doesn't curl.

Now, very lightly, draw with a soft pencil a rectangle in the centre of the paper, about the size you would expect your negative to be - say 5 x 7 inches. Alternatively, you can just mark out the corners of your coating area with 'L' marks, again with a pencil. Next pour a little coloured water into a saucer. Take a flat paint brush, see [4 . Equipment], about one inch

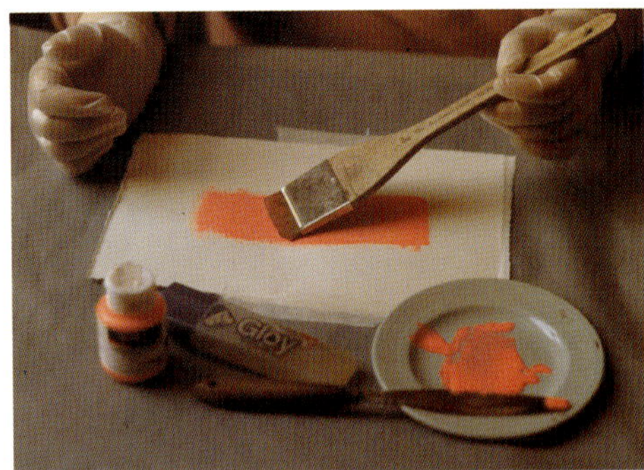

Coating with a brush horizontally....

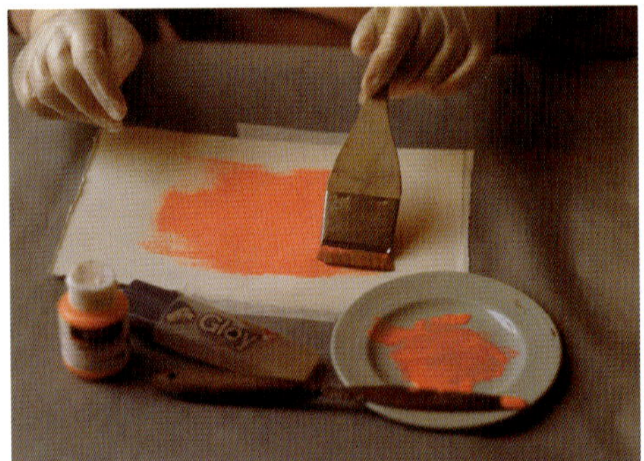

.....and vertically.

wide. Dip it into the liquid, but don't overcharge the brush. Brush the coloured liquid onto the paper within the rectangle, first in horizontal stripes then vertically. Do this gently to avoid abrading the paper surface, and make sure any small puddles are brushed into the paper. If you find you have far too much liquid on the paper, dry your brush on a ball of cotton wool or kitchen towel, and then continue to brush until the rectangle is evenly covered. The paper should absorb the liquid to the extent that when you look across the surface of the paper no pools of liquid remain. At this stage you can carry the liquid across the pencil line to give a small margin of brushed liquid with a ragged edge, (see illustration). When exposed this will give you the brushed edge which is characteristic of so many old process prints. With practice you can eventually control this brushed margin to give your print your own 'trademark' - see illustration. When you feel confident that you have mastered this part of the process, you can safely deal with the coating involved in making salt prints, cyanotypes, kallitypes, palladium and platinum.

The technique for gum printing is slightly different [20 . Gum printing]. You can now hang your paper in subdued light and let it dry. You can speed up the drying process by gentle heat with a hair dryer. If when you hang your paper up to dry, you see small rivulets of liquid running down to the lower edge, you have applied too much liquid. Let it dry naturally. You'll know better next time.

Coating paper is one of the essential skills in working with alternative processes. Make sure you spend sufficient time learning this particular skill. It will pay dividends in the long run.

Note: some 'authorities' on coating paper recommend pouring a small pool of liquid onto the centre of the paper and immediately brushing liquid from the centre to the edges of the paper. There is a problem. Some papers absorb liquid more readily than others and quite often you end up with a print containing a dark irregular blob in the centre, roughly the same shape as your original pool of liquid, where the pool of liquid has sunk quickly into the fibres of the paper. Use this method at your peril!

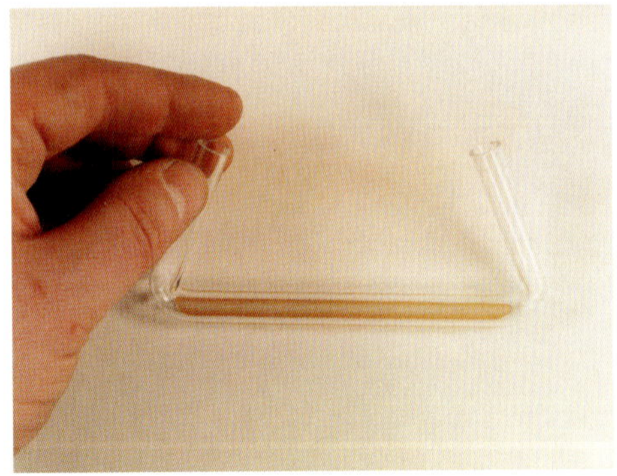

Example of a glass coating rod, showing how solutions cling to it by capillary action.

Coating with a glass rod

This method of coating is the best alternative to brushing. Its main advantage is economy. When you dip a brush into an expensive sensitiser such as platinum, some of the liquid stays in the bristles of the brush and is wasted. With rod coating virtually all the emulsion ends up on the paper - which it is where it should be. The glass rods themselves can be purchased quite cheaply. We recommend a few practice runs before coating with an expensive sensitiser - black coffee makes a good test solution, showing evenness of coating, and allows you to work out how much sensitiser will be placed for a number of passes of the rod. The amount of sensitiser the paper will accept varies according to the makeup of the paper itself, and how well it is sized.

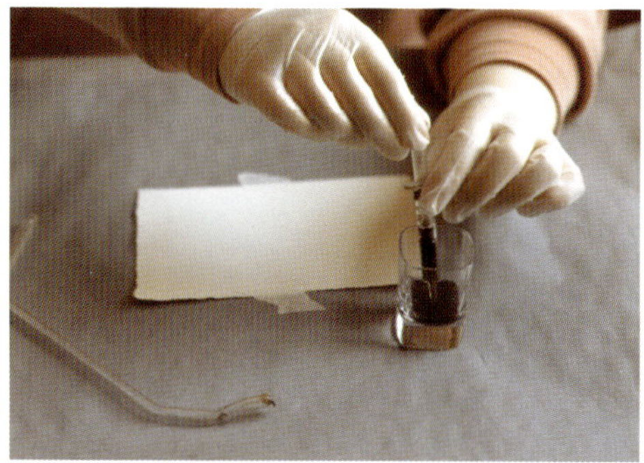

Rod coating. Filling the syringe.

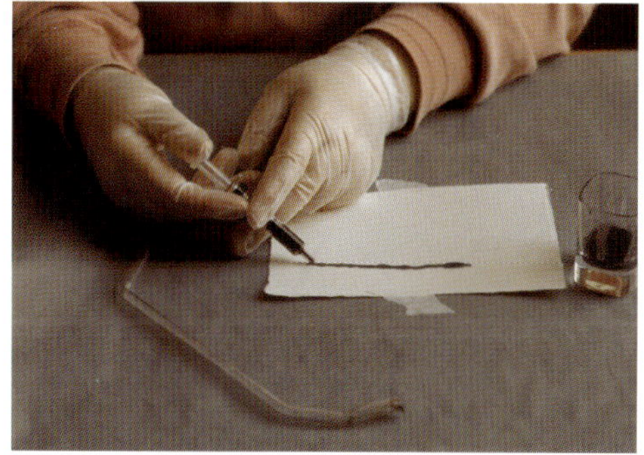

Running a line of solution along the paper.

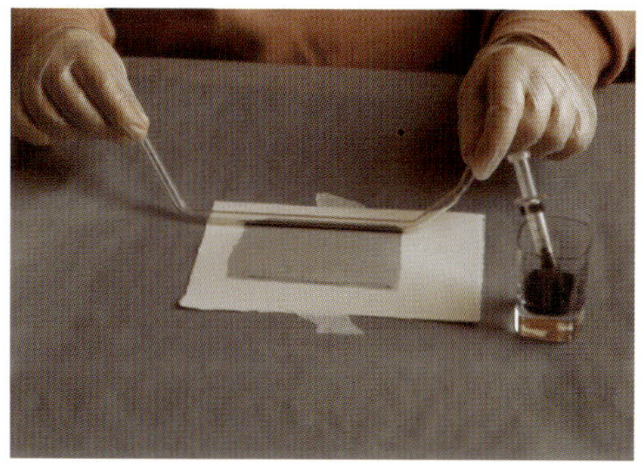

Drawing the rod across the paper to give an even coating. This may be repeated forward and backward a few times to distribute all the solution evenly.

Mark out the size of your image on paper with a pencil (see 'Brushing'). Take a 2ml syringe, depress the plunger, place the end in your container of sensitiser and pull out the plunger until the syringe is three-quarters full. Gently and slowly run the syringe along one edge of the image area, at the same time depressing the plunger. With a bit of practice you should deposit a thin line of liquid on the paper. Touch the rod down on the line of liquid, which by capillary action will immediately cling to it. Now draw the rod slowly down the paper until you reach the bottom of the marked out image area. Lift the rod off the paper, then touch it down again, picking up the line of liquid again. Now move the rod up to the top again. Repeat this sequence perhaps 4 - 5 times, until the liquid is evenly coated and fully absorbed. Finally, lift the rod away and use a piece of blotter to mop up any small amount of surplus liquid. If there is an excessive residue of liquid, use a smaller starting volume. Dry the paper in the normal way.

You may want to make your own rod to suit your own size and specification. In this case take a length of hollow glass rod about 12 inches long and a quarter of an inch diameter, (buy it from a laboratory supplier in Yellow Pages). Now you have to bend it into shape. Hold one end covered with a damp cloth and direct the other end over a gas flame (Bunsen burner, gas cooker jet), so that the heat is concentrated on a point about 2 inches from the end of the rod. This point of the rod will soon glow red and become pliable. While it is still red, hold the end of the rod with a pair of pliers and bend it gently until it is at an angle of 60 degrees to the long part of the rod. It will only bend if the part of the rod where you want it to bend is red hot. When it is bent to the correct angle place the glass on a heat proof surface and allow it to cool. Now repeat this exercise using the opposite end. Make sure the bent ends are at the same angle and in the same plane. Make sure also that the long central part of the rod remains perfectly straight. Especially make sure you take great care - you can give yourself a very nasty burn with glass at these temperatures.

Floating the paper

This involves taking the paper and coating by laying it onto the surface of the sensitiser. This is best done by people who do it day-in day-out for a living, and there are none of those left now.

The real disadvantage to floating paper on the sensitiser, and this applies in particular to silver nitrate, is that continual dunking of salted paper in the silver solution dilutes the mixture and deposits residues in the liquid. This then requires a complicated titration procedure to restore it back to working condition.

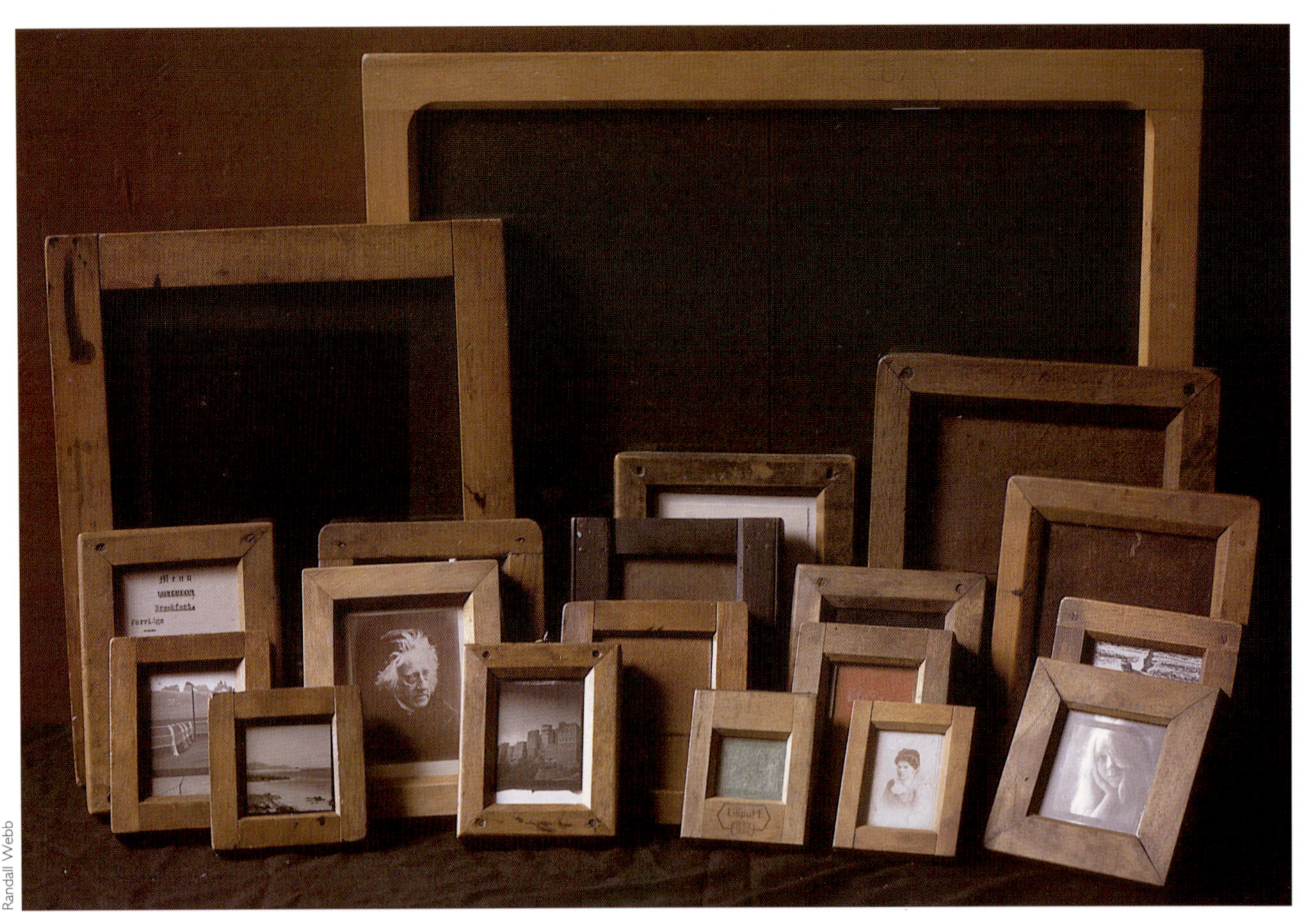

Randall Webb

Old and new printing frames in the traditional hinge-back style, authors collection.

Exposing the print

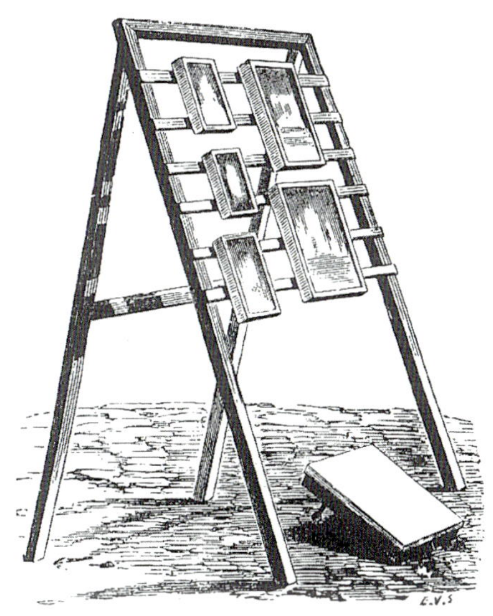
Sun printing in the 19'th century.

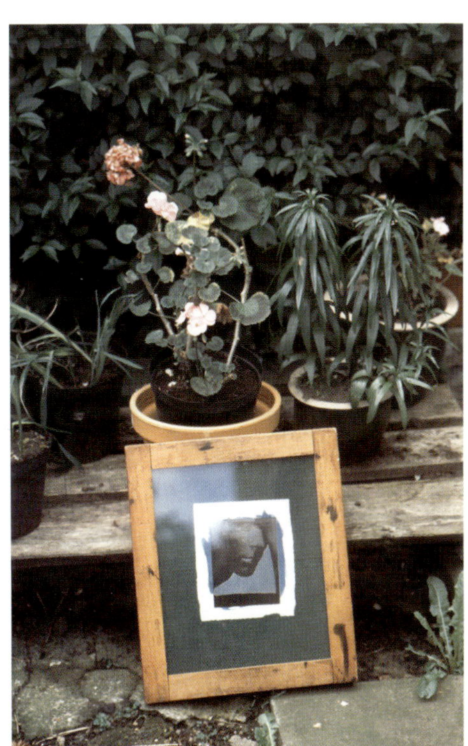
Sun printing in the 20'th century.

The only way to expose prints in nearly all the processes in this manual is by contact under ultra violet light. In the nineteenth century there was no source of UV other than sunlight. On a sunny day in summer the average exposure time could be up to twenty minutes, whereas in cloudy winter weather it could take as long as two or three days. On dry days printing was carried out in the garden and on wet days in a glass covered conservatory. Modern technology has given us a greater choice of light sources, but many people still prefer the authenticity of sun printing. This method is not only historically correct, but is also free. Its disadvantage is its inconsistency. The strength of daylight varies according to time of day and the time of year. It is also subject to cloud cover, fog and rain. For many of the printing-out processes, where you inspect the print at intervals to see if it has 'cooked', this is not so much of a problem, but for some of the processes which need more precise exposure it is not an ideal solution. Substitutes for sun printing now include mercury vapour lamps, sun ray lamps, and UV fluorescent tubes, (see equipment section).

Contact printing with old processes is just the same as contacting conventional negatives. A sandwich is made by placing together in this order:

sheet of glass / negative / sheet of sensitised paper / and a rigid backing.

These are held firmly in contact either with clips or in some form of frame. The traditional printing frame has a hinged wooden back which can be opened one side at a time to check the progress of the exposure (see illustration). It is possible to obtain original versions of the old printing frames from junk shops and car boot sales, or they can be made quite cheaply by the average DIY enthusiast. Otherwise use a clip frame or a picture frame which is easily dismantled. The simplest of all is a piece of plate glass and a sheet of hardboard or MDF board from a DIY store, held together with a strong bulldog clip on each side. The sandwich should be put together so that when it is facing the light source the various components should be in order from the top:

glass (clean and no scratches) **/ negative** (shiny side up) **/ coated sheet of paper** (negative should cover the coated area) **/ backing**

Any variation of this sequence will result in either a black blob on the paper or a clear sheet after processing! Bear in mind that the coated paper must be bone dry before you put it in contact with the negative. If it is not, you stand the risk of ineradicable stains on your precious negative. If you are worried about your negative, then place a clear sheet of thin acetate between the paper and the negative. Thin gauge Mylar (ICI trade name for polyester) is the most effective, see [33 . Suppliers].

Here comes a problem - registration. If you use a hinged back printing frame you can check your exposure by undoing half of the back to check its progress, (see illustration). On the other hand when using a clip frame or glass and bulldog clips you need to fix the negative and paper together

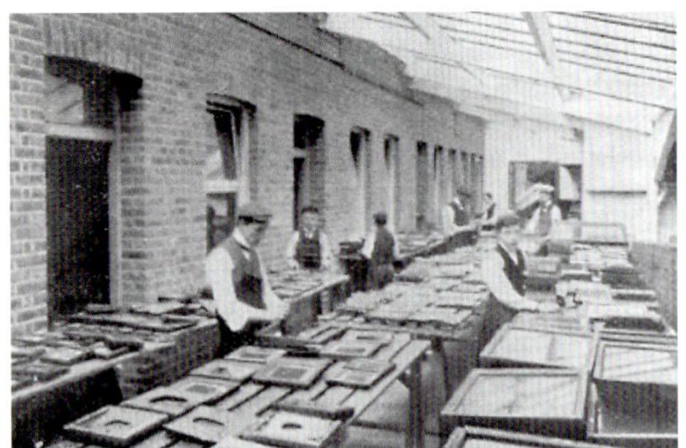

D & P in the 19'th century. Note the glass conservatory roof for maximum brightness.

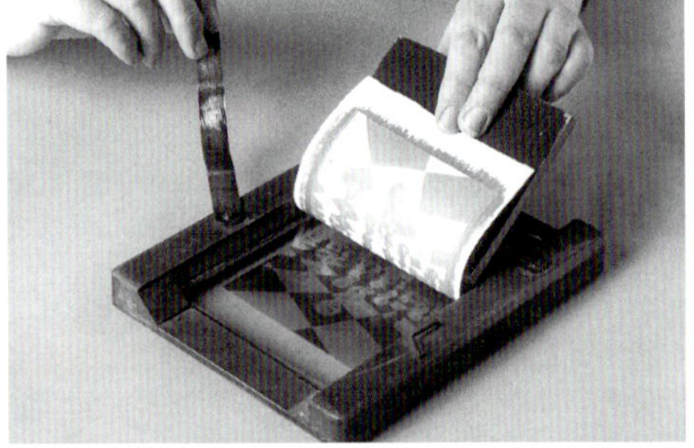

Checking exposure with a traditional hinged-back printing frame. This allows viewing while maintaining full registration.

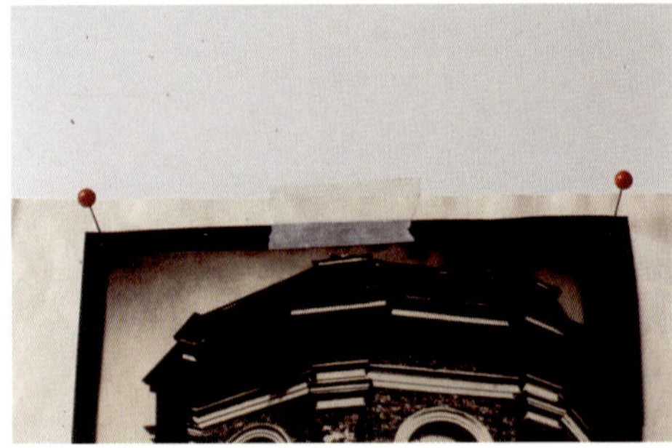

The tried and tested registration method using pins. Any push pin will work.

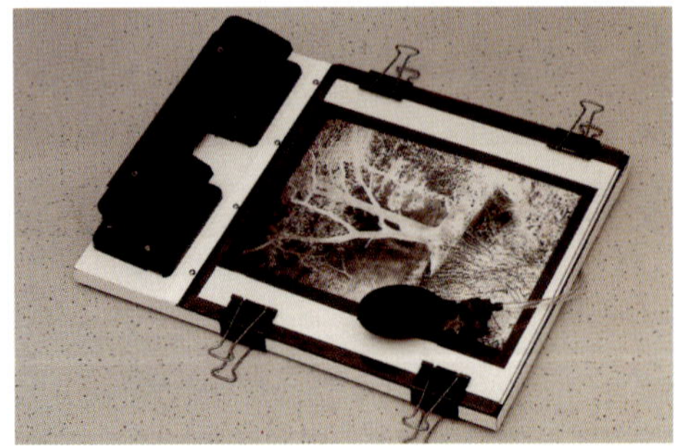

Peter Fredericks innovative register easel design, using air pressure to maintain contact across the platten.

to prevent them from coming out of alignment. Place a piece of Scotch 'Magic' tape along the side of the negative so the overlapping edge adheres to the paper. When you take them out to check the exposure they stay in register. After the exposure is complete the tape can be peeled off gently. Don't use masking tape as this is opaque and will leave an irregular white rectangle on the edge of your image.

There is an added sophistication if you are using multiple coating (eg in gum printing or gum on top of cyanotype). Here you will need to re-register your print and negative between processing stages. You can use a complicated hole punch system, but the time honoured and simple method is as follows. Lay your negative in position on your coated paper and place them both flat on a piece of soft board or card board. Then take two drawing pins and push them through the two top corners making a pin hole through both. Before removing the pins, tape the two together as before. Remove the pins and make your exposure as usual. When the print has been processed and dried, place the paper and negative together and push the pins through both the existing holes and tape the neg and paper as before. You now have the paper and negative in perfect registration. This is better than registering visually, especially when the second coating is somewhat opaque and it is difficult to make out the details of the original image.

A more sophisticated means of registration can be devised by anyone with DIY skills, using a dismantled 2-pin office punch, a piece of hardboard and some tape. A ready made punch on this principle is produced by Peter Frederick, using a 4 hole punch with precision turned registration pins. The pins can be obtained separately if you want to make up your own pin-register easel.

There are two other aspects of exposing old process prints which may be unfamiliar.

First, contrast control. Certain processes, in particular salt and kallitype, can vary in terms of contrast by the quality of light used to expose them. If placed in direct sunlight the contrast in these is less than if they are placed in the shade out of the direct rays of the sun. There used to be a tradition of printing 'plucky' (ie contrasty) negatives in direct sunlight and less contrasty negatives in the shade or on a dull day. The proof of this may be best obtained by means of some trial and error experimenting on your part.

Secondly there is the phenomenon of 'self masking'. This happens when exposing salt prints, kallitypes, platinum and palladium. As the print darkens in the light, the darker shadows act as a barrier to the light and slow down the exposure in these areas, leaving the highlights to continue exposing. This has the effect of separating the tones in both shadows and highlights, giving these processes their characteristic subtle tonalities. We make the obvious assumption that you have in the first place made a negative with details in the shadows and good separation in the higher tones, see [9 . Negatives].

Making contact negatives

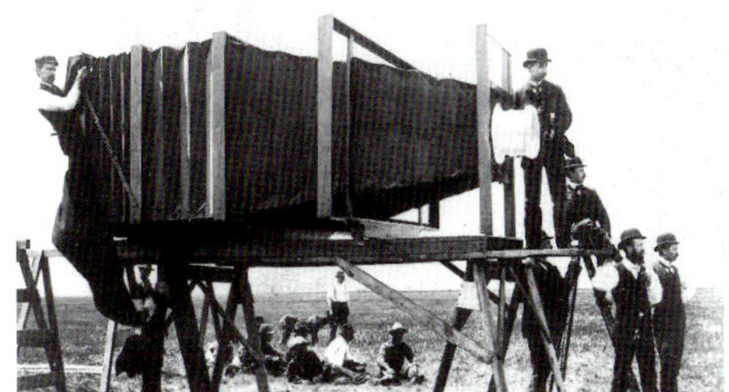

If you need a big negative sometimes the easiest way is to get a big camera.

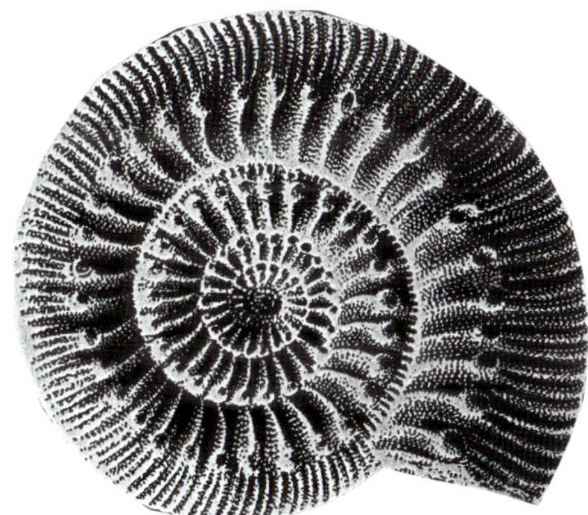

Photocopy on acetate as a negative.

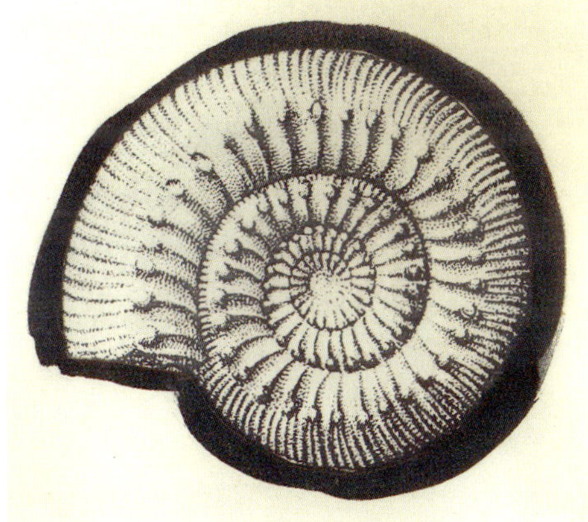

Cyanotype printed from the negative above.

For most photographers contact printing is a chore. Those working with transparencies or colour negatives don't have to bother with it anyway. Black and white workers tend to use contact printing to check that the focussing and composition are correct, and there is a small body of photographers who don't bother with this stage in the process at all.

Zone system enthusiasts use contact printing to check the correctness of their camera exposure and film development by exposing the contact to obtain the first maximum black on the edge of the film. Finally, there are those who make contact prints as a part of their day to day output. Contacting from two and a quarter square, five by four, five by seven, ten by eight, or bigger takes you into a world of precise, sharp and delicate tonalities which are impossible with conventional enlargements.

If you don't believe this claim, then get hold of some old glass plate negatives from a junk shop or jumble sale and try printing them. You will probably need to print them on grade one or two to appreciate their quality.

In any case it will be good practice for what is to come. If you are going to explore the possibilities offered by old processes, then contact printing is the essence and the core of all that you do.

In the earliest days of photography the only way to make a print was to expose it by contact with a negative in daylight. When projection speed bromide paper was introduced at the end of the 19'th century it became possible to make enlargements using a tungsten lamp in an enlarger. However, all the processes in this manual (with the exception of bromoil and bleach etch) demand the use of contact printing. **You cannot make old process prints in an enlarger**.

Therefore it follows that if all printing is by contact, your negative must be the same size as your final image on the print. There is no reason why you shouldn't contact your Nikon negatives onto platinum or carbon provided that you don't mind a 24mm by 36mm image on the wall. By the same token a huge impressive 20 x 24" gum print would require a camera that takes negatives that size as well as half a ton of tripod and a truck to carry them in. A reasonable compromise would be to make an enlarged negative from your 35mm or 120 negs.

Advantages of contact printing vs. enlarging

1 Contact prints direct from camera negatives have an indefinable jewel-like quality which seem to enhance the reality they record. This is assuming reality is what you are looking for.

2 The lack of any enlargement makes the print much sharper, and details much more clearly defined. What you get on the negative, you get on the print.

3 The magnification that goes with enlarging the image also magnifies the

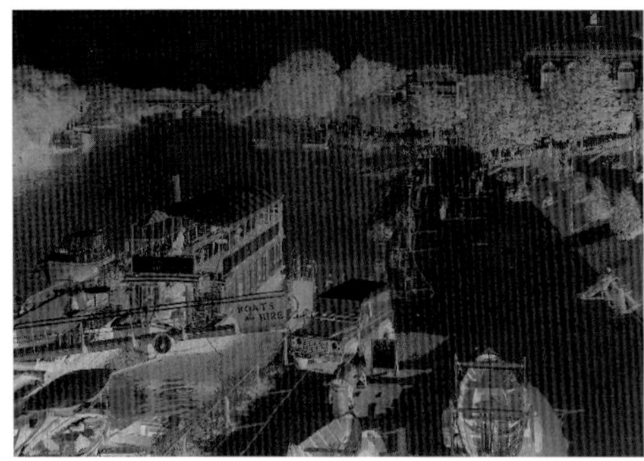

Fig 1 Normal negative. Highlights not too dense and plenty of details in the shadows. The best way of achieving this is by using the classic Zone system method of overexposing one stop and reducing the manufacturers recommended developing time by 20%. This will give you perfect negative for b&w printing and for making interpositives to make into enlarged negatives for old processes..

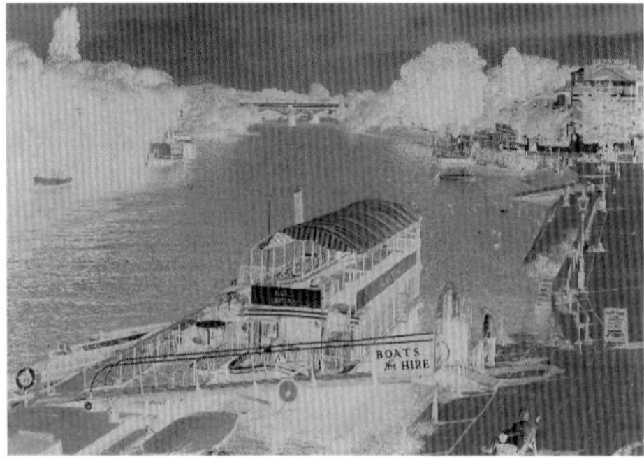

Fig 2 Underexposed and normal development. Somewhat anaemic and not much use.

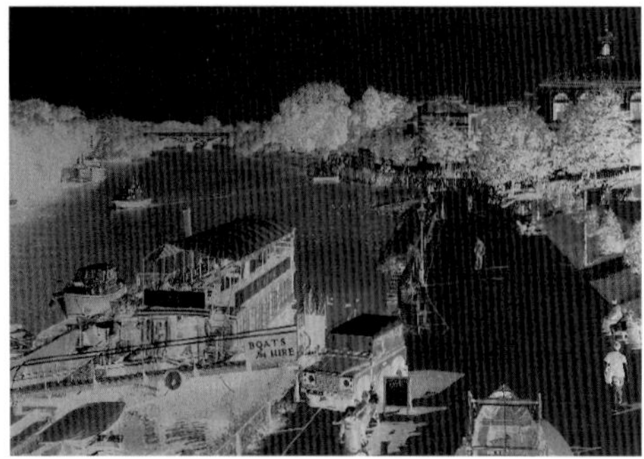

Fig 3 Under-exposed and over-developed. Over dense highlights and thin shadows. This is the sort of negative you get if you indulge in the current fashion for pushing film. It's pretty useless at the best of times, and particularly so for old processes. If you insist on doing this, you should take a long hard look at your negative making technique.

effect of the grain structure in the film. Contact prints have a smooth, velvet-like appearance in the darker tones and a creamy silkiness in the highlights, even if a relatively high speed film has been used to make the negative.

4 Contact prints show a better tonality in the highlights with no 'white wash' effect which occurs when condenser enlargers are used. The latter are subject to the 'Callier effect' which degrades the subtle highlights on the print.

5 A speck of dust on a negative, when enlarged makes a proportionately large white spot on the print. Providing you keep the contact printing frame's glass and the negative clean, this is less of a problem. Small specks of dust stay small. The problems of retouching are thus much reduced.

6 There are no dangers from light and definition fall-off as there are with the illumination systems of some enlargers.

Disadvantages of contact printing vs. enlarging

1 You are unable to change the size of the image on your printing paper.

2 It is difficult but not impossible to dodge or burn in parts of the image.

3 Equally it is more difficult to make superimpositions or montages than it is with an enlarger. On the other hand, with some of the processes described in this manual you can chop up negatives with impunity.

4 Dust is always a problem with large format cameras. Opening and closing the bellows always seems to suck clouds of dust into the camera, and some of it lands on the negative before it is exposed. In due course, this shows as a black spots on the print.

To be historically correct we should make contact prints from our original camera negatives, but as the nineteenth century had not arrived at the concept of 35mm cameras, then we at the start of the twenty-first century have to make compromises and use enlarged negatives for our printing.

But first we should look in much greater detail at the whole subject of making negatives. This is a subject on which every photographer is an expert until you start asking questions about how it is done.

As the hand coated emulsions that we use do not come in variable contrast form, we have to make our negatives of a specific contrast grade to get the best results. So make sure you understand what is meant by the terms 'density' and 'contrast'. Density is the thickness of metallic silver deposited on the film by the action of light falling on it during exposure and consequently the action of development. The thicker the layer the denser the negative and the less that light is able to travel through it. The density of a negative is controlled by both the exposure to light and also by the amount of development it is given.

However the density of a negative should not be confused with the contrast.

Contrast is the result of three different factors.

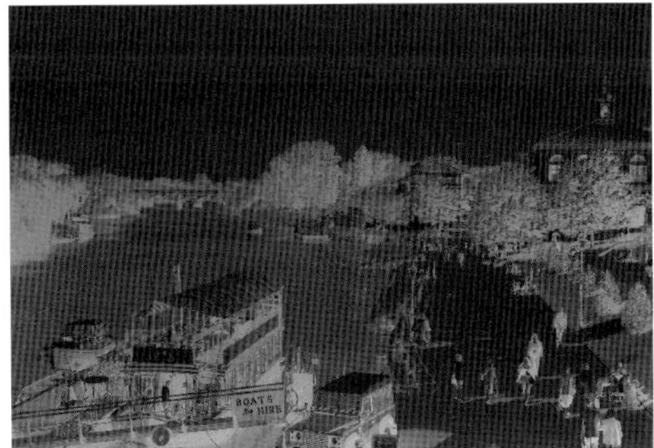

Fig 4 Over-exposed and under-developed. An extreme version of fig 1. Quite useful if you use Multigrade with a no. 5 filter and when making interpositives for some of the old processes.

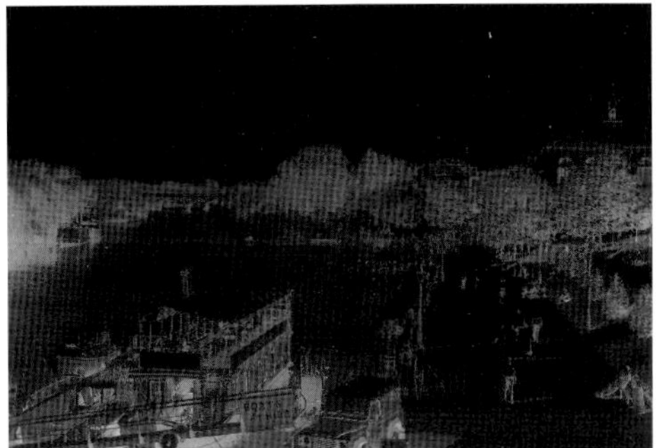

Fig 5 Over-exposed and over-developed. The sort of thing to use for blacking out your darkroom window.

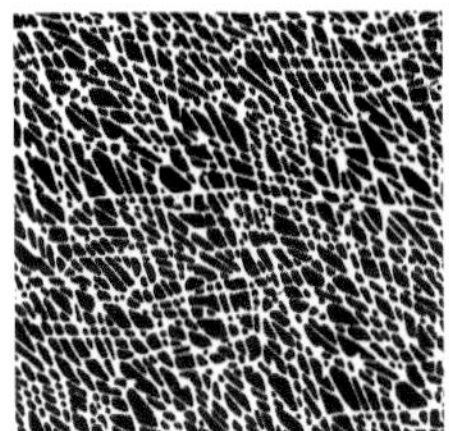

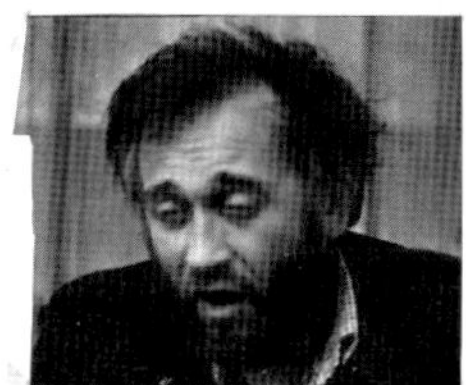

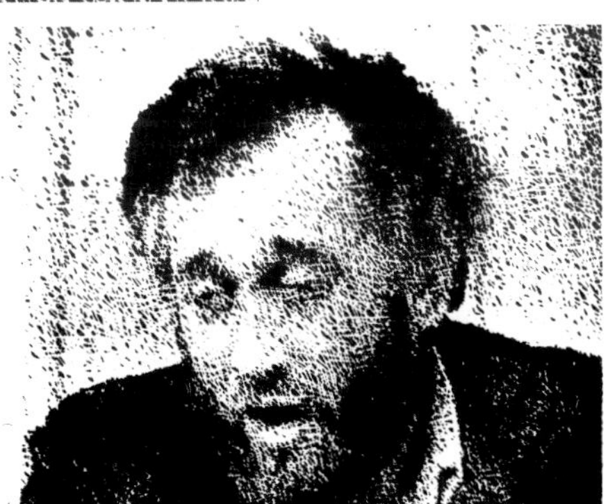

Top right, print from camera negative. Top left, enlarged Letratone screen. The lower image is the lith positive obtained after the Letratone screen is over-printed in sandwich with the lith negative.

1 The lighting of the subject at the time of taking.

2 The inherent characteristics of the film being used.

3 The amount of time the film spends in the developer.

No. 1 is obvious and needs no more explanation.

Films have different features. Fast films tend to be lower in contrast than slow ones and lith films have a very high contrast compared with most other films. The control of contrast that we shall be concerned with most is that of development. As a general principle, the longer a film is developed the greater is its contrast.

If part of a negative receives little light on it (eg. in the shadow area of the scene), when it is developed it will not get any darker however much development it is given. But the parts which have received more light will continue to darken as they are given more development. It is this factor that controls contrast. Another general rule is that the more light that falls on a particular part of a negative, the more it continues to darken in development.

So, if you want a high contrast negative, then you must use contrasty film, and / or developer and develop it for considerably longer than usual.

If we look at the practice of 'pushing' film we shall see that it involves raising the stated film speed which amounts to under-exposure and over-development. This gives us a negative which is contrasty, but which has very little density in the shadow areas and high density in the highlights. One way to ruin a good continuous tone film!

A far better way is to give the negative adequate or generous exposure to make sure all the shadows are properly visible, and then to extend development the negative to whatever degree you need for the process you intend to use.

Another problem that occurs is that of distinguishing between a dense negative and a contrasty one.

A negative may be very dense overall, but in fact be of relatively low contrast. Conversely a very thin, low density negative can contain areas of very high density, and so would in fact be fairly contrasty.

This may be where the use of a densitometer could be justified. Nevertheless, in spite of modern technology the only real way to judge contrast is the craftsman's way. Hold the negative up to the light and make a judgement by eye. Then, if in doubt, make a test strip or several. This is where experience and practice are superior to electronic machines.

Ways of making negatives for old process printing

We can divide films for old processes into two basic types.

1 **Continuous tone film** which includes most camera films and line film.

2 **Graphic arts**, high contrast and lith film.

Camera film

Use this only in cameras, as it is mostly panchromatic. All standard black and white films regardless of size are suitable. If you use standard film

Densitometry

To get a good level of precision into exposure and development some degree of calibration is required, and at the most basic level this means using a step wedge, a range of evenly spaced densities on film base.

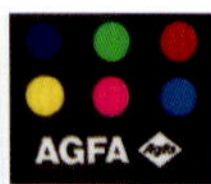

The one shown here is from Agfa, and is remarkably low in price (about £10 at time of writing). The step wedge is exposed onto a sample piece of the film or paper being used. After processing, the densities of this print of the wedge are read with a densitometer. Densitometers are expensive and only perform one job, which is why we don't recommend running out to get one immediately. However, occasional access to one for checking your negative range is useful. The one illustrated is the Macbeth TR924, which has separate heads for measuring transmission (films) and reflection (prints). Density is shown on a digital display.

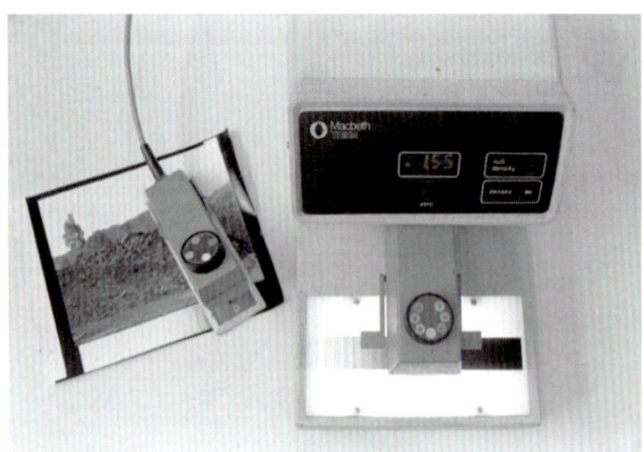

Exposure, that is the light reaching the unexposed film, and the resulting density after the film is processed both pose problems when giving them numerical terms - they can cover an enormous range. To use a number system that is simple to work with, density is measured in **logarithmic** units. It works much like the f-stops on your camera lens. To get ones head around it, think of the amount of light transmitted by the negative, that is the percentage of the light hitting the film that actually makes it through. If 100% of the light is passed, the density will be 0. But every time the transmission is halved, the density increases by 0.3.

Transmittance		Density
1.00	(100%)	0
0.5	(50%)	0.3
0.25	(25%)	0.6
0.125	(12.5%)	0.9
0.063	(6.25%)	1.2
0.031	(3.125%)	1.50
0.015	(1.56%)	1.80

This system relates to that used in exposure, where every doubling of f-stop gives the film half the exposure, and numerically this is also shown by an increase of 0.3. The name for this is the log of exposure, or more briefly **Log E**. So both exposure and density are measured in similar units, and can be related to each other with a simple graph, (next page).

developers you may have to increase development by up to 100%. You can increase contrast without spending too much time in the dark by using the different dilutions offered by Kodak's HC110, or use D19 which is also made by Kodak. You could also make up your own as published in books such as 'The Darkroom Cook Book'. These usually show formulae which do not contain metol.

Colour slides, colour negatives, chromogenic films (Ilford XP2, Kodak TMAX 400 CN) reversal (Agfa Scala) and Polaroid negative film, all are potential source material.

Slides and reversal film need only one step in the enlarger to make an enlarged negative, but most colour material is difficult to control in terms of contrast. This is better done at a later stage. So if you want to contact this straight from your medium or large format camera you may have problems with some processes. Also when colour slides are translated into black and white negative they do not have the same tonal range as those from black and white originals (despite what some people say).

There is one other way of using camera film and that is to process Kodak T-Max 100 film in Kodak's T-Max 100 reversal kit. This gives you a positive T-Max 100 film which can then be turned into an enlarged negative in one step in the enlarger.

Enlarged negatives

If you need to make prints larger than the size of your camera negative you will have to make enlarged negatives on sheet film. This is a practice which was rarely - if ever - found in the last century but if you must, you must.

One small note about using ortho sheet film of whatever size. Don't be intimidated by it. It's really no different from paper except that it is on a transparent base whereas paper is translucent. Cut it with scissors and process it in paper developer under a red safelight.

Using continuous tone & line films

Sheet films generally come in sizes from 5 x 4" upwards and are supplied by most leading film manufacturers. The only real distinction that can be drawn between 'line' and 'continuous tone' film is that line film works to a higher contrast for a given development. Both types can be either **orthochromatic** (blue & green sensitive) or **blue sensitive**, so check your safelight is the right one. The most useful for continuous tone work are;

Ilford Ortho Plus - this is continuous tone, very versatile and quite fast at about 80 ISO, so it can be used in a large format camera.

Agfa N31P - officially discontinued at the time of writing, although Agfa has enough stock to last some years. Excellent tonal separation, the standard film used by some professional labs making platinum prints.

Kodak Precision Line Film - good value for money, about half the price of other films, although inherently high in contrast.

Bergger Ortho (BPFO) - blue sensitive continuous tone film, with the advantage of being available in small packings, (10's in A4 & A3).

Y axis - **Density**

This is the plot of the densities in the exposed and processed copy made from the step wedge.

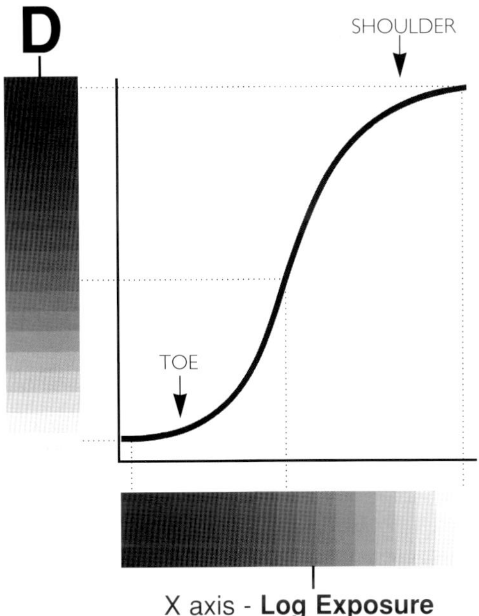

X axis - **Log Exposure**

This is not as complicated as it sounds; it is taken by plotting the range of densities in the original step wedge itself.

Densities of the original wedge, and readings of prints made from it are plotted against each other as a graph, called a characteristic curve. This is a way of examining changes that take place during the printing process. In an ideal world the plot would be a straight line, but the inevitable distortions that take place usually end up with the copy showing compressions in tone, a **toe** in the shadows, and a **shoulder** in the highlights. Lots of information can be drawn out of a characteristic curve plot, including contrast, density range and speed. Even if you do not have access to a densitometer it is useful to include a transmission wedge alongside your negative when printing. Visually, quite a bit can still be taken from the copy on the print.

Important values are **Dmax**, the maximum density measured on film or paper, and **Dmin**, the minimum density. When making negatives for old processes, we need to control the **density range**, the highest and lowest densities in which you want to see detail in the print. With a densitometer you can measure the highlights and shadows which contain these end values, and calculate the net density by subtracting the Dmin from the Dmax value. The table here relates ideal net density range to conventional paper grade values.

Paper Grade No.		Net Density Range Required
Low Contrast	0	1.40 plus
	1	1.20 to 1.40
	2	1.00 to 1.20
	3	0.80 to 1.00
	4	0.60 0.80
High contrast	5	0.60 and less

Just to confuse the issue, most lith film can be used as continuous tone film if it is developed in paper developer diluted slightly more than recommended by the maker, (for more details see below on lith film).

The simplest and the quickest method which you can use to practise with and to familiarise yourself with the system (but not necessarily for your finest exhibition prints), is to first make a standard black and white print on resin coated glossy paper, about 10 x 8" size. Take this to your nearest photocopy shop and ask them to make a negative copy on acetate. This is a normal operation for them and will only cost a pound or two. This will be your first enlarged negative and if you damage it you can always get another one.

Now let us look at using line film. In addition to your usual enlarging equipment you will need either a plain contact printing frame or a clean sheet of plate glass with buffed edges, and not more that 10 x 12". Most line and lith film is dark red on the front and pink on the back. Not very easy to see the difference in a red safelight. Learn to read it by gently rolling over the corner so that the back overlays the front. The back is darkest. After a bit of practise it gets easier.

1 Make a 10 x 8" resin coated glossy print, or use the one you made for the photocopy. When it is dry and in red safelight, place it face down onto a sheet of line film which should be on the baseboard of the enlarger, pink (or front) side up. Cover it with the piece of glass. We assume you have adjusted the enlarger to illuminate the whole area of this sandwich. Open the lens fully and make a test strip covering a quarter of the sandwich every 20 seconds. With a normal enlarger the light should penetrate the translucent resin paper and make an image on the film in about 40 to 60 seconds.

Take out the film and cut it into four strips at right angles to the strips you made during the exposure. Develop these strips separately in paper developer for 1, 2, 3 and 4 minutes respectively. Fix, wash and dry. Now you can assess them simultaneously for exposure and contrast.

If they are not what you need you can make the necessary adjustments until they are, either by exposure or development or both. This method is by far the best way of making enlarged negatives. We will, however give you some useful alternatives.

2 Contact print your camera negative on to a small piece of line film (make the usual exposure and development tests first). When it is dry trim the resulting positive to fit your enlarger negative carrier and enlarge onto a sheet of line film of the size you require.

3 If you have access to a large format enlarger, enlarge your camera negative onto a piece of line film say 5 x 4" or 5 x 7" and then enlarge that onto a larger sheet of line film as necessary.

4 Enlarge your camera negative onto line film up to the size you need for your final image. Then contact print this positive onto another sheet of line film of the same size. This method uses a lot more line film but the interpositive is very easy to retouch with dyes.

Films for different purposes

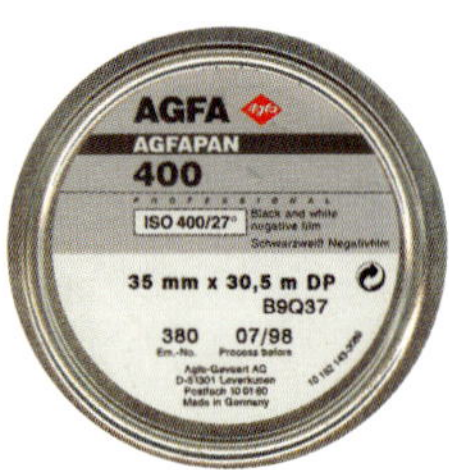

General purpose ***panchromatic*** film, sensitive to all colours of light. Use it in a camera for making your original negatives. Comes in a wide range of speeds and formats., inc. Kodak TMax and Tri-X, Ilford FP4, HP5 and Delta, Agfapan APX.

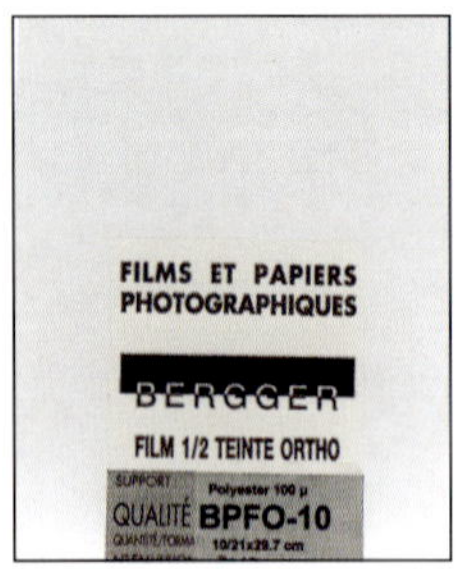

Bergger BPFO continuous tone slow orthochromatic film, suitable for most of the processes in this book. Available in packs of 10, A4 & A3.

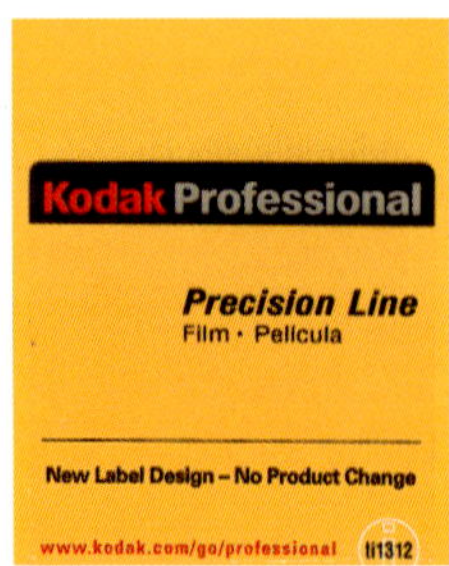

Line film, high in contrast but not to the same level as lith film in lith dev. Can be used for many processes in this book, especially those needing hard negatives, such as platinum. Makes include Kodak LPF7, Bergger BPFB, Maco ORT 25 (in 120 & 35mm).

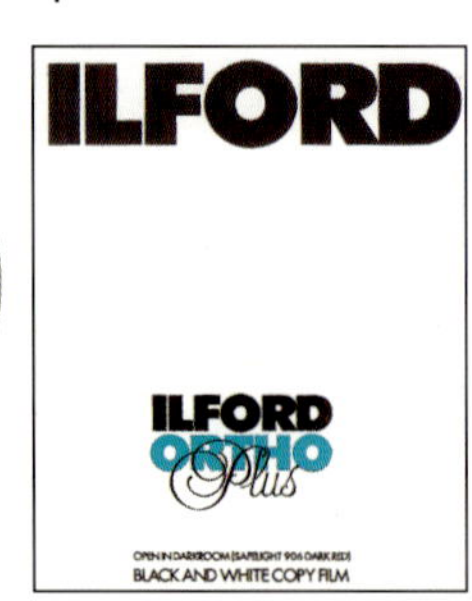

High speed ***orthochromatic*** sheet film, sensitive to the blue and green parts of the light spectrum, but not red, so can be used in a red safelight. Good for making big negatives from smaller formats, and fast enough to use directly in a large format camera.

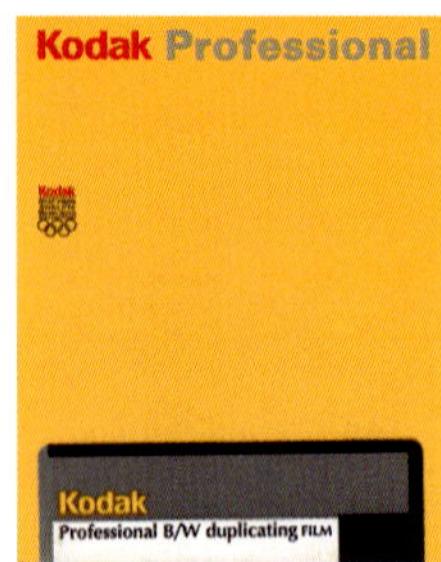

Special Kodak ***direct-duplicating*** sheet film for making a duplicate negative in one step. Very useful when making an enlarged neg. from smaller formats.

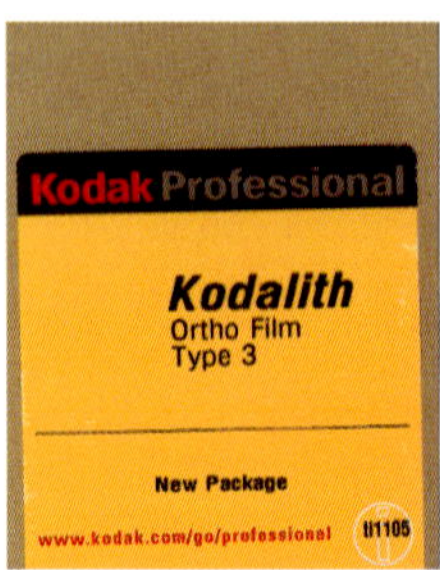

Lith film, ultra-high contrast when developed in lith developer, continuous tone in standard developers. Orthochromatic, needing red safelight. Most common make is Kodalith Ortho.

5 Project positive camera images (slides, TMax 100 reversal processed film etc) in the enlarger on to line film. This uses only one stage.

6 Use **Kodak Direct Duplicating film**. This is a reversal film and gives you a negative direct from a negative and a positive from a positive. Like slide film it goes lighter the more exposure it receives. A few tests may be necessary. It comes only in 5 x 4" and 10 x 8" sizes and is developed in paper developer using a mix slightly stronger than for paper.

7 Make a positive print on resin coated paper to your final image size. Contact print this onto another sheet of RC paper and you have a paper negative. Use Multigrade on filter setting 1 or 2. It will obviously take longer to expose under your light source. It is best used outdoors in the summer sun for making gum prints. Cyanotypes could take several days!

8 Take the best print you have from any particular negative and photograph it on a large format camera with standard camera film. Develop the film to the degree of contrast needed for the process you intend to use. Or make several exposures to get a range of different negatives.

Using lith film

Lith film is known variously as high contrast orthochromatic film or graphic arts film. When processed in the appropriate developer it produces only two tones. Black and clear film. All the intermediate tones that you would expect on a continuous tone film are pushed to either end of the scale. Thus the dark greys become black and the light greys become clear film. Lith film is supplied in sheets from 5 x 4 up to 20 x 24 inches. The main manufacturers are Kodak, Agfa and Bergger. The best known is Kodak's Kodalith, using the code 2556. The Bergger film is coded BPFB, and is conveniently supplied in packs of 10 sheets A4 and A3. You need to use a lith developer to obtain the highest contrast, and this is supplied in two parts usually labelled A and B. The two parts are mixed in equal parts and when kept separately will last indefinitely. When the two are mixed they will go off in a matter of hours. The most readily available developers are **Kodak Super RT** (powder) and in liquid Champion **Novolith,** and Fotospeed **Lith Developer LD20**. Lith film should be developed in lith developer at 20° C for at least two and a half minutes to obtain the full contrast.

Another possible source of supply of film is from local printers (the printing press variety). Many of them still use lith film for making printing plates and will quite often sell a few large sheets for a modest fee. Make sure to take a light-proof bag with you when you go.

We have said that lith negatives are essential for certain processes including photo-etching, silk screen, bleach etch and some fabric printing. But lith film can be used for other applications which increase the range of your creative output considerably. Bear in mind that lith and graphic arts film is not only versatile but very tough. It will put up with an enormous amount of abuse. As it is not precious original camera film it can be chopped and scratched, and if you spoil a lith negative you can always make another quickly.

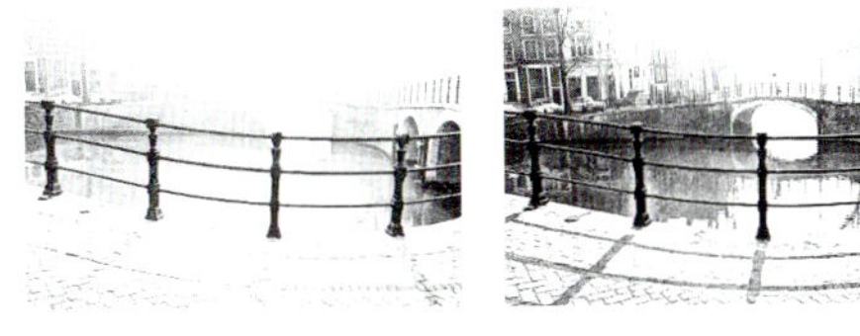

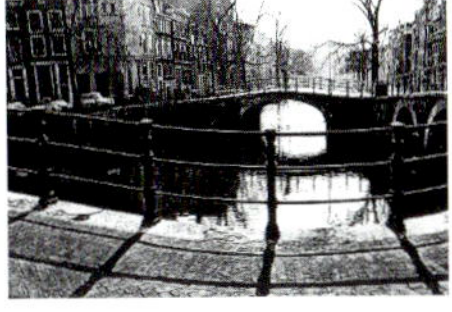

The same camera negative enlarged onto lith film to make positives. These are all given different exposures, eg 2, 4, 6, 8, 10, 12, 14, 16 and 20 seconds. A selection of the three most suitable separations is made, and these are enlarged onto bigger lith film as required to make negatives.

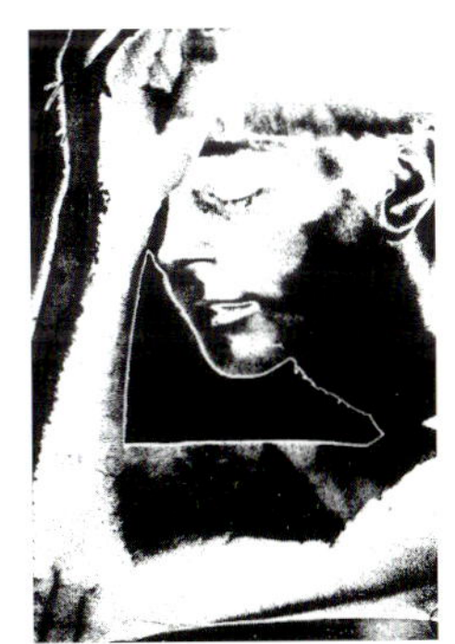

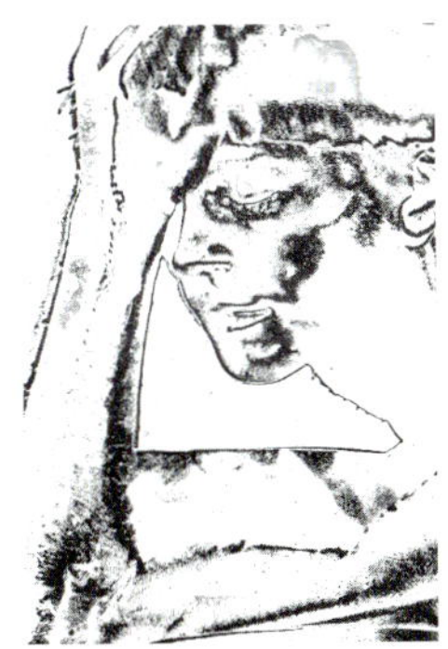

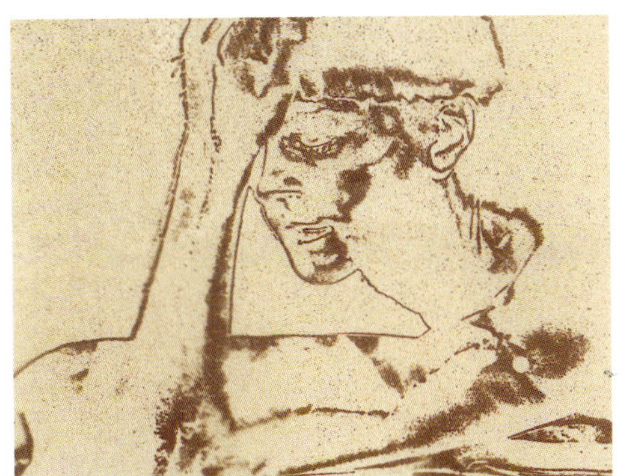

Top left & right, various stages of sabattier and bas relief. Lower image, Kallitype from negative version of above.

Applications

1 To make straight black and white only negatives you can enlarge or contact print from negatives or slides. You can also move from negative to positive and back again by contact or enlarging from one sheet of lith film to another. The more you do this the more stark the contrast becomes. Practise with it to explore its full potential.

2 Lith film can be manipulated to produce a **continuous tone effect**. This sounds illogical at first, but it has been done for over a hundred years in the printing industry to make the plates for printing photographs in books and newspapers. When a process such as photo etching needs to show a continuous tone image, but can only cope with a black and white negative or positive, we break up the lith image into a pattern of very fine dots. To the naked eye this looks like continuous tone, but if it is examined under a lens the fine dots show as only black and clear film, (see illustration p.41).

This is done at the enlarging stage as a rule. Either a sheet of Letraset tone pattern is placed over the film before exposure on the enlarger baseboard, or, more effectively and more cheaply, a sheet of non-reflecting picture frame glass is used. This can be bought from any glass merchant.

3 Sabatier effect and bas relief. The easiest way to make a sabatier or pseudo-solarisation is to make a resin coated glossy print the size of the final picture and when the image starts to appear in the developer, switch the main room light on for a second or two. Make sure the edge of the dish doesn't cast a shadow on the print. Continue to develop the print for its normal time. You should now have a print with a faint, dark image. However dark or disastrous it looks, contact print it on to a sheet of lith film until you get an image.

This can then be contact printed on to another sheet of lith film or given the same treatment with film as you did with the paper. There ain't no rules. For a bas relief effect make a negative and a positive sabatier image (any size) and then tape them together with Scotch tape so they are slightly out of alignment. Contact print this sandwich on to lith film as many times as you wish.

4 Tone separations. Make a series of contact prints or enlargements from negatives or slides. Give each one a different exposure eg 2 seconds, 4 seconds, 8 seconds, 16 seconds 32 seconds etc. Enlarge these positives on to lith film to the size you require but this time give them identical exposure after making a test strip for maximum black. Once you have focused the enlarger at each stage do not adjust it as you may disturb the registration.

5 Finally, **lettering**. It is now very simple to incorporate lettering onto any alternative printing process. Print on a sheet of typing paper the lettering you need having produced it to the correct size and font from a computer and an ink jet printer. Contact print this print on to a sheet of lith film and use this negative to incorporate in your image [12 . Kallitype]. There are, of course, infinite variations on these techniques, but it is up to you to explore them.

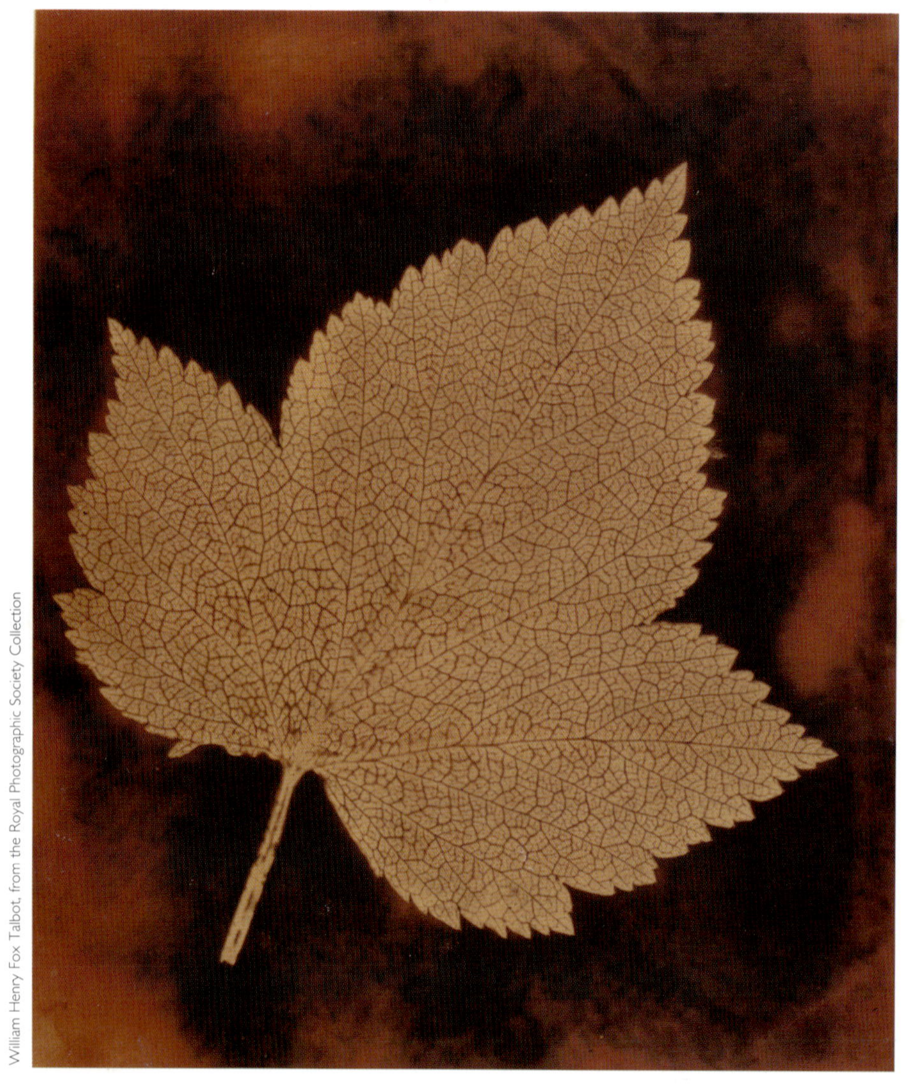

William Henry Fox Talbot, from the Royal Photographic Society Collection

Leaf. Waxed paper negative, 188x156mm.
Talbots earliest experiments involved laying leaves, flowers, lace etc. on sensitised paper, exposing them to the sun and fixing the darkening action at the relevant stage.

PHOTOGENIC DRAWING.

Some Account of the Art of Photogenic Drawing, or the Process by which Natural Objects may be made to delineate themselves without the aid of the Artist's Pencil. By Henry Fox Talbot, Esq. F.R.S.

[From the *Athenæum*.]

In the summer of 1835 I made in this way a great number of representations of my house in the country, which is well suited to the purpose, from its ancient and remarkable architecture. And this building I believe to be the first that was ever yet known *to have drawn its own picture.*

The method of proceeding was this: having first adjusted the paper to the proper focus in each of these little *cameræ*, I then took a number of them with me out of doors and placed them in different situations around the building. After the lapse of half an hour I gathered them all up, and brought them within doors to open them. When opened, there was found in each a miniature picture of the objects before which it had been placed.

To the traveller in distant lands who is ignorant, as too many unfortunately are, of the art of drawing, this little invention may prove of real service; and even to the artist himself, however skilful he may be. For although this natural process does not produce an effect much resembling the productions of his pencil, and therefore cannot be considered as capable of replacing them, yet it is to be recollected that he may often be so situated as to be able to devote only a single hour to the delineation of some very interesting locality. Now, since nothing prevents him from simultaneously disposing, in different positions, any number of these little *cameræ*, it is evident that their collective results when examined afterwards, may furnish him with a large body of interesting memorials, and with numerous details which he had not had time either to note down or to delineate.

Was Fox Talbot being just a touch tongue-in-cheek when he described it as 'this little invention'? Extract from an article in the Athenaeum reprinted in 'Mechanics Magazine' in 1836.

Even if you never make another print in any other process it is worth trying to make a salt print. From an historical point of view you will be able to share the pleasure and excitement that Fox Talbot experienced at the dawn of a technology, and that has since in some way touched the life of virtually everyone on the planet.

You will be able to recreate very closely the conditions in which Fox Talbot invented photographic printing.

With a little household salt, some silver nitrate, a few sheets of drawing paper, some fixer, and a small dose of sunlight you will be able to make a print just as Fox Talbot did.

Advantages

This process produces a rich reddish brown image on a fine matt surface with delicate highlights and deep detailed shadows.

It has the look of a palladium / platinum print at a small fraction of the cost.

If processed properly the prints are archivally stable. (Many of Fox Talbot's original prints from the 1830's look as though they were made last week).

As salt printing is the earliest form of photographic print making, you will enjoy a satisfying sense of history, or at least the feeling of standing in the great man's shoes for a few hours.

Disadvantages

Good results depend on the making of a contrasty negative. A certain amount of practice is needed therefore to get it right. Salt printing involves two separate coating operations which are time consuming.

Silver chloride sensitisers are very susceptible to contamination from stray chemicals in the water and the paper (plus your hands and the work bench). Again the need for clean working must be stressed. Silver nitrate causes stains on hands, clothes and work surfaces which are difficult to remove. It used to be applied as a cure for warts. So if you see anyone with brown stains on his or her hands you will know that they either make a lot of salt prints or they have a severe case of warts!

Shopping list

Chemicals

Sodium chloride - the same stuff as household salt, although we don't recommend the table variety which includes additives we don't want. Sea salt from the supermarket is fine, or buy sodium or ammonium chloride from a chemical supplier.

Silver nitrate.

Citric acid (from the homebrew section of your local chemist).

Gelatin (optional - see method section) - from any supermarket, although photographic grade is purer.

If the print is to be gold toned you will need gold chloride 1% solution

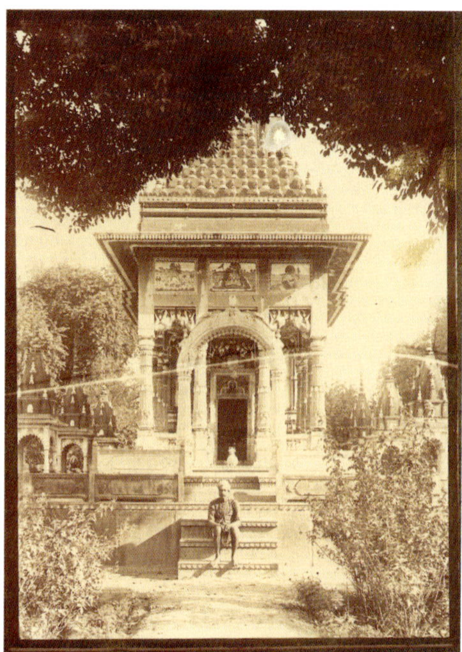

Salt print taken from a glass plate originating from India in the 1890's. This called for a very long exposure, as it was over-developed in solution temperatures of 35° C.

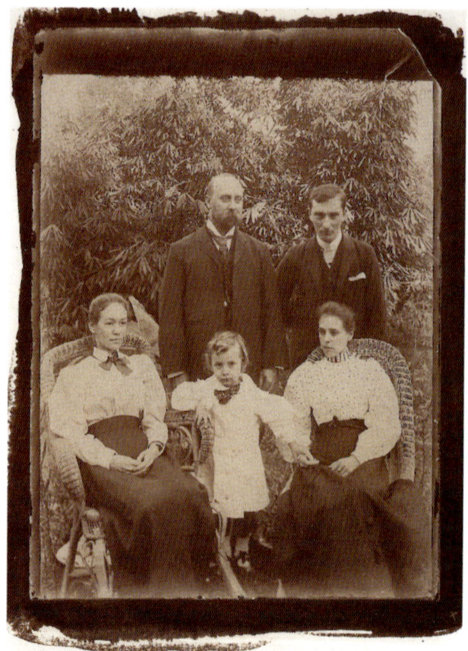

Modern salt print from a late Victorian plate negative. Anyone who thinks image manipulation is an invention of the computer age is mistaken; from the strange variations in focus it is clear the background has been inserted after the portrait was taken.

and borax, or you could use a ready made gold toner - either way it's expensive.
Plain hypo (sodium thiosulphate).
Sodium carbonate.
Hypo clearing agent or wash aid.

Graduated measures - 1 small (up to 50ml), 1 medium (up to 600ml), 1 large (up to 1 litre).

Hinged back printing frame (at least 2 inches larger on each side than your image size), or a picture frame that can be easily taken apart and put together again.

Two flat hake brushes - 1 inch wide or larger. See [7 . Coating].

Good quality water colour or drawing paper. Fabriano 100% or 50% cotton, Rives, Arches, Cranes, or Saunders are all suitable to start. Hot or Not pressed surfaces are the best of all. Try to avoid the temptation to experiment with hand made or heavily textured papers until you are more familiar with the process.

Four **developing dishes** to take your choice of paper size.

Scales which will measure dry chemicals in amounts as small as 2 gm.

Chemical stirring rod.

Roll of Scotch magic tape (translucent).

Ultra violet lamp or daylight / sunlight (cheaper and quicker).

Supply of running **cold water.**

Hair dryer or small **fan heater.**

Sheet of plastic and some old newspaper to protect your working surface.

Set of **print tongs.**

Small **washing line** (plastic coated) and some clean **clothes pegs.**

Small (250ml) **brown screw top bottle** from your local chemist to store your made up solution.

Small china **saucer.**

Small plastic **funnel.**

Negatives

Salt printing, like platinum and palladium is a 'pure' photographic printing process and since the only method of transferring an image from a negative is by contact, you will probably find that more satisfactory results are obtained by using camera negatives rather than enlarged contact negatives. This is a case where small is quite often beautiful. It is difficult but not impossible to reproduce accurately the tonal range, the sharpness and the granularity of the original camera negative by the methods described, (see section on negatives). The ideal negative should be well exposed with good detail in the shadows, (definitely no pushing). It should be well developed - 50% to 100% more than the manufacturer's recommendation for that particular film and developer combination. Try to avoid highlights that are 'bullet proof' without any separation in the

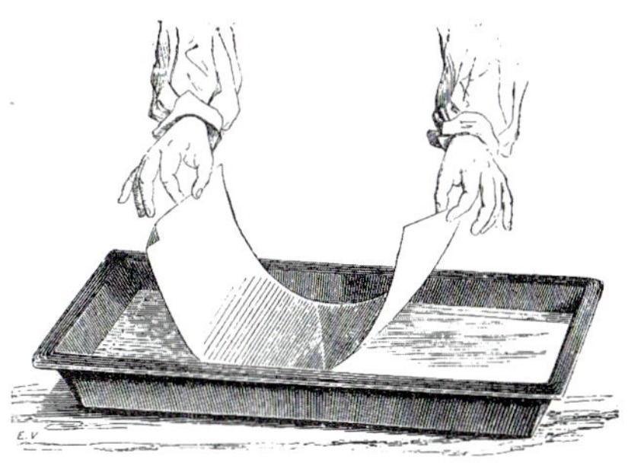

Traditional method of salting paper, immersing paper in salt water.

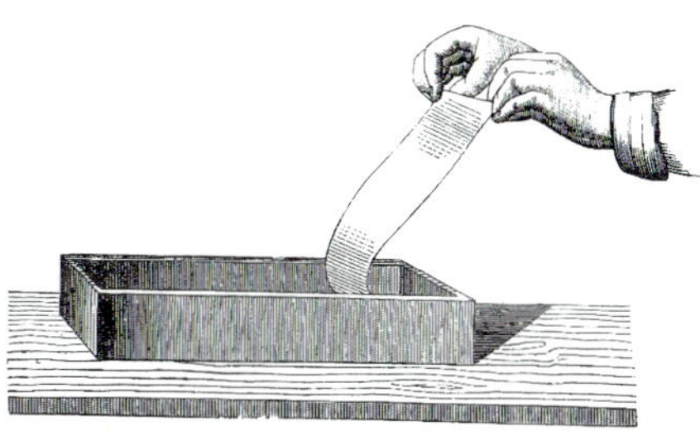

An alternative way of immersion.

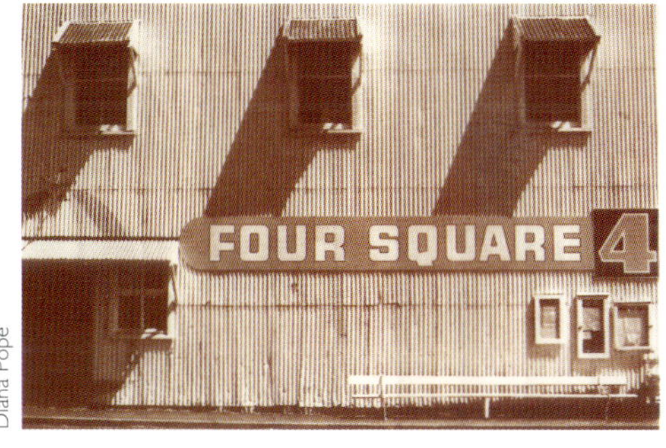

Diana Pope

Supermarket, New Zealand. Contact printed from high contrast line film enlarged negative.

highest values. Get used to printing from 2¼ square, 5 x 4" or 5 x 7" negatives, and if you can get your hands on a 10 x 8" camera then that would be a bonus.

If using a densitometer, aim for a negative with a nett density range of at least 1.7 to 1.9, or an end density of between 2.0 and 2.2. Using the visual method you will need a negative that just about produces an acceptable print on conventional paper using a Multigrade filter 0 or 00, or its equivalent. You can, of course, make perfectly good - allbeit murky - prints using negatives of lower contrast, and these depend a good deal on the original subject matter and the sort of effect you are looking for. Knowing how to do it properly in the first place will give you greater confidence.

Method

The chemistry of salt printing called for a certain amount of lateral thinking on the part of William Henry Fox Talbot. The particular silver halide that he needed on the paper to produce a clear, well defined print was silver chloride. Unfortunately this substance does not dissolve in water or any other solvent to enable it to be brushed onto paper. Silver nitrate does dissolve, but on its own reveals a thin, low contrast and uninspiring image. The great man got round the problem by taking sodium chloride (common salt as you would put on chips) and dissolving this in water. He then soaked the paper in the salt water solution and let it dry. Then he brushed on a solution of silver nitrate in water and dried this. Thus he had on his paper:

Sodium chloride
Silver nitrate

A chemical reaction took place giving him:

Silver chloride
Sodium nitrate

The silver chloride darkened on exposure to light and the sodium nitrate was washed down the sink during processing. Subsequent experiments gave him the correct proportions of salt and silver to give him a satisfactory image. With some refinement of the chemicals in the sensitiser and more sophisticated paper, this is the method we use today to make a conventional black and white print.

Salting the paper

Mix a 2% solution of salt water ie;
1 litre of cold tap water.
20 grams of sodium chloride (sea salt from the supermarket), **or**
20 grams of ammonium chloride (from a supplier of photographic chemicals).

Pour this mixture into a **clean** developing dish, immerse the paper of your choice in it and let it soak for about five minutes. Hang the paper up to dry overnight. Alternatively, let it drain and dry it with a hair drier or a small fan heater. Avoid using the gas cooker jet! An old microwave oven no longer used for cooking food makes a very useful drier. The paper at

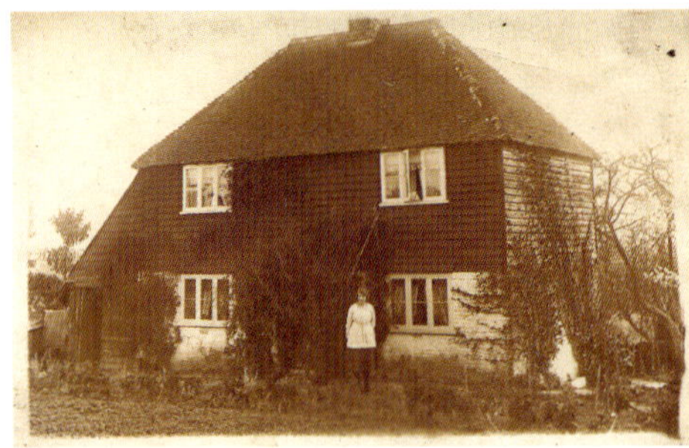

Modern salt print from negative of black and white snapshot, dated 1916. A good way of dealing with family photo archives.

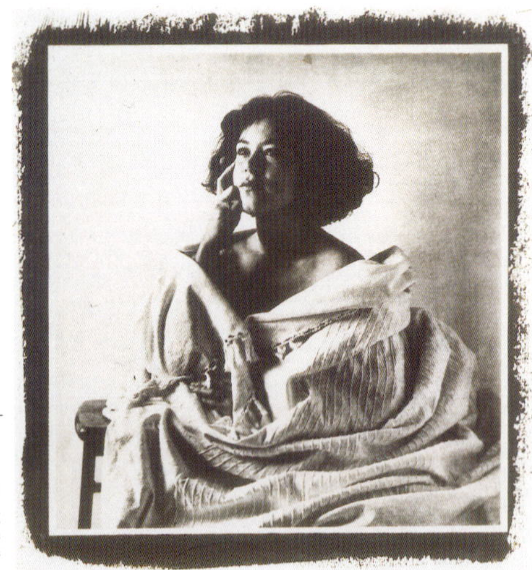

Maria de Fatima Campos

Salt print. Resin coated positive print contact printed onto line film, which was developed to a high contrast level, finally printed onto sensitised mould made paper. This demonstrates it is possible to produce a high contrast salt print.

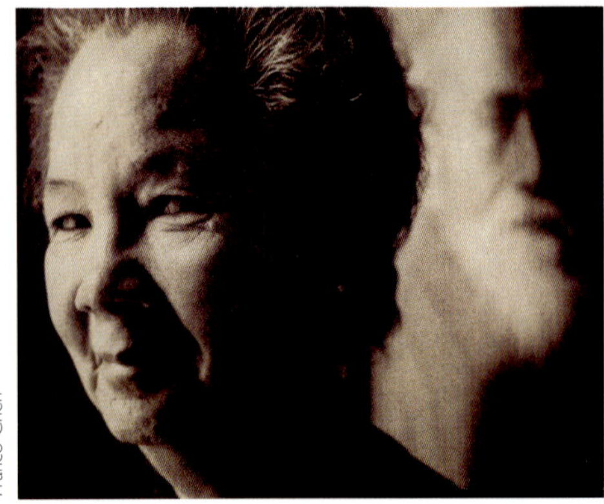

Franco Chen

Original RC print contacted onto line film, printed onto Fabriano paper. The contact negative was of relatively low contrast, although the subject lighting was contrasty.

this stage is not light-sensitive, so this operation can be carried out in daylight. You can also make as many sheets of salted paper as you will need for future use as they will not deteriorate.

Next:

Mix 2 separate solutions;

50 ml distilled water.
12 grams silver nitrate.
Take care, silver nitrate spills easily.

Then mix;
50 ml distilled water.
6 grams citric acid.

When both are completely dissolved mix them both together and pour into a small brown screw topped bottle ready for use. The citric acid acts as a preservative and stops the silver coating from darkening before you can get round to printing it. Only coat enough paper with the silver solution that you intent to use immediately.

Now you are ready to coat the salted paper with the silver. This must be done in subdued daylight or normal tungsten room lighting. Avoid working in a room with fluorescent light. Using the methods described in the section on coating, apply the silver / citric acid to the paper with either a flat brush or a glass rod. Dry the paper with a hair drier or fan heater.

Printing

At this stage the coating is virtually invisible, so mark the back of the paper with a pencilled mark (X or B) so that you know which is back and which is front. Now take your negative and place it dull (emulsion) side down on the coated side of the paper. Place this sandwich in your printing frame or clip frame in the following order from the top:

Glass / Negative (emulsion side down) **/ Paper** (coated side up) **/ Printing frame back**

Make sure that your coated paper is absolutely dry or you will spoil your negative with permanent brown stains.

Place your printing frame - glass side up - in daylight, sunlight or ultra violet lamp (see exposure section). Within a few minutes the brushed silver coating outside the edges of the negative will darken. At regular intervals of 3 or 4 minutes unclip one part of the hinged back of the printing frame and check the progress of the printing. Make sure that you don't move the negative and print out of register. If you are using a clip frame don't forget to tape the edge of the negative to the paper, [8 . Exposing]. When the print is exposed to the point that all the tones are correct, making sure that the highlights have sufficient detail, take the frame out of the light and remove the print. You should have, if everything has gone according to plan, a rich reddish brown image with an irregular dark border caused by brushing the silver outside the confines of the negative. The brushed edges are one of the constant and endearing characteristics of old processes.

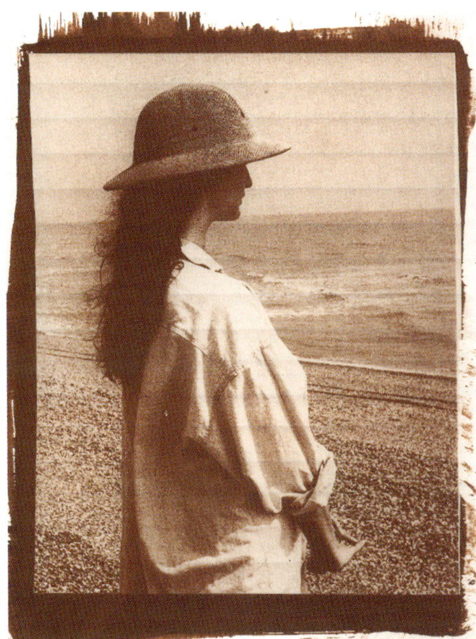

At Dungeness. Unfixed salt print, showing the brighter purple before it is stabilised.

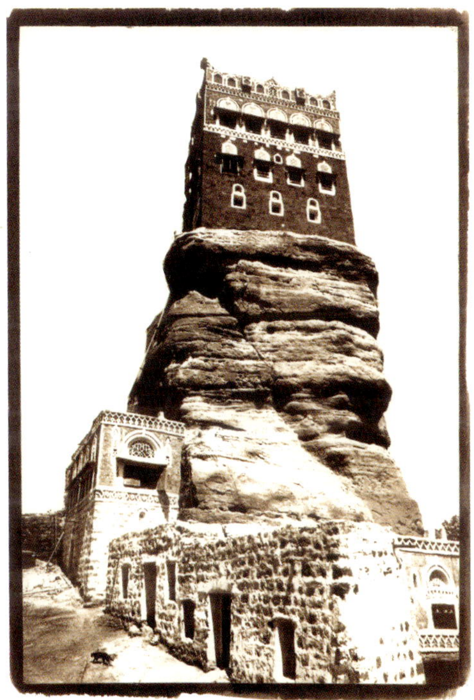

Sultans palace, Yemen. Negative direct from colour slide. For more dramatic effect the sky was blocked out with photo-opaque to give a white sky.

Processing

This consists of washing to get rid of excess silver nitrate, followed by fixing and a final wash.

First prepare the fixing bath. Mix;

500 ml cold tap water.
25 grams sodium thiosulphate powder.
2 grams sodium carbonate.

Sodium thiosulphate has always been wrongly known as **hypo**. Do not confuse it with **hypo clearing** which is for the final print wash. It is at this stage that you decide whether you want to gold tone your print. If you do, then first read the section below on gold toning. If you don't want to gold tone then continue as follows. But do remember that unlike other toning processes, it is better to gold tone a salt print **before** it has been fixed.

In subdued daylight or tungsten room lighting, place the exposed print face up in a clean developing dish and wash in running water. The unused silver nitrate will turn the water slightly milky. When this milkiness disappears the washing is finished. Use a minimum of 4 - 5 minutes. Take a dish filled with the fixing bath and immerse the washed print face up for about 5 minutes. The colour of the print will change in the fixer to a somewhat unattractive ginger brown colour. **Don't panic.** It will go back to its original colour when it is washed and dried. When fixing is complete wash in running water for 30 minutes or use this sequence:

5 minutes **wash**.

5 minutes in **Kodak Hypo Clearing Agent** or Galerie Washaid.

5 minutes **wash**.

Hang up to dry. Avoid using a squeegee to remove excess water as the surface of the print is quite delicate. Do not use a conventional flat bed fibre paper drier. If you need to dry it in a hurry, use a hair drier or fan heater. A less satisfactory method of fixing is to use standard rapid fixer (Hypam etc). The drawback to using this is that the high activity of rapid fixers tend to bleach the image. If you are forced to use this method you should dilute the fixer by twice the manufacturer's recommended amount (e.g. 1:18 rather than 1:9).

When the print is dry, retouch and mount as required.

To avoid the possibility of yellow stains appearing on the print at a later stage, it is not advisable to use chemical methods for retouching, especially mixtures such as Farmers reducer. Remove any black spots with the point of a sharp scalpel. To remove white spots use water colours. Try red and burnt umber mixed to match the print colour and apply with a fine spotting brush. Any serious blemishes on the negative should be removed with Spotone or Farmers reducer before printing.

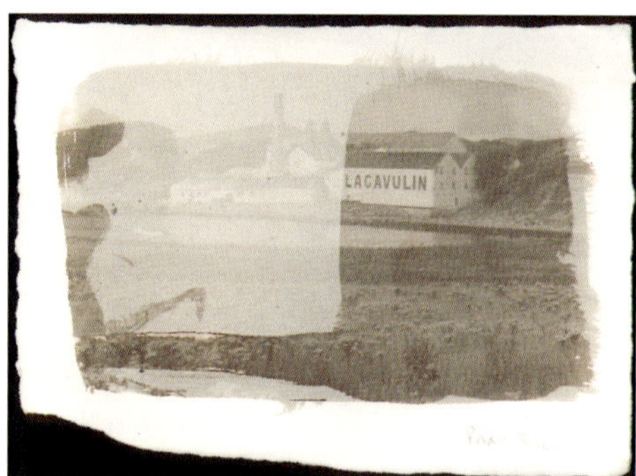

Inadequate salting. The light area is silver nitrate only, and the dark area is silver chloride.

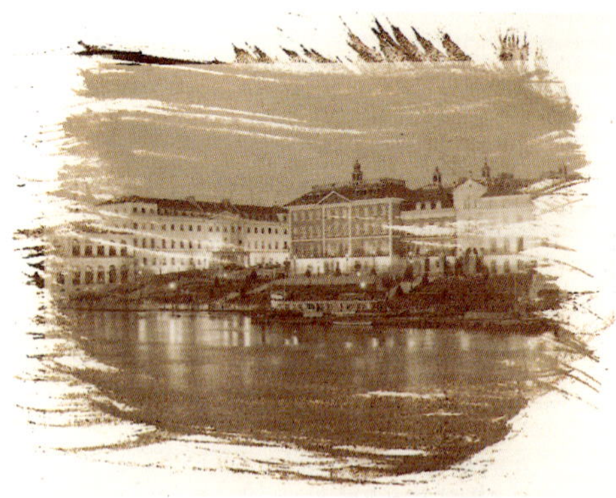

Inadequate silver coating. Contains silver chloride and plain paper.

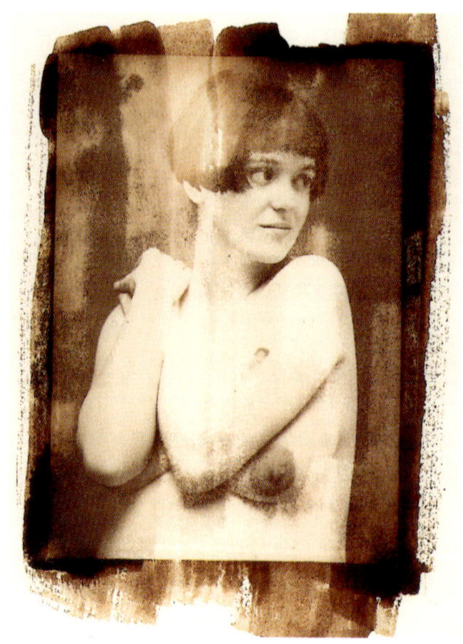

Another example of inadequate silver application.

Trouble shooting

Lack of contrast or veiled and muddy highlights

This is the most common problem and is usually the result of using a negative of too low a contrast. If the negative gives an acceptable result on Multigrade with a 0 filter then it is likely that your negative is still too soft. Make another negative and give it even more development than before. Or see section on contrast control.

If your negative is OK then you may have not put enough citric acid as a preservative in the silver sensitiser.

The last possible cause of muddy prints may be due to having left too much time elapse between sensitising the paper and exposing it. Whatever the books say, make sure you expose your paper as soon as it is dry. Leaving it in the fridge or a rolled-up piece of foil for a few days doesn't really work.

Uneven coating

The secret here is to distinguish between problems arising from the salting stage and the silver coating stage. If the prints shows areas of irregular light patches where the image is very thin and lacking in any shadow depth, then you have failed to get the salt mix to soak into the paper. You are effectively printing silver nitrate instead of silver chloride. If you have persistent problems with this you can either try using a different paper stock (preferably one that has not such a hard size) see section on paper. Or you can try using the salt mixture at a higher temperature - say 35° C which usually has the effect of softening up the paper. On the other hand a print which contains areas of blank paper within the image indicates that you have not coated the salted paper sufficiently with the silver nitrate mixture. The answer to this is to take more care with the silver coating.

Chemical contamination

Silver nitrate reacts with just about every other chemical in the universe. Which is why we use distilled water to make the silver mixture. So if your finished print is covered in various coloured stains - usually yellow brown or grey - then a little detective work will reveal whether the uncoated paper was accidentally contaminated, or whether the stains appeared for a number of other reasons. These include: dirty brushes, dirty dishes, dirty workbench, dirty hands and sloppy working in general.

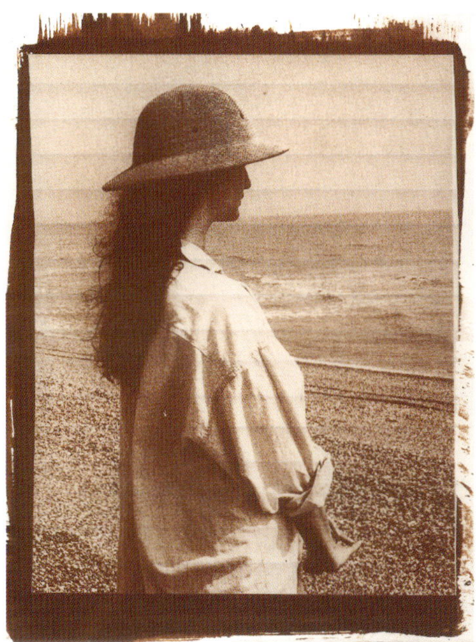

At Dungeness. Unfixed salt print, showing the brighter purple before it is stabilised.

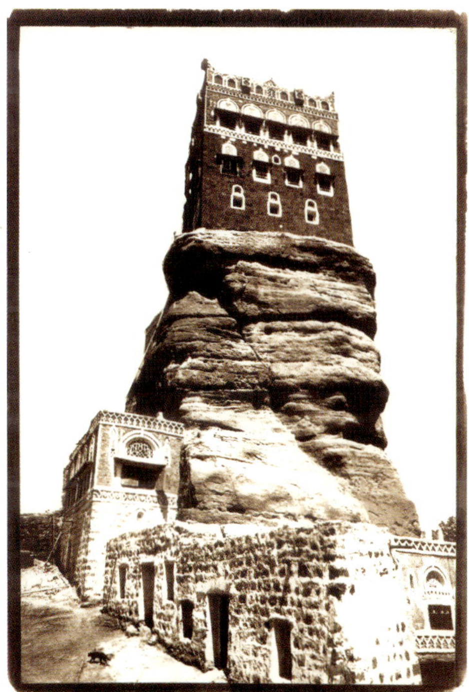

Sultans palace, Yemen. Negative direct from colour slide. For more dramatic effect the sky was blocked out with photo-opaque to give a white sky.

Processing

This consists of washing to get rid of excess silver nitrate, followed by fixing and a final wash.

First prepare the fixing bath. Mix;

500 ml cold tap water.
25 grams sodium thiosulphate powder.
2 grams sodium carbonate.

Sodium thiosulphate has always been wrongly known as **hypo**. Do not confuse it with **hypo clearing** which is for the final print wash. It is at this stage that you decide whether you want to gold tone your print. If you do, then first read the section below on gold toning. If you don't want to gold tone then continue as follows. But do remember that unlike other toning processes, it is better to gold tone a salt print **before** it has been fixed.

In subdued daylight or tungsten room lighting, place the exposed print face up in a clean developing dish and wash in running water. The unused silver nitrate will turn the water slightly milky. When this milkiness disappears the washing is finished. Use a minimum of 4 - 5 minutes. Take a dish filled with the fixing bath and immerse the washed print face up for about 5 minutes. The colour of the print will change in the fixer to a somewhat unattractive ginger brown colour. **Don't panic.** It will go back to its original colour when it is washed and dried. When fixing is complete wash in running water for 30 minutes or use this sequence:

5 minutes **wash**.

5 minutes in **Kodak Hypo Clearing Agent** or Galerie Washaid.

5 minutes **wash**.

Hang up to dry. Avoid using a squeegee to remove excess water as the surface of the print is quite delicate. Do not use a conventional flat bed fibre paper drier. If you need to dry it in a hurry, use a hair drier or fan heater. A less satisfactory method of fixing is to use standard rapid fixer (Hypam etc). The drawback to using this is that the high activity of rapid fixers tend to bleach the image. If you are forced to use this method you should dilute the fixer by twice the manufacturer's recommended amount (e.g. 1:18 rather than 1:9).

When the print is dry, retouch and mount as required.

To avoid the possibility of yellow stains appearing on the print at a later stage, it is not advisable to use chemical methods for retouching, especially mixtures such as Farmers reducer. Remove any black spots with the point of a sharp scalpel. To remove white spots use water colours. Try red and burnt umber mixed to match the print colour and apply with a fine spotting brush. Any serious blemishes on the negative should be removed with Spotone or Farmers reducer before printing.

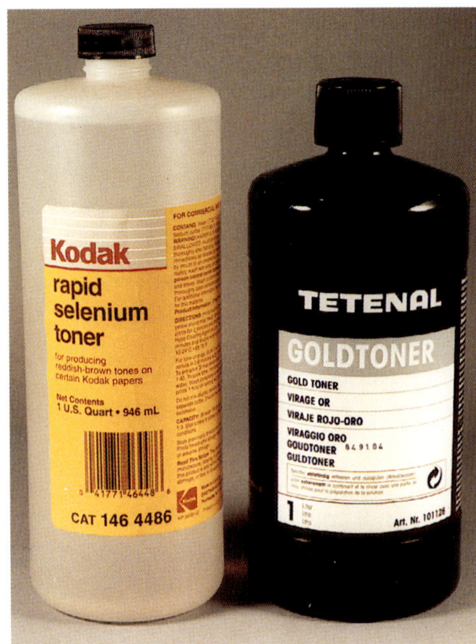

Ready-made gold and selenium toners, valuable after-treatments for salt, kallitype, and indeed any silver-based process.

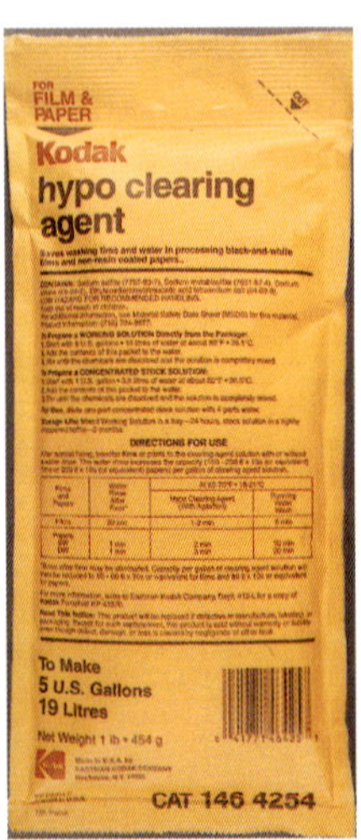

Hypo clearing agent is one of the most useful, and incidentally one of the cheapest, ancillary chemicals used in photo processing. As a rule of thumb it cuts washing time by 2/3, so can be used when trying to cut wash times to the minimum. However if you can give a longer wash time the improved efficiency will ensure an 'archival' standard. The Kodak product is the cheapest and best known, others include Ilford Galerie Washaid & Tetenal Lavaquick.

Variations

Here are a few variations which are not essential but which have become part of the salt printers repertoire over the years. The procedures which we have described so far are perfectly adequate to produce an authentic salt print. The additional items that follow amount to ways of fine tuning your technique if you so wish.

Gelatin sizing

As we mentioned in the section on paper some water colour papers are very absorbent and let the silver emulsion soak into the fibres. This gives the print a dull matt finish and has the effect of reducing the contrast. Some papers contain a 'size' which is included at the manufacturing stage and prevents the absorption of the silver emulsion. If you wish to size your own paper for salt printing use this method. The gelatin mix contains the sodium chloride, which is of course used for salting the paper.

Salt mix with gelatin size

300 ml water
2 g gelatin
6 g sodium chloride

Take the gelatin - powdered from the supermarket or preferably photographic quality. At any rate, use the plain powder, not raspberry flavour cubes! Put it in 100ml of the water and let it soak for 15 minutes. When it has swollen pour the remaining 200 ml at 45° C and mix until it has dissolved. Then add and dissolve the sodium chloride.

While it is still liquid brush it onto your paper with a flat brush or put the gelatin in a flat dish and immerse the paper in the liquid for about 30 seconds and then let it hang to dry. Make sure whichever method you use avoids getting bald patches on the paper.

If you immerse it in the gelatin, run the paper over the edge of a plastic ruler as it comes out of the dish. This will prevent air bubbles forming on the surface of the paper. You will probably need three hands to do this. When the paper is dry you can coat it with the silver mix and continue as before.

The unused gelatin mix will solidify when cold and will last about a week. If you wish to use it during this time to salt any more paper, then place it in a hot water-bath until the mixture becomes liquid and coat your paper as described above. The use of gelatin size on salt print emulsion tends to change the final colour of the print giving it a slightly colder colour.

Floating

You may find that some books on the subject of salt printing describe an alternative method of coating the paper with the silver solution. It consists of taking a dish of silver nitrate and citric acid solution slightly larger than the piece of paper you are printing on and floating your paper on the surface of the liquid for about 30 seconds. It has the advantage possibly of putting an even coat of silver on the salted paper but it also has a number of undesirable features.

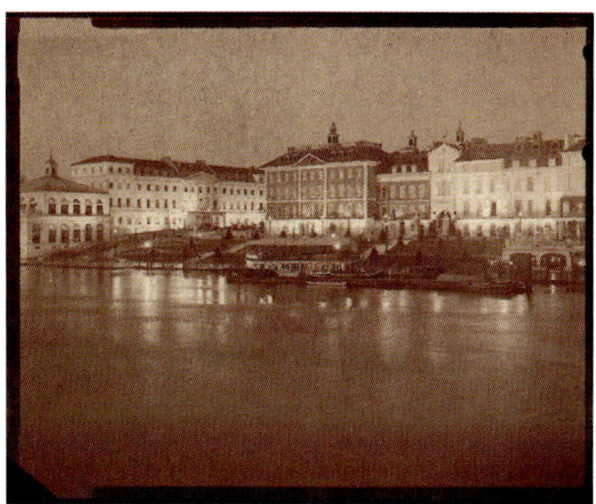

Salt print, fixed but untoned.

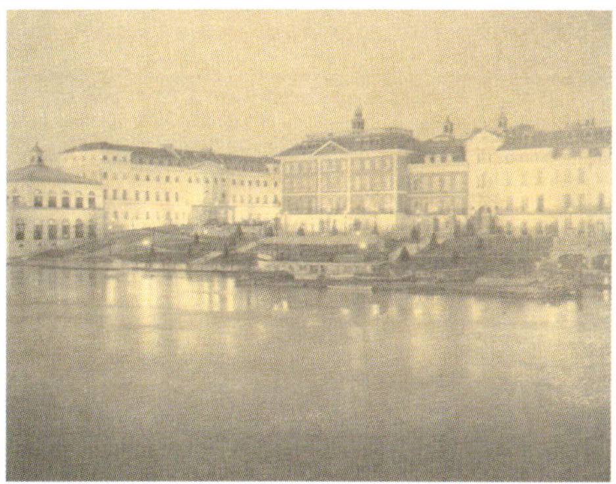

Straight salt print as above, but subsequently gold toned, resulting in subtle blueish overtones.

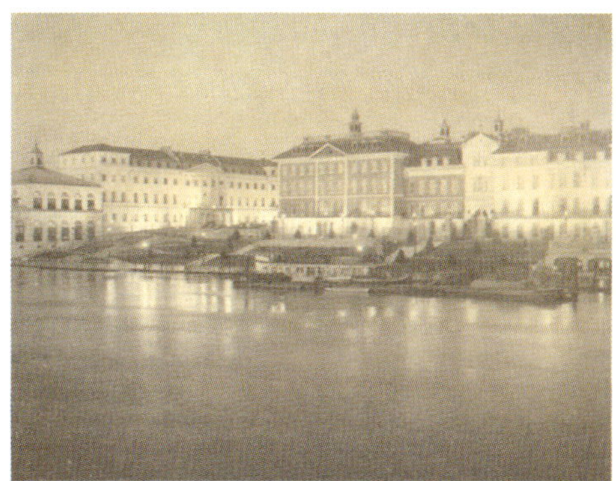

Gold toning for a longer period gives maximum colour shift.

1 It is best done by people who do it all day for a living, (very hard to find any now).

2 It takes an awful lot of silver nitrate.

3 The silver bath becomes contaminated and the silver content reduces with each sheet of paper coated. Replenishing it needs a complicated titration process.

4 It is very messy.

This method is best avoided despite what the earlier authorities say, and we advise you to stick to one or more of the methods described in the section on coating paper.

Gold toning

Gold toning was standard practice for salt printers in the nineteenth century. It had two effects on the print. First it preserved the finished silver emulsion from atmospheric pollution, and therefore from discolouration and fading.

Secondly and probably more importantly, it produced subtle shifts of colour in the print. The normal reddish brown of an untoned salt print could become a much warmer red, or it could move to a colder grey tone. Its main disadvantage today is the high price of its main ingredient - gold chloride. However if you are going to investigate all the possibilities of this, the earliest printing process, then you will probably feel that the expense may be justified by the results.

Two things to bear in mind:

Gold toning of salt prints is best done after the initial washing and **before** fixing.

Under no circumstances allow the fixing bath to get into the gold toning bath. It could be an expensive mistake.

When the print has been exposed and washed as usual place in the toning bath for between 6 and 12 minutes. When the colour of the print has changed to your satisfaction, remove and wash for a few minutes in running water then fix, wash and dry as for ordinary salt print.

Gold toner formula

Dissolve 3 g borax in 400ml of water at 40° C.

When this is cool mix in 6 ml of gold chloride 1% solution.

Note: gold chloride is usually sold as a 1 - 2% solution. Don't bother buying it in powder form. The best way to measure the effect of the toner is to cut an old print into narrow strips (4 or 5) and to put them altogether in the toner and then take them out one at a time at intervals of two minutes. Remember, the more silver there is on the print the more gold you will use up toning it. So if you have a large and very pretty brushed edge all round your print, it is going to cost you dearly.

Apart from making gold toner up to formula, there are some excellent ready made gold toners on the market, the best known and most widely available being Tetenal Gold Toner, sold in 1 litre bottles.

Inadequate salting. The light area is silver nitrate only, and the dark area is silver chloride.

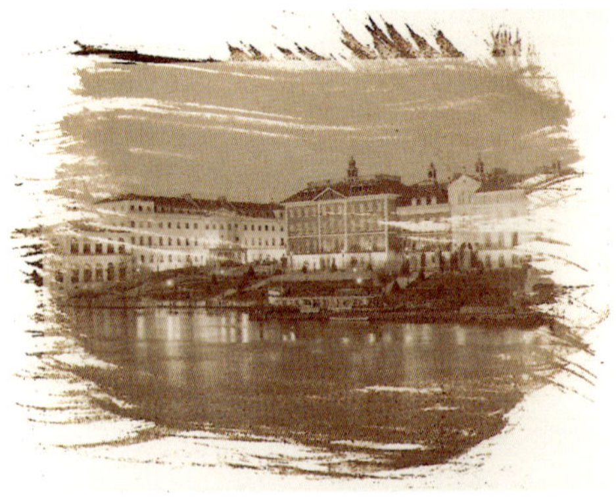
Inadequate silver coating. Contains silver chloride and plain paper.

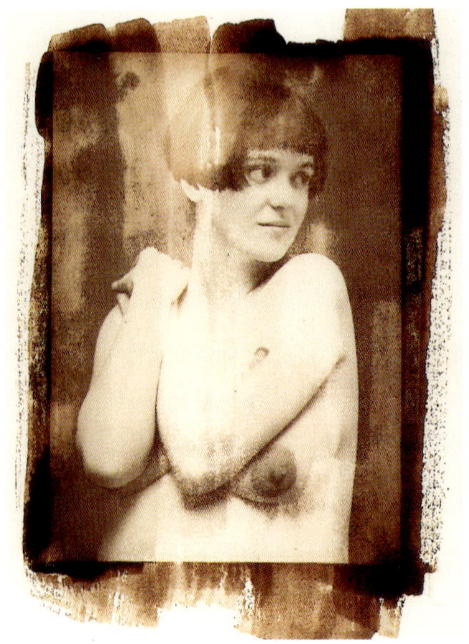
Another example of inadequate silver application.

Trouble shooting

Lack of contrast or veiled and muddy highlights

This is the most common problem and is usually the result of using a negative of too low a contrast. If the negative gives an acceptable result on Multigrade with a 0 filter then it is likely that your negative is still too soft. Make another negative and give it even more development than before. Or see section on contrast control.

If your negative is OK then you may have not put enough citric acid as a preservative in the silver sensitiser.

The last possible cause of muddy prints may be due to having left too much time elapse between sensitising the paper and exposing it. Whatever the books say, make sure you expose your paper as soon as it is dry. Leaving it in the fridge or a rolled-up piece of foil for a few days doesn't really work.

Uneven coating

The secret here is to distinguish between problems arising from the salting stage and the silver coating stage. If the prints shows areas of irregular light patches where the image is very thin and lacking in any shadow depth, then you have failed to get the salt mix to soak into the paper. You are effectively printing silver nitrate instead of silver chloride. If you have persistent problems with this you can either try using a different paper stock (preferably one that has not such a hard size) see section on paper. Or you can try using the salt mixture at a higher temperature - say 35° C which usually has the effect of softening up the paper. On the other hand a print which contains areas of blank paper within the image indicates that you have not coated the salted paper sufficiently with the silver nitrate mixture. The answer to this is to take more care with the silver coating.

Chemical contamination

Silver nitrate reacts with just about every other chemical in the universe. Which is why we use distilled water to make the silver mixture. So if your finished print is covered in various coloured stains - usually yellow brown or grey - then a little detective work will reveal whether the uncoated paper was accidentally contaminated, or whether the stains appeared for a number of other reasons. These include: dirty brushes, dirty dishes, dirty workbench, dirty hands and sloppy working in general.

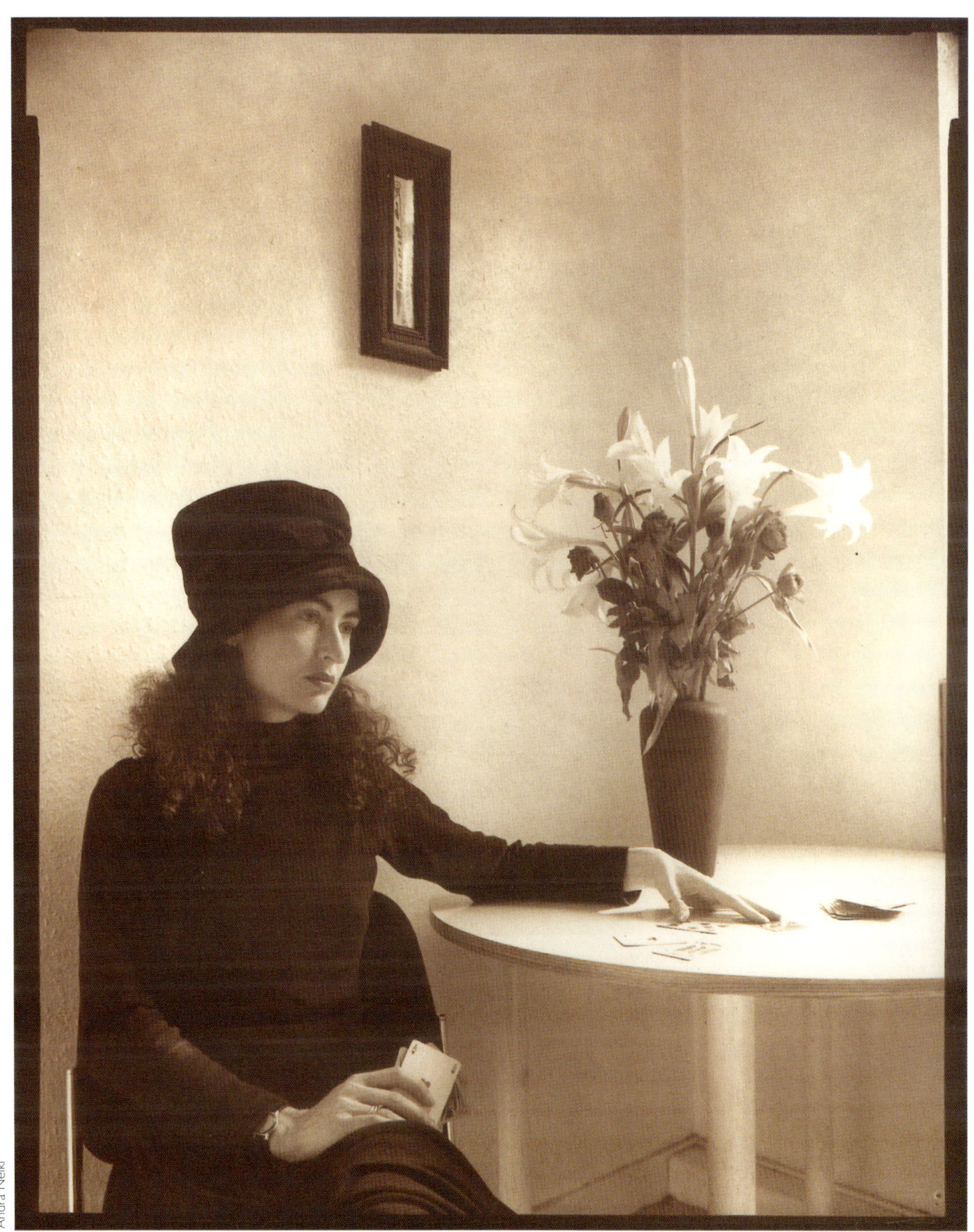

Andra Nelki

Salt print by direct contact from 8 x 10" camera negative.

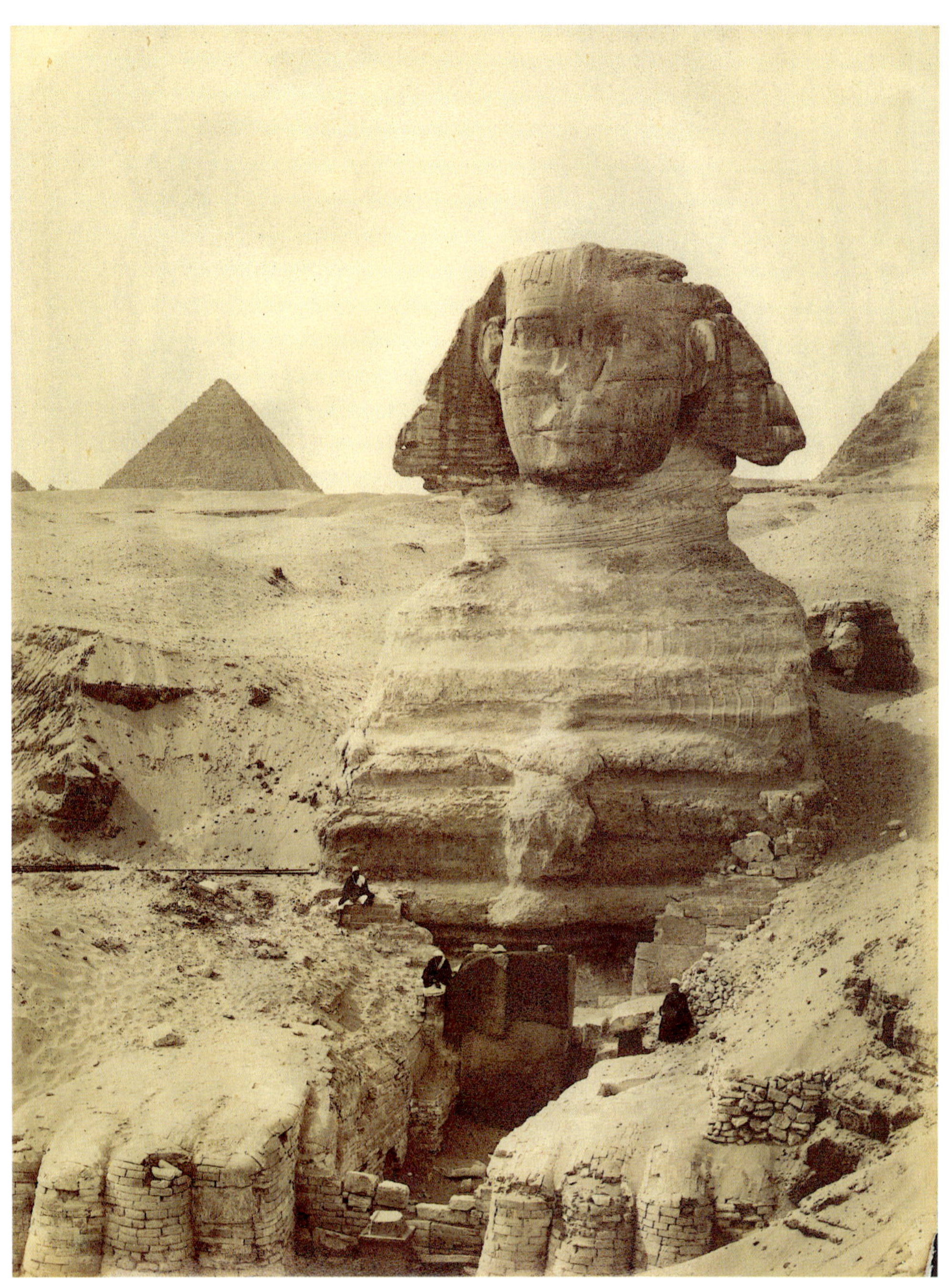

Albumen print from 1870's, possibly by Beato, authors collection.

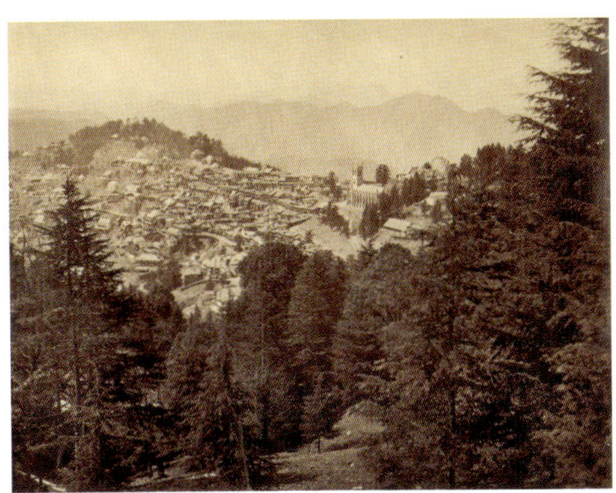

A view of Simla, 1860's. An albumen print by Samuel Bourne, of Bourne & Shepherd, the well known studio photographers of New Delhi.

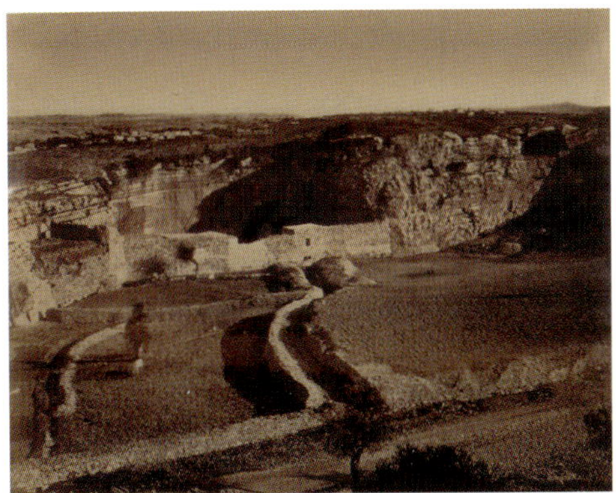

Jeruselem Grotto. A view of the Holy Land in the 1870's by Bonfils, the French photographer who travelled extensively in the middle east, producing vast numbers of albumen prints

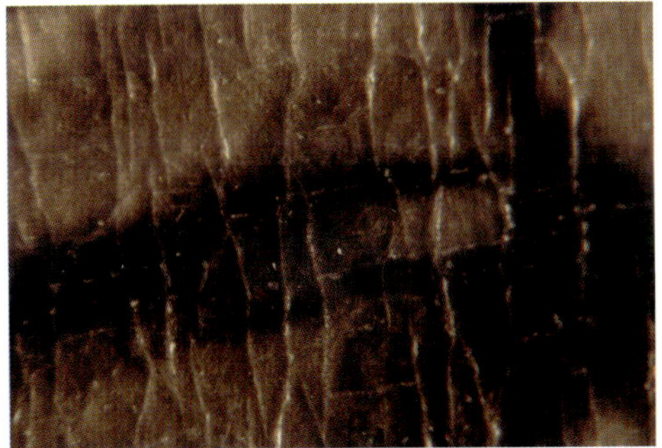

Close-up of the albumen image opposite, showing the fine cracks which appear in the surface of an albumen print as it ages.

Albumen prints were the common currency of photography for over 30 years during the middle part of the nineteenth century, just as resin coated Multigrade is for the latter part of the 20'th. To a Victorian they would not have been remarkable as a process, and today they are an interesting curiosity if only because they use egg albumen as one of the materials with which to coat the paper.

Many albumen prints in museum collections are distinguished by their large size and by their spectacularly wide range of tones and fine detail. This is less a tribute to the quality of the printing medium than the fact that the use of albumen coincided with the use of glass plate negatives, some of which measured up to 20 x 16 inches. Topographical photographers such as Frith used these large negatives in their travels to the Middle East and India. A contact print from such a negative would obviously give a print of very superior tonality and sharpness. The problem with salt prints was their tendency to absorb the chemistry into the fibres of the paper which resulted in a dull and sometimes lifeless image. So a new way of holding the sensitiser on the paper had to be found. The use of a sizing material to give a glossy surface to the paper was introduced by Blanquart-Evrard in the late 1840's. The substance he used was albumen, more commonly known as egg-white. The beaten egg white mixed with sodium chloride was coated onto the paper, which was sold in packets just as it is today. The albumen paper was coated with silver nitrate immediately before printing, giving a modified salt print, with a glossy surface which appeared to appeal to nineteenth century taste more than the matt surfaces of other processes. Much of the albumen paper was made in Dresden in Germany. Armies of women were employed to separate egg yolks from the whites, beat the egg whites and spread the solution onto paper. In one year a factory in Dresden used over one million eggs and it was interesting to note that many magazines of the time featured recipes which used egg yolks as their main ingredient!

Advantages

The glossy surface of the print gives a brighter image, the impression of deeper shadows and greater resolution of fine detail.

As the silver image lies on the albumen surface of the print rather than deep in the paper fibres, it is possible to use a greater range of paper types and surfaces.

It is also possible to coat unusual surfaces such as wood, hardboard and stone. The albumen adheres well to these materials.

Disadvantages

The most noticeable problem that shows on examination of nineteenth century albumen prints is the yellowing of the image, especially in the highlights. This is caused by a chemical reaction between the albumen and the image silver, for which there has been found no successful cure. Fine surface cracking is also a feature of old albumen prints.

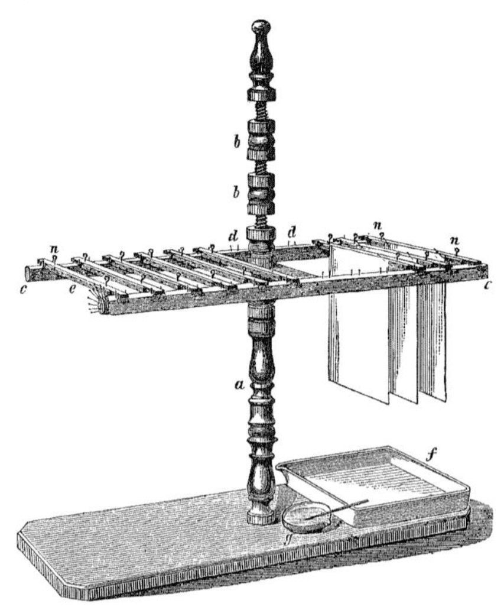

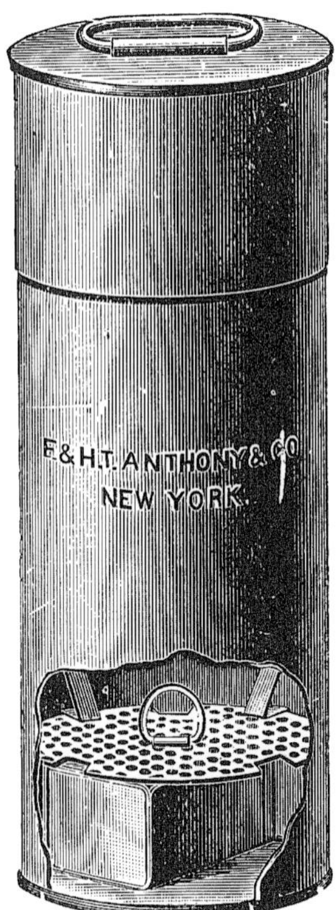

An original drying rack for albumen paper (top) and a calcium storage tube for finished paper (below). The tube had a chamber which was filled with a mixture of calcium chloride and asbestos for maintaining paper at a low humidity.

Egg white goes off quickly and gives off a nasty smell, so any unused stock has to kept in a fridge.

Shopping list

The list of materials you will need for albumen printing is exactly the same as is used for salt printing with the following additions:

One or two fresh **eggs**
or- powdered **egg white** from the supermarket
or- powdered a**lbumen** from an artists suppliers.

Powdered **arrowroot** from a supermarket or artists suppliers - optional.

An **egg whisk and a bowl** to stir the egg whites.

A **recipe** which uses the egg yolks only - rather than throwing them away.

A **fridge** to store the whisked up egg whites if you don't use them all in one go.

Paper

Any paper that works with salt printing will be suitable for albumen. Otherwise try any paper that takes your fancy.

Negatives

As this is basically a salt printing process you should use a negative of the same contrast as you would for salt.

Method

Take one egg. Crack it in half and separate the yolk from the white (a good cook will tell you how to do this). Pour the white into a small measuring jar. See how many mls you have. Now break enough eggs to give you 80 ml of egg white.
Beat the egg whites for a minute or so to break up their glutinous consistency.
Take 20 ml of distilled water and dissolve in it 2 grams of salt as for salt prints.
Mix this solution with the egg white and leave it until the froth on the surface has disappeared.
When most of the air bubbles have gone from the salted egg white you can now coat the paper.

Coating

There are two ways of doing this, the classic way and the easy way.
The traditional way is to float the paper on a dish containing the albumen mix. Take a shallow tray (print tray, baking tray or whatever as you are only dealing with egg, salt and water) and pour the albumen solution into it. Take a sheet of paper and on the top left corner make a small mark with a pencil.('X' or 'F' for front). You will, of course have decided which is going to be front and back. The watermark in the paper will tell you.

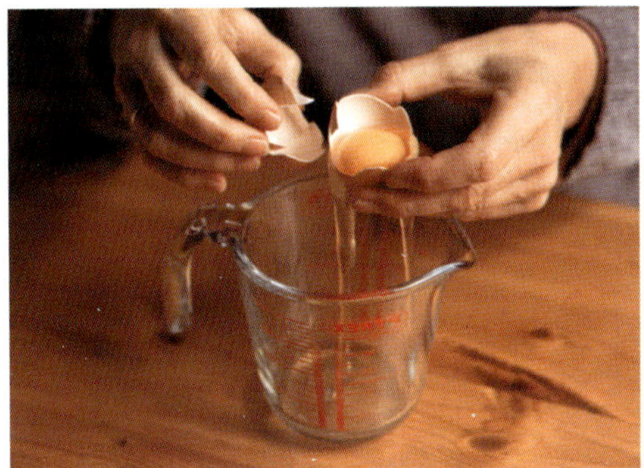

The natural way to obtain albumen.

Now place the paper face down on the surface of the liquid so that it floats on the top. **Make sure it doesn't sink!**

Now remove it by dragging it over the edge of the dish. This will not only take off any surplus liquid but also remove any air bubbles in the solution. Now hang it up to dry. It is not light sensitive and can be kept until you coat it with silver nitrate.

The easier but less historically correct way is to brush the egg white onto the paper. Mark the front with a pencil and then, using a brush (about one inch wide, brush on the liquid, first in vertical stripes then horizontally. Lay off the coating gently so that no brush streaks are left. Then dry it. From this point onwards the process is identical to that of salt printing. That is, coat with silver nitrate, expose, wash, fix, wash and dry. Gold tone if you wish in the same sequence as salt printing.

You will find it easier to get an even coating of silver on the albumenised paper if you dry the paper well and leave it for a day or two to make sure it has properly hardened.

If you don't want to use raw eggs you can use powdered egg or albumen. Make up 100mls of powder and distilled water in the proportions given by the maker on the packet and add 2 grams of salt. Use as before.

Trouble shooting

If you get bits of eggshell everywhere, remember you can't make albumen prints without breaking eggs!

Otherwise all other faults are in common with salt prints, so see that section.

What happens if you don't want an albumen print with a glossy surface? Well, you can make one with a matt finish using a mixture of egg white and arrowroot.

Such was the perversity of the market that after the Victorian public had been offered glossy salt prints in the form of albumen, they decided that matt surfaced albumen prints were what they really needed. So a new surface was developed whereby the albumen coating was combined with liquid starch - in this case arrowroot - which produced a fine matt finish. These alternative prints were usually known as albumen arrowroot prints.

Here, briefly, is the method. Take 4 gm arrowroot (from supermarket) and mix it with a little water into a creamy paste. In a clean saucepan boil 100 ml water containing 4 gm of sodium chloride. Give the arrowroot a final stir and pour it into the water. Let the mixture boil gently for a minute or two and then it cool. When it is cool remove the skin that has formed on the surface and mix the arrowroot with an equal amount of albumen. The albumen this time should contain no salt as enough is already in the arrowroot. Coat the paper and when dry apply silver nitrate as for a normal albumen print.

PHOTOGRAPHIC PRINTING AND MOUNTING.

MESSRS. CUNDALL, DOWNES, & Co. undertake the Printing and Mounting of Negatives, either for Amateurs or the Trade. Specimens, List of Prices, and Estimates for large numbers, may be obtained at 168 New Bond Street, or 10 Bedford Place, Kensington.

ALBUMINIZED PAPER. — Messrs. CUNDALL, DOWNES, & Co. are prepared to supply, either Wholesale or Retail, the genuine Papier Saxe, Albuminized in a superior manner. Sample quires (11×9) by post, 3*s*.

COOKE'S NEW ALBUMINIZED PAPER. —This highly Albuminized Paper has a beautiful, grainless surface, and yields fine Ivory-like Prints; it is therefore specially adapted for Portraits and Stereographs.

J. C. fearlessly invites comparison with any of the high-priced papers in the market.

Price 8*s*. per quire (size 22½ in. by 17½ in.). Sample Sheet, with directions for Use, with Improved Alkaline Toning, on receipt of two stamps.

J. COOKE, Photographic Chemist, &c., 63 Hoxton Old Town.

A PRACTICAL TREATISE ON PAPER PHOTOGRAPHY, made easy for every one, explaining the new Negative Collodion Process on Paper, and Marion's Positive Paper Albuminized by machinery. Positive papers ready sensitized always in stock, which will keep for any length of time. The above Treatise sold at PAPETERIE MARION'S, 152 Regent Street, W. Price 2*s*. 6*d*.

WANTED, a man who thoroughly understands the *negative process*, that would be willing to come upon a small salary and a good commission; he would have a female to assist him if required. Specimens of his own taking, and salary expected, addressed as follows, will meet attention.

Mr. JAMES: Mr. W. T. PARRY, Watch Maker, 19 Whitechapel, Liverpool.

As sensitised albumen paper has a short life, the manufacturing consisted just of coating the albumen. This was then sensitised by coating with silver nitrate solution by the photographer himself. Small adverts from The Photographic Journal, 1862.

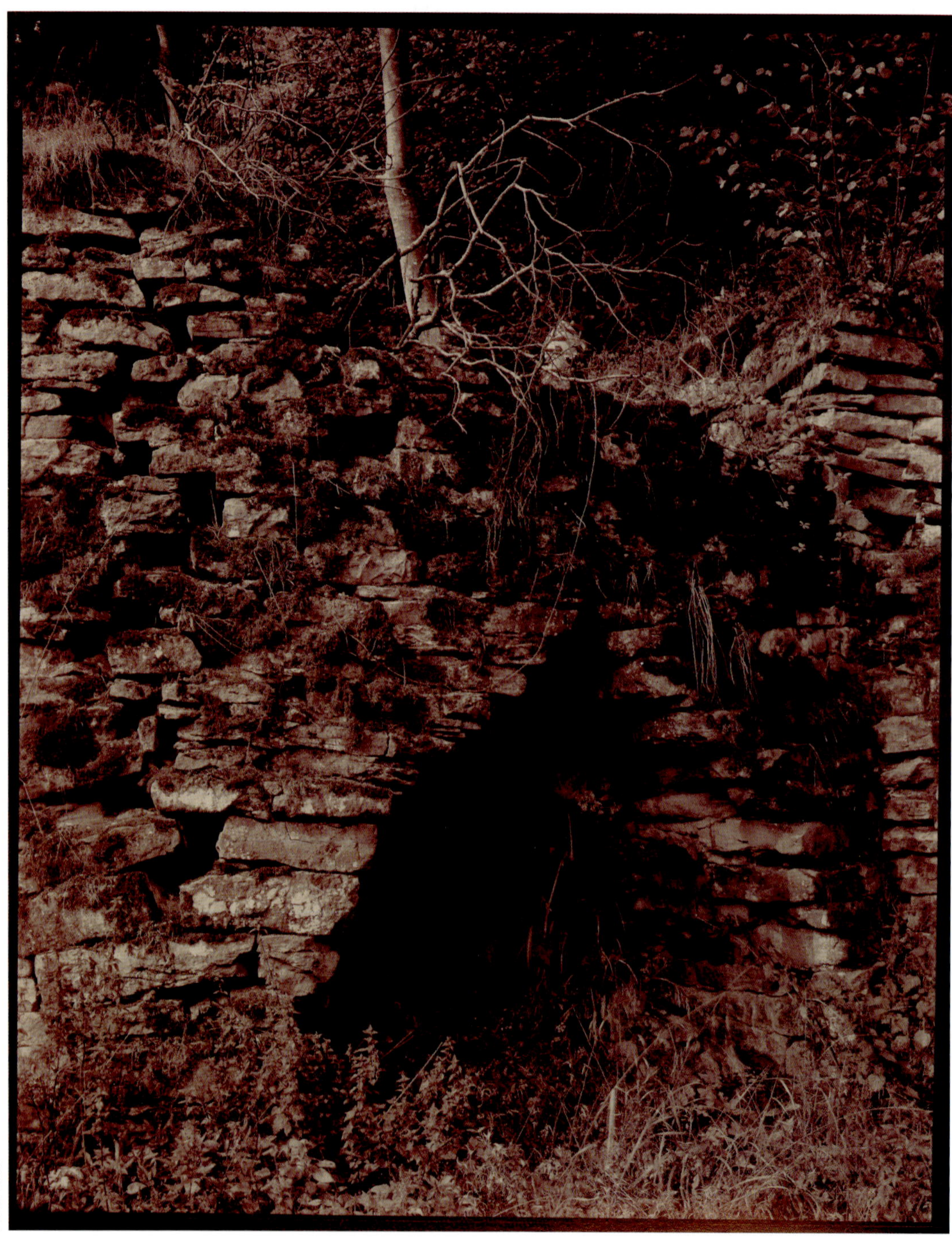

Martin Reed

Centennial printing-out paper, unprocessed, showing the colour formed during exposure.

Printing-out paper 12

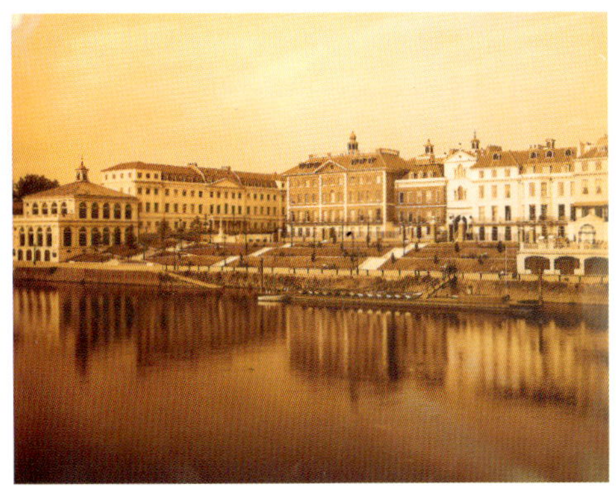

A beautiful colour from a Kentmere made POP, using only standard fixing with no toning. The secret was the considerable over-exposure given during printing, which lightened during fixing to give this result. A normally exposed print will fix to a lighter amber.

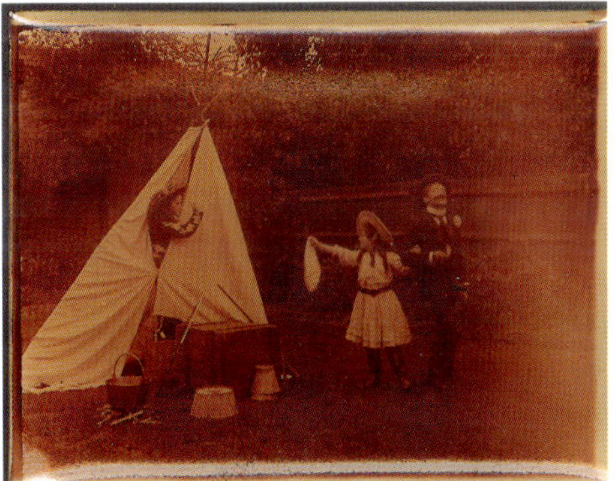

This intriguing performance, taken by an unknown photographer, was printed on POP sometime in the 1920's. Left unprocessed, but kept in darkness, it was found in 1999 with the image still largely intact.

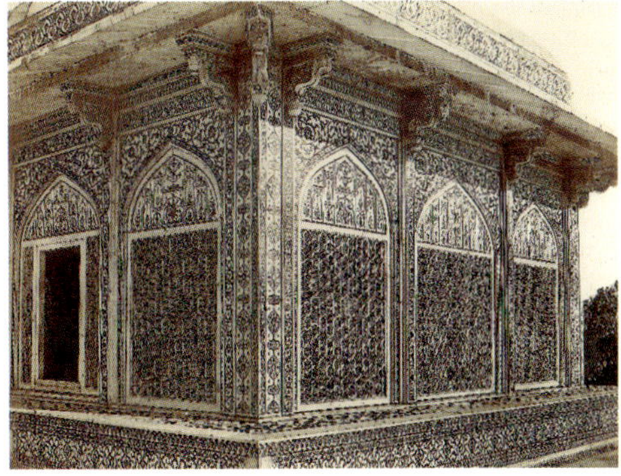

A Victorian photograph on gold-toned POP, showing the clear connections with the albumen process it superceded.

Printing-out paper, usually abbreviated to POP, was the commercial successor to albumen paper, and shares many characteristics with it. The main difference is in the binder, which instead of albumen used gelatin. This progression made possible the use of photographic emulsion on paper, albeit a basic one, in which silver nitrate and a halogen chloride are mixed in a gelatin solution. The slow emulsion formed this way will 'print out' to give a visible image by the action of strong light. The silver nitrate is always in excess, and is not washed out of the emulsion as in modern photographic papers, leaving a reserve of silver which strengthens the image. As in albumen printing, the image is a rich violet colour immediately after exposure. This image is unstable, and will fog if kept in light. To stabilise the print it must first be briefly washed to remove the excess silver nitrate. Fixing can follow, but the image will lighten to an amber colour. To keep most of the purple / brown colour, and a full tonal range, following washing the print should be gold toned, followed by rinsing, fixing and a final wash. Platinum and palladium toning are other options, giving an attractive and subtle brown colour. At the time of writing there are two POP materials on the market, 'Centennial' from the Chicago Albumen Co, and another from the French company Bergger. Centennial is made by Kentmere Ltd in the UK under exclusive contract.

Advantages

It is one of the few historic paper processes still available in a ready-coated form, and if you use it this way you will get a smooth even finish due to the machine coating.

If you have investigated making salt and albumen prints, this is the next step in the evolution of the silver print. If you make your own POP emulsion, you are making a real photographic emulsion, an ancestor of all the modern film and paper emulsions we use today.

Disadvantages

Using ready-coated paper, none. If you are making your own POP emulsion, it has a limited life before coating. The formula here cannot be set and re-melted, and must be coated immediately after preparation.

Shopping list

Equipment as in salt printing.
Silver nitrate, **citric acid** and **gelatin** are needed as for salt printing, but in addition you need **ammonium chloride** and **sodium potassium tartrate**.
If you're going to gold tone you also need either a ready made **gold toner**, or gold chloride 1% solution, plus borax.
Also for the final additives a small amount of **chrome alum** and **alcohol**. De-natured alcohol as in methylated spirits is OK. Vodka might do at a pinch.
Distilled or **purified water** for mixing the solutions.
Sodium thiosulphate for fixing.

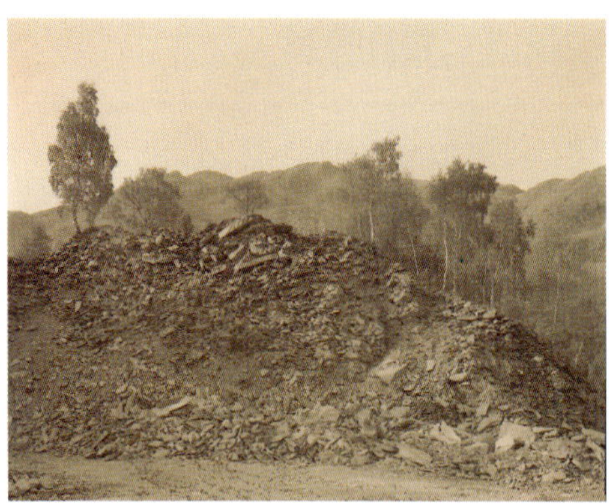

The subtle colours produced on Centennial POP when palladium toned - platinum produces a similar effect. The toner is simple to make up, and can be made from ammonium tetrachloro-palladate (for palladium) or ammonium tetrachloroplatinate (for platinum), dissolving one gram per litre, and acidifying with a little dilute hydrochloric acid.

Method

Make up two solutions:

Solution A

Distilled water	750 ml
Ammonium chloride	3 g
Sodium potassium tartrate	5 g
Gelatin	80 g

Solution B

Distilled water	250 ml
Silver nitrate	25 g
Citric acid	10 g

Raise the water for both solutions to 40° C, mixing the chemicals for each solution at the same time. Add solution B to solution A at a very slow trickle, stirring continuously. The mixed solution should be almost transparent initially, but soon becomes creamy. After ten minutes, add 50ml alcohol. Finally, add 30ml of a 2% chrome alum solution. Filter the emulsion through fabric, cotton wool or glass fibre and coat it before it sets. Using more citric acid will tend to increase contrast.

Coating

The excess of silver nitrate left after the emulsion reaction has taken place allows an image to form spontaneously during exposure, yielding a high density. As impurities in the substance you are coating will also bring this about, this type of emulsion can only be coated on the highest quality papers. Low quality papers will tend to show mottling and black spots. Emulsion spreads easily by brush if the temperature is kept well above its setting point (60° C). Avoid the use of coating rods, which as they contact the surface do not allow a sufficiently thick film to coat the paper. But don't coat too thickly! It won't fix or wash properly. After coating dry the paper well, preferably overnight, in darkness or at any rate very low light.

Exposure is as for salt or albumen printing. After exposure, the print can be made permanent by:

1 After exposure wash in changes of still tap water, until the water shows no traces of milkiness. This indicates that all free silver nitrate has been removed from the emulsion.

2 The prints can now be fixed in a plain sodium thiosulphate (hypo) bath at 20% strength for several minutes - this will, however, change the rich plum colour of the image to a lighter amber. Rapid ammonium thiosulphate fixers will bleach the image to a much greater extent and should not be used. Follow with washing as for a standard print.

3 If the strong image as first formed needs to be retained, a gold toning bath should be used after the first rinse. Treat the print for several minutes, until no further density and colour change takes place and follow with a five minute plain sodium thiosulphate fixing bath, then washing as normal.

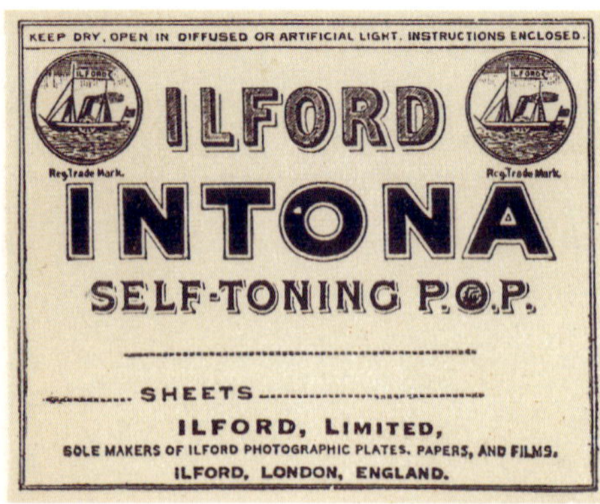

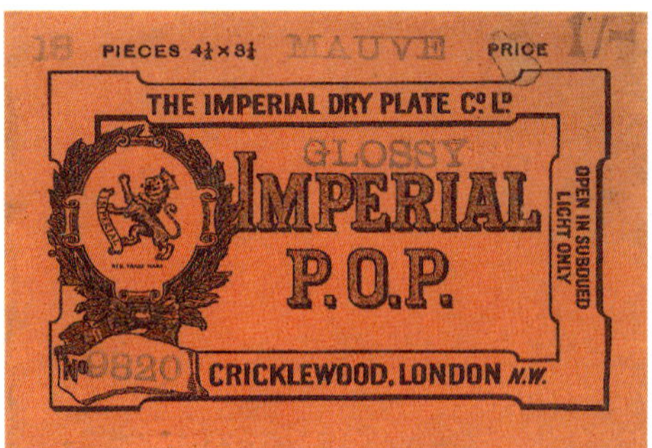

Self-toning printing-out paper incorporated gold salts into the emulsion, and avoided the separate toning step in processing. Many manufacturers were involved in producing the material by the early years of the 20'th century, including Ilford Ltd, who coined the term 'POP'.

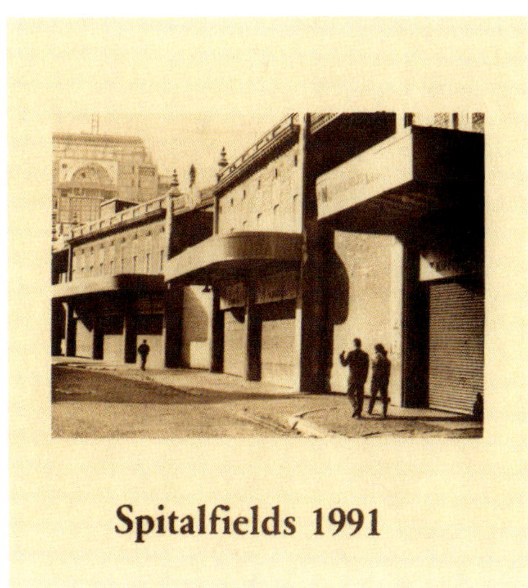

Van Dyke print made on Daler cream cover paper, which is normally used in picture framing. For the lettering, see p. 45, Negatives.

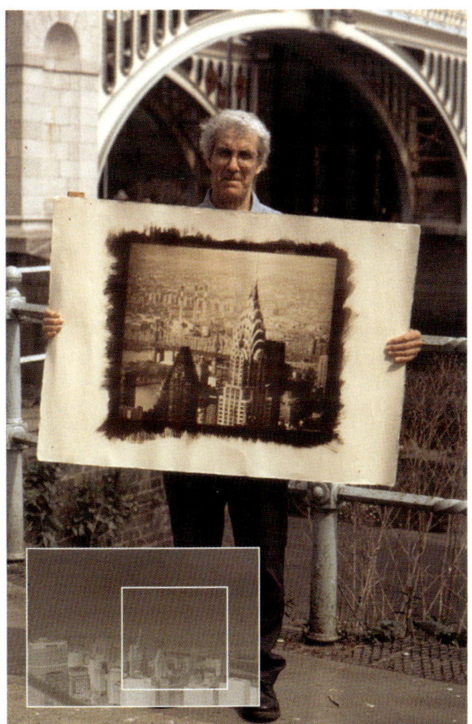

Van Dyke print on Arches Cream Rough paper. Image size 20 x 24", using Dupont lith film from a camera sale. The original camera negative, and the section from which the image is taken is shown inset actual size.

First, a question of definition. There are many newcomers to old processes as well as a good number of veterans, who quite happily spend their time under the impression that they are making kallitypes, when they are, in fact, making the simpler and slightly more recent Van Dyke print. We have reached the point now that the word 'kallitype' has become the generic term for both processes.

For the sake of clarity we shall now reverse the convention and treat the Van Dyke process as the dominant sibling, with kallitype repositioned as the lesser used, more complicated and more expensive of the two. Dissatisfied purists out there will have to live with it. A better overall term to describe both processes would be 'silver / iron' prints.

We have seen that salt prints use silver as their base and cyanotypes are made from compounds of iron. By definition, silver/iron use a mixture of both. Although the potential for making kallitypes existed from the early years of photography, when Herschel, the inventor of cyanotype investigated the possibilities of the process, it wasn't until 1889 that the process was patented. In that year Dr Nicol, a chemist, introduced the kallitype. He went on to patent a large number of variations on the process, to the extent that one wonders if the invention wasn't more important than its application. A few years later the brown or Van Dyke print was introduced, initially in the form of pre-coated paper. It is this that has become one of the most popular of early processes.

Its chemistry is simple and inexpensive, it can be used on a wide variety of papers and fabrics including T shirts, and the method of producing a print is quite straightforward. In the nineteenth century however it never really caught on. The reason for this is probably that it arrived too late.

It coincided with the introduction of gaslight papers which were produced commercially in large quantities, and which eventually led to the universal acceptance of silver gelatin papers as we know them now.

Early accounts of the making of kallitypes always contained doubts as to their permanence, although these warnings were usually accompanied by assurances that they would last indefinitely.

Platinum prints had also made their appearance at about this time, and as it was generally accepted that silver was less stable than platinum, the latter expensive, though equally simple, process overshadowed the silver / iron process.

Many of the variations of the kallitype are outside the scope or the interest of any but the most dedicated student and all rely on one particular chemical - ferric oxalate - for which there is little commercial demand. It is dificult to obtain and toxic. It is, however, essential to the platinum and palladium processes, so when you graduate to those you may try the real kallitype at the same time. Some writers on the subject recommend making your own ferric oxalate, but again this is outside the technical range of most non-chemists. For this reason we suggest you stick to the straightforward Van Dyke process to begin with.

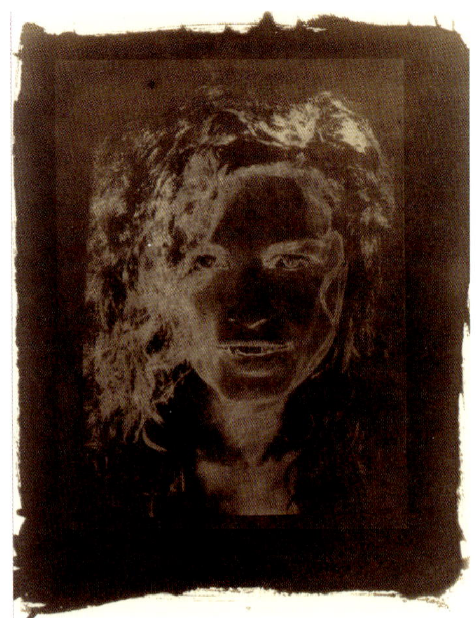

Original camera negative was partially solarised when the lid of the tank was accidentally removed. An inter-positive was made, and from this a new negative. Printed on Arches Cream paper.

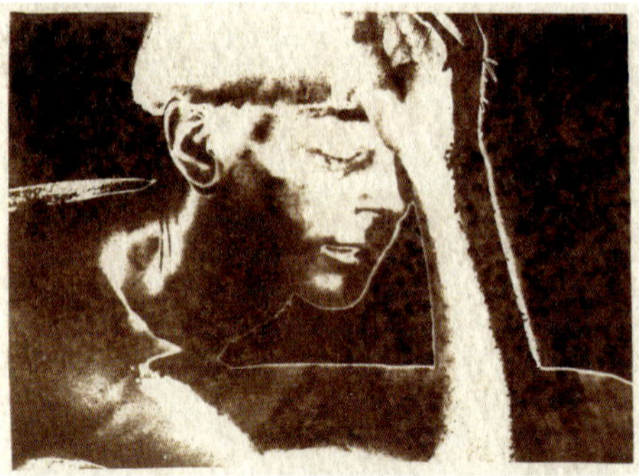

Van Dyke print from manipulated negative, see p. 45.

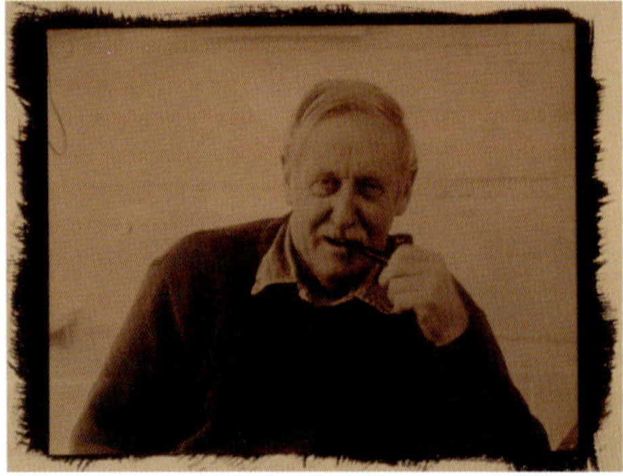

Trevor Bayliss, inventor. Kallitype on Arches Cream paper. Negative on NP31 film, enlarged directly fromAgfa Scala positive.

Some authorities are a bit sniffy about the simple Van Dyke print, claiming that it is not as good as the kallitype. The answer to this is - take no notice. You can spend the rest of your life making perfectly good Van Dyke prints without recourse to the more complex kallitype.

Advantages

Van Dyke prints are quick, inexpensive, easy to manage, and have a minimum of processing operations.

They can be used on a wide variety of paper surfaces and other materials such as cloth and wood.

It is easy to assess the exposure under the lamp as they print out.

They do not require long exposure under the lamp.

It is possible to vary the final image colour depending on the paper you use to make the print.

They need a fairly contrasty negative but not so hard as, for instance, salt prints.

They are a perfectly acceptable substitute for the more expensive platinum / palladium prints.

Disadvantages

There is not much chance of effectively changing the contrast at the printing stage so you have to produce a negative to suit the print.

The true kallitype has much more chemistry and steps in processing.

The literature on the many variations is confusing and quite often obscure.

You could spend years experimenting without producing a decent image!

Ferric oxalate is not very easily available.

Both methods require careful processing to ensure reasonable permanence.

Van Dyke print shopping list

Chemicals

Ferric ammonium citrate (green)
Silver nitrate
Tartaric acid (obtainable from any chemist's shop)
Distilled or purified water
Hypo (sodium thiosulphate)
Potassium dichromate (optional)

Small measuring jar (45 ml)

2 **medium measuring jars** (1 litre).

Stirring rod.

Scales measuring down to 1 gram.

Soft 1" brush or glass rod.

Printing frame or similar.

Brown screw top bottle (250 ml).

Ultra violet light source.

Roll of translucent Scotch tape.

Hair drier.

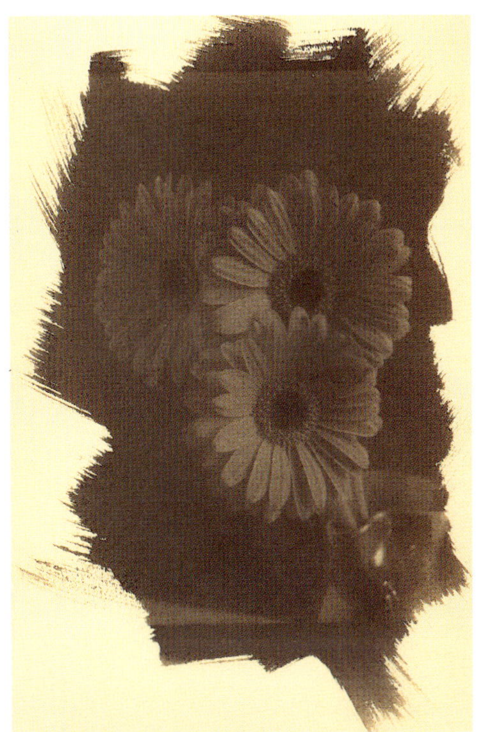

It is not necessary to produce high contrast images with every old process. This, however, may be to some peoples taste a little low in contrast. It is also possible that the brushing is more interesting than the image.

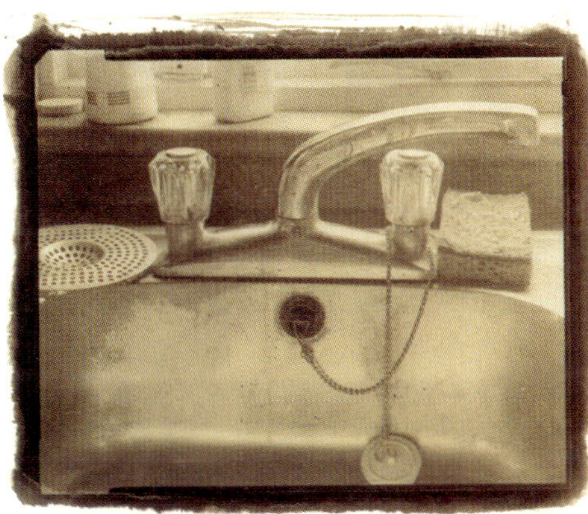

Everything including the kitchen sink. Contact printed from 5 x 4" negative, which was over-developed by 50% to give adequate highlight brightness on the print.

Darlene Honey

Paper or fabric of your choice (see method).

A supply of **running water.**

If you decide to try the true kallitype method you will need the same equipment but a different set of chemicals as follows:
Distilled water
Ferric oxalate
Silver nitrate
Borax
Rochelle salt (sodium potassium tartrate)
Hypo

Negatives

You will need a fairly contrasty negative - the sort that will give a bright print on Multigrade with a no. 1/2 filter. Make sure there is plenty of detail in the shadow areas and that the highlights are well separated and not blocked out.
If you use a densitometer to measure the negative, aim for roundabout 1.6 net density.

Papers for Van Dyke prints and Kallitypes

You have a wide range of papers which will give good results with these processes. In addition you can use fabrics made with cotton, linen, muslin and of course, T shirts, curtains, tea towels, cushion covers and wall hangings.

The type of paper you use will have some effect on the final colour of the print. For example, Arches cream paper will give a very rich chocolate brown whereas Fabriano 50 or 100 per cent will show a slightly redder tint. (Refer to the paper chart for more details).

For printing on cloth and other materials see [29 . Printing on fabrics]

Van Dyke prints

This is very straightforward. Brush on one single solution, dry, expose, wash, fix, wash and dry.
Mixing the chemicals needs a little care.
You will need three small measuring jars.

First, mix solution A

35 ml of distilled or purified water.
Add 10 grams of ferric ammonium citrate (green) - you use the same chemical in the cyanotype process. Stir until dissolved.

Next, solution B

35 ml of distilled or purified water.
Add 2 grams of tartaric acid powder - buy from a home brew supplier. Stir until dissolved.

Finally solution C

35 ml of distilled or purified water.
Add 4 grams of silver nitrate. Be careful not to spill the crystals as they are

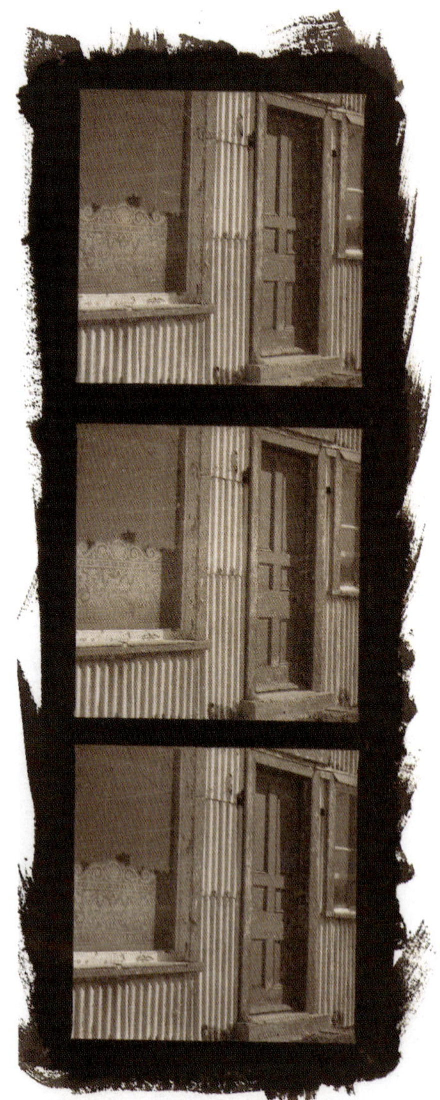

Kallitype printed from strip of 120 film, given 50% plus development on TMax 400 for extra contrast.

highly corrosive and stain everything brown.

Stir until dissolved.

Now pour solution A into solution B and mix thoroughly.
Then add the silver solution C a few drops at a time to the mixture of A and B, stirring all the time until it is mixed. If you don't mix solution C gradually you will end up with a grey sludge at the bottom of the jar and you will need a chemist to advise you what to do next!
Pour the final mix into a brown bottle and label it 'Van Dyke mix' and the date. It should last for months.
Coat your paper with a clean brush making sure it is well brushed into the paper and avoid any puddles of liquid on the surface, (see coating).
Dry with a hair drier or fan heater until it is bone dry. The coating will show as a pale yellow green colour.
All this can be carried out in normal room lighting or in subdued daylight.
Place your negative dull side down on the paper, tack it to the paper in one corner with a small strip of Scotch tape and place it in your printing frame.
Leave the frame in the sun or under a UV lamp to expose.
After a few minutes the brushed edges outside the image will turn a deep orange colour.
After a few more minutes open the frame and check the exposure, making sure to keep the negative in register.
When it looks right it is right, but make sure not to over-expose the print as there is a slight darkening of the image during processing. A little practice will give you a general idea of what you need.
When you think you have the right exposure, remove the print and negative from the frame, detach the print from the negative, and wash the print in cold running tap water for about five minutes.
The image will change to a rather nasty ginger colour. This is normal.
While it is washing make up your fixer solution as follows:

Measure out 250 mls of warm tap water (about 45° C) and dissolve into it 25 grams of plain hypo, see [6 . Chemicals]

Now add to this 250 mls of cold tap water and pour into a dish.

When the washing is complete place the washed print into the fixer, and leave to fix for about five minutes. The image will change colour again, this time to a rich chocolate brown. If you don't have any plain hypo handy you can use ordinary print fixer but mix it at about 1:15, as it can slightly bleach the image.

After fixing wash the print for about 30 minutes in running water as you would a normal fibre print. Then hang it up to dry. You can speed up the drying by hanging it up to drain for 15 minutes and then dry with a hair drier. When it is dry the image will have changed slightly to a deeper shade of brown.

Note: the processing can be done in room lighting or subdued daylight.

Retouch white spots with water colour, and dark spots with a sharp scalpel.

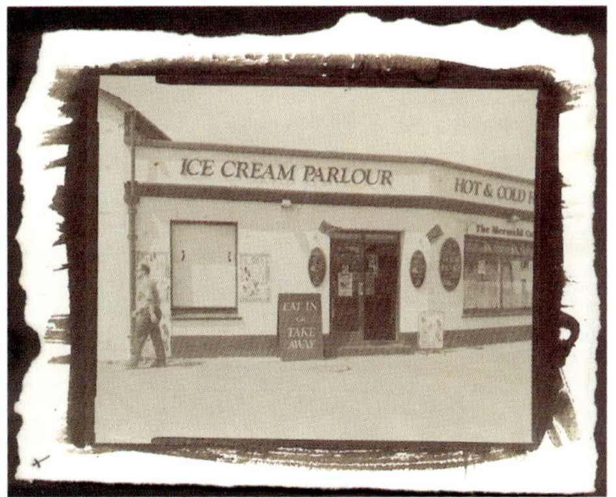

Ice cream parlour. Freshwater, Isle of Wight. Kallitype printed by direct contact in sunlight from 5x4" camera negative.

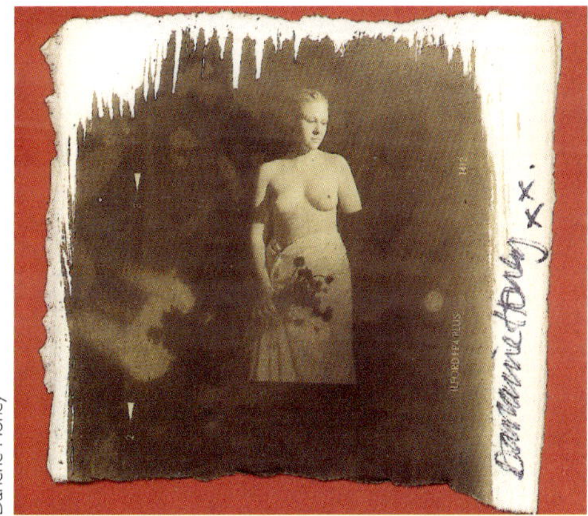

Darlene Honey

Venus. Van dyke print on Fabriano paper. Note the hand written dedication.

Trouble shooting

Some of the sensitiser washes off during washing or fixing.
You have brushed the liquid on too thickly and it has dried as a crust on the paper. Keep washing and hope for the best!

The print is too dark.
You have over-exposed it. Give it less exposure next time.

The print is too light.
You have under-exposed it. Give it more exposure next time.

The print is muddy and lacking contrast.
Make a more contrasty negative. (See [9 . Negatives].

The print is too contrasty.
Make a less contrasty negative. See [9 . Negatives]. You could try giving it more exposure to fill in the highlights. It might work!

The print has stains or patches of uneven colour on it.
This is probably caused by uneven washing or fixing. Be more careful next time.

Kallitype

The problems associated with this method are the relative unavailability of chemicals, the fact that you have to develop the image before you fix it, and most of all the plethora of wildly conflicting published accounts on just about every aspect of the process.

If you want to turn a perfectly simple means of making a photographic print into an unnecessarily complicated operation, then this is the one for you. If you want to try your hand at being a photographic chemist then by all means give this method a go. Be warned - you may end up making your own chemicals. On the other hand, if you wish to remain a humble photographer then stick to the previous Van Dyke method. The choice is yours. The procedures are very similar with the two exceptions that kallitype will need more chemicals and lengthier processing steps.

Method

The choice of negatives and paper are the same as for Van Dyke prints.
Take 50ml distilled water and into it mix 10 grams of ferric oxalate, see [15 . Platinum & palladium].
Take 50 ml distilled water and into it mix 5 g silver nitrate. Put them separately into brown bottles. These comprise the sensitiser.
Now mix the developer;
Take 500ml hot water at 65° C.
Stir in 35 g borax, and keep stirring until it has completely dissolved, (this takes longer than you think).
Then add 50 g sodium potassium tartrate (commonly called Rochelle salt).
Keep stirring until it is clear.
Now add 1.5 g tartaric acid and stir until dissolved.
Pour into a dish and let the mixture cool.

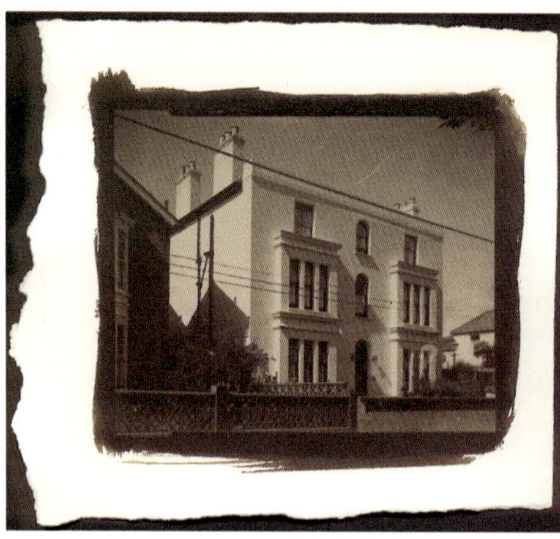

Kallitype contact printed directly from 5x4" negative.

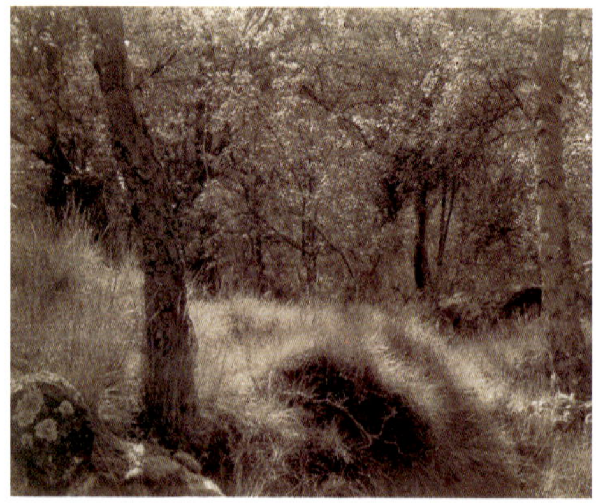

Mike Ware

Argyrotype

Developed by Mike Ware, the Argyrotype can be considered to be a modern relative of the Kallitype, and is similarly based on iron chemistry. Argyrotype chemistry has some subtle sophistications, and is designed to be more 'user friendly' than the traditional Kallitype, and with more consistent permanence. The iron compound employed is ammonium ferric citrate, and is used in conjunction with sulphamic acid and silver (I) oxide. This is normally considerably more expensive than silver nitrate, but can be quite easily produced by reacting silver nitrate with sodium hydroxide. The process is very paper specific, and only the best cotton fibre paper, free from all additives is suitable. The normal colour on high quality paper, example above, is a rich purple / brown similar to Kallitype and Van Dyke. Full working details are on Mike Wares web site, address in [33 . Resources]. A ready-made Argyrotype sensitiser is made by Fotospeed and available through dealers.

Finally the fixer.

Take 500ml warm water (50° C).
Stir into it 25 g plain hypo. Stir until dissolved.
Some writers still include ammonia in the mixture, while others think it is not a good idea. When in doubt, leave it out.
Measure out equal amounts of the ferric oxalate and the silver sensitiser, say 5 ml of each, and mix them well.
Now follow the same routine as with the Van Dyke process. That is, coat the paper, dry it, place it in the printing frame and expose. At this point it will not 'print out' as the other processes did. Instead you will see a faint image which will only arrive at the correct tonal values when it is developed. A useful guide to exposure is to look at the deepest shadows in the faint image, and when they take on a slightly purple tinge, the exposure is very close to being correct. You will need to resort to a little trial and error. For a negative of reasonable overall density it will take about 3 or 4 minutes to expose in bright sunlight. On a cloudy day or under a UV lamp it may take twice as long.
Place the exposed trial print into the dish of developer and leave for about 10 minutes to allow for the background colour to clear. If the exposure was correct the full image should appear in 10 or 20 seconds regardless of whether it has been correctly exposed. Rinse the print in running water and transfer to the fixer. After 10 minutes fixing, wash for 30 minutes in running water. Now assess the print. If it is over or under-exposed try an old-fashioned test print as you would in normal black and white printing!
All other aspects of processing, retouching and trouble shooting are the same as with Van Dyke prints.

A final note on washing

There has been a continuing debate on the question of the permanence of silver / iron prints. The answer to this is that the more residual fixer that is removed from the paper during processing, the less chance that the image will fade in time.
We pass on the method used by Noel Myles, whose Van Dyke print appears on page opposite.

Wash in running water, (preferably in an archival washer) for 2-3 hours. Place in a bath of Kodak Hypo Clearing Agent for 5 minutes, then straight into selenium toner (Kodak) at a dilution of 1:200, and leave until a noticeable colour change occurs (about 20 minutes). Wash again for one hour.

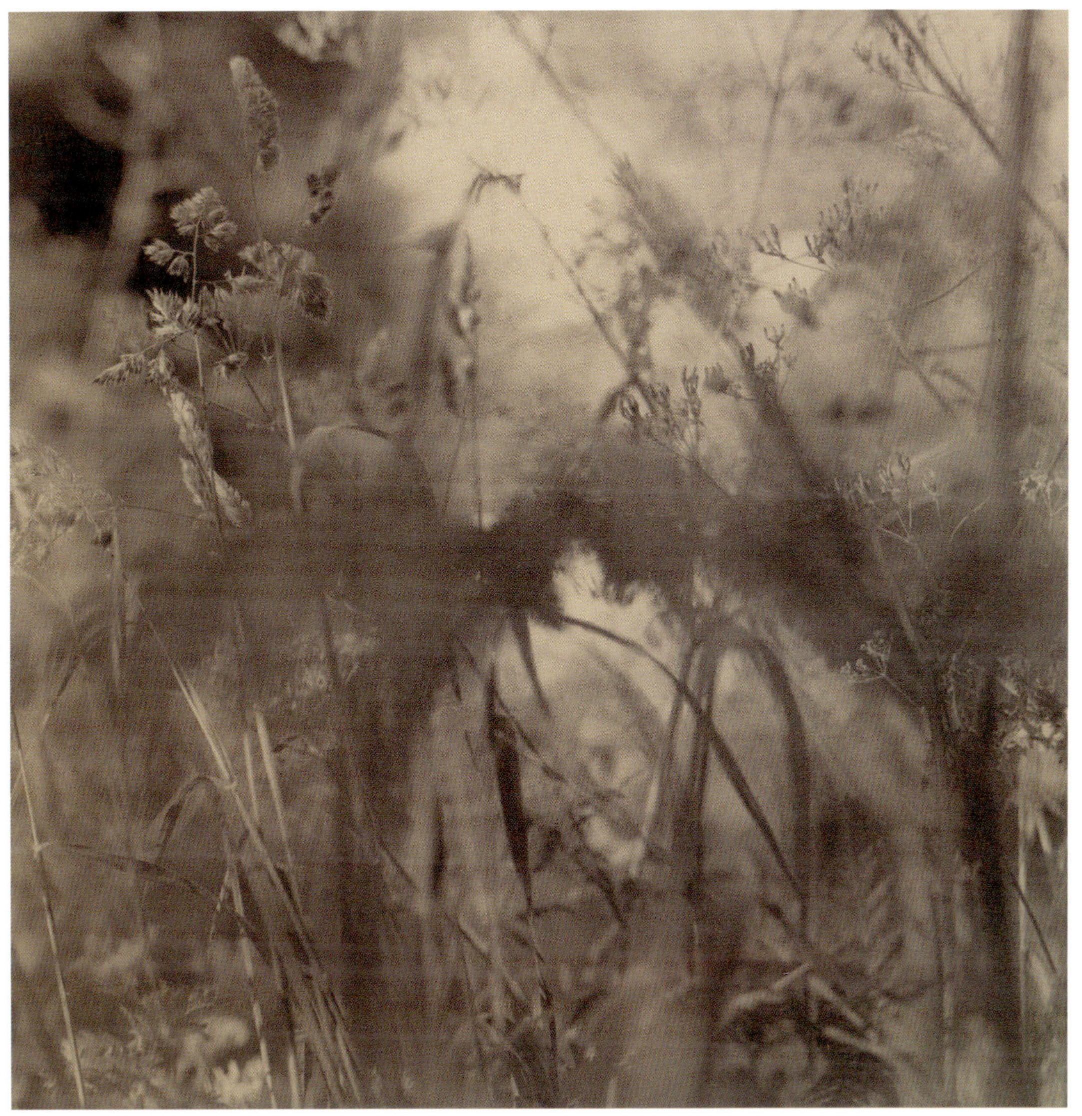

Noel Myles

Kallitype

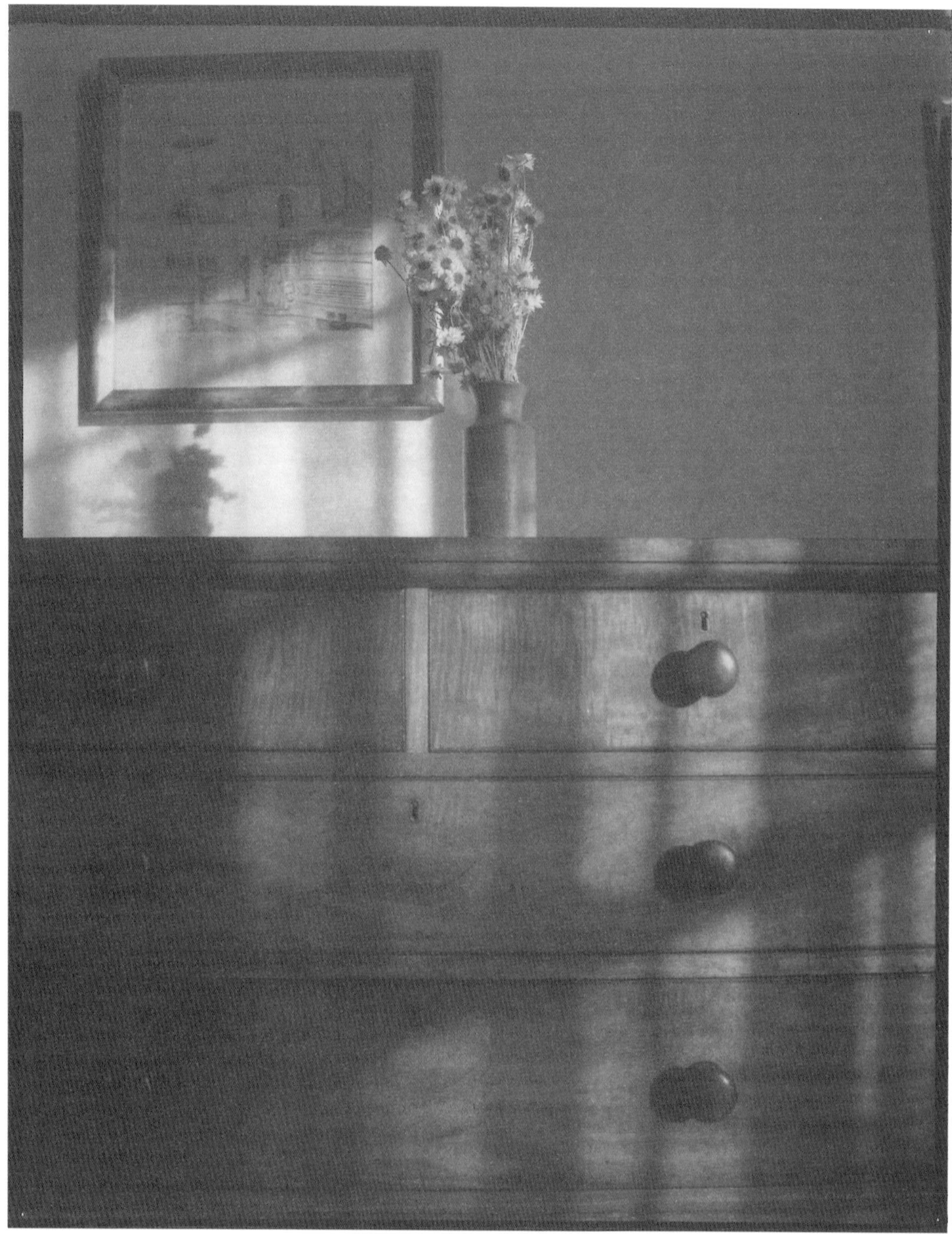

Andra Nelki

Cyanotype

Cyanotype 14

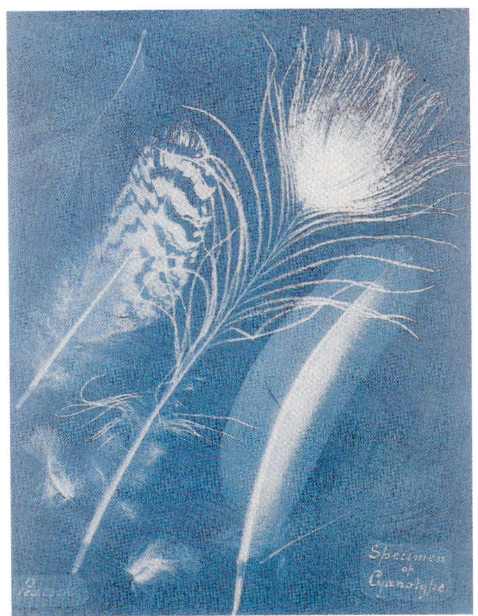

One of the early cyanotype photograms produced in 1845 by Sir John Herschel.

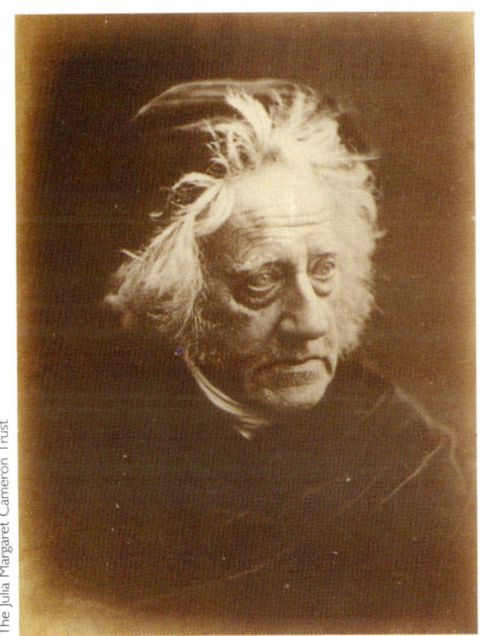

The Julia Margaret Cameron Trust

Sir John Herschel, the inventor of Cyanotype, from the albumen print by Julia Margaret Cameron.

The astronomer Sir John Herschel published his account of the cyanotype process in 1842. He was a friend of Fox Talbot and his researches into light-sensitive materials had run on similar lines to Talbot's. However, as his inquiries were motivated by purely scientific considerations rather than for the possibility of commercial or artistic success, there was no real rivalry between them as there had been in the case of Talbot and Daguerre. In addition to his reputation as a scientist, Herschel's main claim to fame was his discovery of sodium thiosulphate as an effective means of fixing a photographic image on paper and thus preventing it from fading. This substance, erroneously known as sodium hyposulphite or more commonly hypo, was crucial to the development of the new science of photography and has been an essential item in every darkroom to the present day. Many of the early inventors had concentrated their efforts on compounds of silver to obtain an effective means of producing a photographic image. Herschel on the other hand used his wide scientific knowledge to explore other areas of research, and arrived at a method which used two simple compounds of iron to make his light sensitive material. The resulting print was prussian blue or cyan in colour, and was known as cyanotype. It was the first of the early photographic processes to be used to illustrate a book. Anna Atkinson, a mutual friend of Herschel and Talbot, had been making studies of algae and other plant forms and found it very difficult to make accurate and detailed drawings of the specimens that she had collected. The cyanotype process was used as a method of producing photograms of her collection, and the result was published as a series of part works. Her book pre-dated Talbot's book 'Pencil of Nature' by some months.

The virulent blue colour of the cyanotype made it unsuitable for portraiture and was never really popular for pictorial purposes. However it was a cheap and quick form of photocopying, and eventually was used extensively for copying architects' and engineers' drawings until they were superseded by dyeline and other processes. Hence the description 'blueprint'. There was one sad irony about Herschel's invention. Although he had invented photographic fixer, his own cyanotype process did not require hypo to fix the image. Once exposed to sunlight the print needed only washing in plain water to secure a permanent image. Cyanotype fell into disuse for pictorial photography, and apart from a slight revival at the end of the 19'th century was not used to any extent until the middle of the 20'th century.

Advantages

It is cheap to mix and easy to use. A very effective way of introducing children and newcomers to photography and the principles of light sensitive materials.

It is permanent and needs only two chemicals.

It does not need to be fixed in the conventional way.

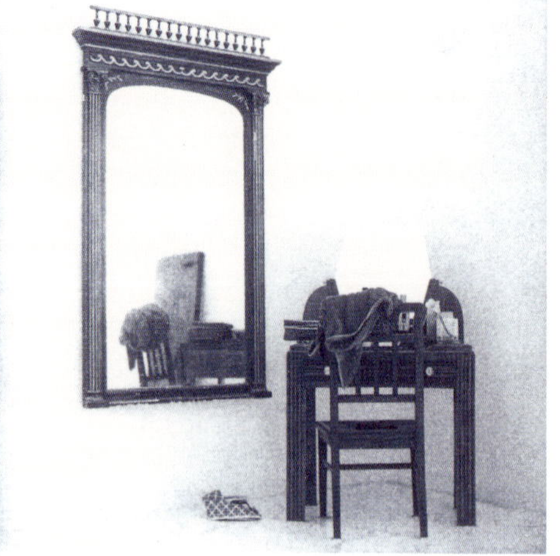

Noel Myles

Modern cyanotypes produced from medium format via enlarged negatives.

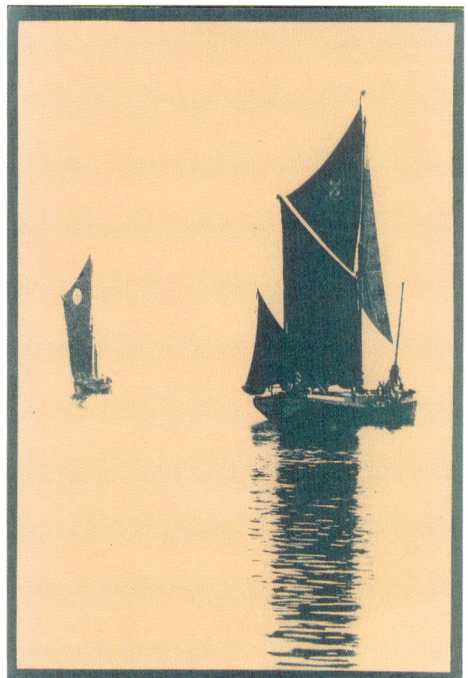

Cyanotype from 35mm negative, enlarged onto line film, and all intermediate tones eliminated with Farmers reducer. Printed on Daler cover paper.

It can be used to print on a variety of materialsm - paper, cloth, wood, ceramics, etc.

It is not degraded by the acid content of papers and can thus be printed on cheap non acid-free materials.

It can be over-printed with other processes eg. gum, platinum, silk screen.

Detail is rendered very finely, and the process can be used for various graphics, dot screens and small negatives.

Low cost makes it ideal for making very large prints and photograms.

Disadvantages

The virulent prussian blue colour makes it a bit wearing to look at and is not wholly suitable for wedding pictures, portraits and landscapes.

Its susceptibility to alkaline substances renders it unsuitable for printing on the current range of politically correct acid-free buffered papers. If printed on cloth, T shirts etc. it cannot be washed in normal washing powders.

Its colour can be varied by the use of toners, but they tend to reduce the permanence of the image.

Exposure even in bright sunlight is quite slow compared with many of the other processes.

Shopping list

Chemicals

Ferric ammonium citrate (green).
Potassium ferricyanide (**not** ferrocyanide).
Hydrogen peroxide (30 vols. from any chemist or hairdresser's supplier).

Graduated measures - 1 small up to 50 ml, 1 medium up to 600 ml, 1 large up to 1 litre.

Chemical stirring rod.

A roll of **Scotch magic tape**.

Hinged-back printing frame (at least two inches larger on each side than your image size).

A cheap 1 inch **paint brush** from any hardware store. See section on coating.

Paper - the cheaper the better - any colour other than black or deep blue! Avoid expensive acid free or buffered papers, as these could make your picture fade before your eyes. Also see [30 . Printing on other materials].

Developing dish to take your choice of paper size.

Ultra violet lamp or **daylight/sunlight** (cheaper and quicker).

Supply of **cold running water.**

Hair drier or small fan heater.

Sheet of plastic and some **old newspapers** to protect your work surface.

Set of **print tongs**.

A small **washing line** (plastic coated) and some clean plastic **clothes pegs**.

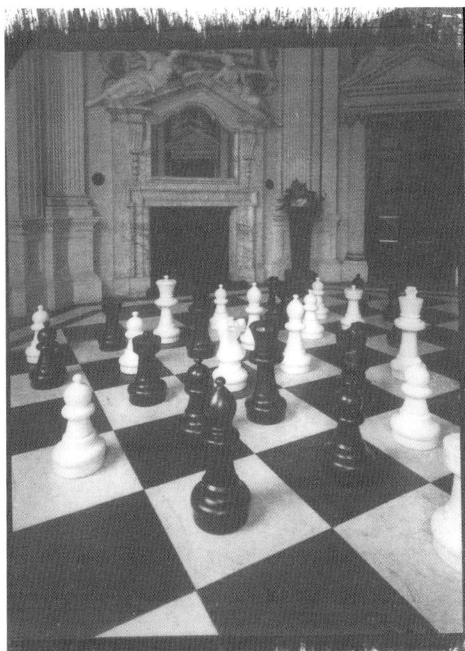

Cyanotype from direct contact with 5 x 4" negative.

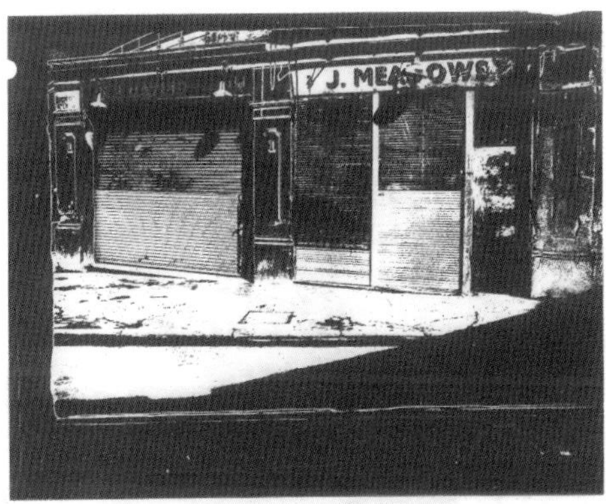

Cyanotype from negative via interpositive using Sabattier effect.

Two small (250ml) **brown bottles** from your chemist to store your made up solution.

Small china **saucer**.

Small plastic **funnel.**

100 ml of old film or paper developer.

Negatives

There are two ways of approaching the production of cyanotypes. As they are capable of resolving very fine details on quite smooth paper you can make crisp sharp and well defined prints from camera negatives from 10x8" right down to 120 format or even 35mm. One well known cyanotype worker does good business selling 120 format prints mounted on large cream mounts. You don't need a spectacularly contrasty negative for this so a camera negative of reasonable contrast works very well. The alternative is to make larger sized contact negatives either as continuous tone or with the full range of graphic effects such as solarisation, dot screens, half tones, cliché verre or montage. These prints can later be overprinted with gum, platinum or silk screen if necessary.

If you are using a conventional continuous tone negative aim for a net density range on a densitometer of about 1.4. If using the visual method , make a negative that will produce an acceptable print on grade one Multigrade paper. Cyanotype sensitiser is somewhat more contrasty than salt or kallitype and therefore needs plenty of details in the shadows and the highlights must not be blocked. If you use lith film for graphic effects then these guidelines obviously do not necessarily apply.

Method

Cyanotypes are very simple to make. Here is a brief summary:
Mix two chemicals in water, brush on to paper, dry, expose under a negative, wash for a few minutes in cold water and hang up to dry.

The following stages can all be performed in normal room lighting or subdued daylight.

Cyanotype mixture

Mix (a) 10 g ferric ammonium citrate (green) - don't use the brown variety - in 50 ml tap water. Pour into 250ml brown stoppered bottle.

Then mix (b) 4 g potassium ferricyanide in 50 ml tap water. Pour into a second brown bottle.

Mix equal quantities of (a) and (b) - say 10 ml of each - and pour into a china saucer ready for coating.

Now a further note on your choice of paper.

Any cheap cartridge or drawing paper will do provided it does not contain alkali. Make sure it has sufficient wet strength to withstand soaking in water for five or ten minutes. If you want to make a print on the front page of the Financial Times (it can be done) don't pick it up by the corner when it is wet - it falls apart.

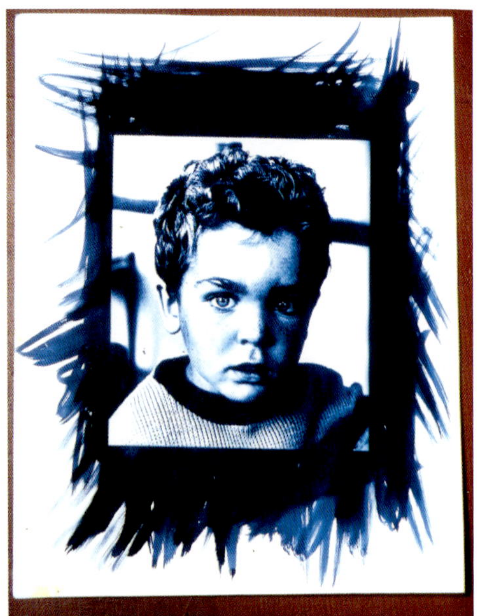

Little boy at Dungeness. Cyanotype on cheap cartridge paper. It illustrates the effect of wild brushwork.

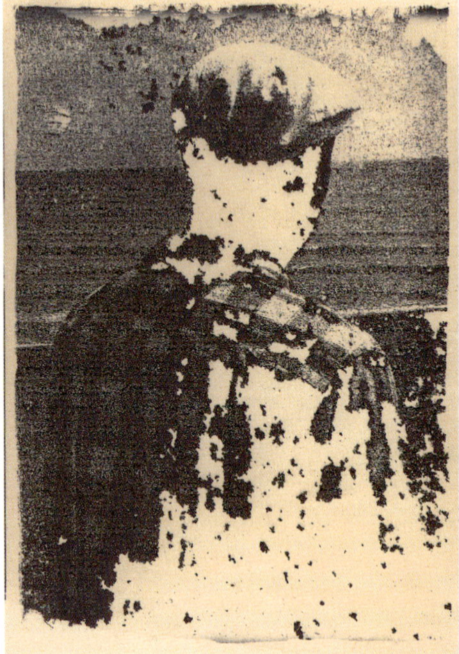

Rick at Dungeness. This negative was made from an interpositive on lith film, broken into dots by means of non-reflecting picture glass [9 . Negatives]. The positive was negligently left in a dish of water for three days, and the emulsion began to accumulate as sludge in the bottom of the dish. The print was subsequently rescued, dried, and printed as a cyanotype.

A good choice of paper is studio backdrop paper- either white or coloured.

Coat your paper, see [7 . Coating].

Caution:- Don't put too much liquid on at first. Don't leave puddles on the paper before you dry it as this will form a crust which will peel off later. If you do put too much on then wipe off the surplus with a piece of cotton wool or a scrap of kitchen roll.
Your paper should now be covered with a pale yellow-green coating.
Dry immediately with a hair drier or small fan heater.
Load the negative and coated paper in your printing frame and if necessary tape them together, see [8 . Exposing the print].
Place the frame under an ultra violet lamp or sun light, and in a few minutes you will see the brushed margins of the print turn from yellow-green to dark green and then to blue.
Open the hinged back of the frame or take your clip frame apart at five-minute intervals to check the progress of the exposure. Resist the temptation to take it out when it looks right. At this stage it is still not fully exposed. The maxim for cyanotypes is that if it looks right it is under-exposed.
Continue exposing until the shadows take on a gunmetal grey appearance and only the brightest highlights remain yellow green. It is a fairly slow business and even in bright sun the exposure can take up to 30 minutes.
After exposure you can separate the paper from the negative and wash it in a dish with frequent changes of water until all the yellow background has disappeared, and the image including the brushed edge is bright blue.
If you wish you can now hang the print up to dry. As it is exposed to the oxygen in the atmosphere the iron in the iron compounds present will oxidise and turn a deeper shade of blue. A quicker and more theatrical way of accelerating this step is to pour a teaspoonful of hydrogen peroxide in the wash water and rock the dish for a few seconds. The image will very rapidly turn a rich shade of prussian blue. Rinse the print in cold water and hang it up on the line to dry. Don't use a squeegee or a flat bed fibre paper drier. If you are in a hurry use a hair drier or a small fan heater.

Troubleshooting

Your print is too light.
Underexposed. Try again with another sheet of coated paper, this time leaving it for at least 50% longer under the light. Don't throw it away. You may be able to use it later when you can try printing a gum print over it, using the residual blue image as an undercolour for the gum.

Your print is too dark.
Overexposed. Try another one with less exposure. It is possible to salvage it by extending the washing time to up to an hour. Too much washing tends to wash out the blue colour, leaving a cold grey image.

Correctly exposed but print has fogged highlights.
Either the negative was of too low contrast. Use a contrastier neg.

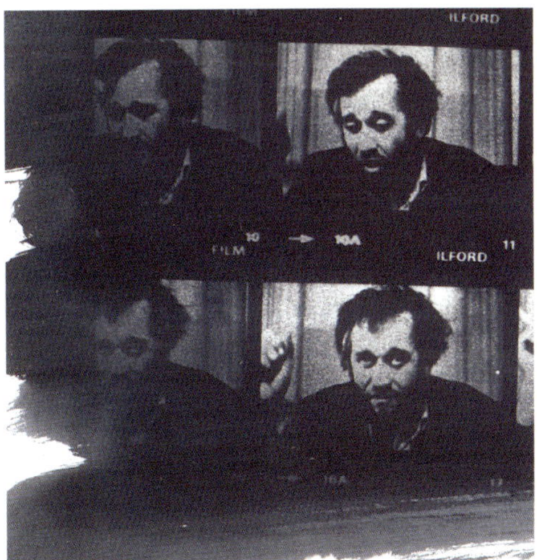

Cyanotype from enlarged 35mm contact print.

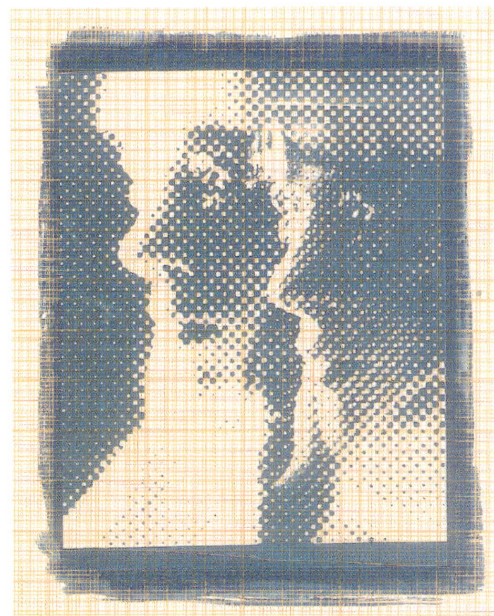

Cyanotype made from enlarged dot-screen negative, printed on old sheet of graph paper used as wrapping paper.

or the sensitising mixture has gone off. Mix some more. Cyanotype is a pretty rugged process so there is not much else that can go wrong.

Further notes on coating the paper

Since cyanotype is so easy and so cheap it may be worth while trying a few alternative ways of coating your paper. Here are a few outlandish suggestions.

1 Dab the mixture on with a piece of cotton wool or kitchen towel.
2 Roll it on with a foam paint roller.
3 Spray it on.
4 Slap it on with your hand, (use protective gloves).
5 Take a piece of muslin or loosely woven cloth, dip it in the liquid, wring out the excess solution, place the cloth on the paper and roll it gently with a roller.
6 Put the paper on the floor. Stand on a chair and let drops of liquid fall on the paper (aim carefully) so that it splatters on the paper. Then hold the paper on its edge so that the liquid runs down the surface. As it starts to soak in blot it gently to avoid puddles.
7 Brush the liquid on your bicycle tyre and ride your bike over it, (technique courtesy of Quentin Ball and possibly Tony Hancock).
8 Cut a seven foot length from a roll of white paper, coat it using a wide emulsion paint brush and let it dry in the dark. Lay it on the lawn and lie on it surrounded by your possessions (glasses, false teeth, jewellery, flowers, the cat etc.) When it is exposed, hang it up and wash it down with a garden hose and peg it on the washing line to dry. Perfect personalised wallpaper!

The possibilities are endless.

Toning

There are published formulae for toning cyanotypes but as they use unnecessarily toxic chemicals we will leave you to investigate these yourself. Anyway, who in their right mind would want to make a brown blueprint?

Having said that there is one non-toxic answer to toning cyanotypes. Try the cold tea treatment. Make a strong pot of tea (not Earl Grey), pour it into a tray and let it cool. Immerse the dry print in it for about ten minutes or so. The tea will physically stain the paper, giving it a rich cream colour, whilst the blue tones will become much richer and darker - a big improvement on the standard nasty cyan. Leave it in the dish until it arrives at the right colour, take it out and let it dry. It is possible that the tannic acid has a chemical reaction on the cyanotype mix. But who cares? The result is more important than the means of achieving it.

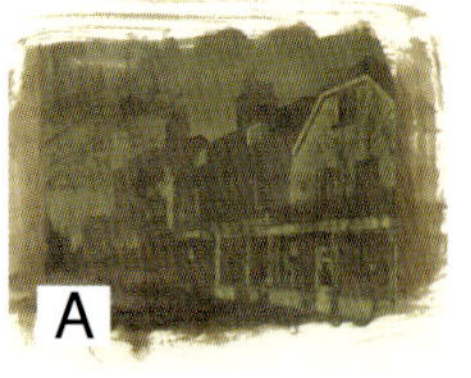

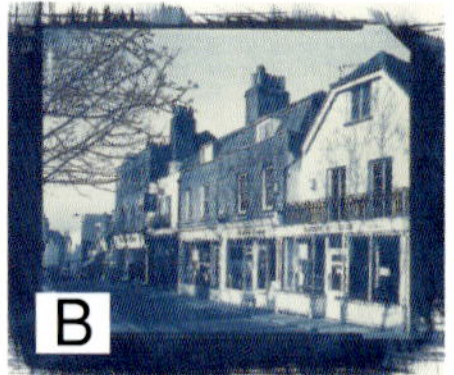

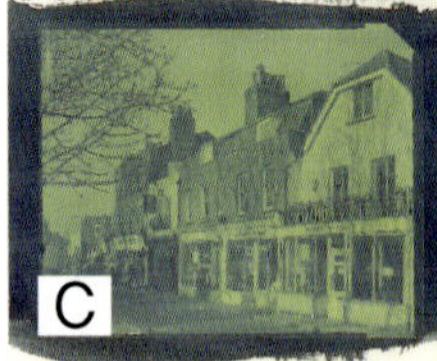

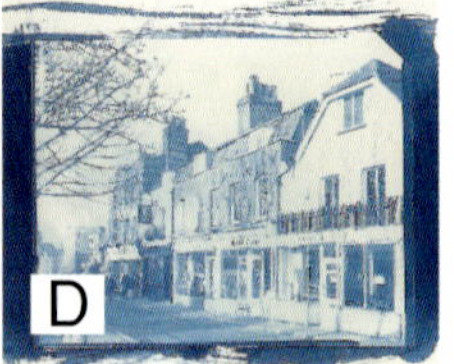

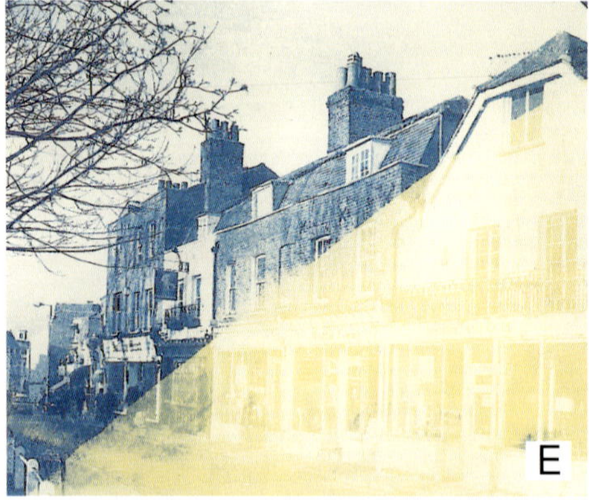

A - Correctly exposed cyanotype before washing.
B - Correctly exposed cyanotype after washing.
C - Under-exposed cyanotype.
D - Same print after washing.
E - The right hand side of this cyanotype has been brushed with household bleach.

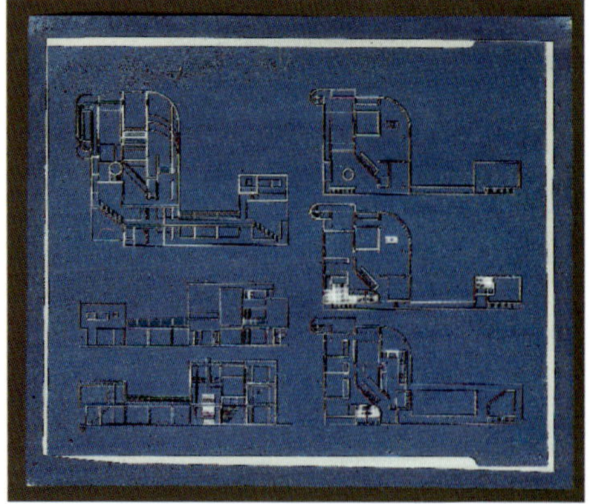

Cyanotype - traditional architect's drawing or Blueprint.

Retouching

To remove any small white spots use water colour and a small retouching brush. Match your blue colour carefully before attacking the print. Alternatively use a coloured pencil such as Caran d'Ache. Avoid using any form of dye in case it contains any alkali which would bleach the blue emulsion.

To remove dark spots, the best treatment is to abrade the surface of the print gently with a scalpel blade. You can, of course, bleach the spots with an alkali - anything from domestic bleach to film or paper developer will work this way, but you run the risk of leaving a brown or yellow stain on the paper if you do. And finally you may have wondered why film or paper developer were included in the shopping list; they contain alkali, and when mixed with water are good for washing your measuring jars and dishes.

Cyanotype 2

Cheap and simple, Herschel's traditional cyanotype has been in use for more than 150 years. There is always another way to skin a cat, and Mike Ware devised a modern cyanotype method that addressed a number of niggling unsophistications in the original method. The principal differences are that the type 2 method is faster, should be absorbed into the paper more easily, and show less tendency to stained highlights and washing out of the tone. If you are trying to work with cyanotype in a 'fine print' discipline you may find this method is worth the extra time and trouble involved. The downside is the greater level of preparation in the making of the sensitiser, and a higher level of toxicity in the chemistry involved. The iron salt used is **ammonium iron III oxalate**, not a chemical widely available and which varies in price dramatically, depending on source. The other chemicals are pretty standard fare, potassium ferricyanide and ammonium dichromate. The method needs detailing thoroughly, so we are not attempting it in the limited space here. We suggest you consult Mike Ware's web site, address in [33 . Resources] which contains the full manual for the process. Meanwhile opposite is one of Mike Wares own images printed with this process, the original being on 'Buxton' paper, designed specifically for iron processes.

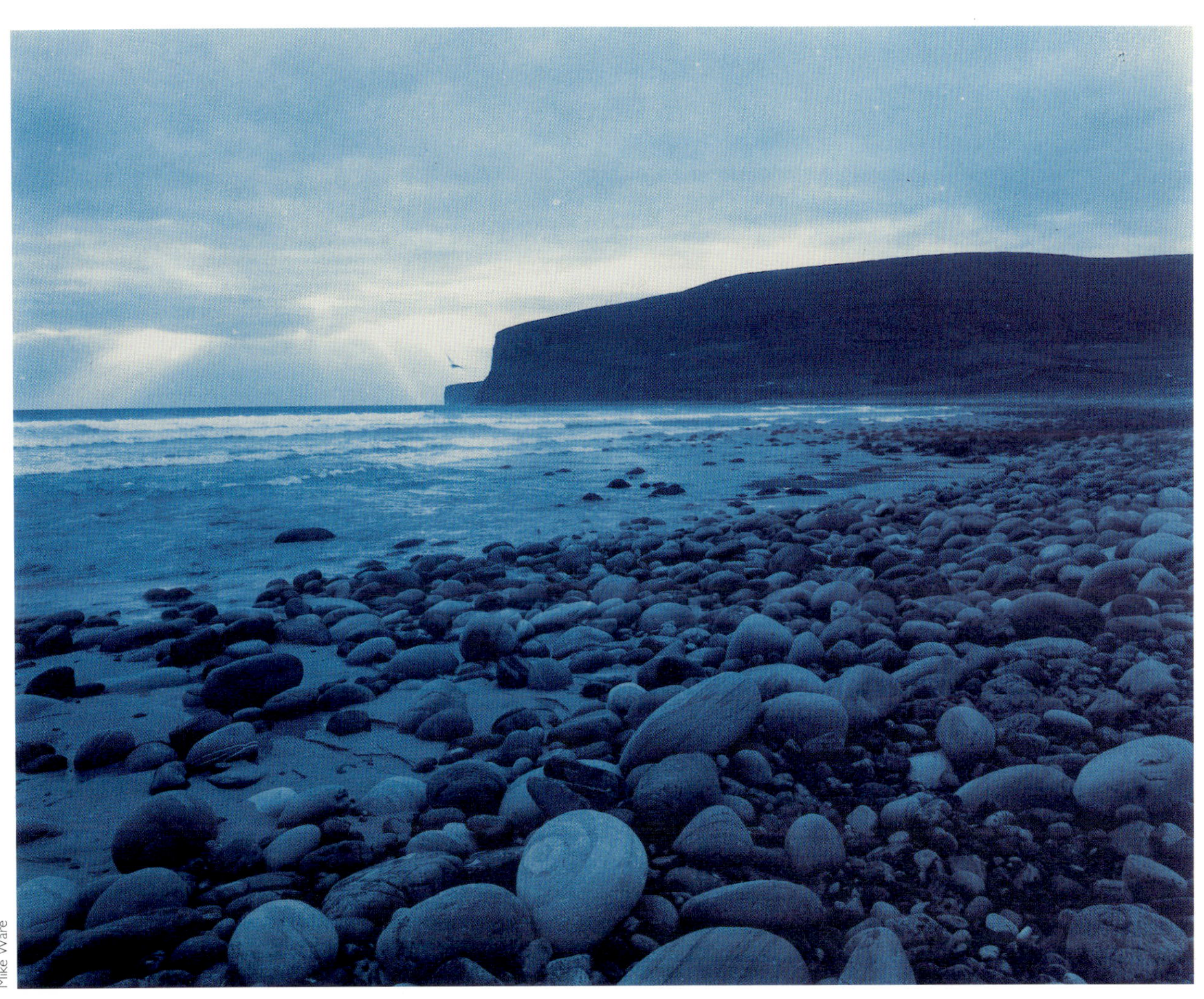

Mike Ware

Rackwick Bay, Hoy. Cyanotype using the Cyanotype type 2 process.

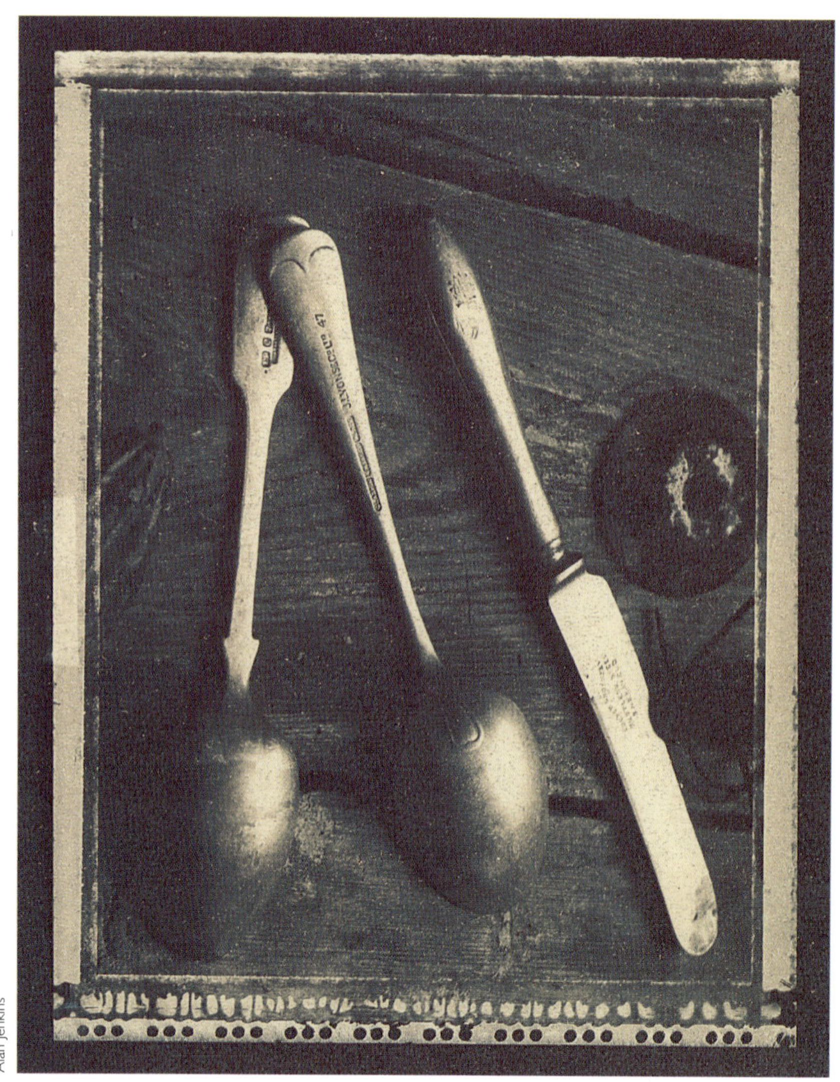

Alan Jenkins

Cyanotype toned in cold tea, producing a delicate blue-green on cream paper, which was originally white and was stained by the tea.

Pellet prints 15

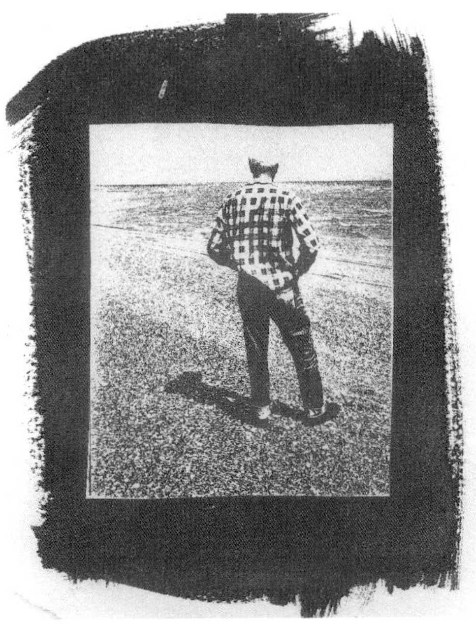

This is a very short chapter. Pellet prints are also known as positive cyanotypes and were invented by a Mr H. Pellet, about whom mercifully little else is known other than he registered his invention in 1878. The process is very similar to a straight cyanotype with two basic differences.

As it is a positive process you can make a positive print from a film positive. This saves a step in the enlarged negative stage. Simply enlarge your camera negative onto line or lith film to obtain a positive and use this to print your Pellet print. Secondly, the exposed print has to be developed before washing, unlike the cyanotype which only needs washing in water.

Shopping list

Gum arabic - from any art store. Buy in liquid form in a bottle. **or,** PVA glue, (Gloy etc from stationers)
Ferric ammonium citrate (green)
Ferric chloride
Potassium **ferrocyanide**
Sulphuric acid 10%

Method

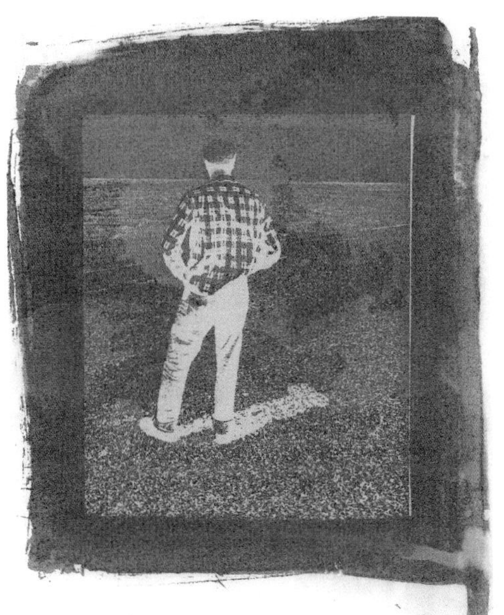

There is a slight problem. The top picture is what we should have obtained from a lith positive. What we got was the lower one. If any reader wishes to investigate this further they may.

Mr Pellet never published his formula. The method that we have shown is the result of educated guesswork by his contemporaries. Please bear with us if they seem slightly potty.
Mix three solutions as:

A) 10 ml gum arabic or PVA glue in 50 ml water
B) 25 gm ferric ammonium citrate in 50 ml water
C) 25 gm ferric chloride in 50 ml water

Take the three solutions and mix them in the following order and proportions.

Solution A 20 parts
Solution B 8 parts
Solution C 5 parts

When it is thoroughly mixed, coat it on your paper, dry it and expose it as you would do for cyanotype. Remove it from your printing frame and wash it for a minute or two in running water. Now you can develop it to bring out the characteristic prussian blue colour by putting it in a dish of 20 grams potassium **ferrocyanide** in 100 mls water. When the blue colour has reached sufficient depth, clear it for a few minutes in a dish of 10% sulphuric acid mixed 1 plus 5 with water, wash and dry.

You, meanwhile, can congratulate yourself on having made a print by one of the most obscure processes known to the photographic world.

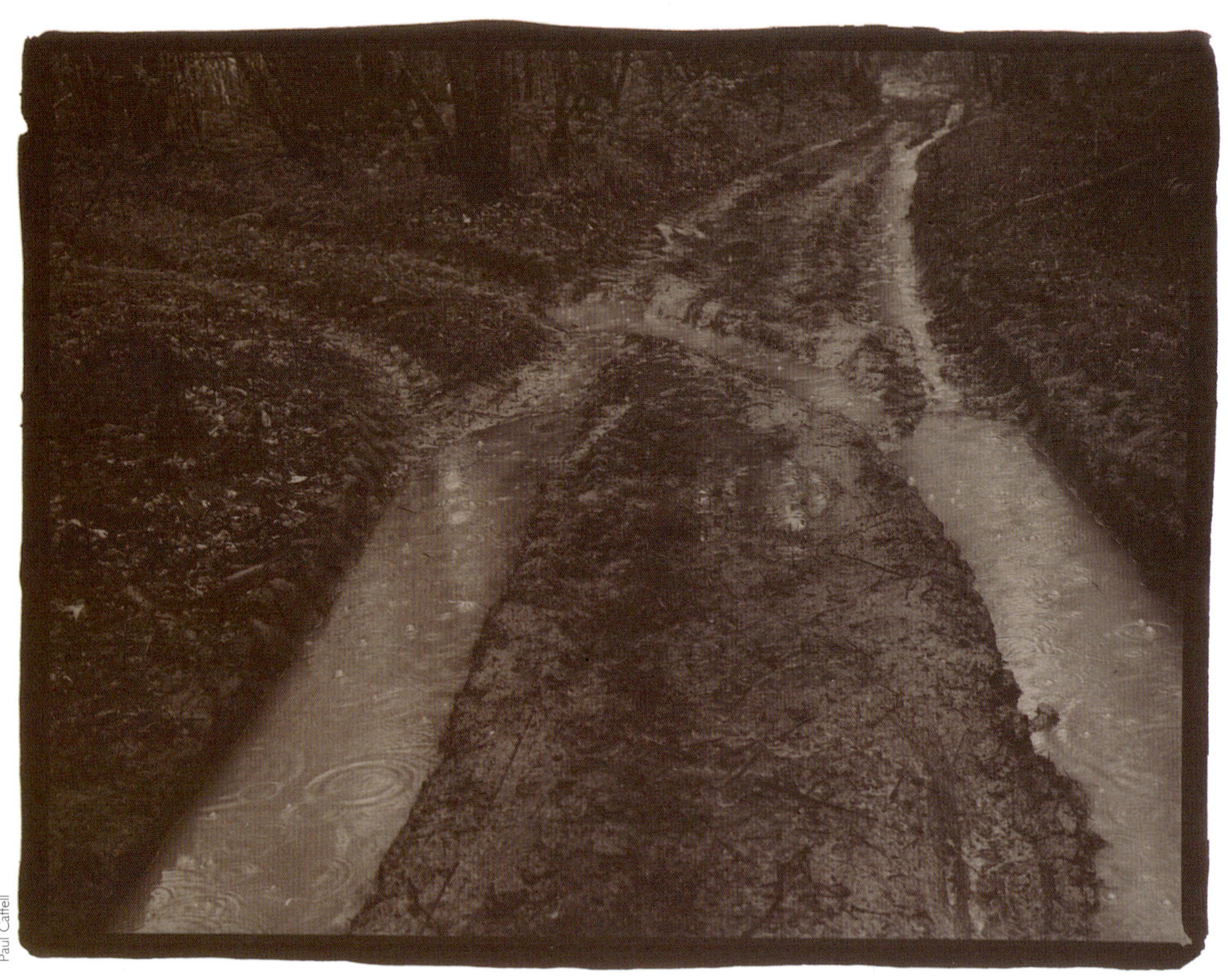

Paul Caffell

Modern platinum / palladium print produced by the specialist platinum laboratory, Studio 31.

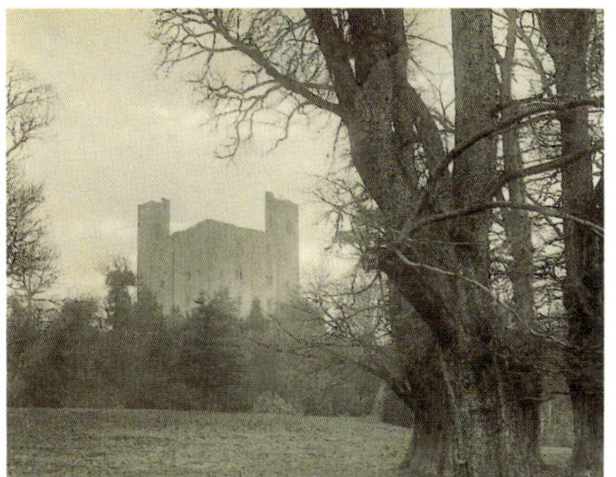

Two platinum prints from the late 19'th century.

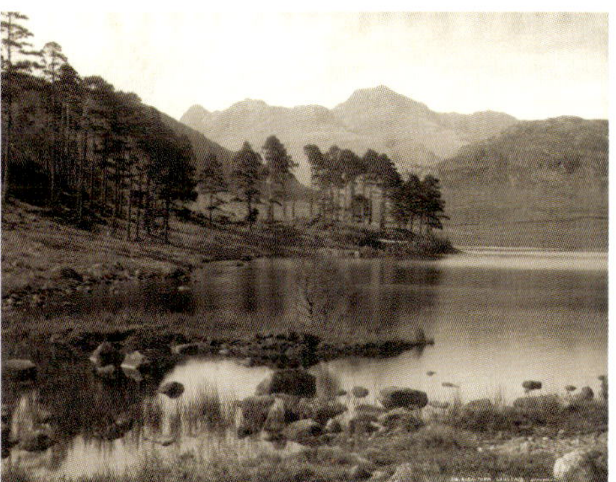

To test if an original platinum print is genuine place a tiny drop of hydrogen peroxide on a dark corner of the print, and if bubbles rise, it is. Then wipe it off. This is a non-destructive test.

At the mention of these processes many photographers throw up their hands in alarm and say things like 'they're too difficult to use', or 'they're too expensive for my exhibition work.'

There has been a sort of mystique built up around them which is largely unjustified. This may have been circulated by platinum printers to enhance their reputation or worse, to put lesser mortals off the scent completely. Although the start up cost of buying the platinum or palladium salts is much higher than the equivalent amounts of silver, it is certainly no more a shock to the wallet than having prints made in a lab from colour slides.

As far as difficulty is concerned, if George Bernard Shaw could do it, then so can any competent photographer. If, however, you aspire to be a master printer using these processes, you will need a lot of practice to make high quality prints. This applies to most things in life. Dick Arentz, the distinguished American printer once observed that platinum printers accumulate a shelf full of platinum prints which are not quite good enough for exhibition but which are too good to throw away.

The use of platinum for photographic purposes had been investigated by Herschel at an early stage in the development of photography, but it was not until 1873 that William Willis devised a practical means of producing platinum paper. In 1879 the Platinotype company put platinum paper on the commercial market. In 1887 a Captain Pizzighelli introduced his ready coated platinum paper which could be printed out and 'fixed' with muriatic acid (known now as hydrochloric acid).

The cachet of using a precious metal and the superb quality of the images produced by it led many well known photographers to adopt the process. Among them were Emerson with his studies of life in rural Norfolk and Frederick Evans with his series of pictures of English cathedrals. Later Steichen, Stieglitz, Paul Strand and Edward Weston worked extensively with the process.

During the first world war platinum metal was declared a strategic war material and was hard to obtain. After the war a cheaper substitute, palladium was used. The use of the platinum / palladium process gradually died out, partly because of its high cost. After the second world war it was revived by a new wave of platinum printers. Prominent among these were Laura Gilpin, Irving Penn, George Tice, Robert Mapplethorpe and Dick Arentz. On both sides of the Atlantic there are now a few specialist labs which work in platinum and palladium. The lack of pre-coated paper has meant that material for the process has to be hand coated, as for many other alternative processes. However there is a recent exception to this, as an American company has introduced a pre-coated paper marketed under the trade name of Palladio.

Advantages

It is a very stable process, as the image is as permanent as the paper it is printed on. The best way to destroy it is to dip it in nitric acid, set it alight

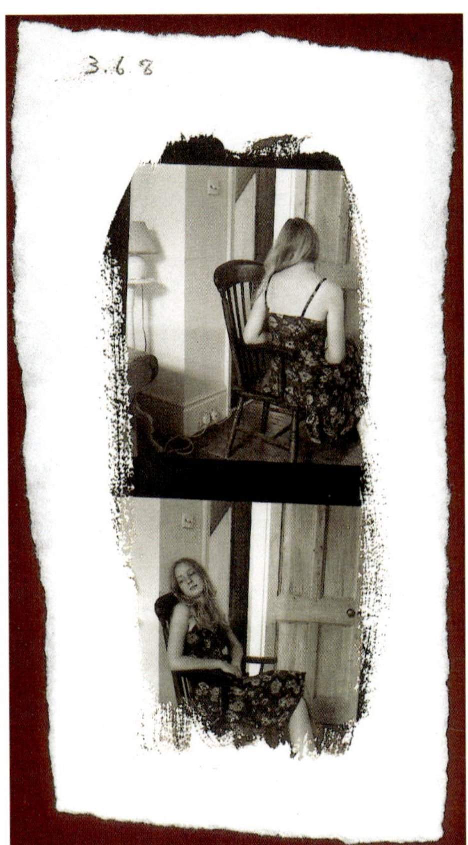

Palladium print on Buxton paper. This is in fact a test strip which seemed good enough to frame and put on the wall. Note the mixture in pencil at the top.

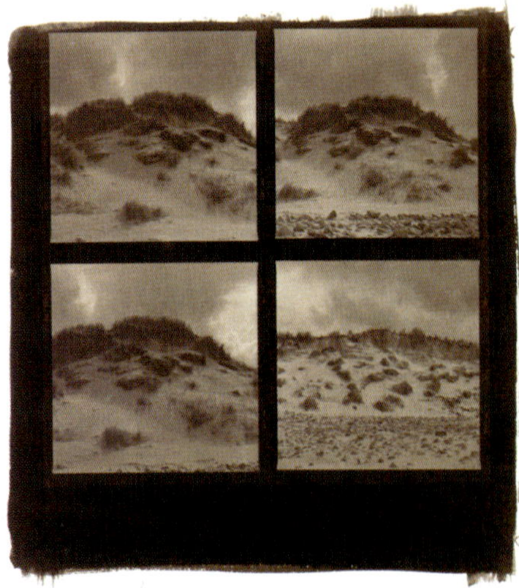

Benbecula sands - Hebrides. Palladium print. Two strips of 120 film, originally intended to be printed on grade 2 fibre-based enlarging paper.

or throw it in the waste bin! It contains a very delicate tonality in the highlights. The range of tones is evenly distributed from dark to light, giving it a distinct physical presence. It is possible, by varying the proportions of the constituent chemicals to vary the range of contrast, allowing the use of negatives of different contrasts. It can be used on a reasonably wide range of paper colours and surfaces.

Disadvantages

It is relatively expensive. It has to be contact printed, using a negative the same size as the final image.

Compared with conventional papers it has less depth of black and resolves less sharp detail. It cannot achieve the same cool blue black tones of conventional papers.

If we compare platinum with palladium, the latter is warmer in tone, produces richer blacks and needs a higher contrast in the negative to produce the same contrast in the print. One possible drawback to palladium is its tendency to solarise during printing. This may or not be a virtue depending on taste.

Shopping list

Chemicals

Potassium chloroplatinite powder for platinum prints. In 1999 the approximate cost is 17.50 US $ per gram, buying 1-10 grams. Five grams will make 24 ml of solution. With care you should be able to coat about forty sheets of 10 x 8" paper with this amount.

Palladium chloride- for palladium prints. Current cost is about 9.50 US$ dollars per gram. 5 grams will make 55 ml of solution, which will ultimately coat about 80 sheets of 10 x 8" paper, so it is not that expensive.

Sodium chloride (common salt) - for palladium sensitiser.

The rest are common to both platinum and palladium.

Ferric oxalate

Potassium chlorate

Potassium oxalate or **ammonium citrate** or **potassium citrate**

Phosphoric acid (an ingredient of Coca Cola) **or**

Oxalic acid (poisonous) **or**

EDTA (tetra sodium salt) **or**

Hydrochloric acid (10% solution)

1% **gold chloride solution** (optional).

Distilled water.

4 developing dishes - preferably ones that have not been used for any form of silver printing.

Small soft short haired brush (see method section) **or** glass coating rod.

Thermometer.

3 print tongs - not previously used for silver printing.

Plastic stirring rod.

Scales.

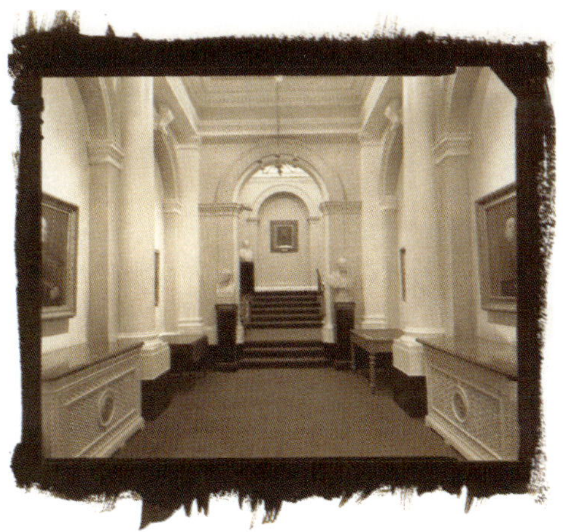

Burlington House, London. Palladium print from 5x4" negative, made to print on grade 2 fibre paper.

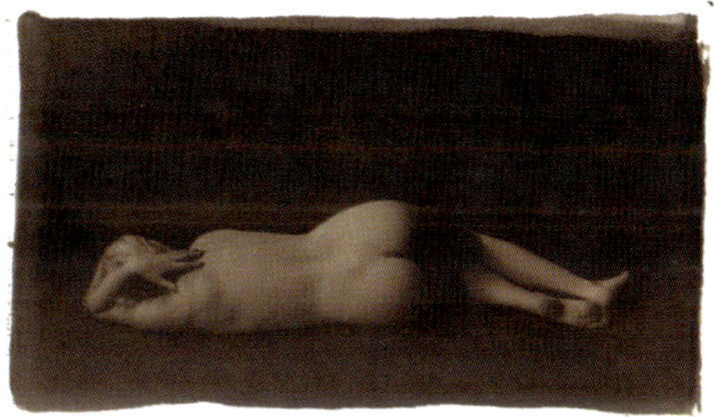

Palladium print from 10 x 8" negative, deliberately overprinted and low contrast.

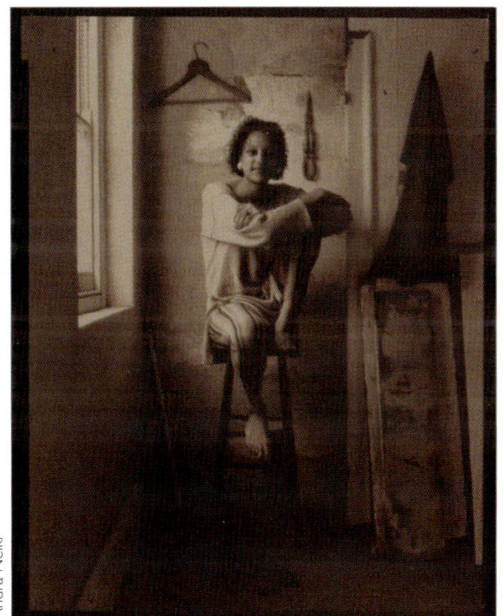

Andra Nelki

Modern platinum / palladium print on the pre-coated Palladio paper.

Four 50 ml **brown bottles** with plastic screw tops from any pharmacy.

Four 2.5 ml **plastic syringes** (without needles!)

Measures; 45ml & 1 litre.

A **hair drier** or **fan heater.**

Masking tape or **Scotch tape.**

Printing frame (see equipment).

Sunlight or UV lamp.

Gelatin (optional).

Paper towels.

Pencil.

Negatives

There has always been an assumption that platinum and palladium prints need very high contrast negatives, the sort that demand a chisel to enable you to see through them. This is not strictly true. It is perfectly feasible to print from camera negatives that will produce good results on normal grade two paper by manipulating the chemistry, (see examples). The ideal negative should contain slightly higher contrasts than required for printing on grade 2, but more importantly, the negative should contain a wide range of tones from light to dark, (no pushing Tri-X to 1600 ISO please!) The table on mixing the chemicals in the method section explains this. On the other hand a lower contrast negative will give you a print with a range of subtle mid tones that are characteristic of classic platinum and palladium prints. Devotees of the grade 5 school may well find that they have to re-learn their techniques and their aesthetics.

Paper

Dick Arentz once remarked that if anything goes wrong with the platinum process the most likely culprit will be the paper you have chosen for printing on.

Many papers used for old processes are buffered to a mildly alkaline state for reasons of archival permanence. Platinum and palladium on the other hand are stable and perform better on unbuffered neutral paper. Fortunately there is now on the market a range of papers well suited to the medium. We suggest you start by trying some or all of the following:

Arches Platine - made specially for the purpose.
Buxton - made to Dr Mike Ware's specification.
Crane's parchment - cream based.
Fabriano Roma Michaelangelo - hand made.
Fabriano 100% and Fabriano 50% also work well.

If you wish to get away from the pure photographic look and work with coarser tonalities and broader strokes then try some of the other papers on the market. If you have trouble with your bank manager, make small prints. Many of Paul Strand's best images were no bigger than 5 x 7".

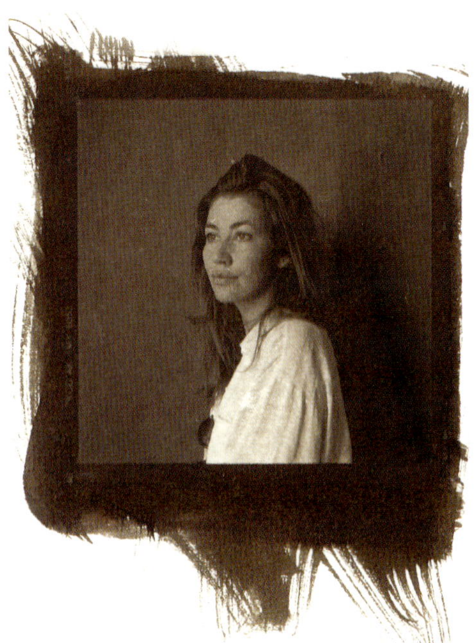

Shiobhan. Palladium print direct from 120 negative.

PLATONA

(REGISTERED).

The ILFORD Platinum Paper

IN TWO VARIETIES, ROUGH and SMOOTH.

Platona is a GENUINE Platinum Paper.

PRICES IN SEALED TIN TUBES

(BOTH VARIETIES).

Size		Quantity	Per Tin.	With Postage.
4¼ × 3¼	...	20 pieces	1/8	1/10
5 × 4	...	20 ,,	2/4	2/6
6 × 4¼	...	20 ,,	3/3	3/5
6½ × 4¾	...	20 ,,	3/8	3/11
8½ × 6½	...	20 ,,	6/4	6/7
10 × 8	...	10 ,,	4/7	4/10
12 × 10	...	10 ,,	7/-	7/3
15 × 12	...	10 ,,	10/6	10/9
24½ × 17	...	2 sheets	4/9	5/-
		6 ,,	13/9	14/1
		12 ,, (½-quire)	27/-	27/5

ILFORD, Limited,

ILFORD, LONDON, ENGLAND.

Note the prices!

Method

First a few thoughts on the process.

For all practical purposes platinum and palladium act in a very similar way, and so we shall treat them as equals in terms of processing. The chemical mixes differ, in that platinum prints use platinum salts and palladium prints use palladium salts. Slight shifts in image colour and contrast we shall deal with as we come to them.

Instead of measuring our sensitising solutions in milligrams we shall be working with drops from a syringe or glass dropper. We mix three solutions, and to control the contrast of the print take various combinations of the three solutions to arrive at the most suitable degree of tonal contrast.

We have included a table to guide you through the permutations that we hope will give you a good result. But at the end of the day the only criterion that matters is that if it looks right it is right. Any art or craft depends on the artists' instinctive judgement, and the application of rigid scientific rules seems an unnecessary and pointless imposition.

So, use the table to guide you through the early stages of learning the process, and then make your own decisions later.

Make up the coating solutions. The best way to mix these chemicals is to pour the necessary amount of warm distilled water into small 50 ml brown screw top bottles and then add the powdered chemical to the bottle. Shake the bottle at regular intervals until the liquid is clear. This may take some hours. Dick Sullivan of Bostick and Sullivan, who sells platinum materials, suggests putting the bottle in the back pocket of your jeans and dancing to your old Chubby Checker records. When you have mixed each solution, pour it into a small (100ml) brown bottle with a plastic lid and label it as indicated below.

Solution A

Ferric oxalate 15 g
Oxalic acid 1 g
Distilled water 55 ml

The chemicals dissolve more quickly if the water is about 40° C.
Label it PL/A

Now make an identical solution and label it PD/A.

Solution B

Type 1 For platinum prints. Mix as follows and label your bottle PL/B.

Ferric oxalate 15 g
Oxalic acid 1 g
Potassium chlorate 0.33 g
(Get the potassium chlorate weighed by a chemist or someone with accurate scales)
Distilled water 55 ml

Type 2 For palladium prints. Mix as follows, and label your bottle PD/B.

Ferric oxalate 15 g
Oxalic acid 1 g

Potassium chlorate	0.66 g
Distilled water	55 ml

Solution C

Type 1, for platinum prints. label PL/C.

Potassium chloroplatinite	5 g
Distilled water	25 ml

Type 2, for palladium prints label PD/C.

Palladium chloride	5 g
Sodium chloride	3.5 g
Distilled water	50 ml

This may seem painfully obvious but we should now have six small bottles marked as follows:

PL/A, PD/A, PL/B, PD/B, PL/C, PD/C.

We now have all our chemicals clearly marked ready to use for coating the paper.

Unless you are absolutely desperate to make platinum prints we suggest you stick to palladium to start with. In that case you leave out the platinum mixes. So you will have three bottles marked **PD/A**, **PD/B** and **PD/C**.

Now we make a test print to see roughly how the system works. One thing to avoid is trying to make large prints at this stage. Stick to medium format or 5 x 4" negatives. Resist the temptation to make huge enlarged negatives from your 35mm negs until you know what you are doing!

You will need a small plastic cup or a small glass (a small sherry glass will do) and four plastic syringes. Assume we will use a normal negative (grade 2). Referring to our mixture table we will need **7** drops of **P/D A**, **5** drops of **PD/B**, and **12** drops of **PD/C**. You will notice that mixtures A and B added together always equal the amount of mixture C. Mark your syringes (felt tip pen or Dymo tape) **A**, **B** and **C**. Leave the fourth one blank. Take your syringe A, place it in the bottle A, and carefully draw into the syringe about 1 ml of liquid. Place it over the cup or glass and gently squeeze the plunger allowing 6 drops to fall into the cup. Squeeze the unused liquid back into the bottle and **replace the cap**. Wash the syringe in distilled water.

If you are nervous about this procedure, do a dummy run with some coloured water until you get the hang of it. It is best to hold the syringe firmly in both hands and press the plunger firmly and slowly. This will prevent the liquid squirting out and splashing.

Now do the same with bottle B and syringe B and adding 5 drops to mix A in the cup. Next take bottle C and syringe C measuring 12 drops this time and add to A and B in the cup. Now take the unmarked syringe and place it in the liquid. Carefully draw up all the liquid and then squeeze it back into the cup. Repeat this twice, and all three solutions will be thoroughly mixed together. Clean the syringe.

Take a piece of paper you intend to use for your print, which should be slightly larger than your negative. Coat it with the mixture using a brush or

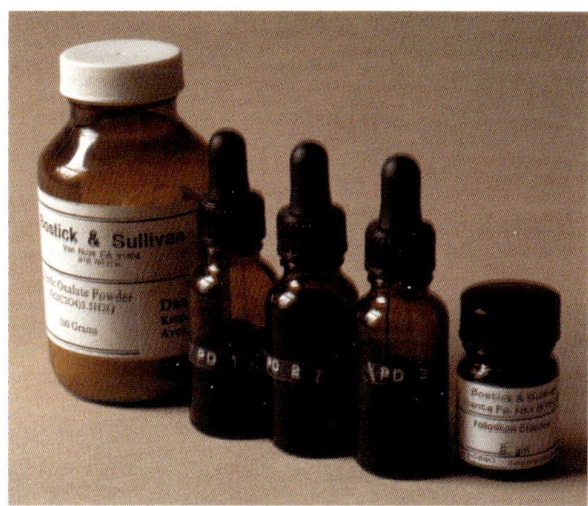

Platinum and palladium coating materials..

Contrast Table

The contrast of platinum and palladium sensitisers can be changed by changing the proportions of the three solutions. The use of a table to work out the different amounts needed would appear less important than many authorities give us to believe. The simple answer seems to be that a negative developed and exposed to print on Multigrade filter 2 or 3 is the most suitable. However,, if you have in the course of your investigations made negatives which are of very low or very high contrast, the table below should be useful. There is no need to follow it slavishly. There is no substitute for test strips. Nor is it necessary to print every thing at the level of grade 5.

You will find that palladium prints will need a negative slightly more contrasty than that needed for platinum. Again, testing is more important than mathematics.

The columns below, reading left to right are:

C - The contrast of the negative, MG - the Multigrade paper equivalent to obtain a good print on standard paper. A, B and C are the amounts of sensitiser in drops.

C	MG	A	B	C
Very high	0	20	4	24
High	1	16	8	24
Normal	2	14	10	24
Low	3	10	14	24
Very low	4	8	16	24

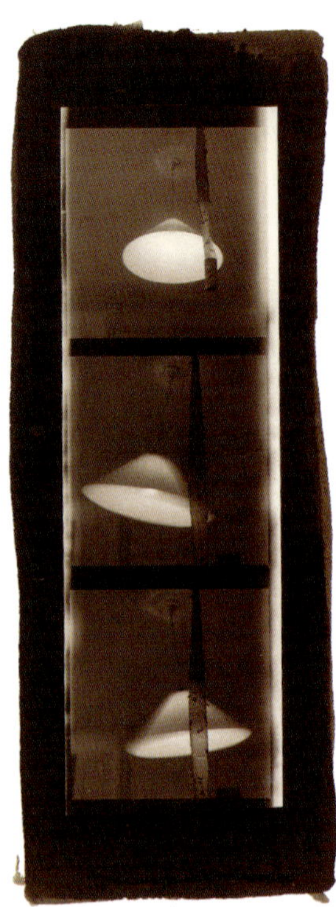

Lampshade. Palladium print, direct contact from strip of 120 film. Image by Darlaine Honey, print by author.

Platinum / palladium 2

This is a revision of the traditional platinotype, devised by Mike Ware, and removes some of the problems of the original method. The most significant difference is that ferric oxalate is substituted by ammonium iron (III) oxalate, a more stable and economical compound. The platinum or palladium salts used are ammonium tetrachloroplatinate and ammonium tetrachloropalladate, which remain just as expensive as their counterparts in the traditional method. The main difference in usage is that most of the image forms during exposure, and adjustments can be made by monitoring the buildup of density. There is a certain degree of self-masking during exposure, as the emerging image reduces shadow density formation while the highlights print in. Humidity is a major controlling factor, and must be adjusted by pre-humidifying the paper in a chamber at a controlled relative humidity. One major benefit is that a higher maximum density is produced relative to the traditional method, removing the need to double-coat for high density. The chemicals used for clearing are also much less toxic. Full working details of the process are on Mike Ware's web site, address in [33 . Resources].

glass rod, [7 . Coating]. Dry it with a hair drier. The coating will dry to a bright orange colour. Now you are ready to make a test strip. Place your negative on your coated paper, and place in a printing frame under your light source. Expose it at two minute intervals, covering a part of the negative with a piece of opaque card until five sections have been exposed (total ten minutes). Take the strip out of the frame. You should see that the image has started to print out, showing a faint brown image on the orange surface. Now you are ready to develop the strip.

The three commonest developers are:

Potassium oxalate	60 g
Distilled water	200 ml (Best at 40° C)

or

Ammonium citrate	100 g
Water	100 ml

or

Potassium citrate	100 g
Water	100 ml

Mix these to make a syrupy solution, then add 700 ml water.

Potassium and ammonium citrate (according to some chemists) appear to be interchangeable in this case. Whichever developer you decide to use (we recommend the ammonium or potassium citrate as it is safer) should be poured into a dish and the test strip immersed in the developer as quickly as possible to avoid developer streaks. The image will appear immediately. Leave it there for about a minute and then wash it in running water for a minute or so.

Now the strip is ready to be cleared. The clearing solution can be either;

Phosphoric acid	20 g
Water	1 litre

or

EDTA	80 g
Water	1 litre

or

A 1% solution of hydrochloric acid. Make this by adding 100 ml of 10% hydrochloric acid to 1 litre of water.

Pour a third of the liquid into each of three glass bottles marked Clear 1, 2 and 3. Take three developing dishes and fill each with the contents of one bottle. Place the strip into the first dish and leave under the solution for five minutes. Then transfer to the second dish for five minutes and repeat in the third dish. By this time the unused coating will have cleared from the highlights and you can wash for thirty minutes and dry. Now check your test strip for the correct exposure and contrast as you would a conventional print. If the contrast is too low or too high make a new coating solution using the mixing chart. Don't try mixing extra chemicals to an existing mix. Rather, use that for a negative of suitable contrast. Once you have arrived at the correct exposure time and contrast, make a proper print.

Notes on processing

1 No need to discard the developer after use. Even if it turns a dark brown colour it will still go on working.

2 Clearing baths. When bath no. 1 discolours, discard it and transfer the contents of bath 2 to 1 and bath 3 to 2. Pour fresh solution into bath 3 so that you maintain a sequence of fresh solutions.

3 Platinum prints tend towards a cooler grey colour, while palladium moves towards warmer brownish tones.

4 Some colour shifts can be obtained by warming the developer up to 40° C. (Use a water bath - not the gas cooker). Some experimentation can be tried when you become more familiar with the process.

5 Alternatively you can use a mixture of platinum and palladium in solution C. For example 6 drops platinum and six drops palladium.

6 For a really exotic mixture try adding a couple of drops of 1% gold chloride to solution C.

7 Your choice of paper will also affect the final colour of your print. A range of colours from cool black to sepia through reddish-brown is possible by ringing the changes on your paper.

Retouching

Use water colours and a fine brush for white spots and a scalpel for dark ones. Avoid dyes. Bleaches won't work!

Presentation

Framed under a window mount looks best. Whether you leave the brushed edges showing or whether you crop down to the edge of the image is entirely up to personal preference.

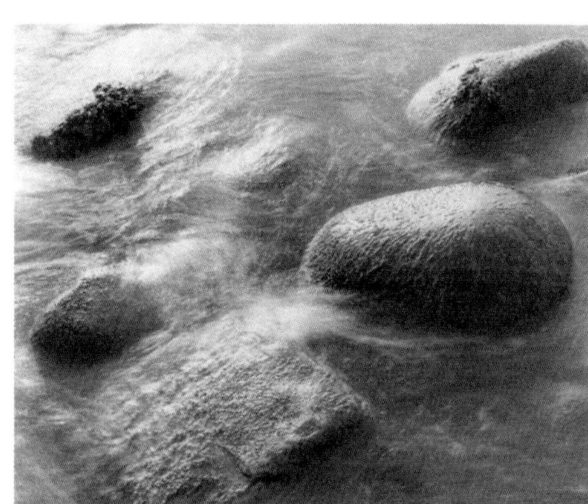

Mike Ware

Chrysotype process

As well as the cyanotype, Herschel devised several processes, and one that produced images in colloidal gold he termed 'Chrysotype'. This was never established as a practical process, due to technical problems in controlling contrast, colour, and fogging of the image. Although there were intermittent attempts during the 19'th century to sort the process out, it was not until Mike Ware tackled it in the late 20'th that methods for controlling the unpredictable gold chemistry were devised. Chrysotype should not be confused with gold toning, which is applied to previously existing silver images. The Chrysotype is a pure printing medium, and can be controlled to produce a wide range of colours, including subtle pink, magenta, brown, purple, violet, blue and green tones. Stability, as one would expect, is on a par with platinum. The procedure is similar to platinum or cyanotype, with a contact exposure to UV light or sunlight, followed by wet processing, washing and drying. However, at the time of writing, Mike has still not revealed the working details! His image above is offered as a tantalising example. Keep watching his web site.

Trouble shooting

Prints too light
Not enough coating. Try mixing solution C with an equal amount of distilled water and give a second coat after the first one has dried.

Printing time too short
Expose for longer.

Uneven coating
Too little coating, see above. Possibly the wrong coating instrument. Practice a bit more before you coat in earnest. May be unsuitable paper, try another type.

Grainy prints
Try warming the developer.
Too much solution B. Use contrastier negative.
Brushing was too vigorous. Use a softer brush and be gentler with it.

If all this doesn't work, change your paper.

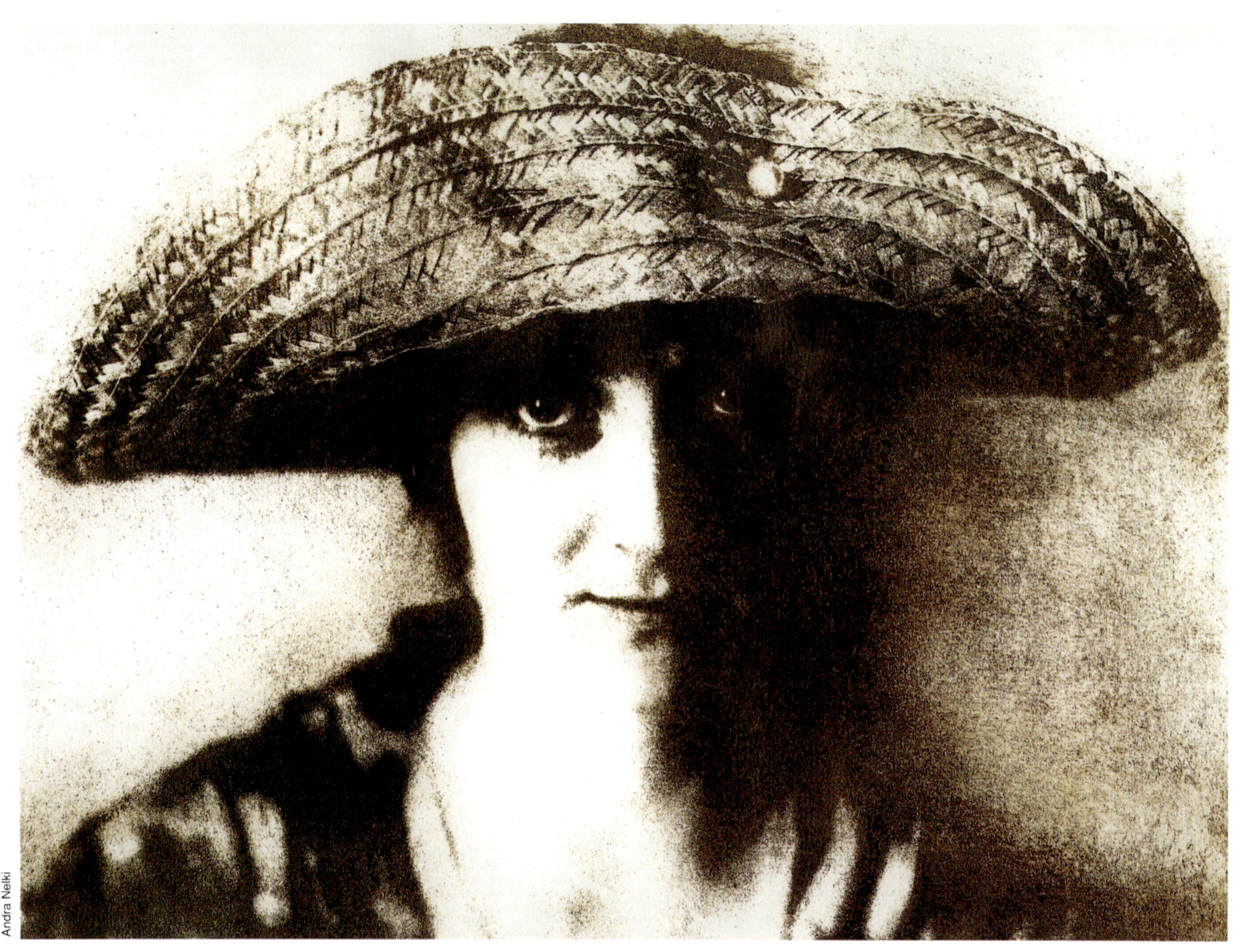

Andra Nelki

'Maria' - Bromoil print on Kentmere Document Art paper.

Bromoil 17

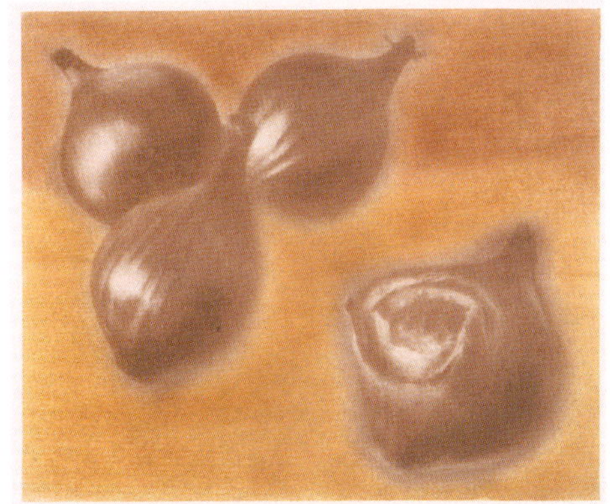

Mair Ellis

Bromoil transfer, using Kentmere Document Art paper for the original.

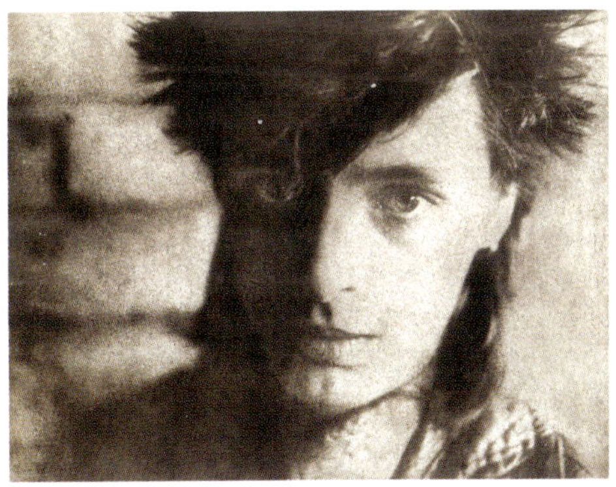

Rock musician. Bromoil on Kentmere Document Art paper.

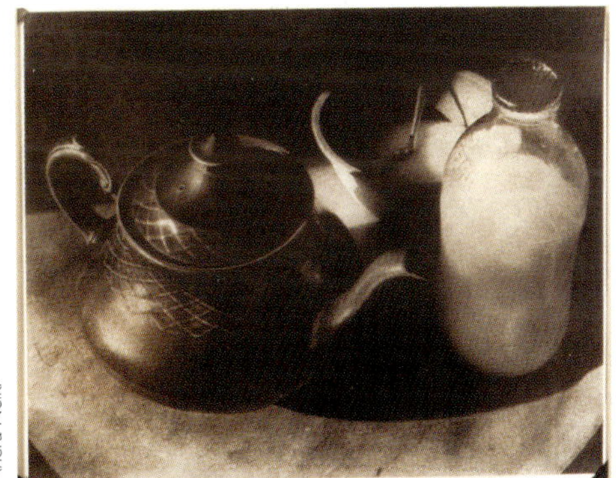

Andra Nelki

Bromoil on Kentmere Document Art paper.

Bromoil is the odd one out in comparison with most of the other early processes. The most obvious difference is that it is not a contact printing technique. The starting point of a bromoil print is a conventional bromide print made in the normal way in an enlarger, thus doing away with the need for an ultra violet light source. Once the print has been developed, fixed and washed, the treatment is carried out on the gelatin coating of the exposed print. This obviously is a radical departure from even the other gelatin and dichromate processes such as gum and carbon. This is the stage at which the photographer crosses the border into the domain of the artist and art printmaker. The silver image is replaced by printers ink (any colour you care to mix), and the original photograph is transformed into a paper 'plate' which can be used in an etching press to be transferred onto hand made paper, see [17 . Bromoil transfer]. One of the advantages of bromoil is that having made the initial bromide print you can carry out all the remaining work on the kitchen table or in a studio in full daylight.

The effect of light on a mixture of gelatin and potassium dichromate had been known from the earliest days of photography, but the application of this principle to make the bromoil print was not made until 1907. Since then it has tended to be associated with leisured amateurs - quite often retired civil servants or bank managers. Possibly because it is not an entirely photographic process a number of myths and misconceptions have grown up around it. Sadly, much of the literature on the subject reflects this desire on the part of its users to maintain some sort of secrecy. Special inks and brushes made from polecats tails (costing a fortune), appear regularly as part of the mythology. The aesthetic has been pretty strange as well. Bromoil tends to be a dark process - if you brush black ink onto a piece of paper you can't reasonably expect delicate high key results first time. The process also lends itself to a certain amount of manipulation, but always of the worst sort. Telegraph poles and wires can be delicately removed from misty rural landscapes and dramatic cloud effects superimposed onto carefully composed woodland scenes. It is a depressing fact of life that bromoil has been used to this day to perpetuate some of the worst aspects of nineteenth photographic pictorialism. On the other hand, it is one of the few old processes which have never really fallen into disuse. Exhibitions held by the Royal Photographic Society and the Salon have ensured a constant supply of small black and white bromoils despite their authors' total unwillingness to come to terms with 20'th century imagery. The only drawback to making more of the process was the apparent difficulty of obtaining some of the materials. The main supplier of bromoil inks brushes and chemicals - Sinclairs in London - closed in 1970 or so, and for some time the process seemed to be fading into obscurity. Now, at the start of the 21'st century there are new materials coming onto the market and the process is experiencing a major revival.

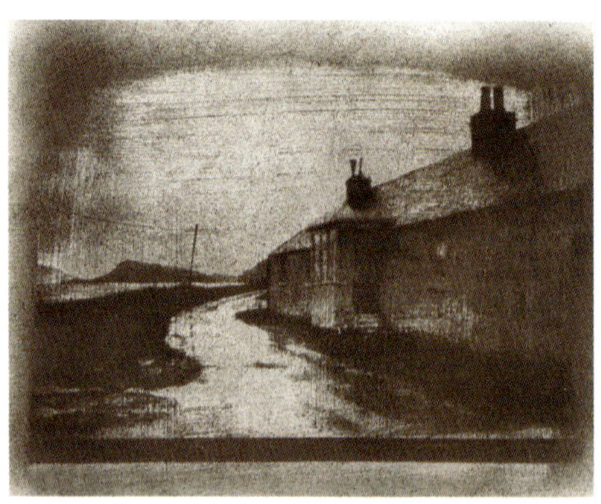

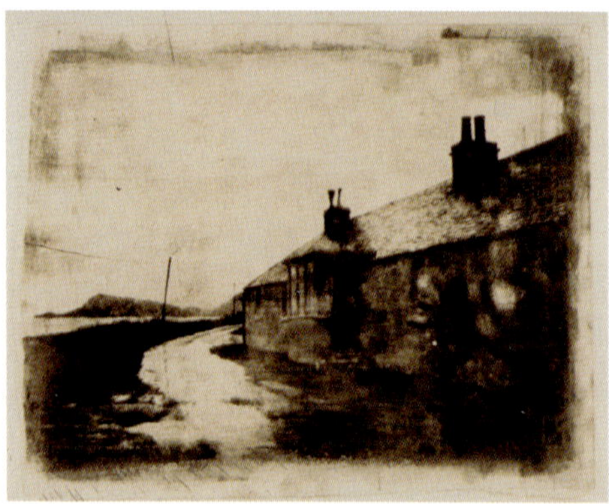

Knoydart, Scotland. Both prints were made by enlarging onto Fabriano paper, coated with Silverprint SE1 liquid emulsion, and then inked as a normal bromoil. The top one was inked with a brush, and the lower one with a rubber roller.

Advantages

The resulting print is beautiful, with rich solid ink on paper, dark glowing shadows and subtle highlights.
The print is made on bromide paper in an enlarger.
There is no need for an enlarged negative.
There is no need for an ultra violet light source.
After the original print is made all other work can be carried out on the kitchen table in full daylight.
Permanence. The image consists of ink on paper instead of degradable silver and will not be susceptible to atmospheric pollution.
It can be made in any colour or with careful application, in a variety of colours.
It can be transferred in an etching press on to any paper base of your choice or onto fabric.
The image can be manipulated either at the enlarger stage or at the inking stage.
It is possible to make a small limited edition of transfer prints on hand made paper. This includes delicate papers that cannot be used in the other processes because of their tendency to disintegrate during the usual wet processing.
The inking process (see method) is very restful and therapeutic!

Disadvantages

The process involves a certain amount of craft skill. Quite a bit of practice is needed to get really good results (but not as much as learning to drive a car or use a computer).

You will be using unfamiliar materials which are not stocked by photographic dealers.

Printing ink is messy. Stock up with Swarfega!

Shopping list

Photographic printing paper - see a full explanation in the section 'Making the print'. We suggest you start with 10 x 8" size until you become more skilled.
250 ml bottle of **liquid emulsion** if you are going to attempt making your own paper.

Sheets of **water colour paper** - Fabriano or Saunders 150 gsm will do.

Standard print developer, PQ Universal or similar.

Plain hypo (sodium thiosulphate)	250 g
Potassium bromide	100 g
Copper sulphate	100 g
Potassium dichromate	100 g

Acetic acid 10% solution **or** hydrochloric acid 10% solution - 500 ml of whichever is most easily available.

3 measuring jars, 1 litre size.

3 Developing trays one size up from your print size. Don't use the ones you use for normal b&w printing.

Liquid emulsions

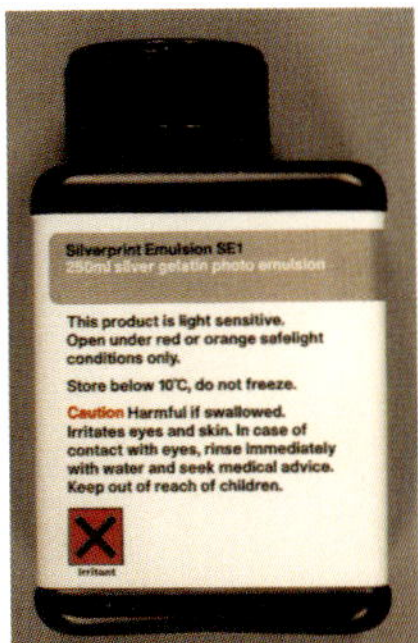

Using a liquid emulsion, in the context of the rest of this book could be construed as cheating - unlike most of the processes we are dealing with here it is enlarging speed, and processed through standard black and white chemistry. It is, in fact, an identical emulsion to that used on conventional enlarging paper, but in the bulk form allows you to coat on a paper of your own choice, or a wide variety of other surfaces, such as wood, glass or ceramic. Techniques for using emulsion are dealt with fully in a companion volume 'Silver Gelatin', detailed in the bibliography.

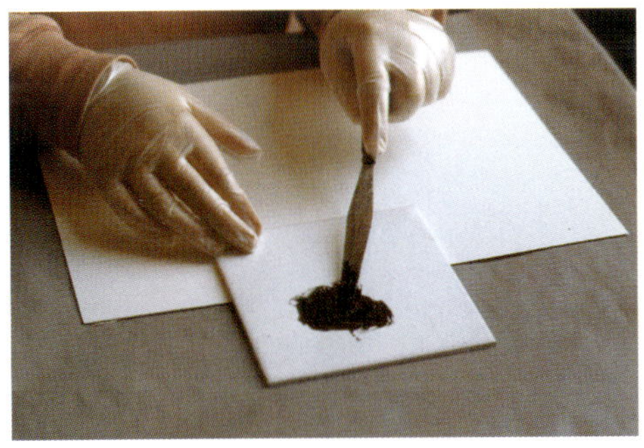

Mixing the ink on the pallette (a ceramic tile or piece of glass).

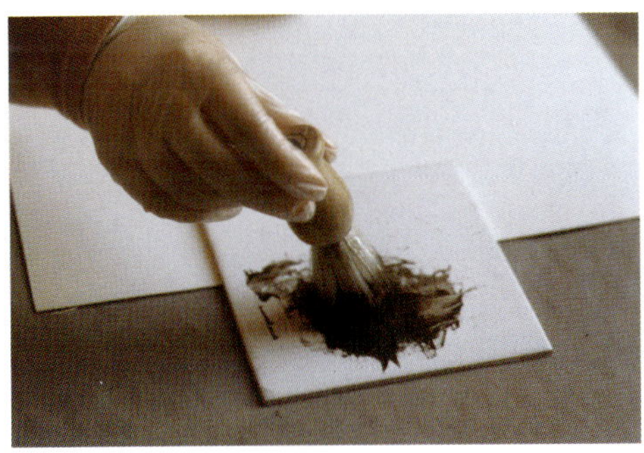

Loading the brush.

At least **6 paint brushes** between one and a half and half an inch wide from your local DIY store. Make sure at least one is a sash brush - that is it has the bristles cut at an angle.

A **cheap shaving brush**. Not the one you shave with!

A new range of inexpensive brushes made specifically for bromoil has recently come onto the market made by Stoddard Ltd.

One or two narrow **fitch brushes** which are used for oil painting (from any art shop). If you get hooked on bromoil you will soon find yourself combing all the shops that sell brushes in search of the perfect bromoil brush. Try the shops that specialise in decorative stencils.

A tin of **black lithographic or etching ink**, 250 gram size. Charbonnel is the best. Ask for **Taille Douce** or **Encre Machine**. See list of suppliers.

Bottle of **white spirit**,250 ml from the DIY store.

A small bottle of **linseed oil** from any art shop.

50 g of **magnesium carbonate powder**. It is very light, so this amount will last years.

A plastic **pallet knife** (if you have a posh metal one with a wooden handle then that is even better).

An old **ceramic tile** at least 6 inches square or an old piece of glass about the same size and as thick as you can find.

A roll of **cotton wool**.

A bunch of **old rags**.

A roll of paper **kitchen towel**.

Lots of **old newspapers** to protect your work surface.

Method

This is a brief summary of the process.

We suggest that you read this section several times until you have familiarised yourself with the basic principles before you start, as it will save time, trouble and nervous breakdowns when you start work in earnest.

A conventional print is made in the enlarger. When it has been developed, fixed, washed and dried it is bleached in a special bleaching bath.

This bleach does two things. Firstly it removes the black and white silver image leaving only a faint yellow green residual image.
Secondly and more importantly it hardens the gelatin in the paper emulsion selectively. This hardening process is usually referred to as 'tanning'. The darkest parts of the image harden to the greatest extent, and the mid tones and highlights are affected proportionately less, to the point where the brightest highlights are unaffected. When the bleaching is completed the print is fixed again, washed and dried.

It is then soaked in water for a short time. At this point the surface of the print undergoes another change. This time the less hardened parts of the

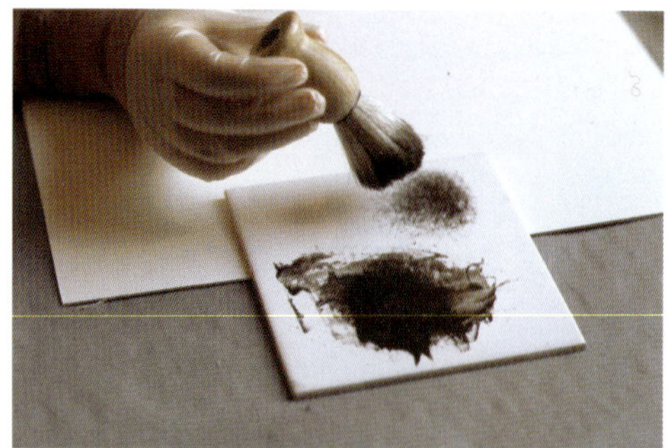

Removing surplus ink from the brush.

emulsion (lighter tones) absorb a minute quantity of water, while the hardened parts (darker tones) absorb proportionately less. Thus we have a photograph in which the range of tones from black to white in the original is replaced with a range of variations in the make-up of the print gelatin, which holds progressively more water as tones move from black to white. It is here that the analogy to lithography holds, using the fact that oil and water do not mix. Oily printing ink (normally used for etching or lithography) is stippled on to the surface of the print with a brush. On the hardened areas which contain relatively little moisture, the ink will stick to the paper. But in the areas which become progressively lighter and hold more moisture, the ink will be rejected by the water, and will leave the surface relatively clear until the point where the brightest highlights will show as white. Eureka! You now have a photograph where the silver image has been replaced in all its original tonal values by permanent, non fading ink. This, in brief, is the basic method of making bromoils and is also the basis for making pigment prints.

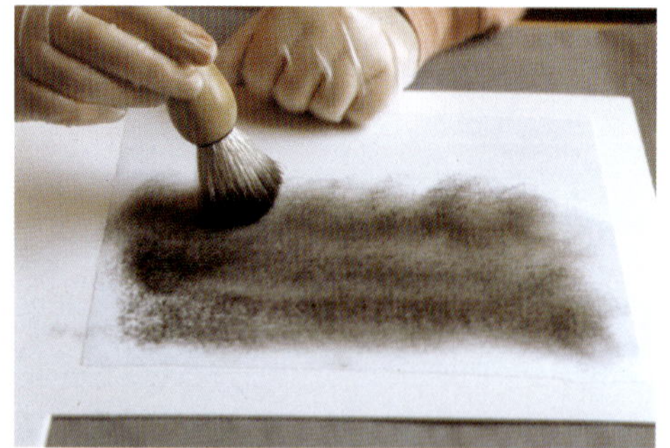

Initial inking of the print using a shaving brush.

Making the print

50 years ago most of the main paper manufacturers produced special paper for the bromoil market. These papers differed from the rest in that they had no extra protective coating of gelatin on the surface or 'supercoating'. Modern papers tend to be supercoated with an extra gelatin layer to prevent scratches and stress marks on the print, and to make them stand up better to the effects of heat drying. At present we have a choice of only a few unsupercoated papers for making bromoils.

Kentmere **Document Art**, which has a mechanically figured surface. It does have the virtue of having been around for years in the absence of anything better.

Kentmere's **Bromoil Classic**, with a smooth matt finish.

Bergger's **BROM 240** bromoil paper which has also been prepared specifically for bromoil printing.

Finally, you can make your own paper by using **liquid emulsion**. This comes in 250 ml bottles complete with instructions.

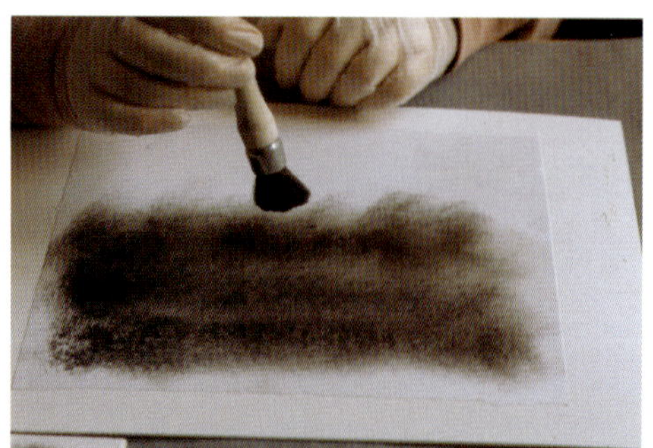

Starting to remove the ink with a finer brush.

Make a few prints, (10 x 8" is a good size to start with and you will understand why when you start inking). Use any camera negative of your choice but avoid those of very high contrast or a 'lith' appearance. The ideal print should look very flat and lacking in contrast. The darkest shadows should contain some detail and should be grey rather than deep black. The mid tones should be well separated and the brightest highlights should have a slightly grey veiled look. In short, the sort of print that would be deemed totally unacceptable by modern printing standards! The current incomprehensible fashion for pushing 400 ISO film to 3200 and desperately overdeveloping it is definitely out. Better to rate 3200 TMAX at 1600 and under-develop it. Develop your prints in any standard print developer such as PQ universal or Neutol, but use a slightly higher dilution than normal ie 1:12 instead of 1:9 and pro rata. Some books on the subject suggest an Amidol developer, but there is no evidence to suggest it is any better or worse than the others.

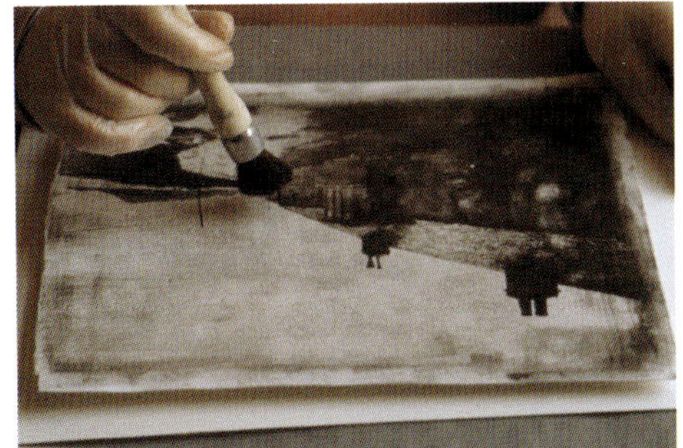

Moving the ink from highlights to shadows.

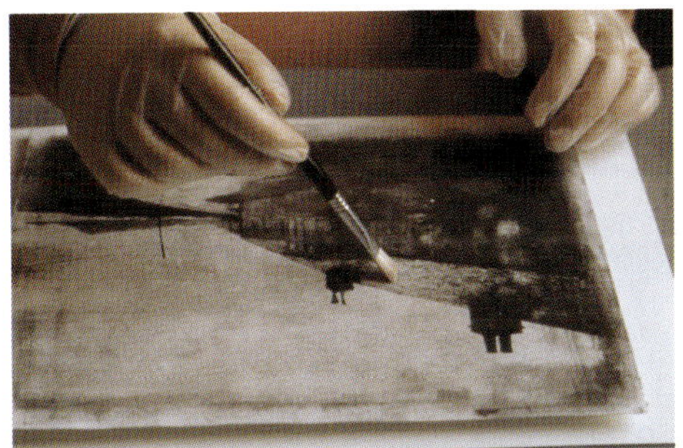

Brightening up highlights with a fine brush.

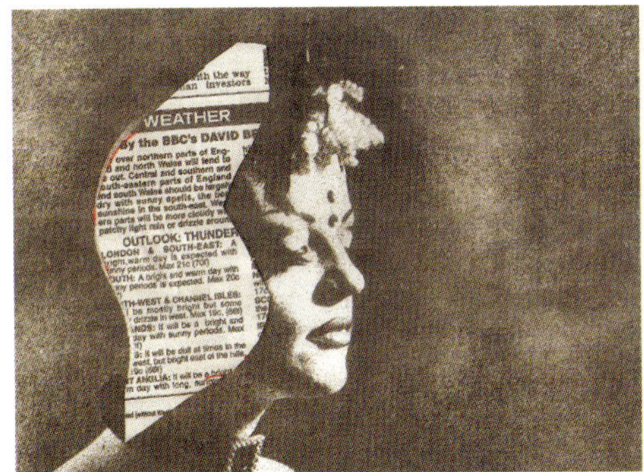

Masking the print for differential inking with damp paper.

Develop them well - 2 minutes at least and rinse for a minute or so in plain water. Don't bother with a stop bath. Then mix a fixing bath as follows:

Hypo (sodium thiosulphate)	25 g
Water	500 ml

We use plain hypo as some rapid fixers have hardening agents in them and may harden the gelatin surface of the print indiscriminately, which would make inking very difficult. Leave the prints in the fixer one at a time for about ten minutes. This bath will do four or five prints before it goes off and has to be replaced. After fixing the prints should be washed in running water as for normal fibre papers, and left to dry. They can be stored until you are ready to bleach them. You do not have to bleach and ink them immediately, you can leave them for months if you wish while you contemplate the next step, bleaching.

Bleaching

Make up a bleach mixture to this formula. (Any problems with chemicals see [6 . Chemicals].

Water	750 ml
Copper sulphate	30 g
Potassium bromide	30 g
Potassium dichromate	2 g
Acetic acid 10% solution	35 ml
or Hydrochloric acid 10%	35 ml

(whichever is most readily available)

Add water to make total volume of 1000 ml.

Take one part of the bleach and add to four parts water. Pour the remaining stock in to a brown bottle, label it and keep it for future use. It lasts for years. Pour the diluted bleach into a dish, soak one of the prints in cold water for a minute or two, and then immerse it in the bleach

After a few minutes the black and white image will fade until it reaches a very pale yellow green shade, or if you are lucky disappears altogether. To make sure it is properly 'cooked', leave it in the bleach for half as much time again as it took to reach the pale tone. If the image appears as a reddish colour then you probably haven't fixed it properly. Dump it and try another one that is fully fixed. Wash the bleached print briefly to get the worst of the yellow stain off (front and back). It now needs to be fixed a second time, as at this stage it contains silver bromide which if exposed to light will slowly darken. (Note, this may be worth looking at later, as a pale grey image under a coloured ink could look quite interesting).

Mix a new fixing bath;

Water	500 ml
Sodium thiosulphate	25 gram

Fix the print for 5 minutes until the yellow stain has gone. Sometimes there will be virtually no image left on the paper. Now dry the print bone dry. This means to the extent that the paper will curl up and crackle. If necessary use a hair drier or leave it on a radiator.

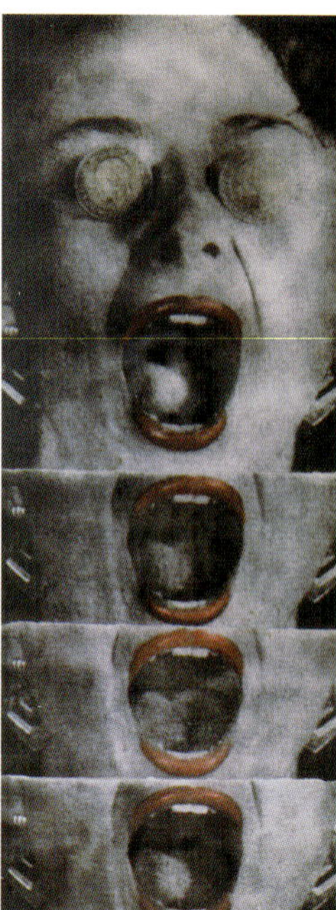

Screaming for Egypt. Bromoil strips pasted onto mount, colour applied with pastel crayon. In the 1930's Fred Judge used to colour flowers in bromoils of municipal gardens.

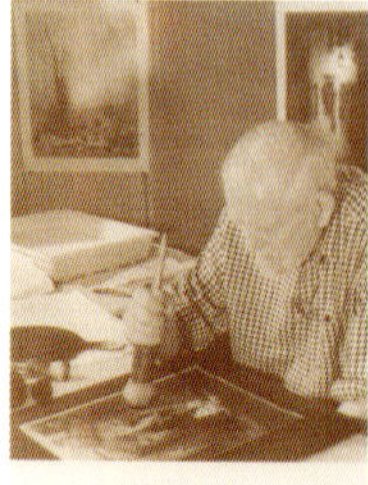

One of the notable figures in the circle of bromoil enthusiasts was the late Norman Gryspeerdt, who worked with the process from the earliest days. Before his death he recorded a video illustrating his techniques, which is available through specialist suppliers.

Soaking and inking

Cover your work surface with plenty of old newspapers. Wear old clothes or an apron.
Lay out your equipment for inking.

You will need:

Selection of **brushes**, (see shopping list).
Ceramic tile or old piece of glass to use as a palette.
Tray containing **water** at 20° C.
Roll of **cotton wool**.
Palette knife.
A piece of **card** or **mounting board** or a piece of **glass** or laminated **chipboard** slightly larger than your print to act as a support when inking the print.
Bottle of **white spirit**.
Some old **clean rags**.

Now place your dry print in the dish of water and leave it to soak for about ten minutes. Make sure that it stays under the water surface, either place small lumps of cotton wool on it or by putting it face downwards, making sure that there are no air bubbles underneath it. Take your 250 gram tin of etching or lithographic ink (see shopping list). Etching ink is rather gritty and litho is fairly smooth, but either will do the same job. When you open the tin you will find on the top of the ink either a circle of greaseproof paper or a disc of polystyrene foam. These prevent a hard skin forming on the ink. **Don't discard them**. With the palette knife, take out a small ball of ink about a quarter of an inch across, and spread it on the palette. Work the ink thoroughly on the palette by alternately spreading and scraping it up to remove any lumps. When it is fairly smooth test the consistency of the ink. This can only be done with a little practice. Spread the ink once more across the palette and lift off the knife from the palette. When you lift it off the ink should separate with a snapping sound and the surface of the ink will stand up looking like fine fibres. If the ink is soft and creamy it is not stiff enough and needs to be reinforced. This can best be done by working a little magnesium carbonate into it. This is a fine white powder which weighs next to nothing. It has no effect on the colour of the ink apart from making it stiffer. Put a small amount of the powder on the end of your knife (about the size of a pea), and work it into the ink. It will soon be absorbed and you notice the ink will become noticeably stiffer. One or two applications should be enough. If, on the other hand, the ink is thick and unworkable, it will need loosening up. Dip a match stick into some linseed oil and dab it on the ink. Work it in and check to see if the ink snaps when you lift the knife. One or possibly two drops will be enough. Any more and you will probably make it too soft. Now take a half or three quarter inch sash brush (the one with the bristles cut at an angle) or the shaving brush and dab it on the ink which you have spread on the palette. Now dab this onto a clean part of the palette. This will be your reservoir of ink. Do not over charge your brush as this will result in putting thick blobs of ink on the paper.

Notes on inking

Several applications of thin ink are better than one thick one.

Make sure the paper remains damp. This helps the removal of the ink from the highlights to the shadows. One of the instructions most of the old books on bromoil forget to mention is the constant re-immersion in water. If you don't, you get a large build up of ink which eventually resembles tarmac! Many of the early works on bromoil make a lot out of increasing the temperature of the soak water and the length of time in the original soaking. You can experiment with both of these if you wish but on the whole it doesn't make a marked difference to the print. One important aspect is the control of contrast during inking. The stiffer the ink you use the higher the contrast becomes. That is, the shadows become darker and the highlights become lighter, while some of the mid tones are lost.

Similarly, the softer the ink the lower the contrast. This latter is caused by the soft ink sticking more to the highlights. If, after a couple of inkings you find the contrast too high, try adding one small drop of linseed oil on the end of a match-stick to your main patch of ink. **Do not do this in reverse. Soft ink must not be applied before you have used the stiffer ink.** Often in warm summer weather the ink softens as it stands on the palette, so that after you have inked up one or two prints, they start to become less contrasty with an overall grey cast. Either mix a little more magnesium powder in the ink, or mix new ink.

Or - leave it as it is, and be satisfied with prints that resemble classic nineteenth century platinums.

Using a roller for inking

Stabbing at the paper with the brush too heavily can abrade the gelatin surface and ruin the print. Using a rubber roller will help you to avoid this.

After the initial inking, take a clean, dry rubber roller or brayer (see pic) and gently roll it over the surface of the print. This obviously covers the the whole print surface much more quickly than a brush. The more pressure you put on the roller the more the ink stays on the print, and the lighter the pressure the more ink is lifted off - especially in the highlights.

Some early workers used rollers exclusively in preference to a brush.

An alternative form of roller is the cheap plastic foam type normally used for painting walls and ceilings with emulsion paint. It tends to give lower contrast and a less grainy effect. Make sure it is dry when you use it.

Masking the print during inking

If you want to hold back or enhance the ink cover on larger areas of the image, cut or tear a piece of paper to the shape needed, dampen it and press it onto the area you need to work on. Now ink over it for the desired effect. See picture, p.93.

Take your print out of the dish of water. It should have soaked for about ten or fifteen minutes. Place it on a piece of clean glass or a piece of card and take off all the surface water with a wad of kitchen towel. Wipe off all the water on the card round the edge of the print. **Make sure there are no droplets of water on or near the print.** Take the loaded brush and hold it upright on the top right hand corner of the print. Press the brush downwards to deposit ink on the print. Then - without lifting it off the surface - move it half an inch down the page. Press again and move it down again. Keep repeating this movement all the way down the edge of the print. **It is important that the tip of the brush remains in contact with the paper the whole time.** When you run out of ink and no more is being transferred to the paper, dab the brush on the main body of the ink, and then onto the reservoir of ink and continue as before.

When you reach the bottom of the page, return to the top of the page, and start inking a fresh line immediately to the left of the first line. Continue inking to the bottom of the page, inking a line at a time - recharge your brush as necessary until you have covered the whole print with a thin deposit of ink. Try at this stage to maintain a thin coating of ink. Do not put thick lumps of ink on the paper as they will be difficult to remove later.

When you have covered the paper, turn it round 90 degrees and start again, repeating the exercise. You will now have a set of vertical ink lines and overlaid on it a set of horizontal ones. It will look a nasty grey mess, but don't panic. All is about to be revealed. Now replace the print in the dish of water and taking a clean unused brush, gently wipe the brush across the surface of the print under water. You should now see the image appear. It will be rather faint but it will be recognisable. What is happening at this stage is that the water is rejecting the ink from the light unhardened areas while the hardened darker areas retain the ink. Take out the print and replace it on the glass or card. **Leave the wet brush in the dish. Use it only under water.** Dab off all the surface water with kitchen roll. Do this fairly firmly - you won't harm the ink at this stage. **Don't leave any droplets of water on the surface!** Take another clean brush and gently scrabble it all over the over the surface of the print. This has the effect of lifting even more of the ink off the highlights and depositing it on the shadows. The image will become somewhat bolder. Do this until no more ink appears to transfer from light to dark areas. Replace the print in the water and you will see the image appear much more clearly. Remove it from the water and dab off the surface water.

Now repeat the whole inking process from the beginning. At this stage, if you think the shadows need to be a little darker, then ink those parts selectively. That will put a little more ink on the shadows and less on the highlights. If you need to lighten the highlights then work on these parts either under the water or with the dry brush. Small areas of highlight can be brushed with the fine fitch brush. Repeat the whole process two or three times and you should have a respectable print.

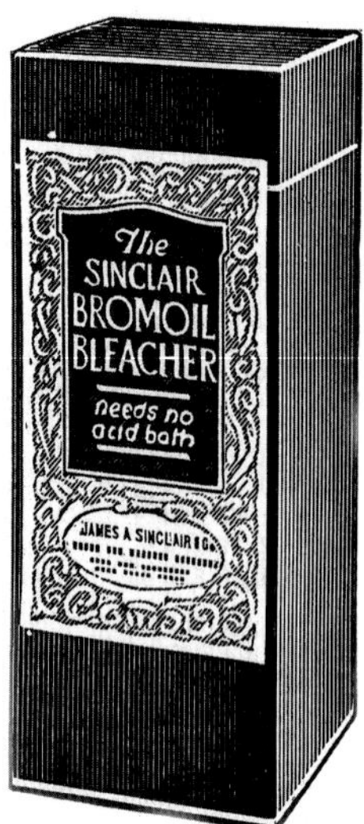

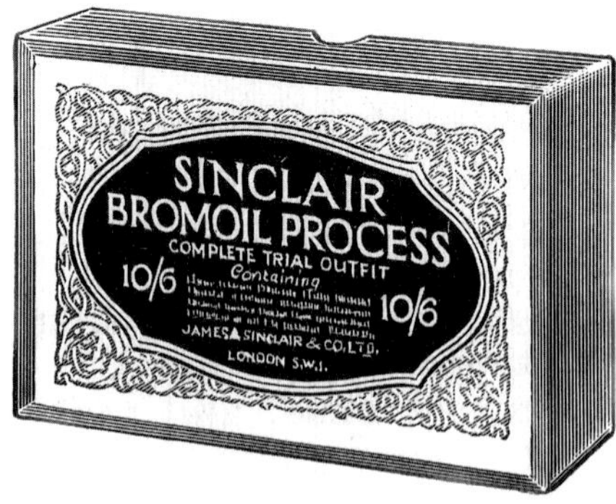

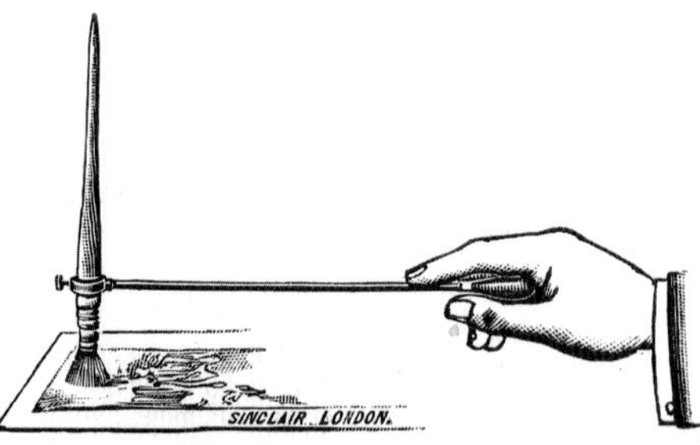

Bromoil practitioners in the early 20'th century were well catered for, and Sinclair especially kept a wide range of specialised Bromoil chemicals and tools.

Trouble shooting

If you have followed the instructions carefully nothing much can go wrong. The main thing to avoid is putting on too much ink at first. When you charge your brush from the reservoir of ink and dab it on the palette, make sure you remove any large blobs of ink which will be hard to take off when you ink the paper. Immerse the print frequently in water, (this is the bit the books fail to mention). Don't leave any drops of water on the paper when you are inking. The water emulsifies the ink and leaves big white spots. Always use the brush gently.

Reversed image

Curiously, many writers on bromoil are hesitant to mention this problem. What happens is that the ink sticks to the highlights instead of the shadows, giving a negative image. There are three possible causes:

1 Contamination with hypo fixer. Ensure adequate washing after both fixing baths.

2 Out of date paper.

3 Room temperature too high. As with carbon, so with bromoil - don't do them in a heat wave.

Finishing and presentation

The paper will dry in an hour or two, but the ink will take a few days to dry properly. The main problem is how to remove the ink left on the white margins of your print. Prevention is better than cure in this case, so when you come to your final inking stage, immerse the print in water, and brush off as much residual ink as possible under water with the wet brush.

When the inking has been completed, clean the margins with a little pad of cotton wool which has been dampened with white spirit. Don't make it too wet, and if necessary, place a piece of card along the edge covering the image. Alternatively, place it behind a window matt to cover your mucky margins. Any brush hairs sticking to the surface can be picked off with the point of a scalpel. Black spots can be touched out with a scalpel and larger spots can be lightened with the tip of an india rubber cut to a point. This is also useful for brightening up highlight areas. White spots can be touched in with ink on the end of a pointed matchstick.

Footnote.

We may have given the impression that bromoil is used as some form of therapy for retired gentlemen. In fact, it is alive and well and has been used continuously since the 1930's.

At the time of writing there is a very active bromoil circle based in the Midlands. This group has been instrumental in maintaining a supply of bromoil paper to supply a continuing demand.

Bromoil Transfer

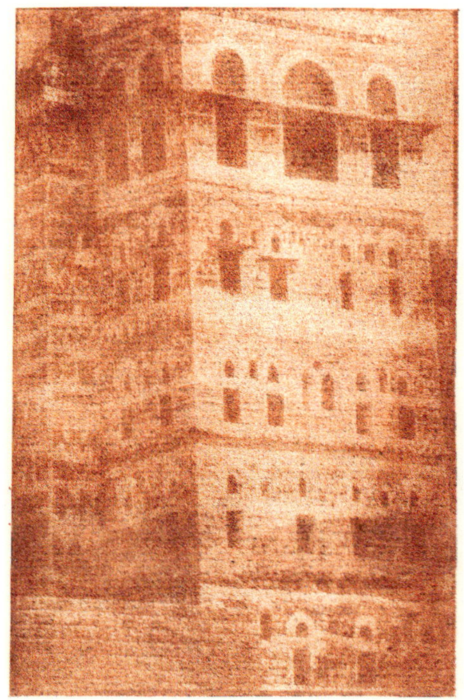

Bromoil transfer using red ink.

This is really no more than a extension of the bromoil process. It could also be called more properly the poor man's lithography. A newly inked bromoil print is placed face to face with another piece of paper and passed through the rollers of an etching press. The extreme pressure exerted by the press transfers the ink (and therefore the image) on to the other sheet of paper. The advantages of this method are:

You can make your transfer print on any paper of your choice.

You don't need a large negative.

You can make a small limited edition from the original bromoil.

The disadvantage is that you need access to an etching press, and the presence of someone who knows how to demonstrate and supervise its use.

Shopping list

A few sheets of **plain newsprint** for packing the press.

A **sharp scalpel**.

A **metal ruler**.

That's all.

Paper. Any paper seems to work. Hand made, mould made. You name it, it works.

Before we start, **please note**. When you make your photographic print in the enlarger, the image should be laterally reversed (ie right to left), because if you don't, when it comes out of the press it will be back to front, and if you have any lettering on the print it will be reversed.

Method

First the etching press.

Most art schools and the art departments of adult education centres will have a press of sorts. There are also a number of printmaking studios that work on a co-operative basis which you could try.

Approach them to see what sort of deal you could do with them for occasional use of a press. The actual time taken to make a transfer in terms of press usage is probably no more than ten minutes at a time. Alternatively, sign on for an etching class and try photo-etching and gravure as well.

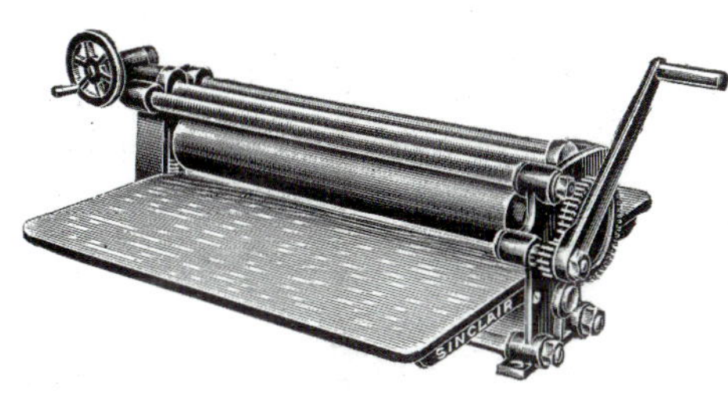

Bromoil press made by Sinclairs, specifically for bromoil transfer. Now, any etching press will do the job.

Many years ago, Sinclairs in Trafalgar Square London, used to sell a special bromoil press. The instructions in all the earlier literature included bolting two large sheets of zinc together among other things. It made it sound more like a car factory than a print studio. Now, a standard etching press is ideal. The press works in a similar way to a clothes wringer. A metal plate on which are laid the bromoil and the transfer paper moves under the roller and out the other side. The pressure necessary to make the transfer of ink can be adjusted on the press. This is where the help of someone with experience of the press comes in.

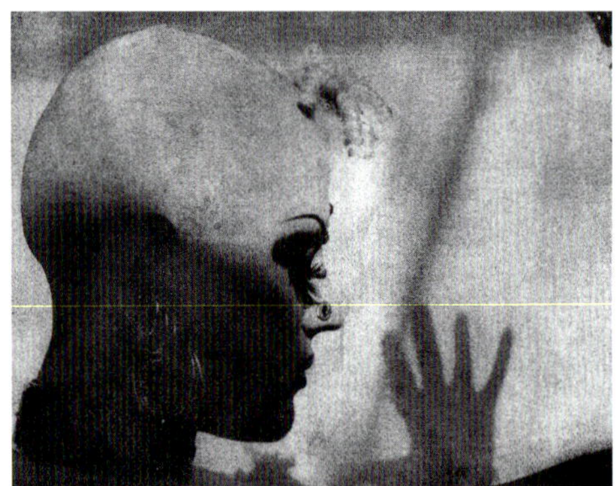

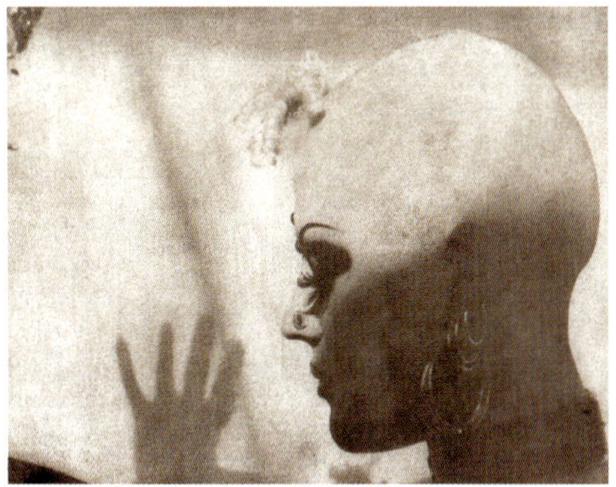

The bromoil transfer (top) and the bromoil matrix after the ink has been transferred (below).

Trouble shooting

If the print is too light

1 The pressure on the press was not heavy enough. Adjusting the pressure of the press is an art in itself and will need a bit of practice. Tell whoever is helping you with the press that it needs to be wound down tighter than for printing an etching plate.

2 The ink on your bromoil has dried too quickly or you haven't put enough ink on.

The bromoil sticks to the transfer paper

1 Your transfer paper may not be damp enough.

2 More likely the pressure on the press was too heavy. Loosen the pressure slightly.

The rollers are turned using a large handle at the side of the press. It is usually turned by hand and is very good exercise. If you are able to ink up your print in the same studio that contains the press, then do so. If not, ink your print, put it between two sheets of very damp blotting paper in a plastic bag, and take it to the press as soon as possible.

Now make sure you find out what the press looks like and how it works, but do not attempt to adjust the press yourself. Do it under expert supervision - always.

First, place the damp inked bromoil on a suitable surface and trim the margins off the print with the straight edge and the scalpel. Take care as the damp paper tears easily at this stage. Now take a sheet of the paper you wish to transfer to and place it in a dish of cold water for a few minutes. Then remove it and blot off all the excess water with a blotter and let it hang on a line for a few minutes. You now have a suitably damp sheet of paper for a transfer. The transfer paper should be larger than the bromoil to give a generous margin to the transfer print.

Now place two sheets of plain newsprint, one on top of the other, on the platten of the press.

In the centre place your bromoil image - face side upwards, making sure there are no creases on the print. On this place your damp sheet of transfer paper. It's a bit tricky getting the print under the paper in the centre. Practice!

Now come the blankets. The press will have two strips of blanket roughly the size of the platten. These, placed over the paper 'sandwich' add to the pressure on it. Take the first blanket which is smooth like felt and place it over the papers. Now place the second blanket, which is coarsely woven, on the first one. Smooth out any creases on the blanket with your hand. Turn the handle of the press without stopping until the platten, blankets and paper sandwich have all gone under the roller to the other side. Peel back the blankets and the transfer paper which now contains your mastepiece. Hang it up to dry and mount it in a window matt. The bromoil from which you transferred the image will look a sorry thing. Pale with just a faint image. Let this dry, and at any time in the future you can soak it and ink it again to make another transfer. With a bit of luck and care you should be able to get a small limited edition of at least 5 or 6 prints, (see chapter 32 for more about limited editions).

Notes on bromoil transfer

One important feature. When the ink is transferred from the bromoil print to the transfer paper, proportionately more comes off the highlights than from the shadows. This has the effect of reducing the contrast of the final print. So try to aim for a reasonably contrasty bromoil if you intend to transfer it.

Retouching can be done with a brush as with bromoils. If you are using several colours you can touch in the gaps between the various colours with pigment and a brush. Nobody will notice the join! Finally when you've mastered transfers on paper, try doing it on cloth. But not on the blankets from the press.

Oil printing

Dichromate coated paper after exposing and before inking.

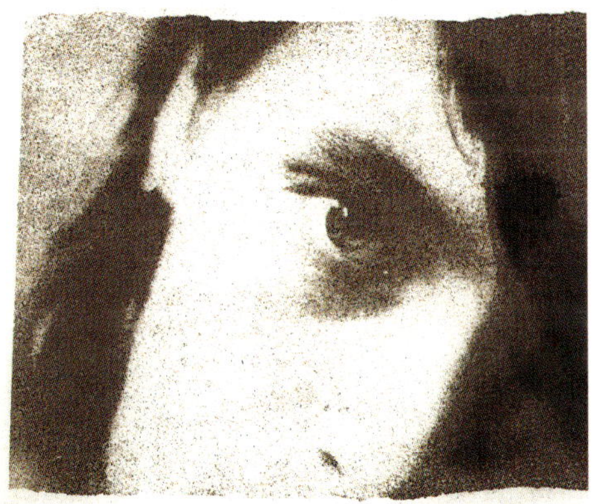

Example of a fully inked print.

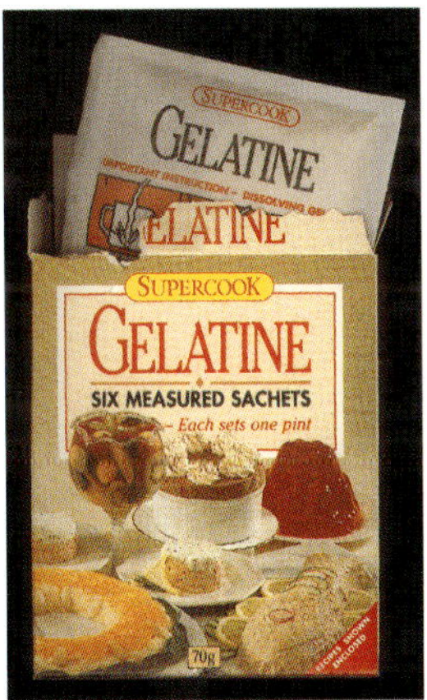

Gelatin can be obtained pretty well anywhere in food quality, although for the best and most predictable results it may be worth obtaining photographic grade from a specialist.

Oil prints are a sort of back to front version of bromoil. Briefly, a sheet of paper (any sort) is coated in several coats of gelatin. A solution of dichromate is brushed onto it and when dry it is exposed by contact under a negative. It is then washed and dried and then inked in the same way as an ordinary bromoil.

Advantage

You can make a print on any paper of your choice without recourse to a press as in bromoil transfer.

Disadvantage

You can't enlarge onto this paper as you could with bromoil, so you have to make an enlarged negative the size of your intended final image.

Shopping list

(in addition to that needed for bromoil).

Gelatin
Potassium or **ammonium dichromate**

Negatives

Make an enlarged negative of high contrast that would print well on Multigrade 0 contrast. Using a densitometer aim for a 1.4 net density.

Papers

Anything you like but as it has to be inked try to use paper not less than 200 gsm. [5 . Papers].

Method

Take a piece of paper at least two inches larger each side than your negative. Coat it with three or four successive layers of gelatin size, (see the section on salt printing for this). When it is dry mix up:

Potassium dichromate	3 g
Water	100 ml

When this mixture is dissolved brush it on the surface of the gelatin until it is covered with an even orange coating. Leave it to dry in the dark. You can heat dry it gently if you wish. Now expose it under your negative in a printing frame as normal. When a faint image appears showing some details in the darker tones, take it out of the frame and wash it in cold running water for ten minutes or so or until the orange dichromate stains have disappeared. Don't worry if you can't get rid of all the last traces. It's not that important. Now hang it up to dry. You can now ink it up just as you did with bromoil. You can store it for as long as you like before you ink. It won't deteriorate. You could if you so desired, make a transfer from it, but why bother. It's on good paper anyway.

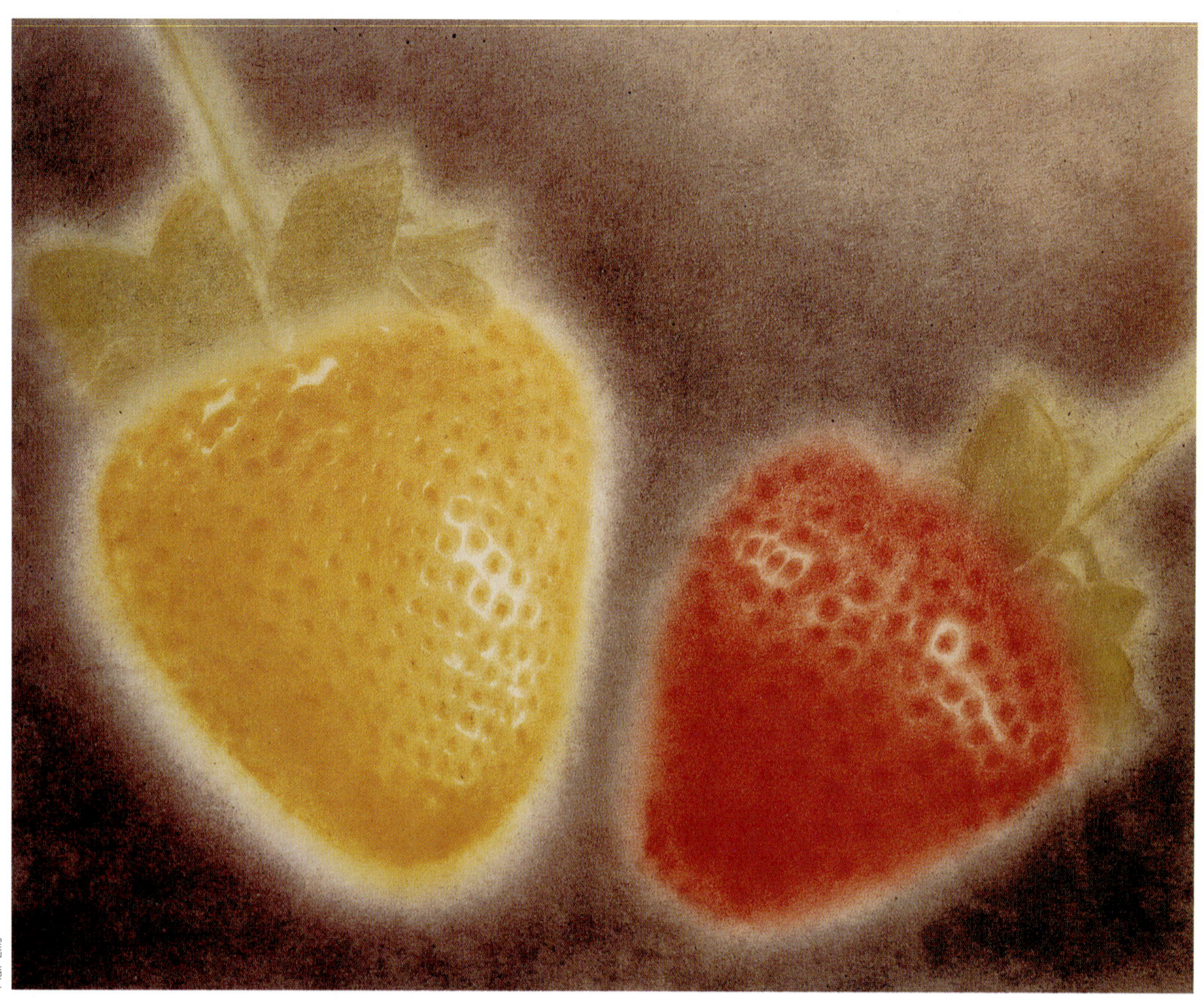

Mair Ellis

Strawberries. Bromoil transfer using a variety of Charbonnel inks. The original was a 5x4" colour transparency converted onto black and white film negative.

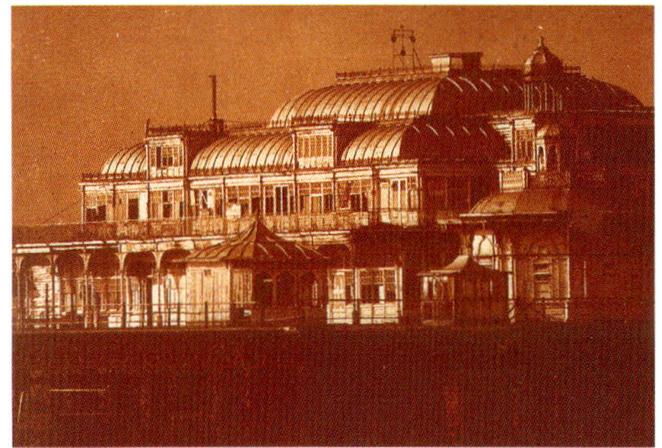

Brighton pier. Carbon print using Autotype carbon tissue. Transferred onto fibre based silver gelatin paper which had been fixed and washed to remove all the silver, leaving only clear gelatin.

Carbon prints were patented as a photographic process in 1864 by Joseph Wilson Swan. However the basic principle goes back somewhat earlier to the invention of gum printing by Mungo Ponton in 1839. As described in the section on gum printing, [20 . Gum printing], a mixture of gum arabic, or gelatin and potassium dichromate coated on a sheet of paper will harden on exposure to light so that the mixture cannot be washed off in warm water. If exposed under a negative only those parts of the emulsion which have received less light through the denser parts of the negative will wash off. Thus a reverse image of the original remains, giving a positive print. In 1855 Alphonse Poitevin patented a method of incorporating a carbon powder (black) in the mixture. This of course produced a print containing a range of tones from black through grey to white. Swans method improved on this by using a pre-coated paper which he called 'carbon tissue'. His method is very little different from what we use now, although 'carbon' is something of a mis-nomer, as a wide range of coloured pigments can be used in the tissue to form the image.

A piece of plain non-photographic paper is coated with a gelatin emulsion which contains pigment of any colour. This tissue is then soaked in a solution of potassium dichromate and dried. When exposed in a contact printing frame under a negative of the size required in sunlight or ultra violet light, the coating is hardened in inverse proportion to the densities of the negative. The exposed tissue is then soaked in cold water and placed in contact with another piece of paper which has been previously coated with a layer of gelatin. After being left pressed together for a short time this 'sandwich' is placed in hot water. The gelatin softens, and the backing of the carbon tissue is gently peeled off leaving an amorphous mass of gelatin on the receiving paper. The image is 'developed' by soaking it in the hot water until the unhardened gelatin in the highlights washes off leaving a continuous positive image. When all the soluble gelatin has been removed it is hung up to dry and mounted - preferably under a window matt.

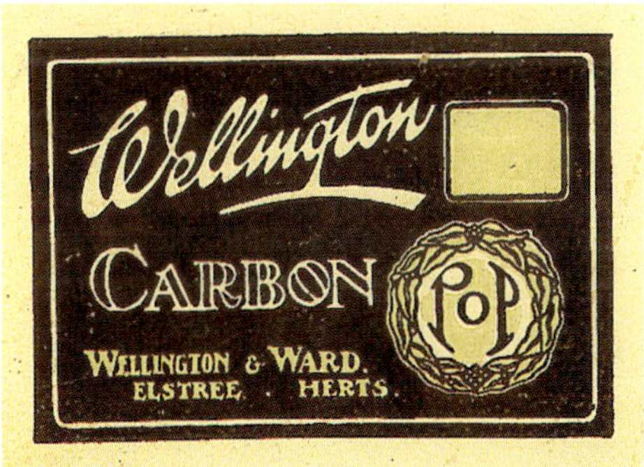

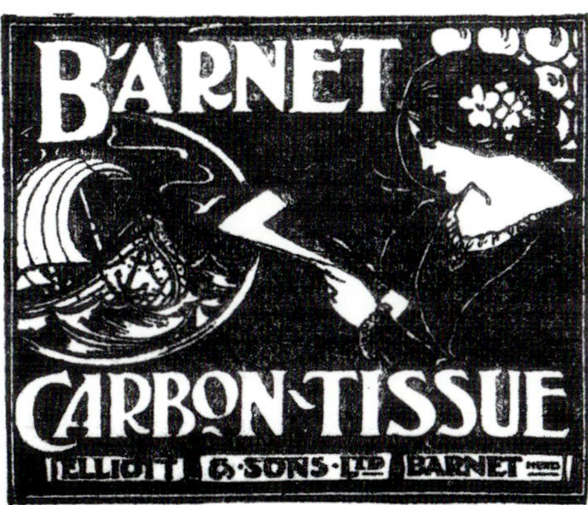

Apart from The Autotype company, Barnet, one of the oldest companies in photographic coating, were early manufacturers of carbon materials. Wellingtons 'carbon' was actually another POP material.

Since the beginning of this century the production of carbon tissue has been dominated by the Autotype Company. They originally operated a factory in Ealing in West London but are now based in Wallington in Oxfordshire. The main use of carbon tissue today is for the manufacture of rotogravure plates for the commercial printing industry, [23 . Photo etching] & [24 . Gravure]. As carbon tissue is used only as an intermediary part of the rotogravure process, it can now be bought from them in any colour - provided it is terracotta red! In the old factory in Ealing, in West London, long strips of carbon tissue were draped on washing lines to dry. Now in Wallington they have fully automated coating machines 'the size of a block of flats'. Much of the early literature on carbon printing was published by the Autotype company and in their 1905 catalogue 30 feet of carbon tissue cost 7/6d, (35p). It's a bit more expensive now.

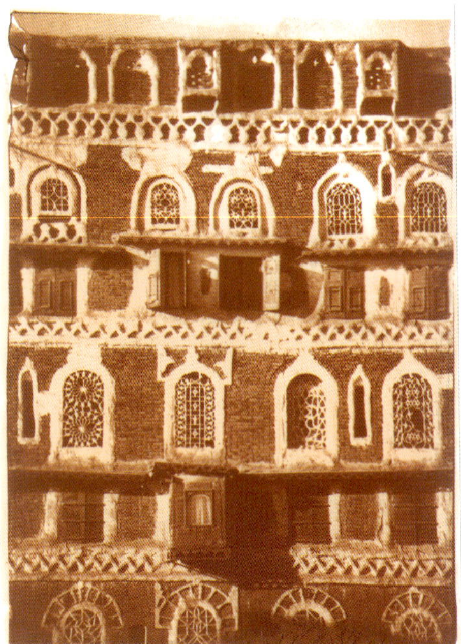

Facade, North Yemen. Carbon print using autotype tissue. Continuous tone negative.

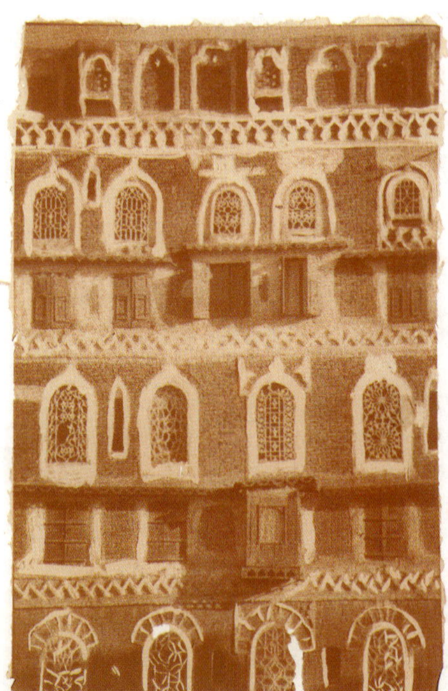

Facade, North Yemen. Carbon print using Autotype tissue. Negative made on lith film, broken up into half tones by the use of a sheet of non-reflecting picture glass placed over the film on the enlarger baseboard.

A modern version of carbon tissue on polyester base suitable for full colour printing is made in the USA by the 'UltraStable' company, and is coated on a plastic base which makes it more dimensionally stable. This is available in yellow, magenta cyan and black, although bear in mind the 'black' is intended for providing the 'K' separation, that is the key black in 4-colour printing, and does not have enough density for the single carbon technique described here.

Advantages

Permanence; your image is made from pigment embedded in gelatin and cannot fade or be degraded by the atmosphere as can conventional silver processes.

Tonal range; carbon shows very extended tonal separation and is capable of giving a very delicate range of tones.

Choice; if you make your own carbon tissue you can make a print of any colour you wish. If you feel the need to explore the full potential of carbon printing you can make four-colour carbons that look like colour prints but without the danger of the colours fading as conventional colour prints do. However don't try this until you have mastered the skills of single colour carbons. Once you have acquired these skills you are well on the way to being able to make a photogravure copper plate to print in an etching press, see [24 . Photogravure].

Unlike most of the old processes it is possible to vary the contrast of the print slightly by chemical means but don't expect the Multigrade range.

Disadvantages

If you want to produce good quality carbon prints on a regular basis you will need a certain amount of patience and the ability to work precisely and cleanly. You will also need quite a bit of practice. Sloppy workers wanting to get it right first time need not apply! Nevertheless the beautiful results that can be obtained with this process make all the effort worthwhile. If you are willing only to use the commercially produced carbon tissue from Autotype you have to be satisfied with only one colour - terracotta red.

You need a fairly contrasty negative to work with - the sort of negative that works best with salt prints.

Making your own carbon tissue is an extra task which also requires some practice. See side box on p. 103. It is best done in the winter when there is less chance of the soft gelatin sliding off the paper.

Shopping list

Potassium dichromate.

Carbon tissue - see method section.

Gelatin - or - a few sheets of ordinary fibre based photographic printing paper (glossy or matt, - it doesn't matter which at this stage).

Roller squeegee with a rubber roller about 6 inches long from any art supplier.

Thermometer.

Making carbon tissue

When you get tired of terracotta red from the Autotype carbon material, what do you do then? Carbon tissue is not a particularly difficult material to put together oneself, using only paper, gelatin and a permanent pigment. This is a recipe for a presensitized tissue. Only carbon black is specified here, but a richer black will be obtained by adding small amounts of other pigments, such as Carmine Red and Quinacridone Violet. The prepared pigmenting solution should be used in one session.

Distilled water	50 ml
Gelatin	10 g
Sugar	10 g

Let the gelatin swell in room temperature water for 30 minutes, and then heat it to about 50° C. Then add;

Distilled water	25 ml
Wetting agent	0.1 ml
Lamp-black	10 g

Now make a 5% solution of potassium dichromate, by dissolving 5 grams in 100ml water. Measure 25 ml of this and add to the gelatin and pigment mixture.

Meanwhile, get the coating surface prepared. This should be a flat waterproof surface, such as a plastic laminated chipboard, or a piece of plate glass. It should be possible to level it easily, either by fitting adjustable screws, or possibly using shims at 3 points. Immerse the paper to be used for the tissue in hot water for a minute or two, then squeegee it hard onto the surface so that there are no bubbles beneath, and no water drops on top. Wipe round the edges of the paper with absorbent towelling, and tape round the edges, fastening it down onto the board. This is to stop the pigmenting solution from reaching the back of the paper. With the pigmenting solution at. 50° C, pour onto the centre of the paper and spread it quickly across the surface - a pocket comb makes a good spreader. As a guide, about 50ml solution will be needed for an 8x10" area, equating to 1 litre per square metre. As it cools the gelatin will quickly set, and the tissue can be removed from the coating board after a few minutes. It should then be hung vertically to dry, attaching weighted clips to the bottom. Drying will take up to about 24 hours, depending on humidity and temperature.

Dish - one size up from the size of the paper you are printing on.

Measuring jugs, in 1 & 2 litre sizes.

Supply of cold water not above 20° C.

Supply of hot water not less than 40° C.

Sheet of glass slightly larger than your printing paper size.

A few **old newspapers** or **sheets of blotting paper**.

Washing line with about six plastic clothes pegs or four metal bulldog clips.

Printing frame.

Metal ruler.

Stanley knife or scalpel.

Roll of **red litho tape** or a small bottle of **photo-opaque**.

A **weight** ie a few heavy books or a 5 litre chemical container (full).

UV light source or daylight.

Scales.

Negatives

These should be of fairly high contrast. Using a densitometer it should be about 1.4 or sufficient to print on Multigrade contrasts 1 or 0. The contrast can be varied somewhat by altering the strength of the sensitiser, (see below).

One important feature of the negative is that if it is an enlarged one, it should be reversed right to left. Ensure this is so at the enlarging stage.

Paper

Use any fibre based photographic paper. When you become more skilful you can use any art paper, but it has to be sized with several coats of gelatin.

Method

We recommend that you read this section carefully several times before you start so that you can anticipate the various stages. Certain parts of the method depend on precise timings.

The most important item in this process is the carbon tissue, purchased in long rolls from Autotype or in sheets from Silverprint. It consists of paper coated with gelatin containing a red pigment. It is also very brittle. When you cut a sheet from the roll lay it on a flat surface and cut it with a straight edge and a scalpel. Take a sheet about one inch larger all round than your image. Now place it in a dish of cold water not warmer than 14° C. This has the effect of softening the paper and the gelatin. After about two minutes in the water hang it up on a line to drain.

Now mix the dichromate sensitiser:
Water 200 ml (not more than 18° C and not less than 10° C).
Potassium dichromate 4 g

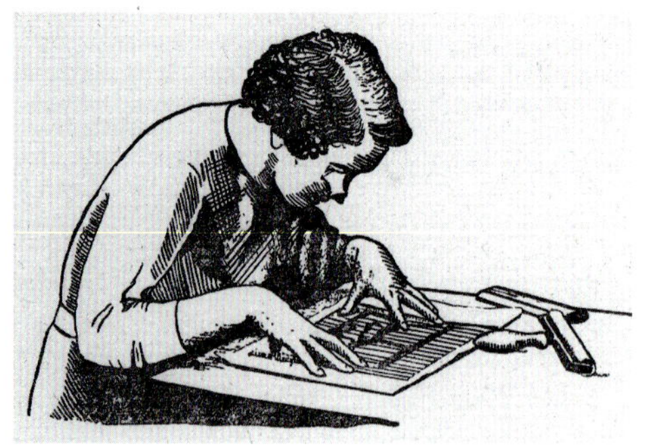

The concentration affects the final contrast. The stronger the mix the lower the contrast and vice versa, within a range of between 3 to 7 grams per 200 ml and pro rata.

Pour the dichromate mix in a dish and place the damp carbon tissue in the liquid, making sure it remains below the surface. After **three minutes** remove it from the dish and hang it on a line with a plastic clothes peg at both top corners. Place an empty dish underneath to catch the drips. Then put a plastic clothes peg at each bottom corner.
The carbon tissue must now dry naturally. **Do not** attempt to dry it with heat.

Sensitise two or three sheets the night before and allow them to dry in the dark. Make one extra sheet to use for exposure test strips.
Before you come to the exposing stage, take your negative and cover the outside edge on all four sides with red litho tape about half an inch wide. (It looks like red sellotape). Otherwise use black paper tape or if you are very careful, paint the edge with photopaque and let it dry.

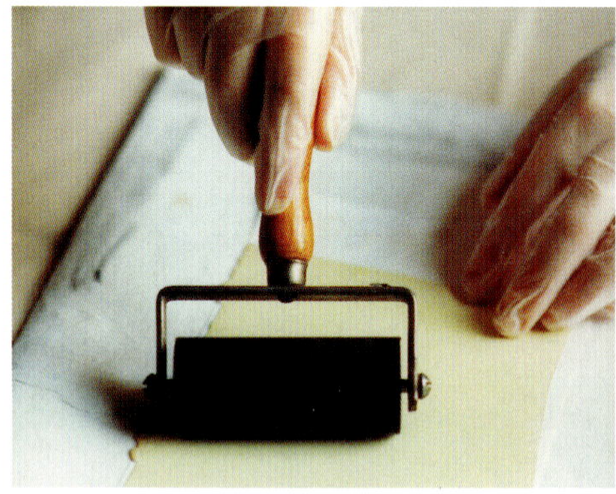

Rolling the carbon tissue face down on the receiving paper.

Now take a whole sheet of the sensitised tissue, and place it red side up under your negative and place it in your printing frame.

Note: the negative should be laterally reversed at this point. You will have already done this if it is an enlarged negative, but if it is an original camera neg you will need to place it on the red carbon tissue emulsion (dull) side up. The reason for this will be obvious later.

Expose the whole sheet as a test strip under your light source. If you use daylight as your source make sure the light remains constant. (No bright intervals with showers). The exposure on an average neg will be between 5 and 20 minutes, so cover up a quarter of the sheet every 5 minutes. When the exposure is finished take out the paper and place it in a drawer or a dark place.

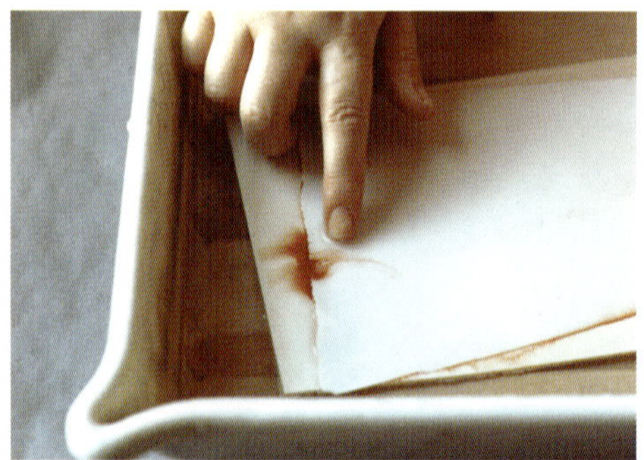

Testing to see if the gelatin has softened enough to allow the tissue and the paper to be separated.

At this point you need to prepare the fibre based paper onto which you transfer your gelatin image from the carbon tissue. Take a piece of fibre based photographic paper (any sort and any surface will do). Cut it to size an inch or so all round larger than the red carbon tissue. Place it a dish of paper fixer for five minutes, and then wash it for about ten minutes. This removes all the silver in the paper and you are left with a piece of paper coated only with gelatin.

Now place the exposed red tissue in a dish of cold water (some of the orange dichromate will mix into the water but it is not important, so ignore it). As soon as the red tissue softens make sure there are no air bubbles adhering to the surface. Then place the wet fibre based paper on top of the red tissue emulsion side down. They are now emulsion to emulsion.

Now withdraw the two together from the dish, holding them together by the two top corners. Make sure that the red tissue is in the centre of the fibre paper and place the 'sandwich' on to a sheet of blotting paper or a few sheets of newspaper on a flat, hard surface. The fibre paper should now be on the bottom emulsion facing up, and the red tissue on the top,

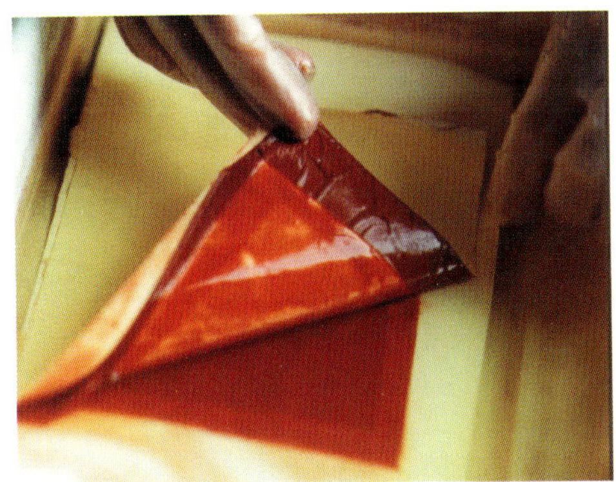

Separating the tissue from the receiving paper.

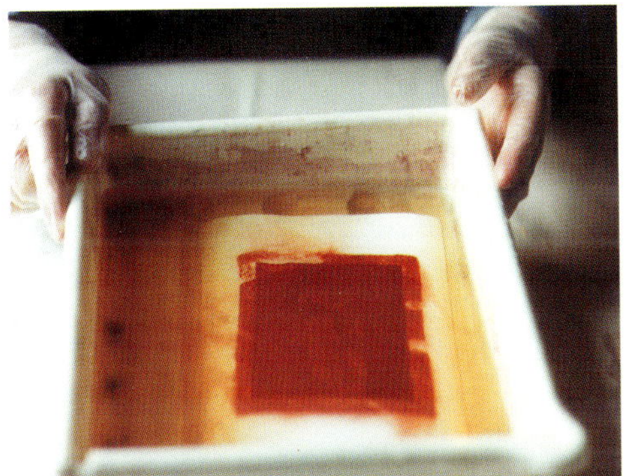

Rocking the dish to wash away the unhardened pigment.

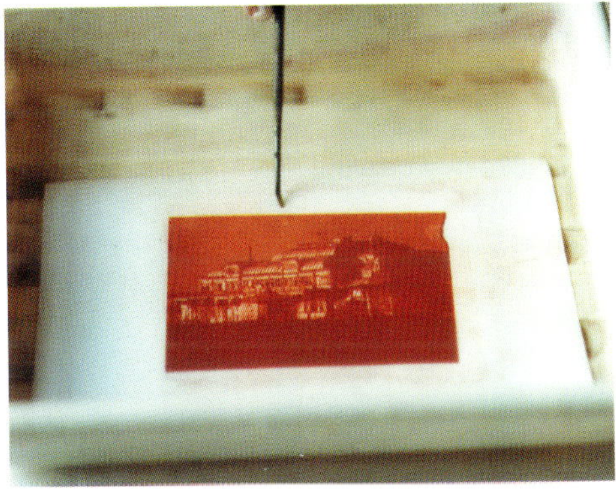

Clearing the margins with a fine brush.

red side facing down. This is an awkward manoeuvre and needs a little practice. It is also essential that no more than **one and a half minutes** elapse between immersing the red tissue and removing it and the fibre paper from the dish.

Now the two papers have to be squeezed together firmly. With the papers resting on the blotter, smooth the surface of the paper backing of the tissue gently with your hand to ensure there are no air bubbles underneath, and there are no creases on the top.

Place another sheet of blotting paper on top of the sandwich and firmly roll it to and fro with a rubber roller squeegee.

Take care not to let the two sheets of paper slip apart. In addition take great care not to make any creases on the red tissue.

With the two sheets of gelatin coated paper firmly bonded together we now have to leave them under a heavy weight to allow the two layers of gelatin to merge.

Place a piece of plate glass or board on top of the sandwiched papers and weigh it down with a heavy object. Heavy books or a full 5 litre chemical container will do.

Leave them like this for about 15 minutes.

Meanwhile prepare a dish of warm water prior to 'developing' the image. What happens in fact is that the warm water will melt the gelatin and the image on the carbon tissue will transfer to the fibre paper underneath. The water in the dish should be as close as possible to 40° C.

When the papers have stood under the weight for 15 minutes remove them (still stuck together), and place them carbon tissue side up in the warm water making sure they stay under the surface.

After about a minute you will see the red gelatin seeping out around the edges. Gently press the edge of the carbon tissue under water with your finger. A little red gelatin should squirt out at the point where you touched it. Let another minute pass.

Now is the critical part when we have to peel one sheet of paper from the other. Keeping the papers under water, carefully peel back one corner of the red tissue with your finger. Slowly and gently, continue to peel off the top paper until it completely detaches from the lower one. Now throw away the top sheet of paper that you have peeled off.

What you should have left in the dish is the fibre paper covered with a nasty red mess. Just inside the edge of the paper you will see a pale rectangular band. This is where your red litho tape prevented the red tissue from exposing.

Leave the paper covered with the nasty red mess in the water and gently rock the dish. After a few minutes you will see the red gelatin slowly lifting off the surface of the paper revealing your positive image in delicate shades of red on a white background. They will, of course, show four distinctly different bands of density where you gave the tissue graded exposure times.

As the gelatin lifts off it will make the water very cloudy. This is a good time to change the water in the dish.

Making sure you have a ready supply of water at the same temperature (40° C). Pour out most of the clouded water and replace it with the clean warm supply. Carefully avoid letting any of the fresh water fall directly on the gelatin image area. Pour it slowly into the corner of the dish. Continue this developing action with one or two more changes of water until you are satisfied with the image.

Carefully drain out all the warm water and very, **very**, gently replace it with cold water. This will go some way towards setting the gelatin. You must appreciate that at this stage the surface of the print is extremely delicate, and the slightest touch with your finger or any other object will remove a chunk of gelatin irrevocably.

After 5 minutes in the cold water remove the print holding both corners on a short side with your fingers, and hang it up to dry with plastic clothes pegs. Do not try to dry it with heat. Let it dry naturally.

When it is dry you can assess it in terms of exposure and contrast. If the contrast is wrong you can change the concentration of dichromate when you make your next solution. Don't throw away the remaining sheets of sensitised tissue, but keep them to practice on. Now you can see why we covered the edge of the negative with red tape. This prevents the edge of the gelatin image from frilling or the gelatin falling off altogether. This is a slow, time-consuming process. If you have a client who wants a carbon print, tell him it will take at least a fortnight!

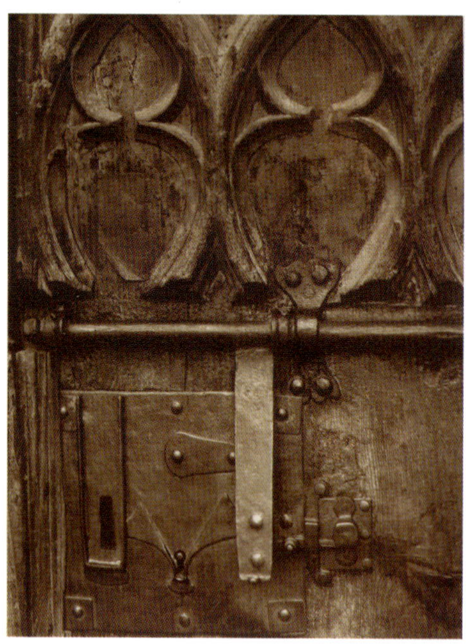

Gelabrome

With connections reaching towards Bromoil printing, gelabrome can be regarded as an interesting variation on Carbro, but requiring no transfer from one support to another, or the use of a pigment tissue. An enlargement is made on unsupercoated photographic paper, and the dried print is taped to a flat boaard. It is then flooded with a solution of gelatin to which has been added Indian Ink as pigment. After drying, the print is placed in a tanning bleach containing potassium dichromate. The reaction between the silver in the print and the gelatin in the presence of the dichromate renders the coating differentially hardened according to the density of developed silver in the original print. Next the print is developed in hot water, the soluble gelatin in the coating being washed away to leave a strong image in an attractive cold sepia tone. The print is finished by clearing, hardening and fixing baths with washes after each stage. The final result has all the qualities of a Carbon or Carbro print, but without the need for large negative, Carbon tissue, or second support.

Troubleshooting

Damage limitation is the most effective form of trouble shooting where carbon is concerned.

Don't make carbon prints in a heat wave and high humidity. Gelatin tends to behave unpredictably in these conditions.

Do make sure you mask the borders of your negative with red litho tape or opaque material. This will stop the gelatin frilling at the edge of the image.

Do stick closely to the instructions regarding the water temperatures at each stage of the process.

Mix a fresh solution of dichromate every time you make a new batch of sensitised carbon tissue.

Gelatin fails to adhere to the receiving paper. One of the most common and frustrating faults occurs when a small section of gelatin lifts off the receiving. This usually takes place on the most visible part of the image. This is either as the result of leaving the tissue too long to soak before transferring it to the receiving paper, uneven rolling when the tissue is transferred, or impatience in removing the tissue from its backing.

Retouching - all you need is a scrap of carbon tissue a little hot water and a retouching brush. Work it out.

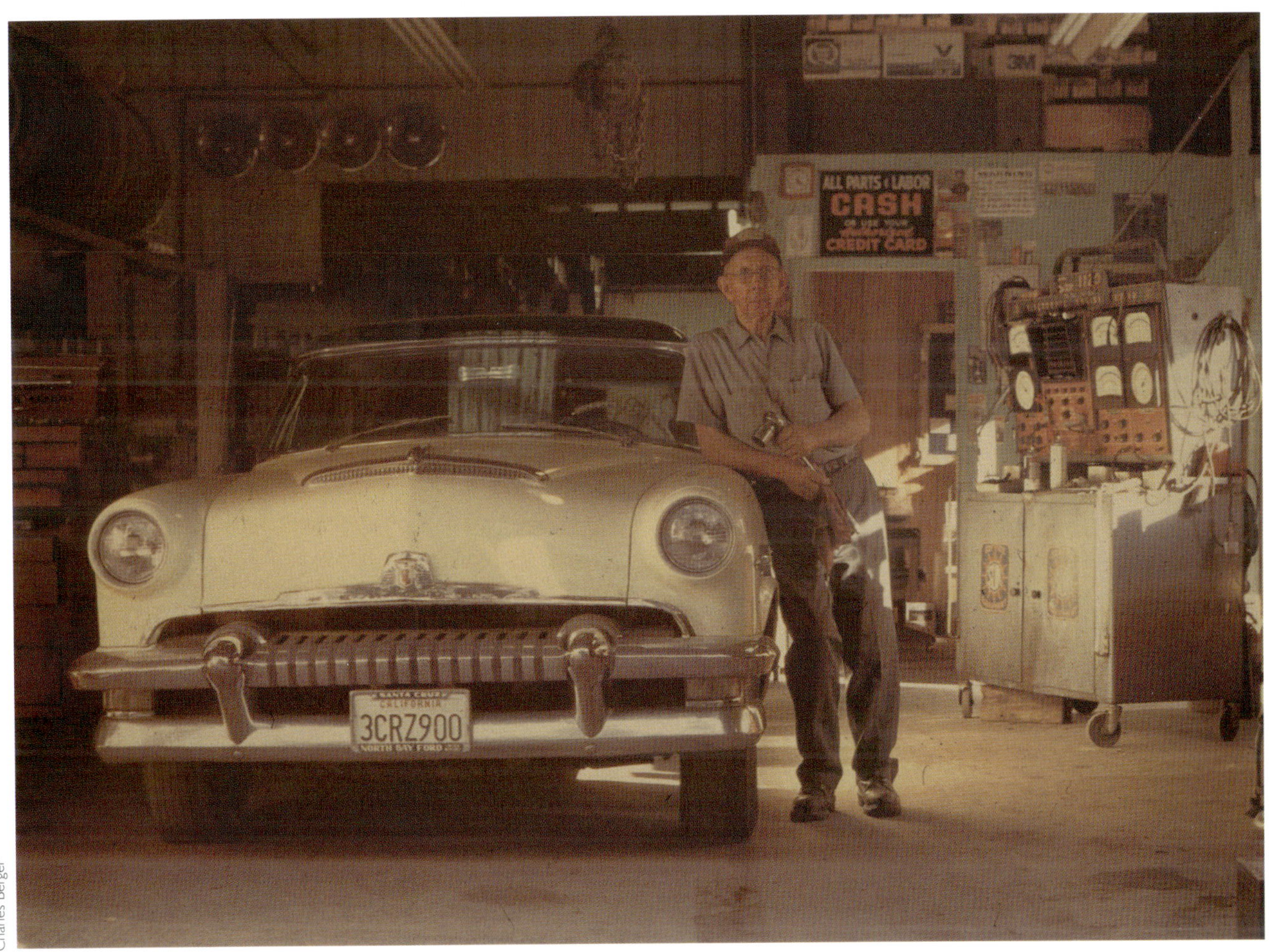

Charles Berger

Four colour carbon print produced by Gerrard Anniere using the four separations of Ultrastable carbon material.

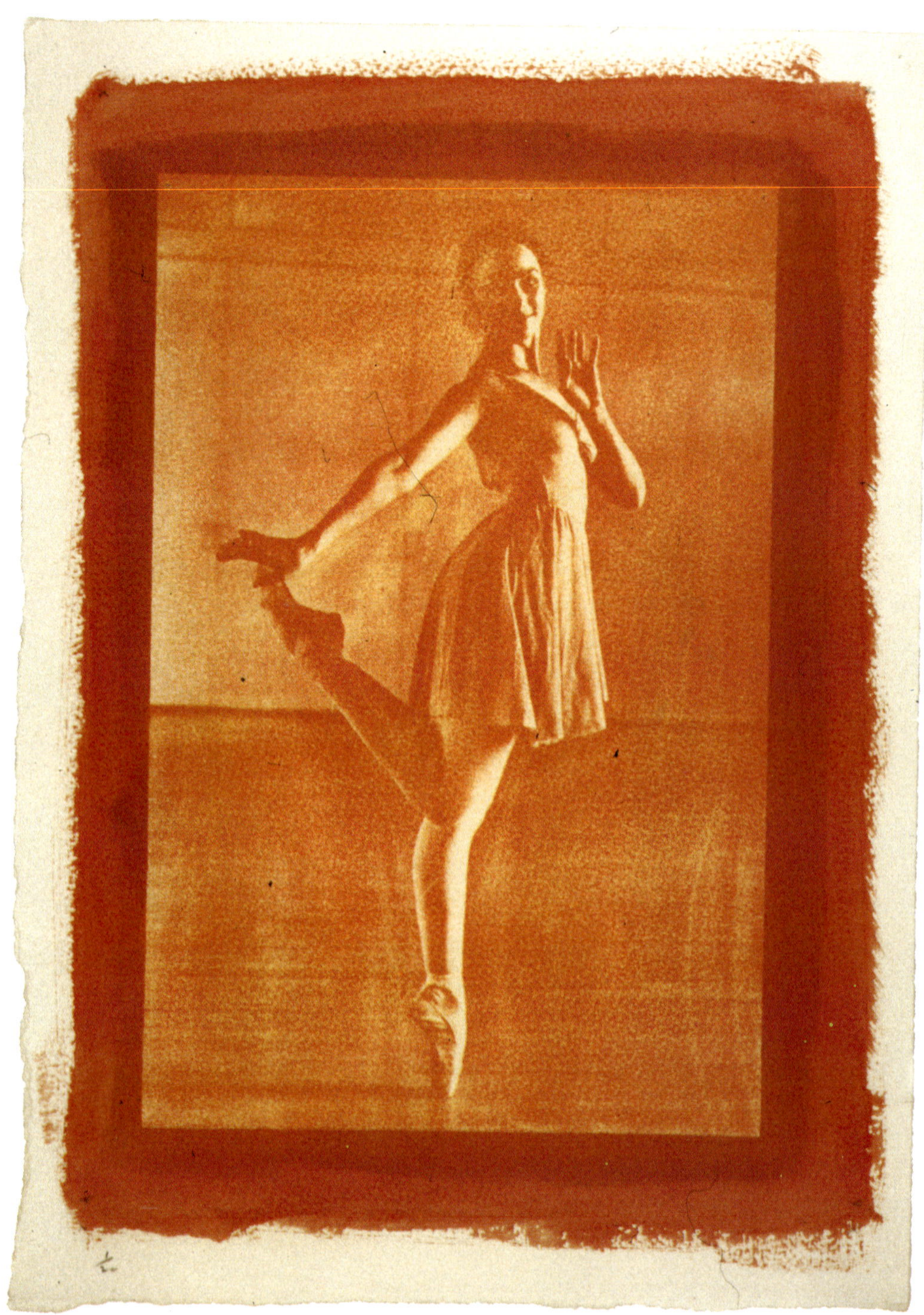

Two-colour gum print, red and yellow watercolours.

Gum printing

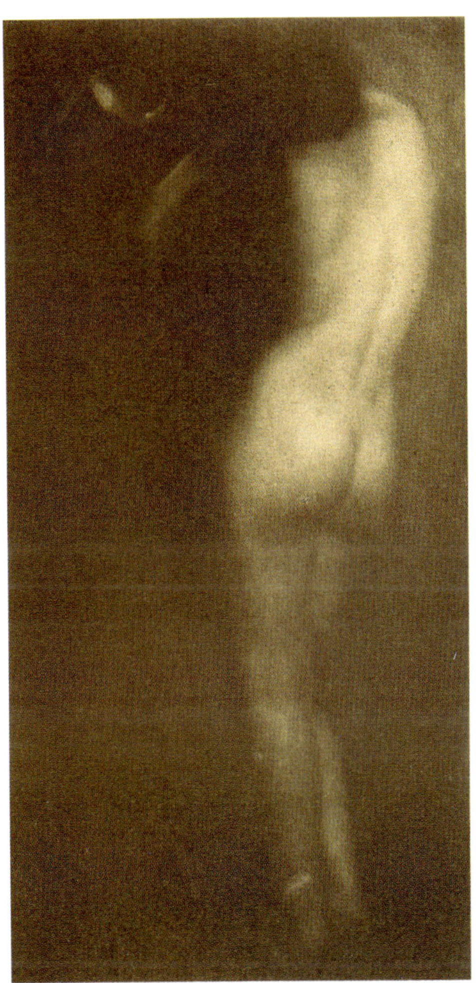

The Little Round Mirror - gum print by Edward J. Steichen.

Gum prints are now recognised as being an interesting way of making colour prints from black and white negatives. However, this appears to be a fairly modern concept. The early exponents of the process at the turn of the century tended to work in brown or black monochromes, but Robert Demachy, one of the leading 'gummists' (yes, they actually called themselves this), used terra cotta pigment for many of his figure studies. Stieglitz who led the 'art' photography movement at the end of the 19th century used blue or green gum emulsion to overprint his platinum prints. The main purpose of this technique was to reinforce the tones in the shadow areas of the picture. Like bromoil, gum printing was a very popular medium with the Photosecessionists. Both processes lent themselves to a considerable amount of manipulation and the use of ink or pigment gave the resulting prints a distinctive painterly appearance. There was also the popular assumption that both processes produced somewhat unsharp images. This fitted in well with the current fashion for soft focus or simply out of focus photographs.

In fact most of the qualities attributed to gum printing were totally misplaced. Contrary to received opinion, gum prints can be made to resolve fine, sharp detail. A gum print made by contact from a 10 x 8" negative shows as much detail as any other type of printing method. The misapprehension that gum prints have always to be fuzzy stems from multiple printing. The lack of accurate registration on each subsequent coating and printing gives the appearance of unsharpness.

The modern day resurgence of gum printing is most probably due, like bromoils, to their lack of pure photographic qualities and to the recent exploration of multi-coating and multiple printing. The fact that they only need one chemical (dichromate), some glue and some pigment followed by washing in warm water, adds to their popularity.

Advantages

Gum prints are quick, easy and cheap to make. It is possible to make a simple gum print from coating the paper to drying the print in less than 20 minutes. They only need one basic chemical - potassium dichromate - in addition to a bottle of glue from an office supplier and a selection of water colour pigments or powder paints.

They require no developers or fixers. Development and fixing consists of washing in warm water.

You can use an infinite variety of colours as well as black. With multiple coating and printing you can make quite sophisticated colour prints from a black and white negative, on the hand made paper of your choice.

Unlike many other old processes, they do not need a negative of very high contrast.

You have a wide choice of papers on which to print. Provided the paper has a reasonably rough surface and has been well sized in the manufacture

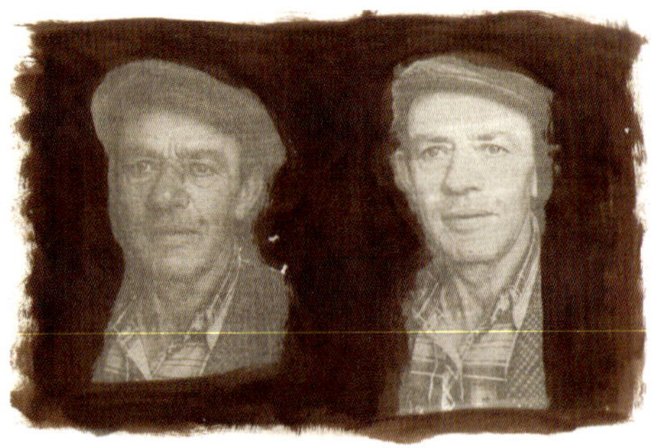

Gum print. Two prints on water colour overlaid with opaque poster colour, which was then exposed without any negative.

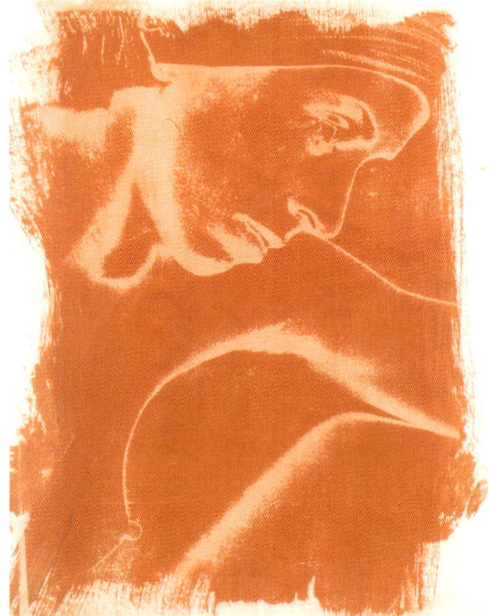

Gum print using water colour from manipulated negative.

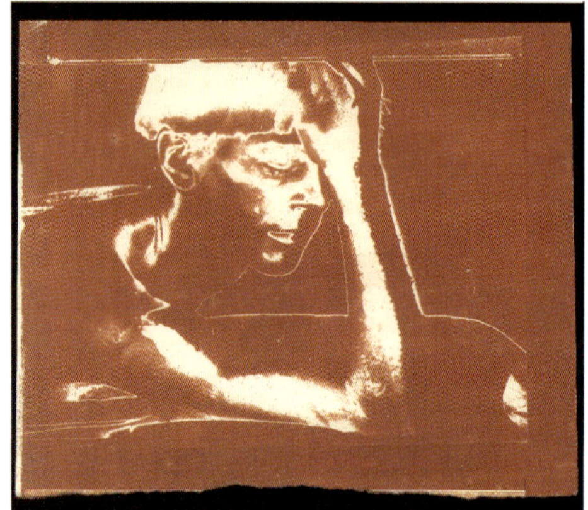

Gum print using opaque poster colour (or mixture of red and black).

the process is not adversely affected by any chemical inconsistencies in the way that, for example, platinum printing is.

The range of effects that can be obtained with this process is very wide. It is possible to go from very pale, delicate water colours to hard, brilliantly coloured graphic designs.

Gum can also be used to good effect by overprinting on other processes such as platinum or cyanotype. It is possible to obtain a painterly quality in the final print. You can print on fabrics and use it as an underglaze on ceramic tiles and other objects.

Disadvantages

If you use watercolours to make your print, they are a very transparent form of colouring and to get the best results you will need to make several coatings to get any depth and richness in the shadows. This involves the use of an effective method of registration in order to lay one colour on another. The 'development' of gums involves soaking the paper in warm water, which tends to remove the built-in sizing of the paper. You will probably find that you have to size the paper with gelatin or glue size between coatings. If you don't take this precaution the pigment will adhere to those parts of the paper which have lost their sizing and give the print the appearance of having been solarised. The use of artists colours and the necessary mixing of colours means that you will find yourself moving into the world of the painter, and you will need to learn some of their techniques. If you are prepared to accept these limitations you will find gum printing a different and very rewarding experience.

Shopping list

Potassium dichromate (avoid any advice to use ammonium dichromate unless the potassium is not available).
Potassium metabisulphite - useful but not essential - see Method.

A small **bottle of glue** (the sort sold by office suppliers such as Gloy or Stephens). Don't bother with the traditional gum arabic. It is difficult to prepare and needs a preservative to make it keep.

Colours. A few tubes of artist's water colours of your choice, poster paints, acrylic, gouache, tempera (in tubes), indian ink, powdered pigments. Any of these will do provided they will dissolve in water. Oil paints are obviously unsuitable.

50 grams of **powdered gelatin** or glue size (from artists suppliers).

Three or four **paint brushes**, 2 inch hake brushes or ordinary paint brushes from the DIY shop will do.

Flat **saucer or small plate** in which to mix the colours.

Plastic **palette knife** or spatula.

Roll of **clear Scotch tape**.

A 5ml **plastic spoon**. The sort that comes with bottles of cough mixture. (use it only for mixing your solution!)

Hair drier or **small fan heater**.

Jennifer. Gum print printed on colour paper from a positive image and using opaque white ink.

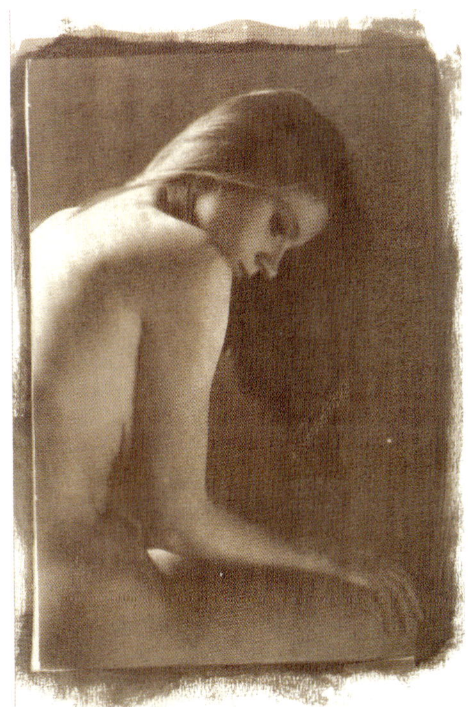

Nude. Three coats of water colour on hard sized Van Gelden paper.

Printing frame.

A few **drawing pins**, dressmakers pins or map pins.

UV light source or daylight.

Supply of **warm water** (40° C).

Developing dish larger than your paper size.

Thermometer.

A few **clothes pegs** or print clips.

A lot of **old newspapers**.

Negatives

You will need to make a contact negative the size of your final image, [9 . Negatives]. You will not need a high contrast negative for this process. One that will produce a good print on grade three or four paper is best. However, make sure that you don't have large areas of clear film on your negative as this will produce very murky shadows on the print. Avoid making your negative from colour transparencies. If you are using a densitometer, aim for a negative with a net density of between 0.7 and 0.9. If you want to make strong graphic images with opaque poster colours, make a negative on lith film developed in lith developer. Try solarising it, or use bas-relief effects, see [9 . Negatives].

You can incorporate print in your image by contacting type on paper onto lith film, see [9 . Negatives].

You can also make a gum from a positive film instead of a negative, see method.

As gum sensitiser is relatively fast, you may try experimenting with a paper negative. See [9 . Negatives].

Papers

Unlike many old processes, especially the silver and iron varieties, gum sensitisers are less likely to be adversely affected by the chemicals incorporated in the paper during manufacture. Thus you have a fairly wide choice of papers to work with. The mixture of glue and pigment has to adhere to the fibres in the surface of the paper when it is hardened during exposure and at the same time must be able to be washed out during development in warm water. It follows that if you try to use the sort of shiny paper used in the making of coffee table books, where the fibres are encased in a layer of china clay, you will find it difficult to achieve a reasonable result. Similarly, if you use an absorbent, soft, fibrous paper, the emulsion will be difficult to wash out after exposure. You may also find that some pigments, green in particular, will stain the paper. In the latter case mix blue and yellow to make green. Developing the print in warm water will dissolve some of the sizing in the paper, especially if you do several coatings. It is therefore necessary to buy a paper which has a noticeable texture, not too smooth and with a relatively hard sizing. Fabriano, Bockingford, Saunders, Rives and Arches will all provide you with good choice of surfaces to work with.

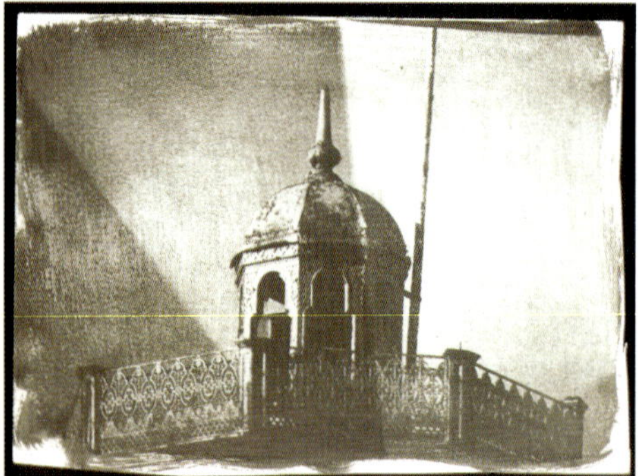

Test strip, blue and yellow watercolour to make green.

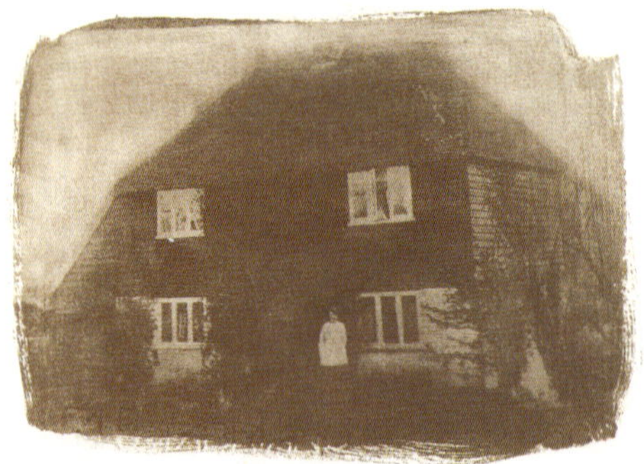

Gum print made with Frankfort black powder pigment. This mixture needs very delicate washing.

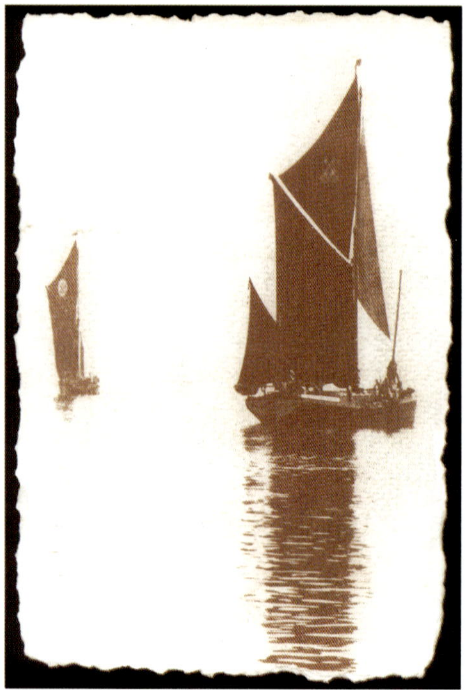

Gum print. Mid tone details in background on negative removed with Farmers reducer.

Some rough textured papers have a surface where the high points of the surface show through the emulsion after processing, which may not always be to your taste.

Some experimenting is obviously required. Please note that some decorative hand made Japanese papers have a habit of falling apart in the warm water!

Method

Here is a brief overview of the process.

Having made a mixture of glue, pigment and liquid dichromate solution, you brush this onto a piece of paper and dry it quickly. Expose it under a negative and then wash it in a dish of warm water until the image clears. Wash it briefly in cold water and hang it up to dry.

That's it, a simple gum print. The variations take a bit longer.

Mixing the chemicals and coating the paper should be carried out in tungsten room lighting or very subdued daylight. Avoid fluorescent light. Gum is much more light sensitive than all the other sensitisers.

First, make up your dichromate sensitiser.

Water	100ml
Potassium dichromate	5 g

Pour this into a small brown glass bottle. It will last for ages. It will dissolve more quickly if you screw the top on and shake it. You can, if you wish, place the bottle in a jar of warm water (40° C) to make sure it dissolves completely. Into a flat saucer or small plate squeeze out from a tube a small amount of water colour about the size of a pea. Add to this a 5ml spoonful of liquid glue, (Gloy works as well as any). Mix them together with a plastic palette knife. They may coagulate into a rubbery mess. Don't worry, this is natural. Then add a 5 ml spoonful of the dichromate mixture and mix together thoroughly. The bright orange of the dichromate will change the colour of mix dramatically. Don't panic. This orange will wash out in the development, and your emulsion will revert to its original colour. Brush the mixture onto a piece of paper covering an area slightly larger than your chosen image size. Then coat a small strip of the same paper. This will be your test strip. When you brush on the coating, do it quickly and fairly thickly, as it goes tacky in a very short time. When you have covered the paper, lay off the coating with firm strokes in stripes, first horizontally then vertically. Then finish off by feathering lightly with the brush so that all the streaky brush strokes disappear, and an even coating remains. Now dry the paper bone dry with a hair drier or a small fan heater.

Then we make a conventional test strip. Place the negative and test strip in your printing frame, (see exposure). Expose in the light covering a quarter of the strip at a time. In sunlight total exposure may only be about a minute or so. Under a UV lamp it may be up to four or five minutes. Make your test strip with these times in mind.

Remove the print from the frame. It does not print out as salt and

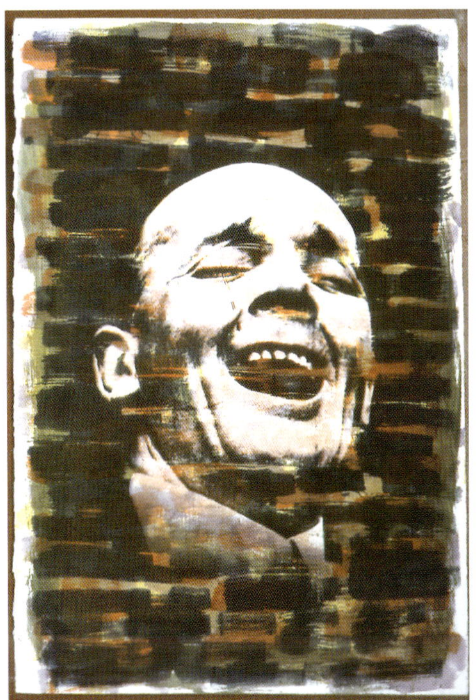

Multi-colour gum print using different colours laid on in blocks and printed with the negative kept in registration.

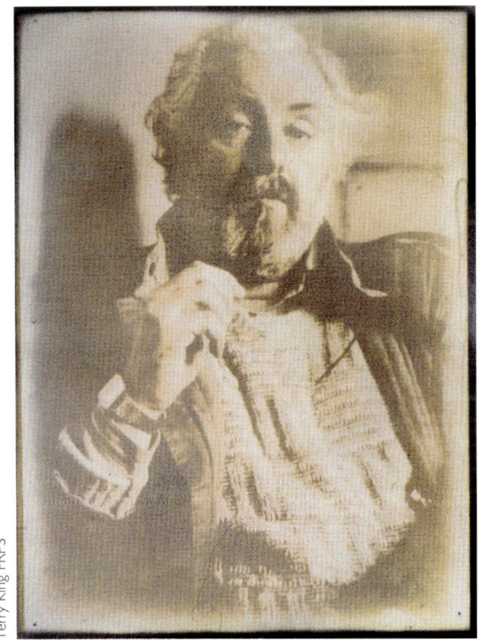

Terry King FRPS

Randall Webb, portrait. Gum print 16 x 20", printed from 35mm negative, using two paper negatives exposed for different times to give separation effect.

kallitype prints do, but you should make out a faint image on the coating of the paper. The strip must now be 'developed'. Take a developing dish of warm water, which should be warm enough to wash your hands in, but not hot enough to be uncomfortable. Immerse the strip in the water and rock the dish gently. In a few minutes the image will start to appear as the unhardened gum and pigment coating lift off the paper. The orange dichromate will also leave the paper revealing your image in the colour that you mixed originally. As the water becomes discoloured by the chemicals, replace it with more at the same temperature. If you are impatient for a result you may speed up this part of the process by either swabbing the paper gently with a soft brush, or in the classic tradition, slowly pouring warm water on to the emulsion to clear the image. Certain persons we are reluctant to name have been known to attack a stubborn gum print with a pot scourer. A means we would not advise except in extreme circumstances.

When all the gum and pigment appear to have been removed place the strip in a dish of cold water for a minute or two. Then hang up to drain and dry. You can heat dry it without any ill effects. Now you can assess the test strip. If it contains just a block of colour with no details you have overexposed it. Try again by halving the exposures. If it is thin almost to the point of clear paper you have underexposed. Try doubling the time. You may find that your first attempt at gum printing may be a little disappointing, as your image does not have the same depth and punch as, say, a platinum or a salt print. This is a normal reaction. But then it is a different process and much of its appeal is its delicate water colour effect. Watercolours are transparent and when applied to paper give a translucent glow to the picture. Poster colours or gouache are more opaque and give a much bolder look. If you want deeper tones and more contrast using water colours you will need move onto multiple printing.

Make your first print with a pale colour, such as yellow, grey or pale red. The less pigment you mix with the gum the paler your colour. Make your print and wait for it to dry. Now using the technique for multiple printing in the section on exposure, coat it with a darker colour and expose, wash and dry. This time make the exposure less (a half or third less than the first). Now only the shadow area will harden in the light, and where the highlights have washed off, the original colour will show through. You will now have more overall contrast and more details in the shadows. There are some pitfalls, however. Repeated soakings of the paper in warm water will quickly wash out the gelatin sizing built in to the paper. As the sizing washes out of the paper, subsequent coatings of gum and pigment adhere to the now absorbent paper particularly in the highlights, giving the visual effect of solarisation. There are two ways of getting round the problem. First find from your paper supplier a paper which is well sized, and able to resist the rigours of multiple printing and soaking. Alternatively, coat the paper between each printing with your own home made sizing solution, (see salt printing for details of sizing paper).

Taking this precaution will make the paper that much more waterproof, and allow successive gum coatings to be applied without staining the otherwise soft paper.

Retouching

As the end result is pretty coarse it doesn't matter too much if there are a few spots on it. If you want to retouch, then use a spotting brush and the appropriate water colour or dig around with a scalpel. Present it behind a window mount but please avoid the urge to use a lurid coloured matt.

A note of caution; Gum printing engenders in its followers a certain amount of obsessive behaviour. Not only do they suffer from the delusion that they may be 'artists' but they are given to long and tedious bouts of making tests. Tests on the mixing of colours, tests on the transparency of colour, exposure times, strength of the dichromate mixture etc. There appears to be no long term cure for this. After all it is only another printing process and probably works best when done instinctively rather than as a controlled scientific routine. Time spent making tests is time wasted which could be better spent making pictures.

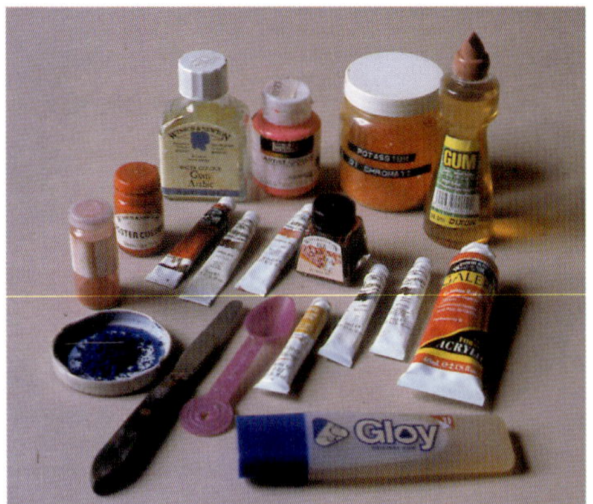

Gum printing materials.

Experiments with lino

A. Wainwright, who wrote a series of guides to the Lake District, once left 12 pence under a stone on a lonely peak in the hope that some walker would find it and buy fish and chips with it. On the afternoon of the day the book was published someone rang the publisher saying he had found the money. We have no wish to repeat that experience, but we will give some clues on the subject of lino cuts with which some enterprising reader can become famous or rich or both.

As far as we know there is no such thing as a photo-lino cut, but the picture on page 117 is half way to being one. We took a piece of lino for lino printing (buy at any art shop) and coated it with a gum mix. Any colour will do. We then printed a graphic image from a lith negative onto the lino and processed it. When it was dry we cut out the plain parts of the lino not covered by the gum image, so that image stood out in relief from the rest. We then took it to the local art school and printed it in their press on Fabriano paper. The main point to notice is that the more detailed the image, the more cutting you have to do. Lino cutting tools are on sale at most art shops.

To take it one stage further, you could etch the lino. Instead off cutting the lino, you spray the gum coated surface with oven cleaner foam. This eats away the uncovered lino in the same way as acid etches zinc plates. Making sure the gum doesn't lift off may be a problem.

If it is, try substituting gum with a carbon print.

Incidentally, this etching effect was discovered by a print maker who was cleaning his wife's oven and spilt some foam on the lino floor.

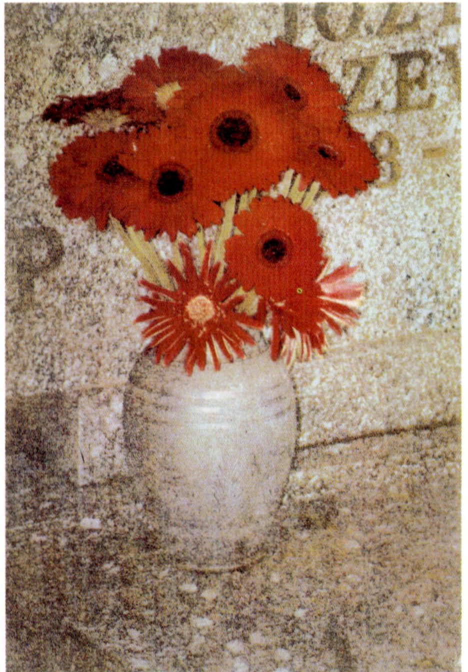

Temperaprint

This modern printing method, devised by Peter Frederick, is another process in which the light sensitivity of the versatile dichromate chemistry is employed. Ammonium dichromate solution is mixed with a binder comprising beaten whole egg. Pigments, which can be chosen from a wide range, are then added. The sensitiser is then applied to paper. After exposure to sunlight or UV light, the print is developed by removing unhardened solution with a soft brush in water at room temperature.

The process is particularly suited to multiple coating, although this requires a dimensionally stable paper base is - Peter Frederick recommends 'Synteape' a spun polyester material.

Casein printing 22

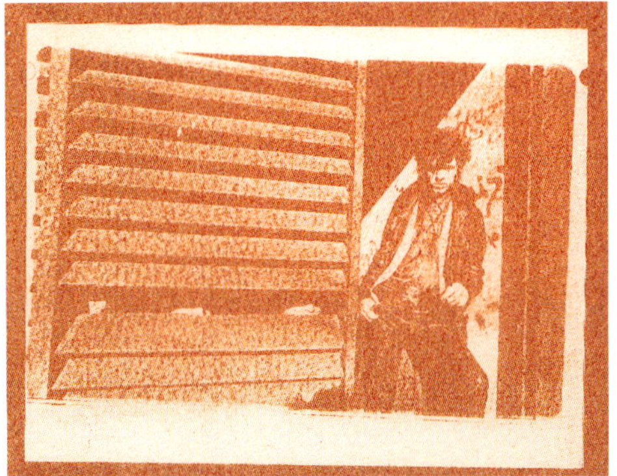

Casein print. This proves that if you use an opaque paint, such as poster paint, it is possible to get rich colours with the casein process.

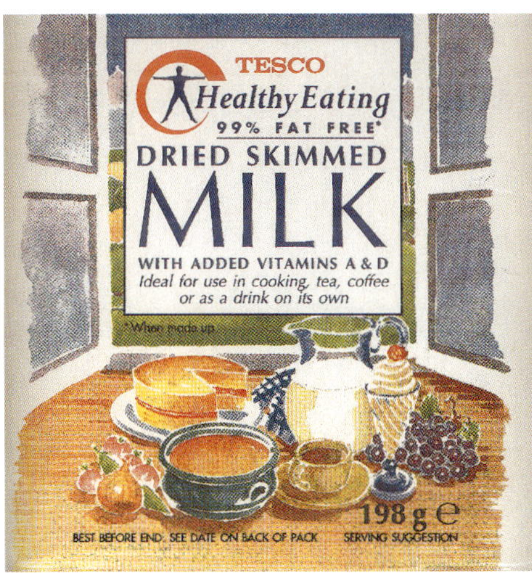

Powdered milk.

One description of casein is: principal albuminous constituent of milk, in which it is found as a calcium salt, obtainable by curdling. From this we can safely infer that curdled milk contains similar substances to those found in egg white. Its only use as far as we are concerned is as a substitute for the gum or glue in making gum prints. Its use was patented in 1908 for photo-printmaking but appears to have been neglected ever since. Making a casein print is exactly the same as making a gum print with one difference. We curdle milk to make the gum, which we then mix as usual with dichromate and pigment.

Advantages

It enables you to say to your friends 'Would you care to see my latest photos which I have just printed with cottage cheese?'
It produces prints with a range of pale delicate tones. If you are into misty watercolours this is the technique for you.

Disadvantages

None really, unless you are allergic to curd cheese. It also takes longer than pouring glue out of a bottle.

Shopping list

(In addition to the one you need for gum printing).
Instant powdered milk (from any supermarket).
Acetic acid (10%) or lemon juice.
Small pudding basin.
Piece of muslin or cheese cloth about 24 inches by 12 inches.
Ammonia (from hardware store).

Making the casein mixture

Mix; 30 grams instant powdered milk in 200 ml hot water (about 60° C). Stir until dissolved and add a few drops of stop bath, acetic acid or lemon juice to make the milk curdle.
When it curdles the white cheese solidifies and separates from the liquid or whey. Now fold the muslin in half to make a 12 inch square and place it over the basin. Carefully strain the curd mixture through the muslin, letting the liquid whey drain into the bowl. Wrap the muslin round the ball of curd and squeeze it to remove any remaining liquid. Empty the whey from the basin and crumble the curd into the empty basin with your fingers.

Take 20 mls water and place **5 drops** of ammonia into it. Slowly mix this into the curd, stirring with a pallete knife until it is like thick cream. Now use this in place of glue to make a normal gum print, as detailed in [21 . Gum printing].

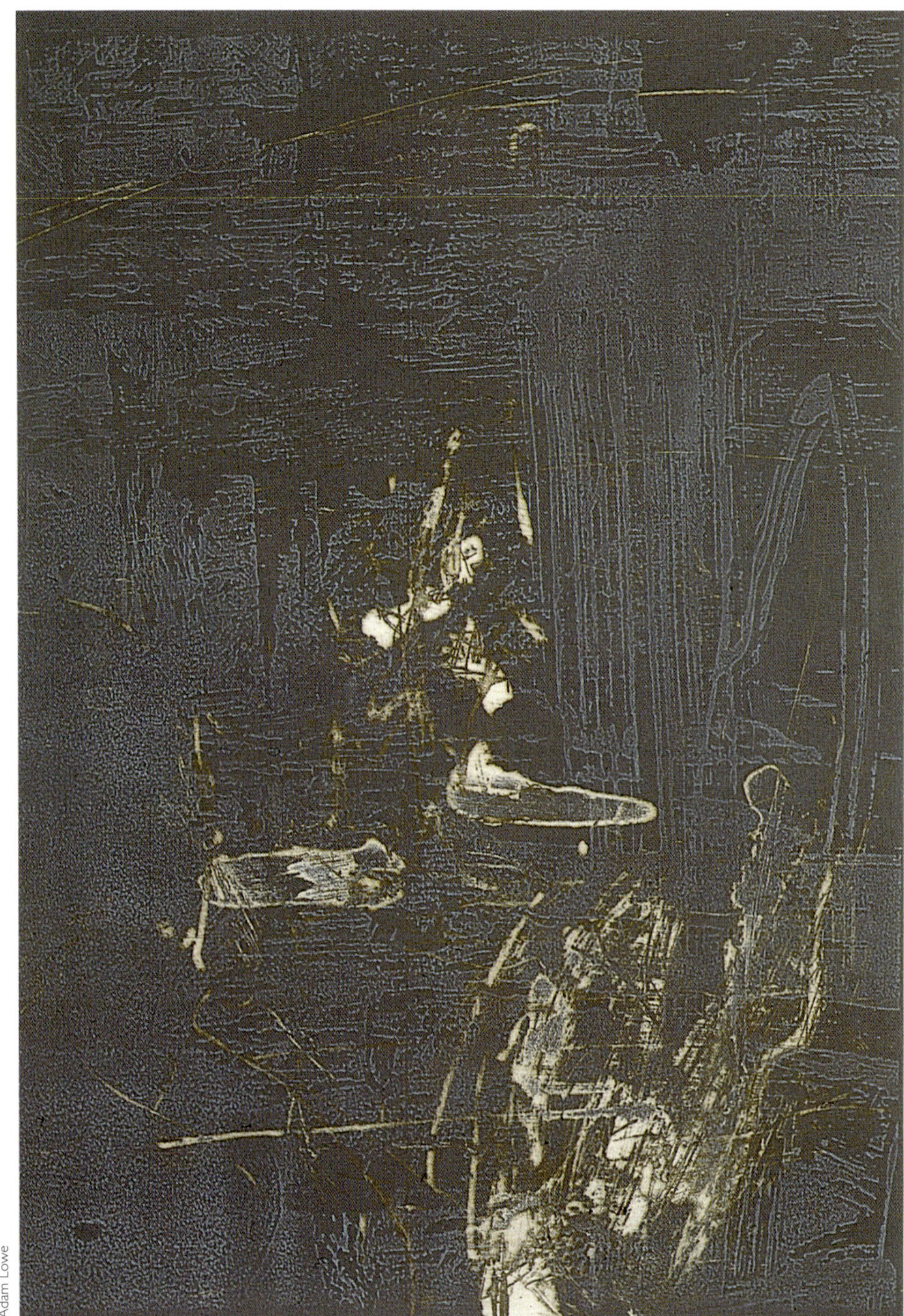

Adam Lowe

Registration Marks VI 1992
Photogravure and etching, 420 x 290mm, from a portfolio of 6 prints published by The Print Centre. The photogravure was made from both photographic and hand-drawn information on Mylar film.

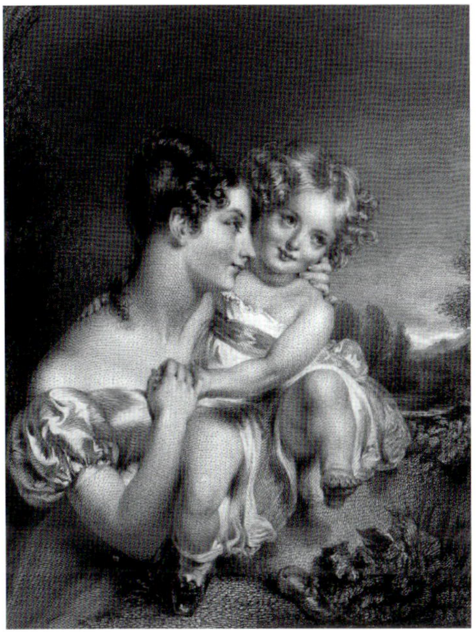

A 19'th century print, engraved by hand on a copper plate. This was capable of a wide range of tones and details and was produced by a highly skilled craftsman.

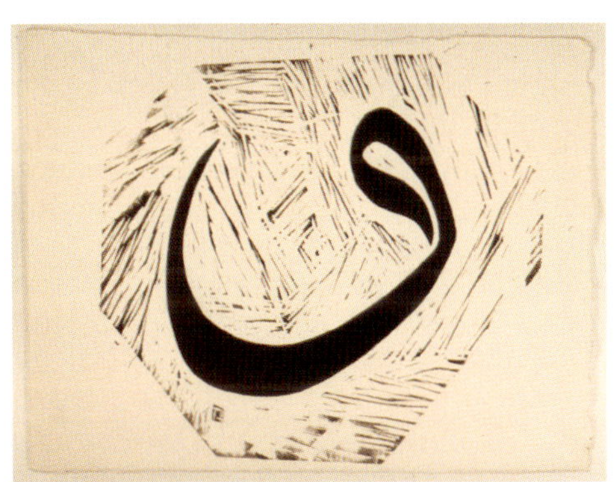

A relief print on lino. The image was printed in gum on the lino and cut by hand. The lino cutting marks are also visible round the image. See chapter 21.

Photo etching, photogravure & photo silk-screen

These last three processes are written from a different standpoint from the others in this manual.

We make the assumption that you have already had, or intend to have, access to a printing studio and some experience of using etching presses and silk screen printing methods.

Alternatively, you intend to learn these methods in parallel with traditional photographic printing.

Or, finally, you may be involved in fine art printing and wish to incorporate photographic images into your work.

In any case it is impractical to teach the disciplines of strictly non-photographic skills within the confines of a manual of this sort.

The use of metal printing plates, etching, aquatinting, stopping out, adjusting the press and mixing inks are all learnt by hands-on experience under the supervision of a skilled printer in a studio environment.

For these reasons these sections will deal only with the photographic applications of the process. We can show you how to put a photographic image on a plate or silk screen. Thereafter you will have to continue the process using the traditional skills available in a print studio.

We feel that the inclusion of these processes is valid, not only because they offer a very interesting and different means of presenting an image, but also because they played a very crucial part in the development of photography from its earliest beginnings.

Niepce, Daguerre and Fox Talbot all used metal plates in their experiments with photography, which in turn allowed multiple reproductions of photographs to be made from the original source material.

Types of printing using a press

Relief printing

This is a method whereby a design is cut - usually on wood or lino - so that it stands up in relief above the surface of the plate. This design is covered in ink and pressed onto a sheet of paper to make a print. Making a photographic based image by this means has not been thoroughly investigated. However, the accompanying illustration shows a photo-lino cut made partly by photographic means and partly by the tried and trusted method of cutting out the lino with a sharp knife. If you want to make a name for yourself, try some experiments with photo lino as sketched in at the end of chap 21.

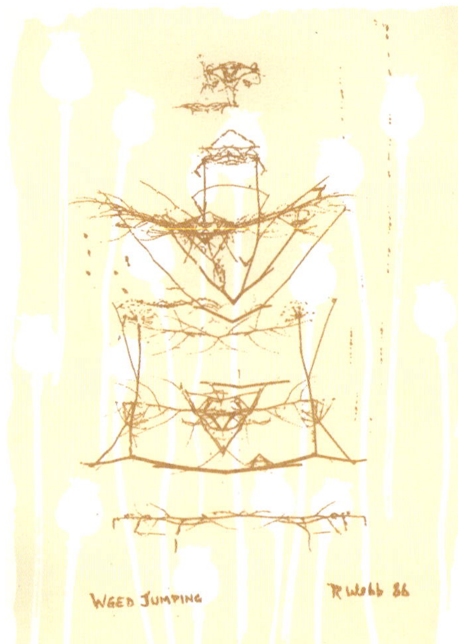

Weed Jumping Photo silk screen. When viewed sideways it is apparent that the weeds are a reflection in water.

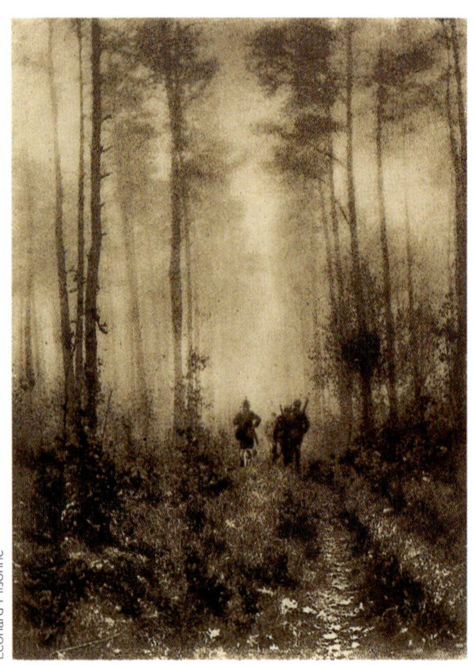
Leonard Misonne

Gravure book illustration from the 1920's.

Intaglio printing

This process covers engraving, etching and photogravure. In engraving a design is scratched on metal plate - usually copper - with a point or needle and then ink is rubbed into the lines made by the needle. The plate is pressed onto a sheet of paper so that the ink is transferred onto it, thus making the print. Again there is no photographic application for this method.

In etching a steel or zinc plate is covered with an acid resisting coating - usually dark varnish - and a design scratched through it with a needle.

The plate is then immersed in acid, and where the plate is exposed by the needle, the acid eats away the plate, leaving the image as a series of indentations on the plate. The varnish is cleaned from the plate, ink is rubbed into the indentations, and the plate pressed onto a sheet of paper resulting in the transfer of the ink to make a print.

The use of etching dates back to the Middle Ages when it was used to make complex designs on suits of armour. From this it was only a small step to inking a flat sheet of metal and printing on paper.

Photo etching uses this basic technique, the difference being that the acid resistant coating is light sensitive, and can be exposed under a photographic positive and developed in acetone.

The characteristics of the plate make it possible to print only pure blacks or whites as on lith film.

Photogravure is a similar process, but uses a sheet of copper covered with a photographic image made on pigmented gelatin as in carbon printing, [19 . Carbon printing]. The etching is carried out using ferric chloride instead of the usual nitric acid in photo etching. With this process you can achieve a full range of continuous tones.

Planographic printing

This is neither intaglio nor relief printing. The image is inked onto the flat surface of a block of polished stone or on a specially prepared metal plate and then pressed onto paper in a press designed purely for that purpose. The supply of stone for use in lithography has now dried up and the limited availability of lithographic presses make the process impractical for photographic purposes.

Photo silk screen printing is also a planographic process. For this, a stencil is made from a photographic image and pressed onto a fine mesh screen. This is placed onto a sheet of paper and ink is pressed through the holes with a rubber squeegee, making the image.

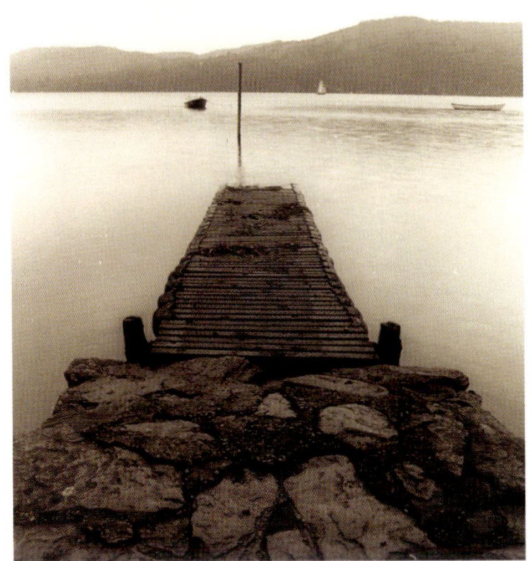

Lake Windermere - straight proof on resin coated paper, from which the etching below was taken.

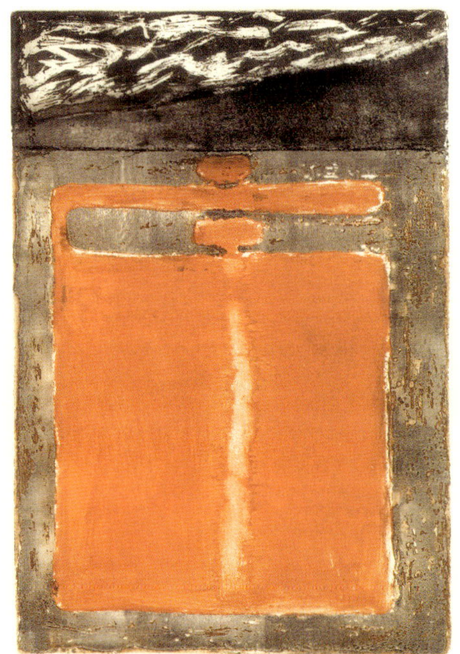

Photo etching from the image above. Only the mountains are recognisable. The plate was given a series of immersions in the acid, and masked in various places with stopout varnish. The pale streak was made by rubbing the inked plate with a finger dipped in white spirit. Influenced by the work of Joseph Beuys.

As we have said before, the idea of placing a photographic image on a metal plate and subsequently printing it, set the parameters for photographic printing from the earliest times to the present.

However, it was not until the end of the 19'th century that photo etching was used seriously.

The use of the half tone screen to make a plate made the reproduction of photographs in books, magazines, and newspapers a viable proposition. By breaking up the photographic image into a series of fine dots it was possible to produce a print with the appearance of a continuous tone image. If you look at a newspaper picture with a magnifying glass you can see the effect.

Magazine illustrations before the mid-1880's were all hand drawn engravings made by artists copying photographs. The use of half tone illustrations led to an enormous increase in the productions of cheap magazines and newspapers. One consequence of this was that many engravers went out of business or had to quickly learn the skills of photographic etching plate making. A similar complaint is now heard from photographers who claim they are losing business through the introduction of computerised digital imaging.

Most magazines and other printed matter are now printed using roto-gravure, where a continuously revolving copper drum is etched and coated with ink in four colours - red, blue, yellow and black, one over the other in a very large and complex press. The etching is now carried out by laser using signals from a computer, so now even photo etching is fast becoming an old technology.

Advantages

Each print you make is a 'one-off' as each inking of the plate is marginally different from the previous one.

However, if you print from the same plate a series of images, these can be numbered and presented as a 'limited edition', which in theory at least, makes each one more valuable, [31 . Presentation.]

The prints are permanent as they are made with ink rather than light sensitive chemicals.

Because they are made with ink and show a slight relief effect on the paper, they have a very distinct physical presence compared with the other processes.

The impression made by the edge of the plate around the outside of the image gives it a characteristic etching appearance, see p.124. This is known as the plate mark, and distinguishes it from other forms of printmaking.

They are capable of an enormous degree of manipulation, both in the photographic part and in the subsequent working of the plate. Once you have acquired the basic skills you can experiment by working on the plate to obtain some very different effects from the ones you are used to.

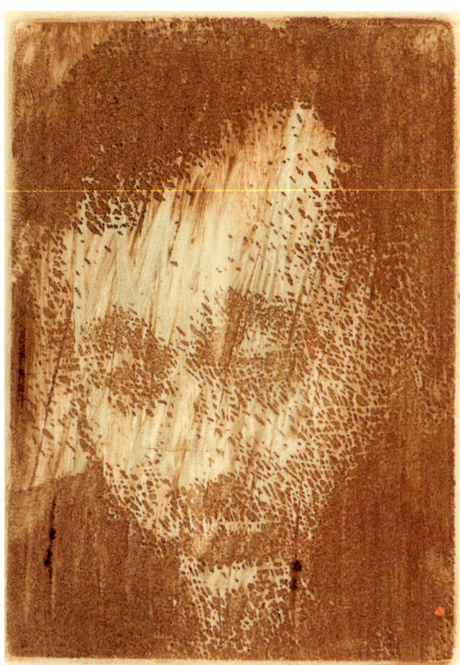

Dave. The lith positive for this plate was broken up into crude half tone by a letratone screen. After inking, the plate was smudged with a matchstick.

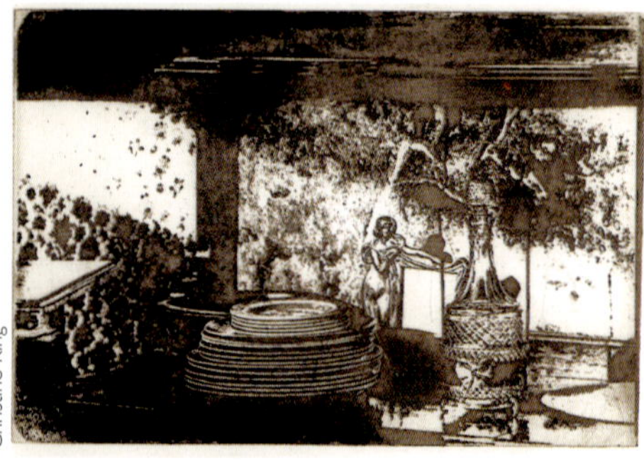

Christine King

Paris Adams. The lith positive for this plate was not manipulated and shows pure black and white.

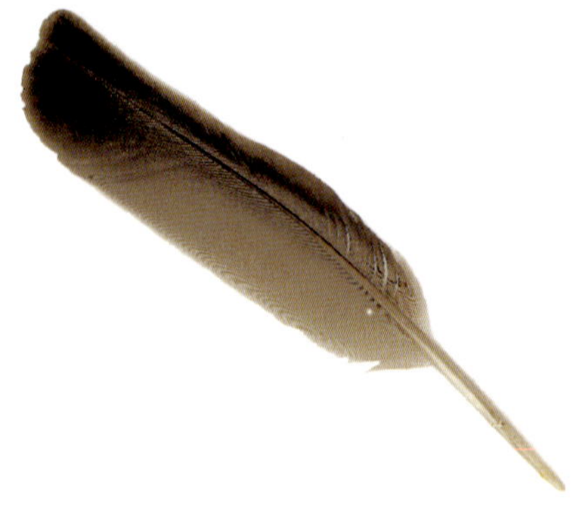

You can, if you wish, use a number of different coloured inks on the same plate to give a multi coloured result.

Once you have made your lith film positive it is surprisingly quick and easy to make a plate, (about 20 minutes is the average, although subsequent hand working on the plate can obviously take longer).

If you are a photographer you can suddenly join the ranks of the real art printers.

Disadvantages

When you buy a sheet of etching plate it has no instructions for use enclosed. This is a craft skill acquired after years of apprenticeship. When the writer first started to make etching plates he was referred by the makers to a man in Birmingham who gave him a few tips on the finer points of plate making!

You get ink all over your fingers and everything else in sight.

The plate developer smells of acetone and stains everything purple.

It takes quite a bit of experience to learn what sort of negative will translate into a good photo etching.

Photo etching used literally without much creative input will produce a print that looks much like a black and white photo on the front page of a daily newspaper.

Shopping List

Lith film 5 x 7" maximum to start with.

Lith developer.

Film fixer.

A sheet of **non reflecting picture glass** from a glass merchant or picture framer, (about 10 x 8").

2 or 3 sheets of **NEG JET zinc plate** 5 x 7" pre-cut. Make sure it is neg jet with a light sensitive coating and covered with a layer of black plastic. There is no way of telling just by looking at it. Double check with the supplier before you pay for it.

500ml of **NEG JET** developer.

500 ml of **10 per cent nitric acid** - don't get the concentrated version as it is unpleasant and corrosive.

A **feather** about 4 inches long - from a chicken or a pigeon - honestly!

A small bottle of **methylated spirits**.

A small bottle of **white spirit** and some **cotton wool**.

Two **developing dishes** slightly larger than your plate and which you can afford to mess up.

UV light source.

Rubber gloves.

The remaining materials you can obtain from the printing studio.

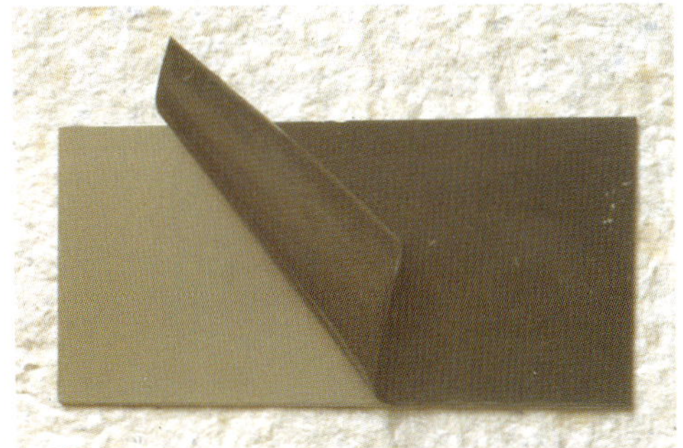

Peeling back the black plastic film from a Negjet plate before exposing.

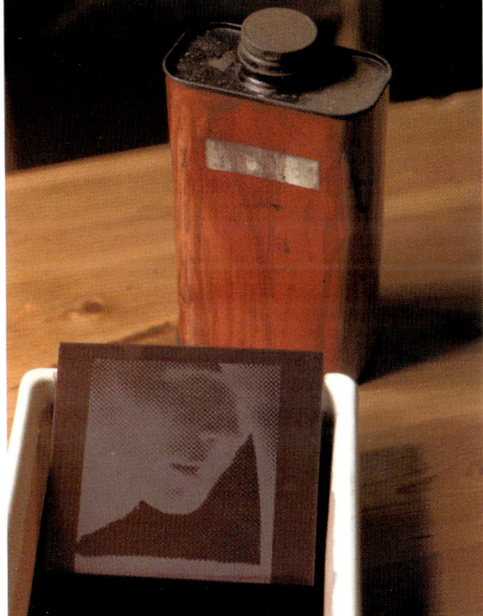

Negjet plate in dish after development. The purple developer stains everything it touches. Use gloves.

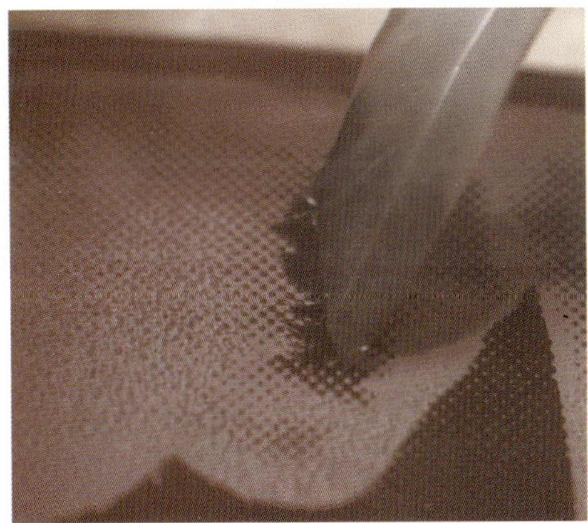

Bubbles on the surface of the plate caused by action of the acid on the zinc, being wiped away with a feather in the traditional manner.

Paper

Be advised by your printing studio. As a general rule use paper made specifically for etching. This is known as waterleaf which means it has little or no sizing in it, [5 . Paper].

Making the lith positive

Take a camera negative of your choice [9 . Negatives], and make a lith positive on lith film in the enlarger about a quarter of an inch smaller all round than the plate you intend to use.

Develop it in lith developer as per the instructions on the bottle.

Fix, wash and dry.

Take the neg jet plate and peel off the black plastic film on the front (not in bright daylight).

The front of the plate with the light sensitive coating is shiny metal and the back is dark green.

Place the film dull side down onto the shiny side of the plate, making sure the clear edge of the film makes an even border round the edge of the plate underneath. Trim with a knife and a ruler if necessary.

Keeping the film and plate in position, place them in a printing frame with the film on top of the plate under the glass and facing the light as you would with any contact print.

Expose in sunlight or UV lamp for about 5 minutes.

What happens at this stage is similar to gum printing. Where the light goes through the clear parts of the film it hardens the light sensitive coating on the plate. Where it cannot reach the plate through the dense part of the film the coating remains unhardened.

Using rubber gloves place the plate shiny side up in a dish containing the purple neg jet developer. Do this stage in a well ventilated area. Leave it in the dish, making sure it is well covered and rock the dish gently.

The hardened areas of the plate will turn purple and the unhardened parts will show through as bright metal.

Do not under any circumstances touch the surface of the plate. Although technically it is hardened, it is in fact still very delicate.

After it has been in the developer for five minutes, remove it carefully and tilt it slightly to let it drain for a few seconds then hold it horizontally under cold running tap water for **at least** 5 minutes.

It is now hard and safe to touch. Carefully dab off any surface water with a kitchen towel and put it aside while you put out the acid.

Pour enough 10 per cent nitric acid into a clean dish to cover the plate adequately and immerse the plate in it purple side up. (use rubber gloves). After a minute or so you will see small air bubbles rising from the clear areas of the plate as the acid bites into the zinc.

Now take the feather and gently brush away the bubbles with its soft edge. Continue this for about five minutes.

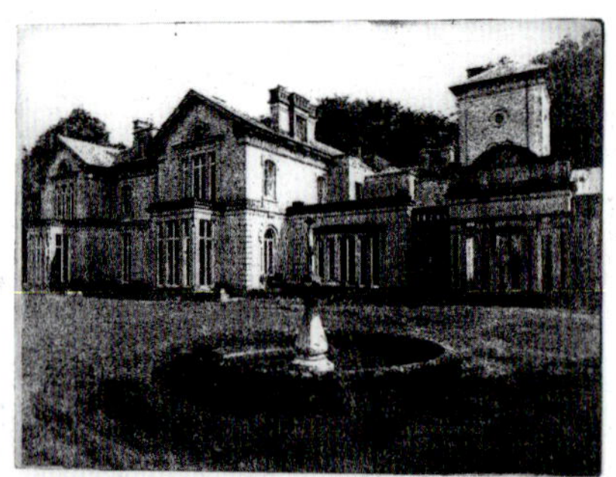

Country house, Cumbria. The lith positive was broken up into half tone by using non-reflecting picture glass on the enlarger baseboard. This has had the effect of maintaining fine details in the building and the long grass.

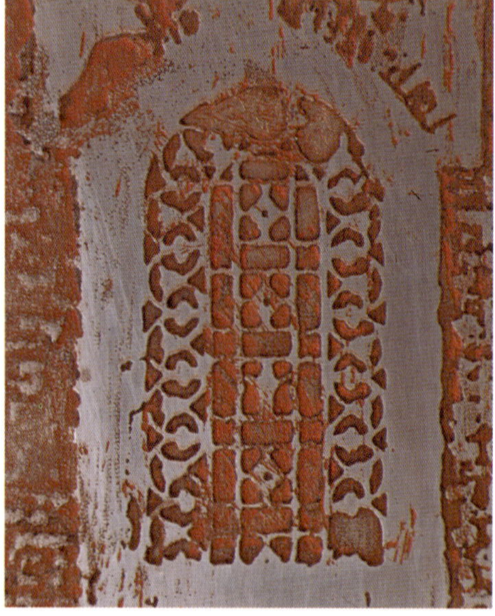

Close-up of etched plate, showing residual ink left after printing.

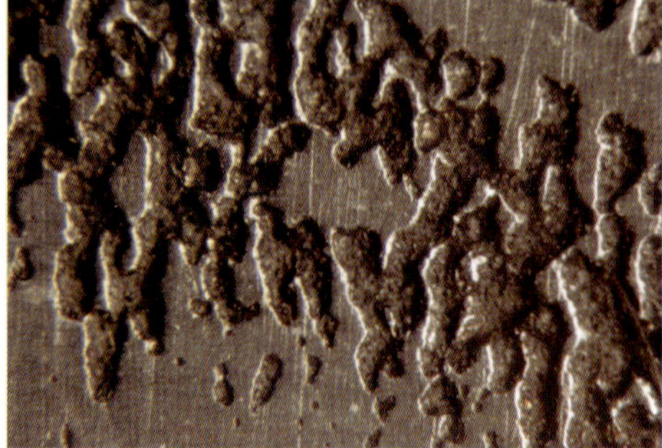

Extreme close-up, through microscope of the surface of an etched plate. Care must be taken that the acid does not undercut raised portions of the plate so that they become detached during printing.

Still wearing the gloves, take out the plate and rinse it in cold water.

Now look at the plate through a magnifying glass. You will see the image as indentations shining silver under the purple coating.

Only experience will tell you how long to leave it in the acid but another 5 or 7 minutes should be enough. It is better at this stage to give it too much than too little.

Rinse the plate in cold water and dry with a kitchen towel.

Now you are ready to take it to the studio, ink it and pull your first proof. There are several things that you should know in order to pass them on to whoever is supervising your printing.

1 Large areas of shiny plate will not be rough enough to hold the ink when it is rubbed on it, and will consequently give the appearance of solarisation. This can be cured by the normal process of aquatinting and replacing in the acid.

2 Do not be tempted to remove the purple coating until you have done all you need in working on the plate. You can print proofs quite easily with the purple in place.

3 You can use stop-out varnish in the usual way on top of the purple resist.

4 When you do need to clean it off prior to the final polishing, rub it off with a generous amount of methylated spirits on an old rag. It takes a little time but keep rubbing.

5 Before you put the plate through the press, you should file down its edges with a file and emery paper to form a smooth bevel. This will prevent the paper from being cut by the sharp edges of the metal.

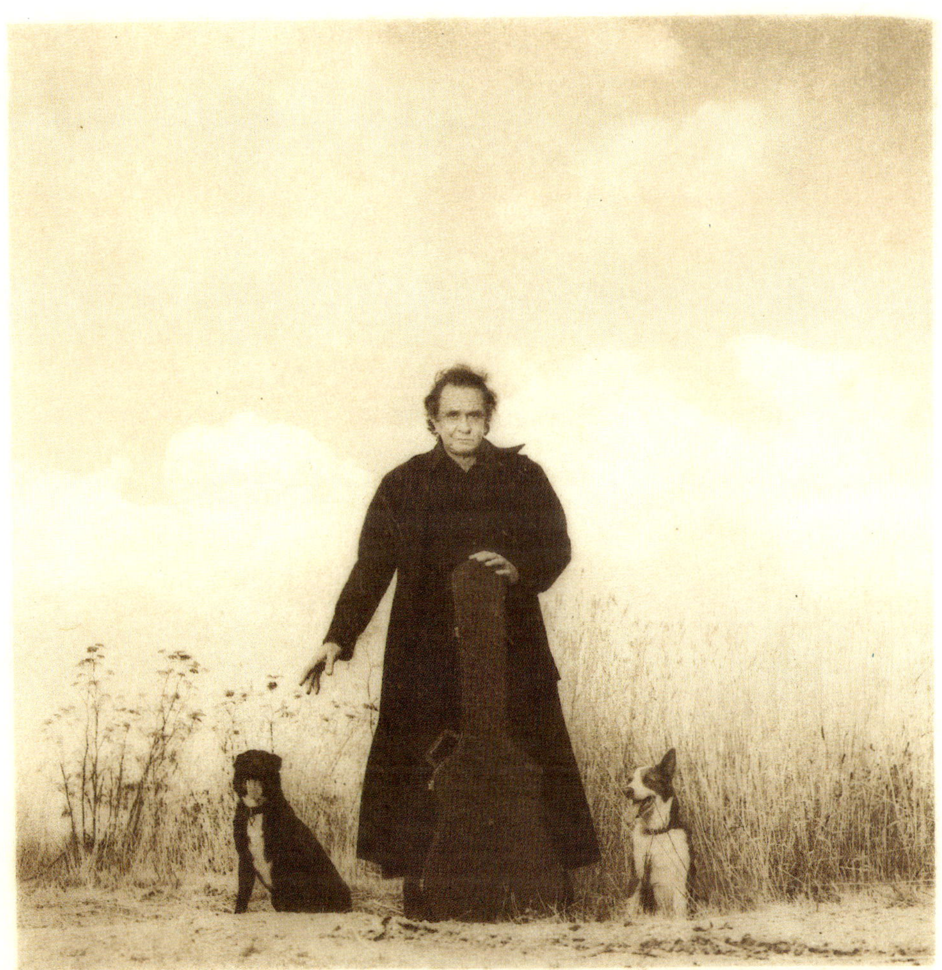

Andy Earl

Johnny Cash. Photogravure on fine Japanese tissue by Amanda Lane.

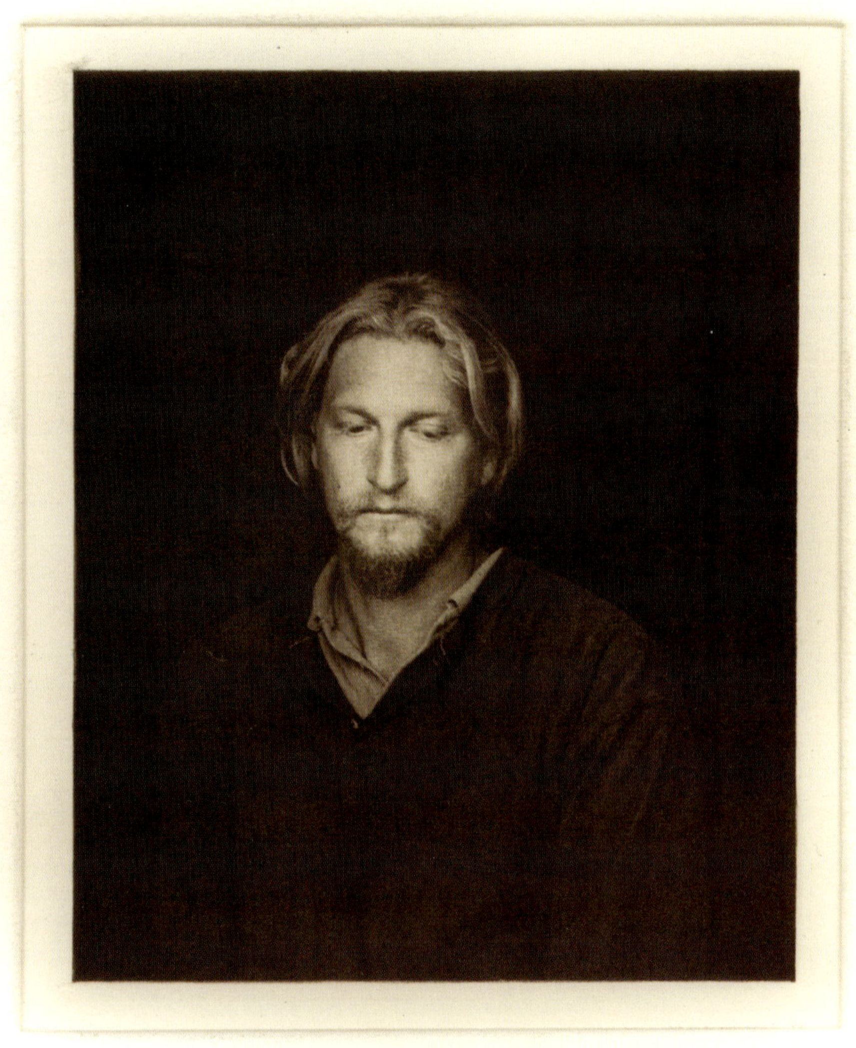

Amanda Lane

Alejandro. Photogravure by Amanda Lane on Hahnemuhle paper.

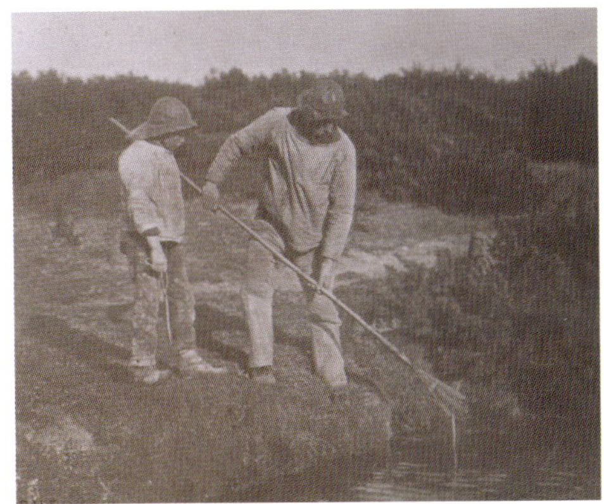

One of Emersons' series of photogravures depicting life in the Norfolk Broads at the end of the 19'th century. Authors collection (offers?).

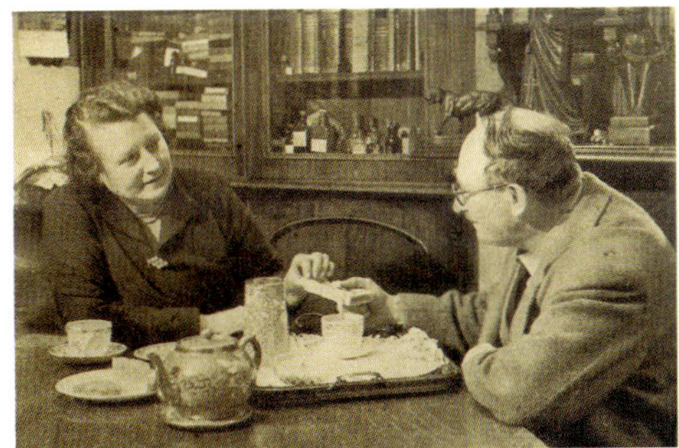

With best wishes
from
Fred + Tim Hawkins

Somewhat surreal greetings card in photogravure from the 1950's.

A few thoughts on the subject of photogravure.

Nobody has ever said that this process is easy. It involves two quite different disciplines and only one is photographic. The second needs the assistance of a qualified printmaker to oversee the inking and printing of the copper plate.

Photogravure originated as a way of reproducing photographs on the printed page. It gives a far superior result to that of the universal half-tone process. It has now been superseded by Duotone and the highly mechanised Rotogravure method.

When it started to be used as a means of making a high quality print on hand made papers at the beginning of the 20th century, it was embraced by the art photography movements.

In the same way that they seized upon gum printing and bromoil as being closer to the old masters than mere camera operators, so did photogravure become the medium for the serious photographer. The fact that it could be issued in the form of a limited edition added to its appeal. At the turn of the century there were large numbers of plate makers and printing studios capable of producing editions on behalf of photographers. Emerson, Stieglitz and many others made editions of their work. It is interesting to see that in the modern auctioneers' catalogues platinum prints tend to realise higher prices than photogravures. This is somewhat ironic as photogravure was always regarded as being very close in its colours and tonalities to platinum. It is possible that the production of limited editions has depressed the prices at auction.

Now, at the end of the 20'th century there are only few skilled plate makers left in the world and if this chapter can persuade just a few people to revive the art of photogravure printing as a fine art, then it will have been justified.

In recent times we have seen two interesting editions of photogravures by well known names. The first was a portfolio by Lee Friedlander on the subject of cherry blossoms in Japan. The brilliance and quality of the light in these prints was outstanding. The fact that the subject matter was outside the usual streetwise urban landscapes that we have come to expect from him made them a valid parallel to his normal work, and more exciting to view.

The second portfolio was by Fay Godwin. They were on good paper and well presented. They looked 'different' from her usual black and white work, but did not have the same silky textures and tonalities and the depth of meaning of her best documentary images.

The moral of this may be that if you establish your own particular photographic aesthetic it may be unwise to play about with it just for the sake of using another process. (If Friedlander ever produces an edition of gravures showing his usual street scenes we may have to revise our opinions).

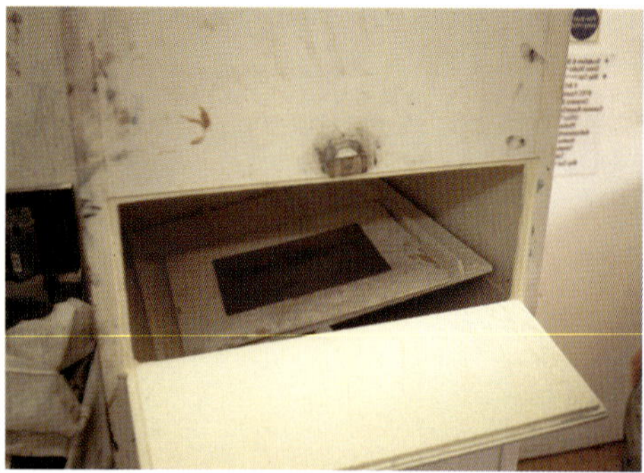

Copper plate in the resin dusting box, ready for the dusting process.

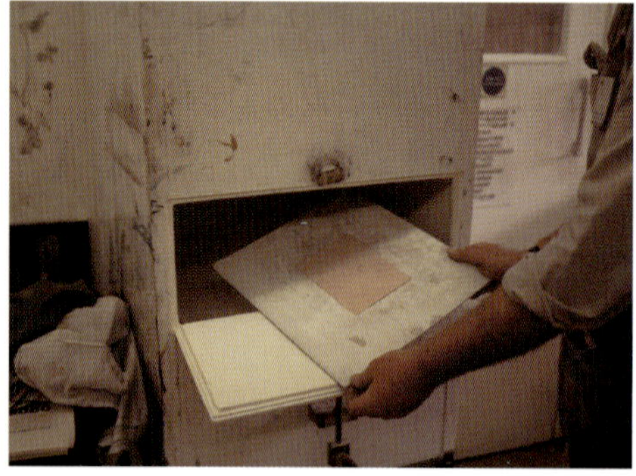

The copper plate being removed from the dusting box. It is now covered in a fine film of resin dust. It is then heated to melt the resin to give an overall grain effect.

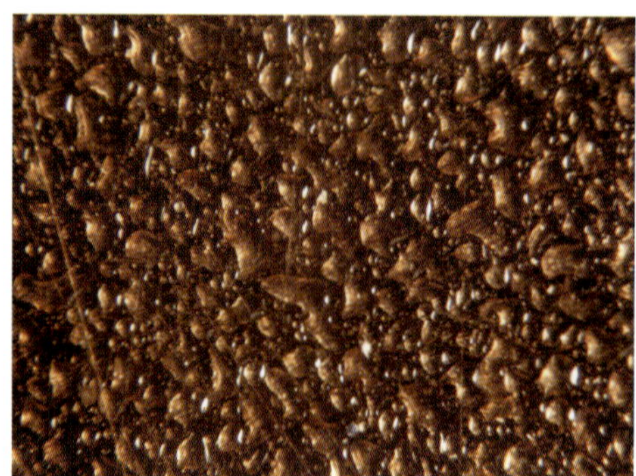

Extreme close-up of the surface of the copper plate after the resin dust has melted and hardened on the surface.

Now.... if you still feel that you want to persist with the process and we haven't put you off for ever, then here it is.

One final note: the method used to place the acid resistant coating on the copper plate is the same as that for making a carbon print, with the one difference that instead of laying down the carbon tissue on paper you put it on a sheet of copper. So if you familiarise yourself with making carbon prints first, you will find making gravure plates that much easier.

Advantages

The image is formed with ink and is as permanent as the paper it is printed on.

As it is printed with ink it has a physical presence that other processes do not.

When properly done it has soft and subtle tonalities.

It has the embossed impression of the plate surrounding the image which like photo-etching, distinguishes it from straight photographic printing.

You can make a legitimate limited edition, [31 . Presentation].

You can print on good quality handmade paper.

You may even imagine you are an artist.

Disadvantages

A photogravure is nothing more than a mechanical reproduction and at first sight looks much like any other black and white silver gelatin print on the printed page. Traditionally it is always presented as such.

It therefore has not lent itself to any manipulation or colour variations as have photo etchings and photo silk screens. This should not deter you from experimenting with colours. However, be careful if you decide to tamper with the final etched plate. On the other hand, there ain't no rules.

The making and printing of gravure plates is a highly developed craft skill and you must expect many false starts and wasted sheets of copper before you can begin to get it right.

Dogged persistence and careful attention to detail are the qualities most needed by a gravure printer.

As in all things photographic, Sod's law works in a mysterious way - especially in the case of gravure.

Shopping list

This list is identical to the one used for carbon printing with the following additions.

Two or three sheets of **copper plate** 5 x 7". Most print departments of colleges or evening class centre will sell them. They usually have a guillotine to cut them to size. Otherwise buy them from specialised art suppliers. [33 . Suppliers]. Make sure the copper surface contains no scratches or pitted marks.

Ferric chloride (see method).

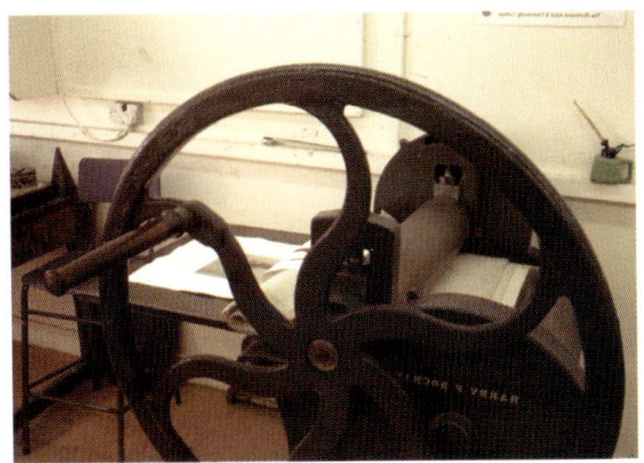

Modern etching press, used for photo etching and photo gravure. Not suitable for lino cuts!

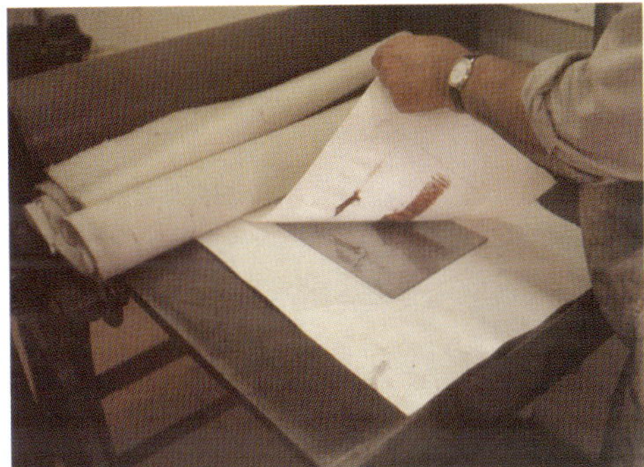

Print being removed from press after printing.

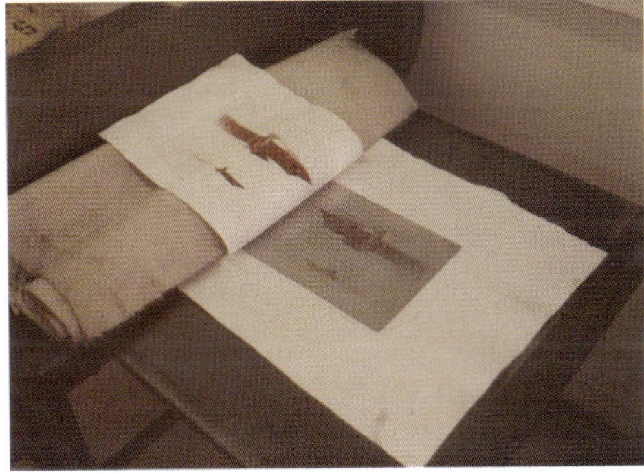

The plate rests on a piece of blotter, or newsprint, which itself rests on the bed of the press. The paper covers the plate, and this is covered by two blankets, which when passed through the heavy rollers force the dampened paper into the indentations in the plate, thus pulling the ink into the paper surface. This illustration shows the blankets rolled back.

In addition to your usual dishes you will need **four dishes** a little larger than your copper plates for the etching baths.

A **hygrometer and a glass jar** to measure the specific gravity of the etching baths, (see method and suppliers).

A pair of **rubber gloves**.

Four 500 ml **screw top plastic bottles** to store the etching baths, a small tin of Brasso and some soft cloth.

Method

Photogravure differs from photo etching in several ways.

It is done on copper plate rather than zinc. The plate has to be covered with a grain - fine particles of resin dust which are melted on the plate to form a rough surface. The resist coating is exposed and developed before it is laid on the plate, as opposed to etching where the resist is pre-coated by the manufacturer and exposed in situ on the plate and developed. The line film image you use to make the resist is a positive, but containing a full range of continuous tones instead of the black and white lith image used for etching. The etching bath is ferric chloride as opposed to nitric acid.

To summarise, this is what happens;

You make what is in effect a carbon print, but instead of placing the carbon image on a sheet of paper you place it on a sheet of copper. When it is dry it is immersed in baths of ferric chloride of varying strengths. The liquid bath softens the gelatin coating and allows the ferric chloride to penetrate through to the copper in order to bite into the surface. The ferric chloride bites deeper into the plate where it goes through the light areas of the image, and less deeply through the dark areas. Thus, when the plate is inked, more ink adheres to the plate in the deeply bitten parts and less in the lightly bitten parts. When it is passed through the press you have varying depths of ink transferring to the paper giving you a continuous tone image.

Preparing the plate

Take a sheet of copper - it is usually supplied with a sheet of clear plastic adhering to the front - and peel off the plastic.

Now polish it with Brasso on a soft piece of cloth. Polish it until it shines like a mirror. This could take some time! Fifteen minutes is probably not long enough. When it is really shiny finish off with a clean soft rag and wash it under hot running water. Do not touch the surface with your fingers. Wrap it in a sheet of clean tissue.

Now the plate has to be grained in an aquatint box. This consists of a large wooden box containing fine resin dust and is standard equipment in all etching studios. A few vigorous turns on the handle on the side of the box stirs up the dust inside to a fine cloud.

Place the plate - shiny side up - on a piece of ply or hardboard (there is one in the box) in a slot in the box and close the lid. After two or three

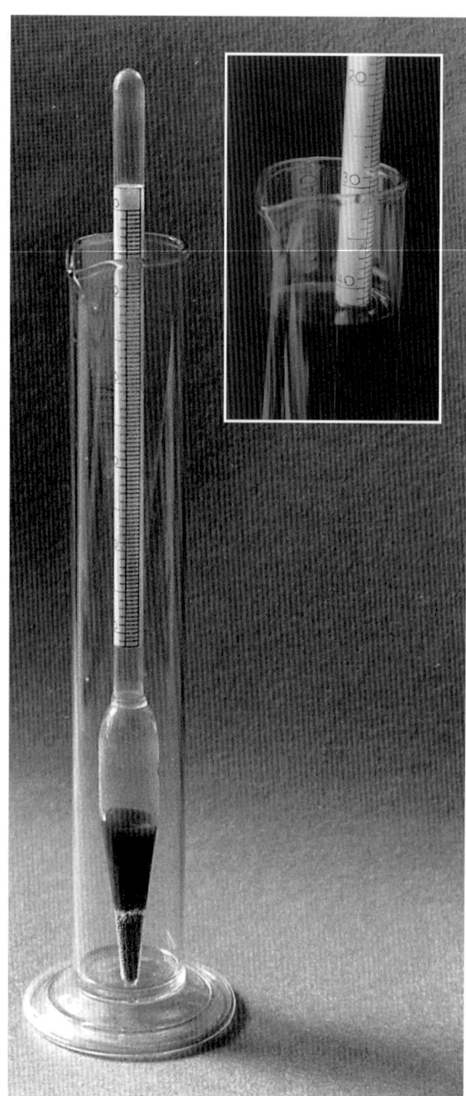

Hydrometer in jar for measuring specific gravity of ferric chloride etching bath in degrees baume. Inset - hydrometer breaking the surface of the ferric chloride solution in the measuring jar. This is showing a specific gravity close to 42 Baume.

minutes open the lid and you will see your plate covered with a fine layer of white dust. Remove the board and the plate carefully, and (without sneezing or touching the surface of the plate) slide a wooden handled metal spatula under the plate and hold it over a heater. In most studios this is an electric ring for boiling kettles.

As the copper gets hot the fine particles of resin melt with a slight whiff of smoke and the surface of the plate reverts to a shiny surface with the appearance of fine sandpaper. Do not over-heat it. Now set it aside to cool. The rough surface allows the carbon tissue to adhere to the copper and breaks the image into half tone.

Make sure you get someone who knows what they are doing to supervise you. It is a routine etching technique. Now refer to the section on carbon printing.

Make a carbon print with the following variations;

Instead of a line negative, make a line positive with continuous tones to the same contrast as required by a carbon print. This is easy. Just put a camera negative in the enlarger and project onto a sheet of line film. Make the line negative including the quarter inch border the same size as the plate. The carbon tissue should also be the same size. Instead of transferring the gelatin image onto paper, place it on the rough side of the copper, making sure that the carbon tissue is placed exactly over the plate with no overlap.

When the image has been developed and the backing paper removed stand the plate on one edge and let it dry in room temperature. **Do not use heat to dry it**. You should now have a plate containing a negative image with a clear border.

If, when it is dry, you find serious imperfections on the surface of the image such as air bubbles, or parts of the image lifting off the plate, wash the gelatin image off with hot water. Make a new carbon tissue and repeat the operation. At this stage, though, you can live with small blips. It is unlikely to be perfect the first time round.

Now you are ready to etch.

Preparing the etching baths.

You will need four dishes of ferric chloride solution of different strengths. The strength or more correctly, the specific gravity of the etching solution is measured in degrees Baume. The normal strength is 45 degrees and the lower the specific gravity the lower the Baume number. Adding water to the solution will increase the dilution and reduce the Baume number. At the same time, the more water that is contained in the solution the faster the ferric chloride penetrates the gelatin and bites into the copper. This fact will have particular significance when you start to etch.

The Baume is measured by a hydrometer. This is a glass rod with a large bubble in the centre and the same as those used for measuring the gravity of home made beer. This one has different calibrations on the stem, unfortunately, (see picture).

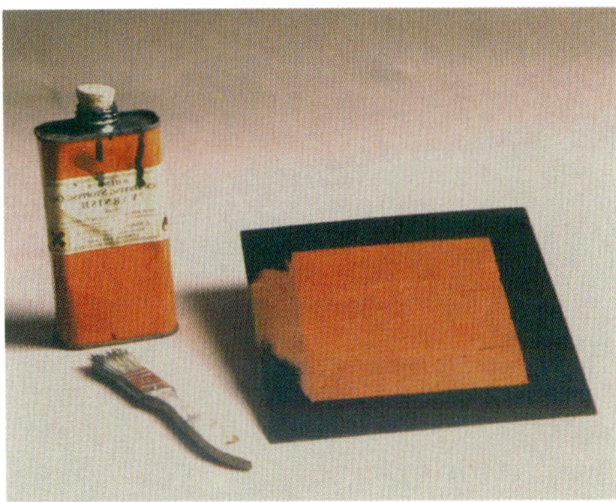

Border of copper plate being coated with stopout varnish prior to being etched.

Letratone screen enlarged onto lith film and chopped into strips to make plate for image on page 131.

We suggest you buy 2 litres of ferric chloride liquid and pour 500ml in to each of four plastic bottles. Mark them as follows;

Bottle 1- **Ferric Chloride 45 Baume**
Bottle 2- **Ferric Chloride 43 Baume**
Bottle 3- **Ferric Chloride 41 Baume**
Bottle 4- **Ferric Chloride 39 Baume**

Now you must adjust the strengths of each solution.

Place the hydrometer in the glass jar that comes with it and pour in enough ferric from bottle 1 to make it float. Where the calibration on the stem breaks the liquid surface note the number. With a bit of luck it should read 45. If it reads more pour the liquid back into bottle 1 and add 5ml of water and stir. Now check again with the hydrometer and keep adding water until it reads 45.

Now repeat the procedure with bottle 2 adding about 30 ml at a time until the hydrometer reads 43.

In the same way adjust bottle 3 to 41 Baume and bottle 4 to 39 Baume.

Ideally they should be left overnight to stabilise but a few hours should do.

Etching the plate

Take the coated copper plate and carefully paint over the clear border with stop out varnish (standard equipment in the studio). Lay a piece of card along the edge of the image if you want a really clean edge, (see picture) Then paint the back of the plate with varnish and stand it on its edge to dry.

Whilst this is drying, lay out your four dishes and with a felt tip pen mark the edge 45, 43, 41 and 39 respectively. Pour the ferric chloride from the bottles into the corresponding dishes. The plate must be etched in successive baths starting with 45 through to 39.

Make sure the temperature of the baths is as close to 20° C as you can.

Etching schedule

At this point you are on your own. There are no real rules on exact etching times, only bitter experience and constant practice.

However, here is a rough guide which should set you firmly on the road to etching a gravure plate.

USE RUBBER GLOVES

45 Baume bath

Immerse the plate in the bath. Agitate the dish gently but continuously.

As the etching liquid starts to bite the plate, the copper will darken under the resist and you will see some shadow details appear. Each band of tonal detail will appear in successive baths.

When the shadows start to show detail, transfer the plate to the 43 bath. If nothing happens in 4 or 5 minutes transfer it to the 43 bath anyway.

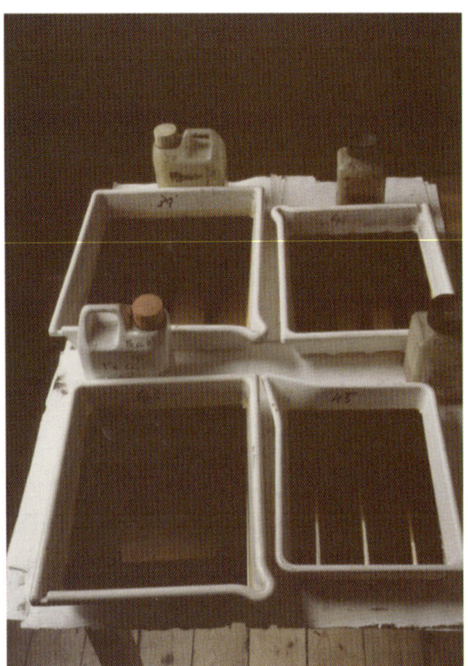

Four ferric chloride baths, specific gravity of each one marked on the dish with felt tip pen.

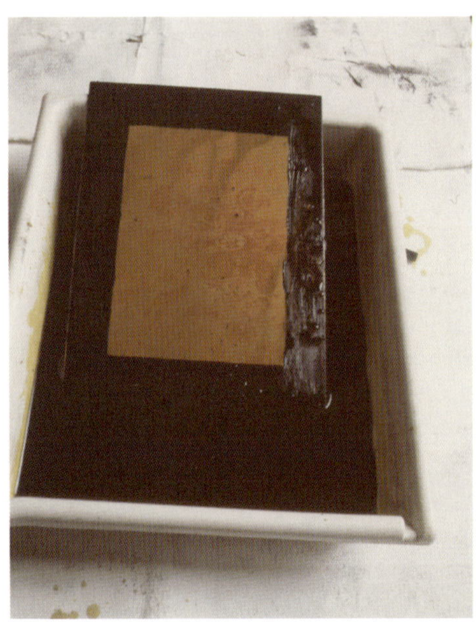

Copper plate with carbon tissue resist in course of etching. The border has been coated with stopout varnish so that when the plate is printed the border will show up as pure white on the print. The rear side of the plate should also be varnished to protect it from the etch solution.

43 Baume bath

Most of the etching takes place here. This one usually takes up to 10 minutes. As the etch proceeds you will see successive lighter tones appear.

41 Baume bath

When only the highlights remain to be etched, the plate goes into this bath to get the final highlight details.

39 Baume bath

You may have to use this one to fill in the final highlights if necessary.

Bear in mind that any part of the plate that you intend to print as white should remain untouched by the etching bath.

When you feel that the etching is complete, and you have a good range of tones in the image, remove the plate and wash off the remaining resist with hot water.

Remove the varnish on the border and the back with white spirit and the resin grain surface with methylated spirits.

The next part of the process involves an equally steep learning curve and should either have been investigated beforehand or should be part of a collaboration between you the photographer and the person who will supervise the inking and printing of your plates.

There will be a lot of testing of exposure and etching in the chloride baths. Get used to the idea of making small test plates and inking them. In this process there are no short cuts.

It is a long but rewarding task.

Before you make your print in the press always remember, as in photo-etching, to file down the edges of the plate to make a bevel. This will prevent the sharp edges from cutting your paper under the pressure of the blankets.

After a quick polish with Brasso, take the plate into the studio, ink it and print it.

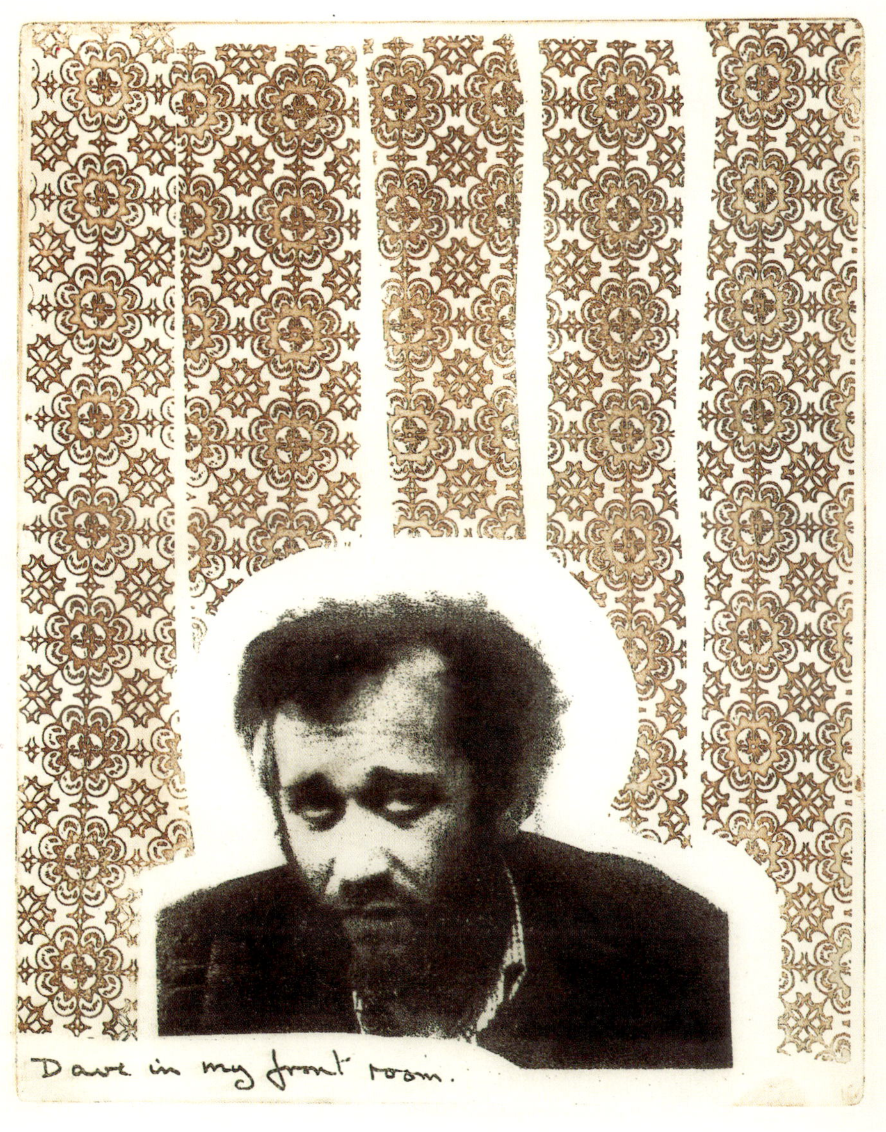

Randall Webb

Dave in my front room. A crude hybrid print. Photo etching. The wallpaper was made by enlarging Letratone screen onto lith film. The film was then cut into strips with scissors and placed onto the plate for exposure. The figure was made on a separate piece of lith film, broken into hallf tone with non-reflecting glass. The title was written on a piece of paper and contact printed onto a strip of lith film. It was then contacted again onto lith film to make a positive. It was then placed laterally reversed on the plate to read correctly on the print.

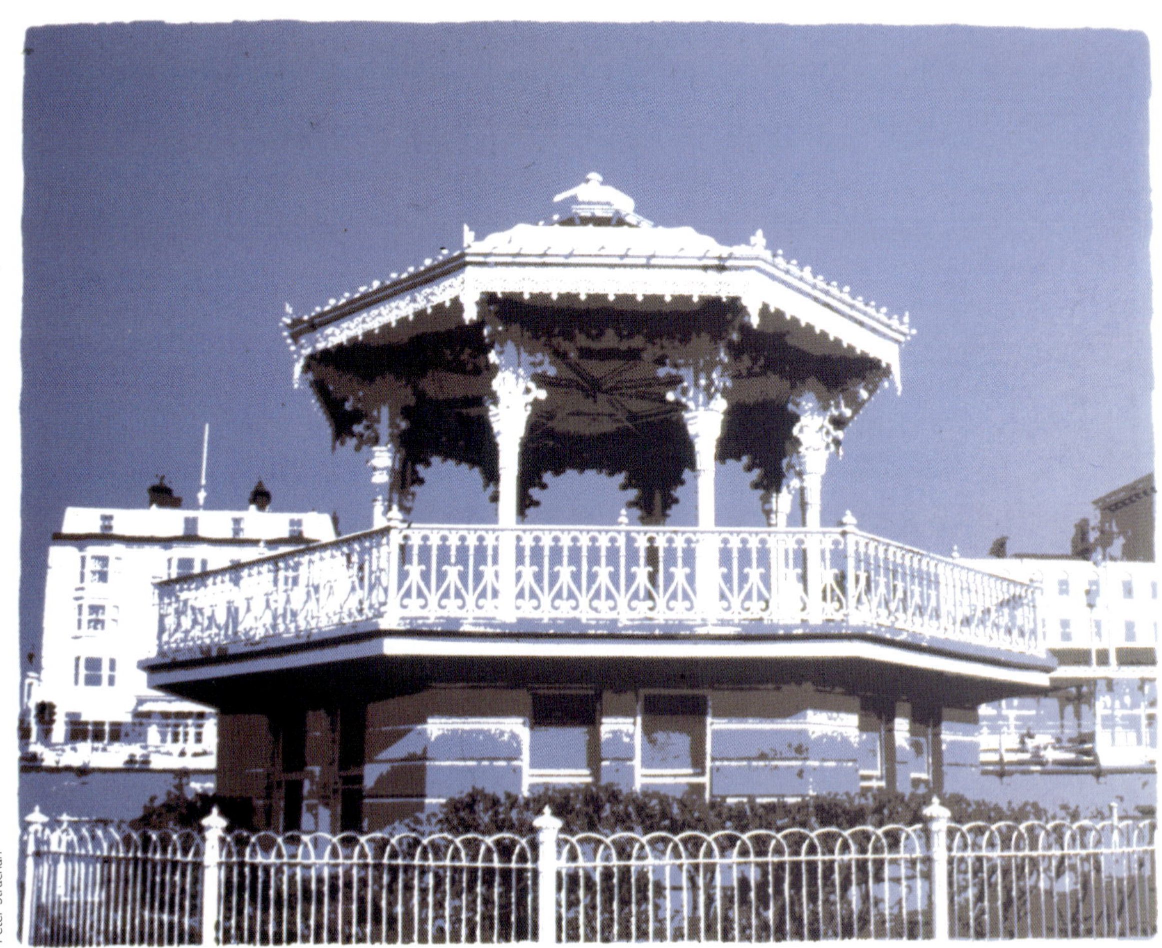

Peter Strachan

Brighton bandstand. Classic example of three colour silkscreen print using lith separations.

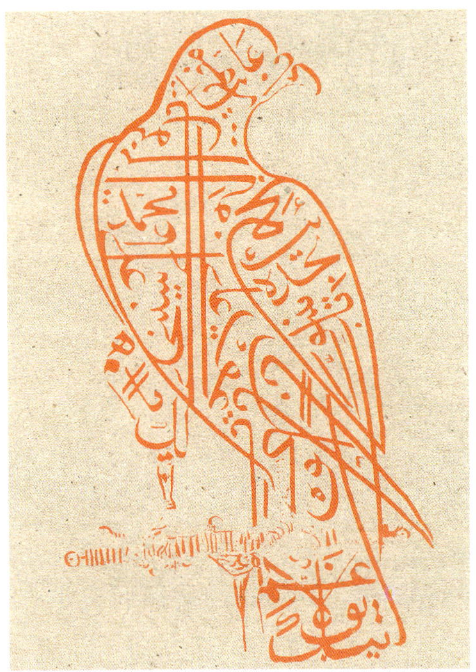

Single colour silkscreen, red ink on grey paper.

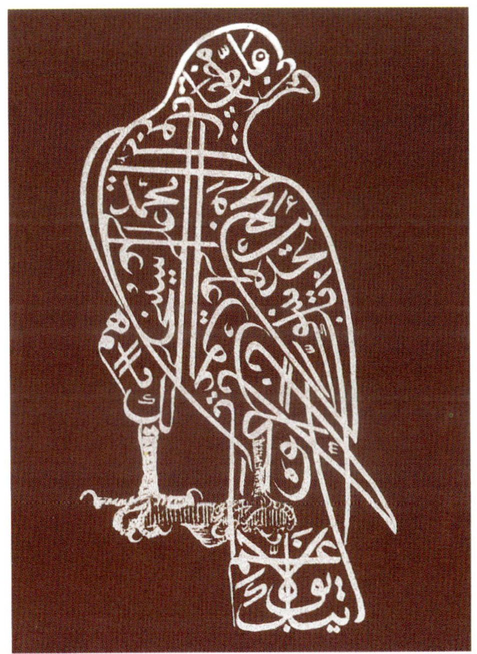

Print from same screen as above, but using white ink on red paper.

It is easier in the long run to regard photo silk screen as a refinement of silk screen printing using hand cut stencils, rather than an extension of photographic printing.

Many students come to the process expecting to make sophisticated half tone and posterised prints, which in the text books resemble full colour photographic prints.

Unfamiliarity with the darkroom work necessary to make the lith film positives, combined with learning the new techniques involved in screen printing make the learning curve rather too steep for comfort. Consequently many people tend to give up before they have really started.

To avoid this problem we suggest you sign up for a course which teaches you the basic principles of hand cut stencils and screen printing. Then, when you have gained sufficient facility with these, you can progress onto making simple photo stencils. After that it is a relatively easy transition to the more complicated versions illustrated in this manual.

A silk screen is simply a wooden frame over which a piece of fine polystyrene mesh is tightly stretched. A design consisting of paper shapes is applied to the underside. The screen is then placed onto a piece of cloth or paper and ink poured on the screen. The ink is squeezed through the screen with a rubber-bladed squeegee. The paper shape prevents the ink from passing through the mesh, but where the mesh is uncovered the ink is squeezed through and adheres to the paper, giving in effect a negative image in ink on the material.

It thus enables a number of prints to be made in a very short time. The commercial uses of the process are varied. Wall paper, furnishing fabrics, ceramics, T shirts and point of sale materials are some of the applications that are used to mass produce images.

Photographic images can be made in the same way. A lith image is contact printed onto a sheet of light sensitive gelatin which is applied to the screen. When printed on paper or fabric with the squeegee the resulting image is a negative photograph in any colour of your choice.

Successive layers can be printed, building more colours and tones at will.

A brief history of photo silk screen printing

The first photo silk screen prints were made in 1915 as a form of alternative cheap commercial printing.

In the 1950's a number of artists in the USA experimented with the process as a means of producing limited editions of fine art prints, but found it difficult to overcome the prejudice of art dealers toward what was considered an inferior medium.

It was not until the 1960's that silk screen as an art form really came into its own when a few American painters and print makers started using the

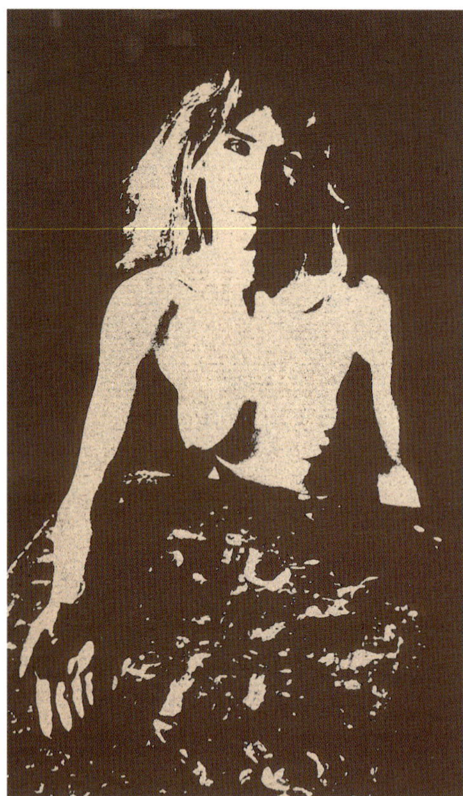

Maryka. Lith negative made from 35mm negative. Ink found in discarded jam jar at back of studio, printed on black studio background paper.

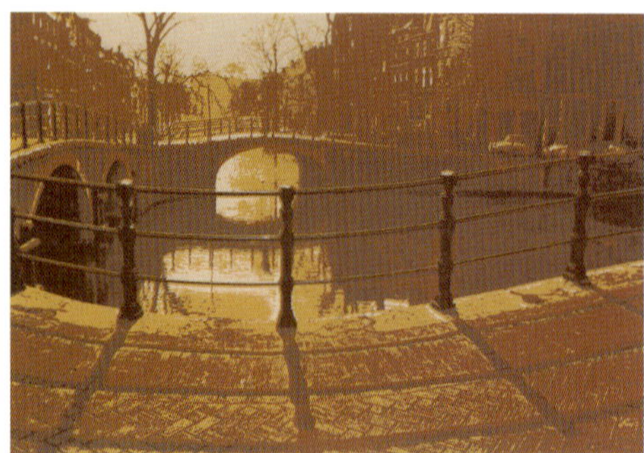

Amsterdam. Multi-printed silkscreen using the lith separations shown in chapter 9.

medium to produce what became known as 'Pop Art'. The best known of these was Andy Warhol with his prints of Chairman Mao and Marilyn Monroe.

Other artists in America included Roy Lichtenstein and Robert Raushenberg, whilst in Britain, Peter Blake, Richard Hamilton (who designed the Beatles' record covers) and R.B. Kitaj popularised the new medium.

Advantages

It is very easy to make a long print run in a short time once the stencils have been set up on the screen. Many printers use the process to make Christmas cards.

You can use any combination of colours, overlaying one image on top of another, combining opaque and transparent inks.

It is possible to print on any colour paper, using light coloured inks on dark paper or vice versa.

You can combine photographic images with hand-drawn ones.

You can make prints in subtle colours that look like gum prints, or at the other end of the scale, dramatic ones in day-glow colours.

Even if you make a mistake half way through they still look good (quite often).

Disadvantages

The time taken to set up each stencil on the screen makes it impractical to make one-off prints.

It is usual to make an edition of 10 or 15 prints with the result that you end up with folders full of editions which you may sell, but which you generally end up giving to your friends.

Don't expect to become an expert in a couple of afternoons.

However, when you start to make good prints it rapidly becomes addictive.

Negatives

Any photographic source material can be used - negatives in black and white or colour, or colour transparencies. They all eventually have to be made into lith images on lith film.

Paper

Use any paper you wish provided it has a reasonably smooth finish. When you start it is cheaper to use machine made cartridge paper, progress later onto mould-made paper such as Fabriano or similar. If you sell prints on cheap paper and they turn yellow after a few months, remember that the purchaser probably knows where you live

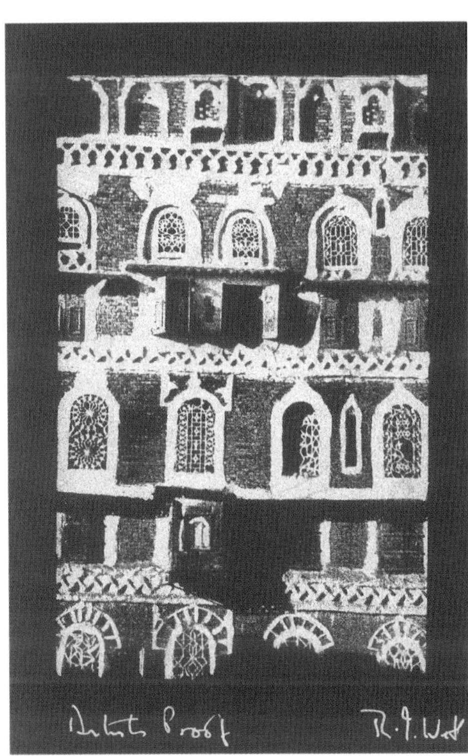

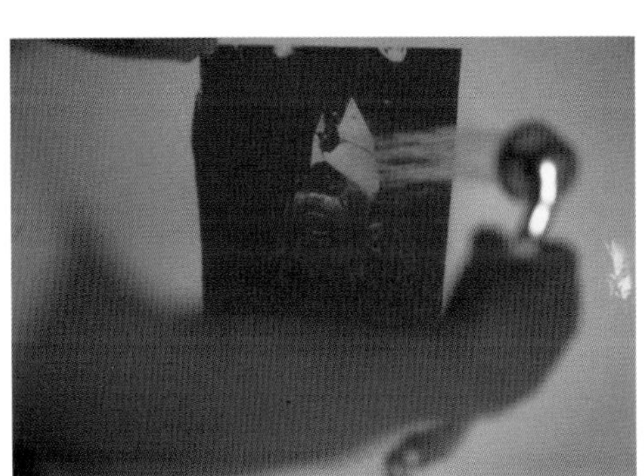

Washing off the the stencil with hot water to remove the unhardened gelatin. The blue stencil is washed off with hot water whilst the red stencil has to be developed in a dish containing water and hydrogen peroxide.

Shopping List

Lith film.

Lith developer.

Film fixer.

Autotype 5 star screen film red (see Method).

Ditto **blue** (see Method).

A **silk screen frame** not bigger than 15 inches square to start. Some books suggest that you stretch the fabric on the frame yourself. This has always struck us as being a pointless exercise as you can buy them ready-made from a supplier who is an expert at it.

250 ml bottle of **blue screen filler**.

250 ml bottle of **hydrogen peroxide** 30 volumes, (check label when you purchase).

Small bottle of **white spirit**.

Bottle of **domestic bleach**.

Pair of **scissors**.

Roll of **plastic parcel tape**.

Rubber **roller squeegee** 6 inches wide.

Flat **squeegee** 12 inches wide.

An **old credit card**.

Lots of **cotton wool**.

Some **old newspapers**.

2 developing dishes 16 x 12".

A **sheet of acetate** 16 x 12".

4 small tins of **opaque oil based printing ink**, white, red, yellow and blue. See [33 . Suppliers].

A small **nail brush**.

A bottle of **cream bathroom cleaner**.

A small **plastic ruler** about 6 inches long.

A **Stanley knife** or scalpel.

Method

In the enlarger make a lith positive by projecting your camera negative onto lith film (not bigger than 10 x 8"). Develop this in lith developer at the strength shown on the bottle, fix, wash and dry. If you use a colour slide instead of a negative, you will of course have a lith negative. This will then have to be contact printed onto another piece of lith film to obtain a lith positive.

Make sure that your final lith positive contains only black tones and clear film. Any half tones will make it difficult when you make the photo stencil. If you can't achieve pure black and white tones from the camera negative you will have to use a roundabout route to boost the contrast.

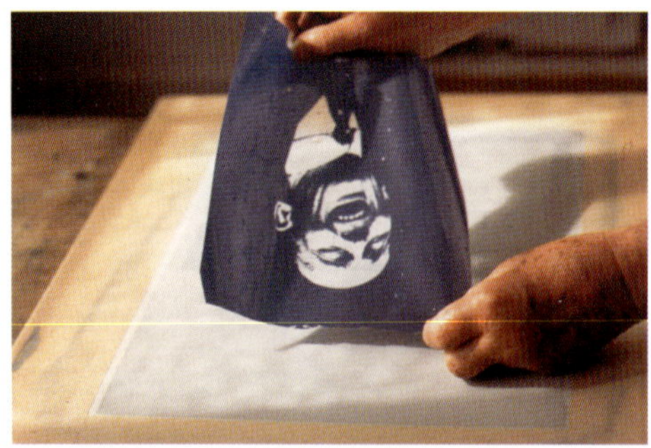

Positioning and laying down developed stencil on the top of the screen, the soft gelatin side downwards.

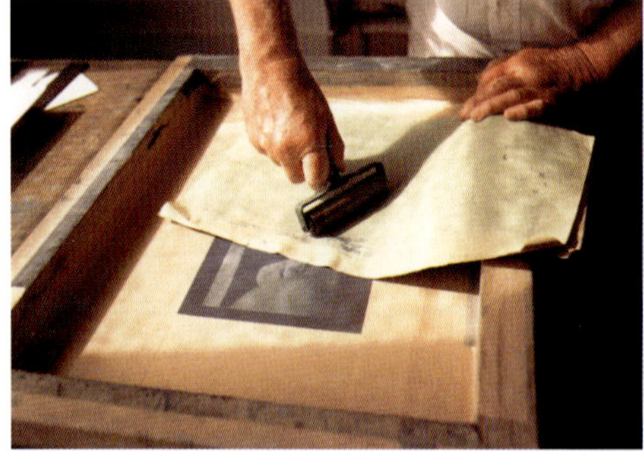

Rolling the screen onto the stencil from the back of the screen in order to make the gelatin adhere to the mesh of the screen.

Take your camera negative and contact print it onto a piece of lith film and when it is processed and dry, take this lith positive and contact print it yet again to arrive at a new lith negative.

Process and dry this negative, trim the edges, place it in the neg carrier of your enlarger and project it onto lith film of the size required (not larger than 10 x 8"). When it is processed you will have a lith positive containing only black and clear film as your image. This little dodge is useful whenever you have trouble reducing a continuous tone image to pure lith tones.

Finally take your lith positive and trim off all the borders with a knife and a straight edge so that only the image area remains.

Note: Any part of the film which is black will show as a colour on the final print and any clear parts of the film will stay as plain white paper.

Preparing the screen

Wash the screen fabric under running water. On the flat front of the screen pour a little cream bath cleaner and scrub it well with the brush. This is 'degreasing' the screen is to ensure that the stencil will adhere firmly. Wash off all the cream cleaner and stand the screen on one edge to let it drain.

Cut off a piece of the red stencil film to a size about 2 inches larger on all sides than the film.

Make a sandwich as follows;
A piece of card or board.
On top of this the sheet of red stencil film **with the dull side of the red stencil film facing down towards the card**.
You are thus exposing the stencil through the back.
Then on this place the lith film in the centre of the red film dull side down.

On top of this place a sheet of glass or alternatively, place the sandwich of card, red film and lith film in a printing frame with the lith film facing upwards against the glass.

Now expose it under a UV lamp. (Most silk screen studios will have a special exposing box for this purpose).

Make a test strip giving exposures of 2, 4 and 6 minutes respectively. Keep the lamp at a standard distance of about 18 inches from the printing frame.

Once you have established an exposure time you can use this for all future stencil making.

Mixing the developer

Mix 150 ml of hydrogen peroxide into 900 ml of cold water and pour into a dish slightly larger than your red film.

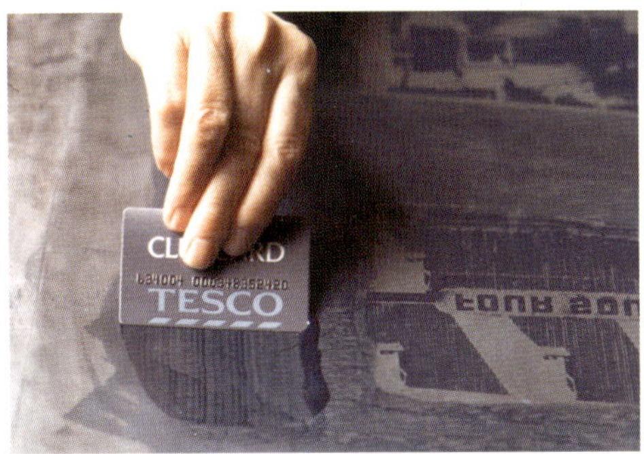

Spreading blue filler on the remainder of the screen not covered by the stencil. This prevents spare ink leaking through onto the printing table. A credit card seems to be the most useful form of squeegee.

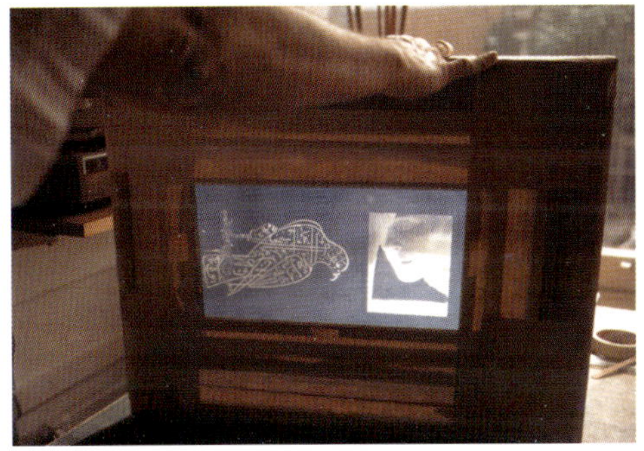

An alternative way of blocking out the spare screen is by covering it with parcel tape or gummed brown paper. Note two stencils on one screen. When one is being printed the other is blocked off with a piece of discarded acetate from the stencil.

Developing the stencil and placing it on the screen

Slip the red film quickly into the dish with the dull side upwards making sure that all the film is immersed.

Now rock the dish gently. Gradually the unhardened gelatin on the red film will be washed away, leaving only the hardened gelatin revealing a negative image in red on the screen. This stage closely resembles the development of gum and carbon prints.

Keep rocking the dish until no more red colour shows in the clear parts of the screen.

Pour away the peroxide developer, which by now will be bright red.

Carefully pour 500ml of cold water into the dish to rinse the screen.

Place the silk screen frame on to the bench or table with the wooden frame to the bench, and the flat side of the screen pointing upwards.

Take the red film out of the dish holding it only by the top two corners and lay it gently on the centre of the screen **with the dull side to the screen and the shiny side facing upwards**.

Make sure it lies flat with no folds or wrinkles. If it is not flat first time, lift it gently and re-position it.

Now dab the film gently with a pad of blotting paper so that the stencil adheres lightly to the screen.

Place a newspaper or blotter on the bench and turn the screen over onto it so that the stencil rests on the paper and the wooden frame faces upwards.

Place a piece of plain paper on the screen covering the area of the stencil and roll the paper gently but firmly with a rubber roller squeegee. Make sure there are no folds or wrinkles on the paper.

Now the gelatin of the stencil has been pressed into the mesh of the screen and when dry will stay in place for printing.

Once the stencil has been fixed to the screen it should be allowed to dry. Heat from a hair drier can be used to speed up the process. As it dries the acetate backing of the stencil will start to detach itself from the stencil and the screen. Pull it gently, making sure you do not take off the gelatine at the same time. Keep the acetate for later use. The area of screen outside the image must now be blocked off to prevent ink spilling through the screen during printing. The blue filler can be spread across the mesh of the screen with an old credit card or similar. Otherwise parcel tape or gummed brown paper can be used. Any retouching of holes in the image can be made with a fine brush and blue filler.

Randall Webb

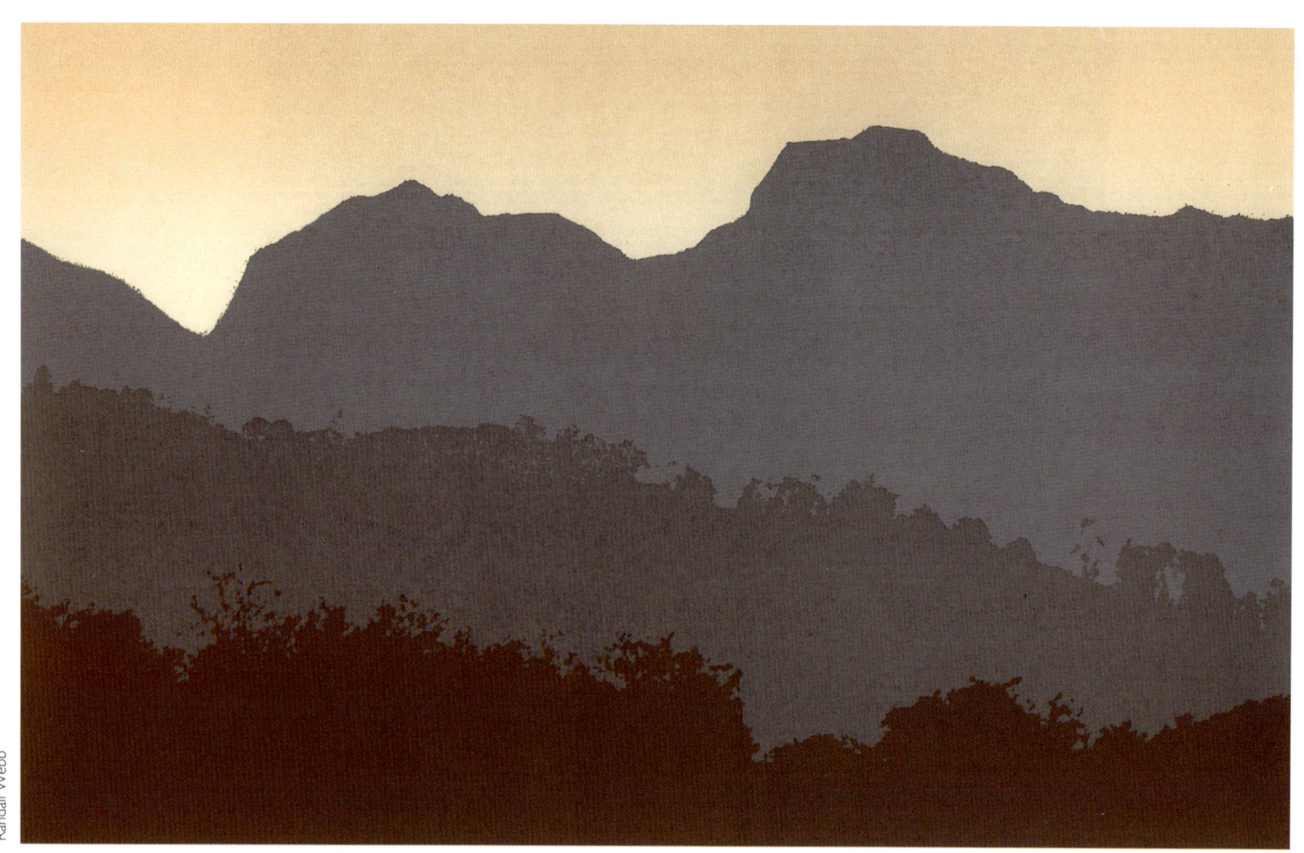

Langdale Pikes. Four colour silkscreen print from an original colour slide.

Miscellaneous Processes

The following three chapters contain a few oddities which are rarely described and consequently less used in comparison with the other processes. They are all photographic processes in the strict sense of the word, whether they use camera based images as a source or whether they are produced by means of one of the early printing methods. What does link them together is the fact that they all seem to be short-cut methods of making pictures which would normally be produced by much more elaborate means.

The **cliché-verre**, a quick way of making multiple copies of hand drawn images.

Bleach etch, a fast way of etching photographic paper to make a colour print.

The **solvent transfer**, an instant colour and black and white photocopying process without using a machine.

They are all fairly simple processes so we have kept the descriptions of them equally simple.

Cliché-verre means literally 'glass picture'. It is also known as glass etching or hyalography (back to the old business of dredging the Greek and Latin dictionaries for fancy names - in this case the Greek word for glass). The method was used regularly to good effect by the French painters Corot and Millet. It is essentially a hand drawn negative and as such is difficult for historians and students of old processes to categorise. Perhaps it illustrates the currently held view that the artist's ideas are more important than the medium through which they are expressed.

Corot and his contemporaries took a piece of flat glass, smoked it over a tallow candle, and then scratched an image in the soot covered surface with a sharp pointed instrument. This was placed onto a sheet of photosensitive paper and exposed in the sun. When the light passed through the clear parts of the glass where it had been scratched, it produced a line drawing in black on a white background. This could be reproduced ad infinitum without resorting to the making of an etching plate and the use of a heavy and bulky printing press, or even more important, without having to pay for the services of a printing studio. If you insist on being completely historically correct you can use the smoked or varnished glass method, but there is a much more flexible improved way of working which give opportunities for many more variations of effects. This involves the use of a sheet of fogged lith film. It may not be quite so authentic but it is close to the spirit of the thing without having to 'invent' a new old process.

Original glass method.

You will need:

A **sheet of thin picture glass**.

A **tallow candle** used to smoke etching and engraving plates(from any good art supplier).

A **sharp point** - needle, scalpel, etching, tool, compass point, great-grandmother's hat pin (a nice Victorian touch!)

Cotton wool.

Cotton wool buds.

Some **wooden cocktail sticks** or used matchsticks.

Any of the materials for making contact prints described in this manual.

Method

Take your piece of glass and hold it over the smoke produced by your lighted tallow candle making sure that the surface is covered by an even coating of soot. Take care not to heat the glass so that it cracks. When you have coated the glass completely, scratch your design in the soot coating using whatever tools you find most suitable. A needle will obviously give the finest line and a scalpel can be made to give a line of

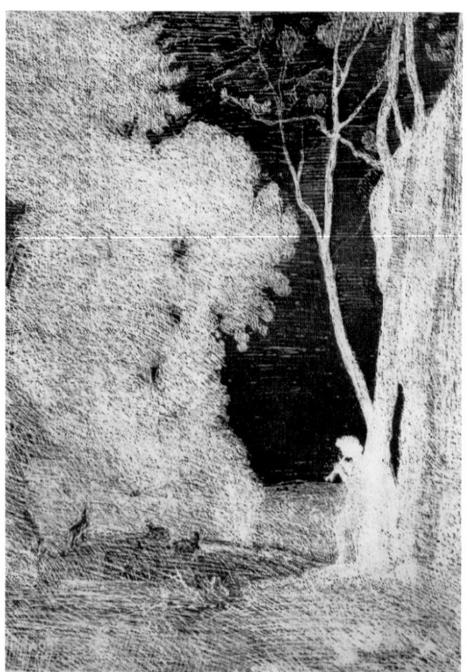

Hand drawn negative by Corot, the 19'th century painter.

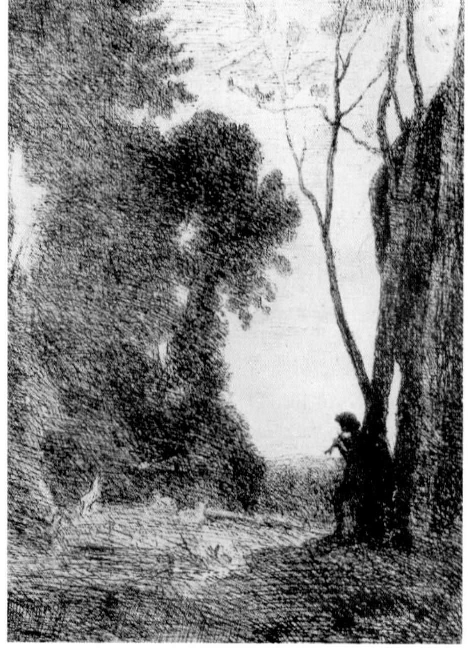

Positive from above negative.

variable thickness by changing the angle at which you hold it. For even thicker lines use a matchstick or a cocktail stick. If you want to remove larger areas, use a cotton wool bud. Now place the plate of glass soot-side up on a piece of paper sensitised with any old process emulsion of your choice. Expose it in the sun or your usual UV light source and process accordingly. You now have an etching without all the fuss it normally entails. However, there are some drawbacks. The soot is messy and rubs off easily. It therefore is not possible to place it face down on the paper to get a good contact. Even if you use thin glass, the thickness of the glass prevents the formation of a really sharp line on the print. (There is a way of fixing the soot covering on the glass but this involves heating the glass and we feel that safety takes precedent over historical authenticity. Instructing our readers to wander about the house holding sheets of hot glass may not be in anybody's best interest).

So we must consider the alternative glass plate method. In this we replace the soot from the tallow candle with either a coating of stop-out varnish (see section on photo-etching) or with modern enamel paint. Photo-opaque, (used for blocking out lith film) is also a good alternative.

Coat the glass with varnish or paint and let it dry. Now scratch your design with a needle or scalpel. If you want thicker lines or large areas removed try experimenting with matchsticks or cotton buds dipped in white spirit for the stop out varnish or cellulose thinners for the enamel. The thinners can also be used for solvent transfers, [29 . Solvent]. The advantage of this method is that you can, when the coating is dry, place the glass face down on the sensitised paper to get a much more effective contact. For every plus there is a minus; if you place the glass face down you get a laterally reversed image. Not much good if your picture contains lettering. In that case you need the improved film based cliché-verre method.

Film-based cliche verre

For this you will need:

Some sheets of **lith film.**

Lith developer.

Standard **paper developer**.

Needles, scalpel, cotton wool, cotton buds, etc as before.

Small quantity of **potassium ferricyanide** and **hypo** to make Farmers reducer.

Poster colour or photopaque.

Small **water colour brush**.

This time we dispense with the traditional glass plate in favour of a lith film negative. Take a sheet of lith film and fog it thoroughly, either under a tungsten lamp for a few minutes or in daylight. Then develop it in standard lith film developer at the makers recommended dilution for three or four minutes so that when it has been fixed, washed and dried it

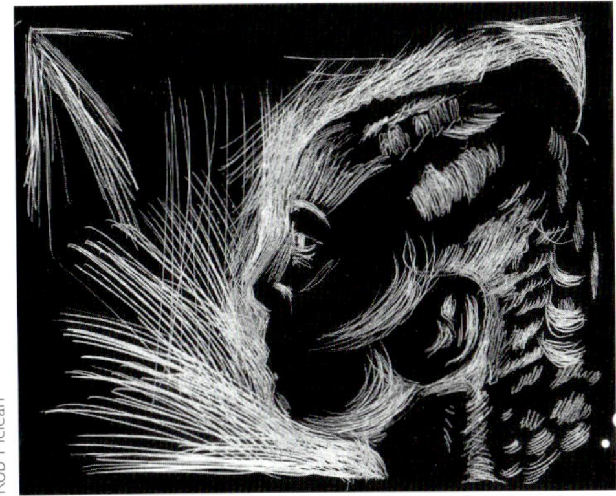
Rob Mclean

Sheet of fogged lith film developed to very high density. Image scratched on emulsion side of film with a scalpel.

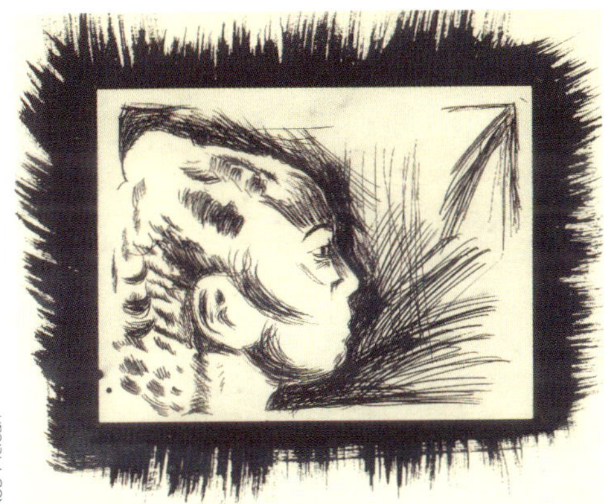
Rob Mclean

Cyanotype positive from negative above.

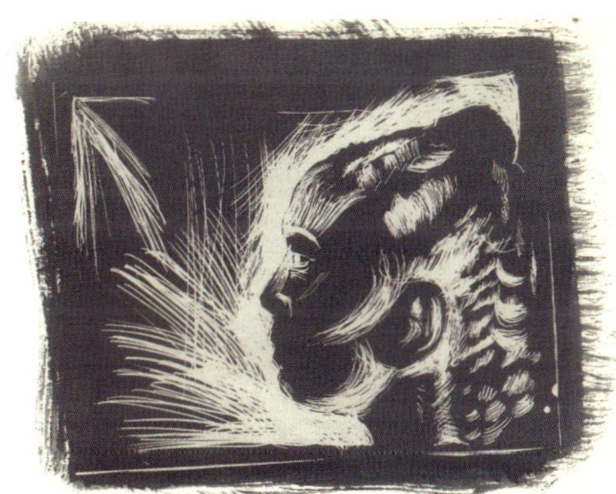
Rob Mclean

Cyanotype negative from positive from negative above.

is completely opaque when held up to the light. You can now scratch through the blackened emulsion (the dull side of the film) as you did with the glass.

If you want thicker lines or to remove larger blocks of tone you can mix up a small amount of Farmers reducer and apply it with a matchstick or a cotton bud or small paint brush. The reducer will bleach the emulsion until you eventually end up with areas of clear film. When the bleaching is reached the stage that you want wash the film and dry it. If you want to reduce some areas of the film to achieve a grey tone effect on the print, then wash the film before the reducer completes its work of bleaching down to clear film.

There is a further variation using the film method. If you want a number of different grey tones on your print as well as black lines on white paper you may substitute paper developer for lith film developer when you prepare your lith 'plate' as follows:

Expose your sheet of lith film as before, but develop it in normal strength paper developer (eg Ilford PQ universal or Agfa Neutol) and develop it to the tone that you require. This can be any degree of translucency that is necessary from very thin to quite dark but obviously not completely opaque. The degree of density is controlled by the length of time you leave the film in the developer. This part can be done by inspection in normal room lighting. Once it's fogged it's fogged!

Now when you expose your scratched film onto sensitised paper you will have black lines (light shining through clear scratched film) on a grey background (light shining through a translucent film).

You can now add an extra tonal dimension by painting areas of the film with poster colour or photopaque, which of course will produce areas of white in addition to your black lines and grey background. As you are using relatively thin film you can print it onto paper face up to avoid lateral reversal without compromising the sharpness of the line.

That is the basic technique of cliché-verre. You will find that it is capable of endless variation and combination. The result of printing on say, kallitype, is quite different from printing on gum emulsion and so on. Two very useful applications of the method are;

Making decorative hand drawn borders round your prints. If you are making a straight gum or salt print or whatever and your large contact negative has a reasonably wide black border, then you can scratch a cliché-verre design on it and it will print simultaneously with the rest of the image.

Let us suppose you have made a cyanotype with a white border (see section on exposing). When it has been washed and dried you make a cliché verre negative to fit round the edge of the cyanotype image. Then you may coat the area round the edge of the image with gum dichromate sensitiser and expose it under the cliché verre neg. Now you have a cyanotype image with a hand drawn decorative border on any colour you want. And so on ad nauseam. How good or how utterly naff it is depends entirely on you and your artistic ability or integrity.

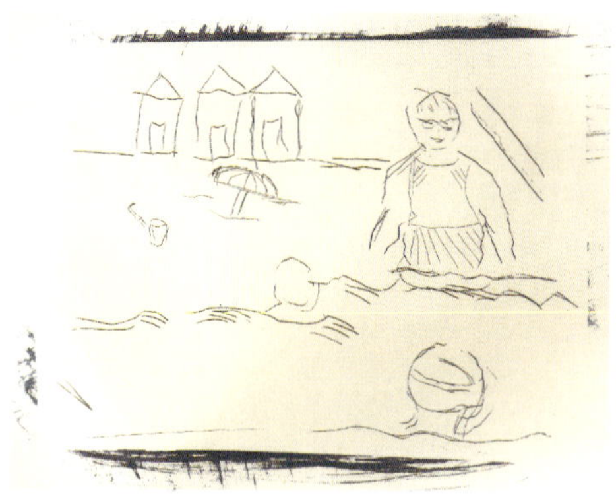

Childs drawing scratched on film with compass point. Printed on gum emulsion.

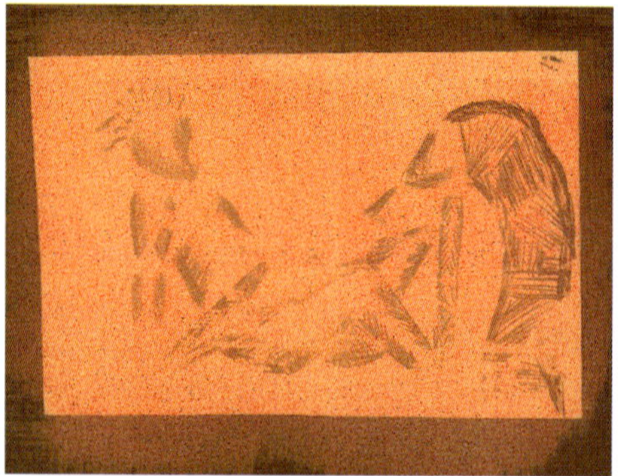

Kallitype with gum overlay.

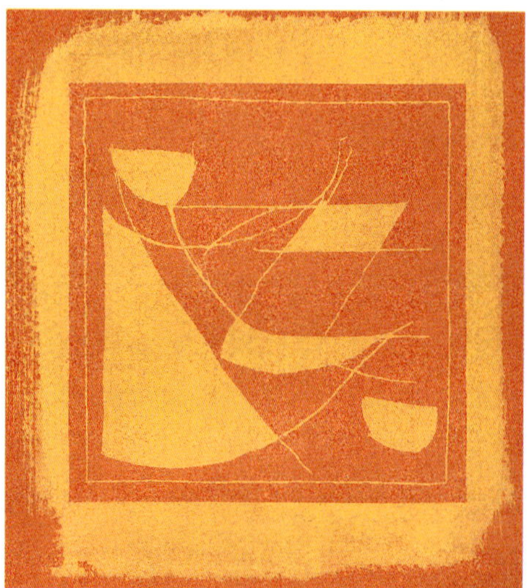

Abstract. Red gum on yellow paper.

The second application enables you to print titles, signatures, dates, or edition numbers on the lower edge of your alternative process print. Write whatever information you want to show on your print on the border of your contact neg with a needle or a scalpel. Alternatively make a small cliché verre negative and tape it to the edge of your main neg. Now when you expose your main neg you will have simultaneously printed your signature, title on the border of the print.

Question: What happens if you are no good at drawing?
Answer: Tough. That's your problem.

However, there is a solution for all those unfortunates who have to become photographers because they couldn't draw. Take heart, Fox Talbot wasn't very good at drawing so he invented photography.

Here is a possible solution. Place a negative which you would like to convert into a hand drawn image in your enlarger and project it on the baseboard as if you were making a conventional enlargement. Now place a sheet of lith film on the baseboard (emulsion - the light side - up). Use it straight from the packet. Don't attempt to process it at this stage. Now, in safelight conditions, trace with a black felt tip pens the major elements of the picture on the film. A black pen will show up on the relatively light toned film. When you have traced enough details for your purpose, take it out of the easel and in normal room light, scratch through the felt tip image with a needle or scalpel. Now develop the film in room lighting in lith developer. The film will go black leaving the clear lines that you have previously scratched in the film. Hey presto! (as they say) you have a hand drawn cliché verre negative. There does not appear to be much literature on the subject of cliché verre but the three best known users of the technique were the French painters Corot, Millet and Rousseau. It is an obvious field for making one's name by original experimentation!

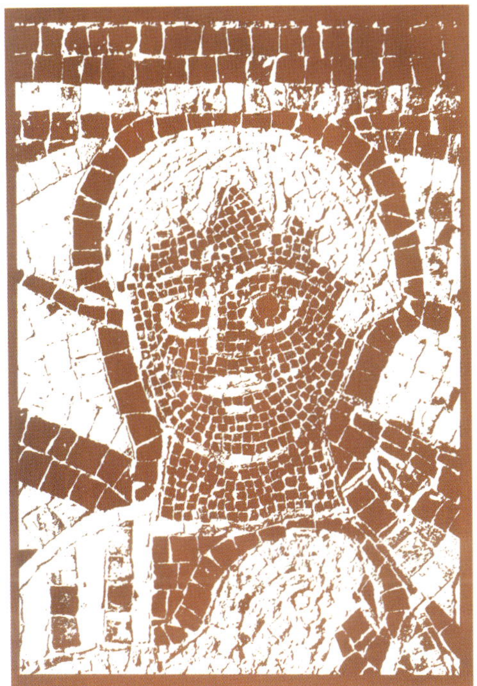

Mosaic - Jordan. Bleach-etch from an original 35mm colour slide. The colour is a mixture of different food dyes from the supermarket.

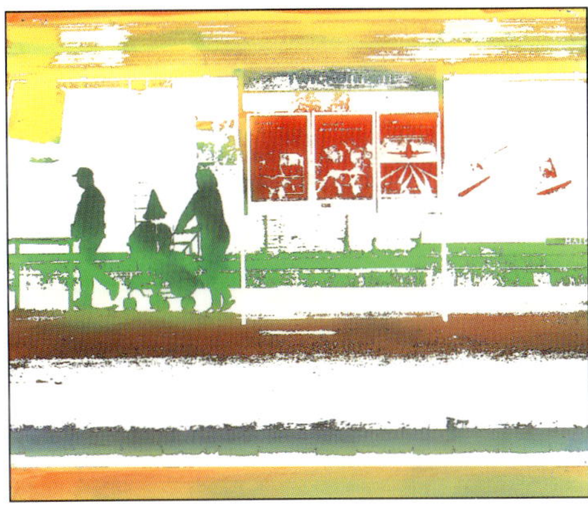

The colours can be mixed before application, or used raw.

This is a somewhat obscure process, not because it is rarely used, but because it is used in an industry unfamiliar to most photographers. Bleach etch is a valuable aid to the exhibition and display business. It makes it possible to produce small quantities of coloured images and lettering on posters and display cards without recourse to the paraphenalia of plate making and commercial printing. As a photographic process it is an equally rapid method of making a coloured image from a line or lith neg.

Advantages

It needs no special equipment and no complicated chemistry. You can choose any colour or combination of colours of your choice.
All the work can be carried out in an ordinary darkroom.
The colour dyes used to make the final print can be obtained from the corner grocer's shop.
It is no more expensive or difficult than ordinary black and white printing.

Disadvantages

There is one. You can only use a high contrast lith or line image. There are no intermediate greys. You can however get round this problem to some degree by using dot or half-tone screens, [9 . Negatives].
Well, two disadvantages really. The bleach etch solutions smell a bit.

Shopping list

Lith film not bigger than 5 x 4".

Lith developer.

Your **usual darkroom dishes and measuring jugs**.

Scales (if you mix your own chemicals).

25 sheets of 10 x 8" of any resin coated multicontrast **photographic paper**.

Kentmere **bleach etch chemicals** or, if you want to mix your own,
Acetic acid
Cupric chloride
Hydrogen peroxide

A selection of **photo dyes** or vegetable dyes used to colour cake icing from your local grocer, (see Method).

Some **cotton wool**.

A supply of **old newspapers**.

Method

First you make a positive image on lith film.
Contact print your camera negative onto a piece of lith film and process it in lith developer [9 . Negatives]. It doesn't matter what sort of image you have, provided the lith positive contains only two tones - opaque black and clear film. When it is dry trim it to fit into your enlarger neg carrier.

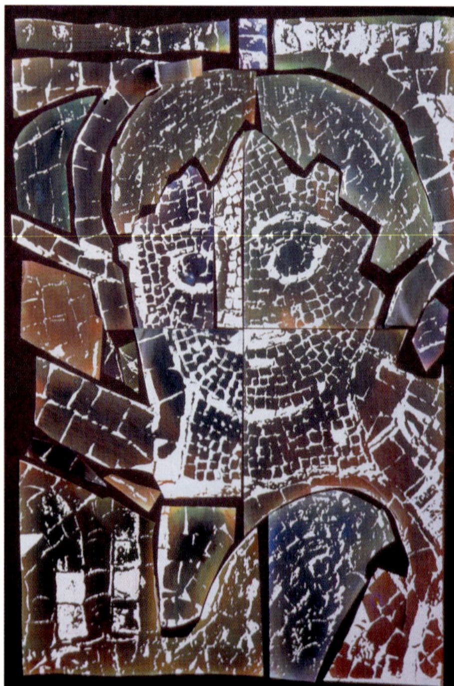

Mosaic - Jordan. From the same colour slide as on p. 143, this time several sheets of RC paper were made, both as negatives and positives. These were then cut up to make a mosaic of the paper itself, and pasted on red card. The vegetable dyes were mixed one on top of the other as they were applied.

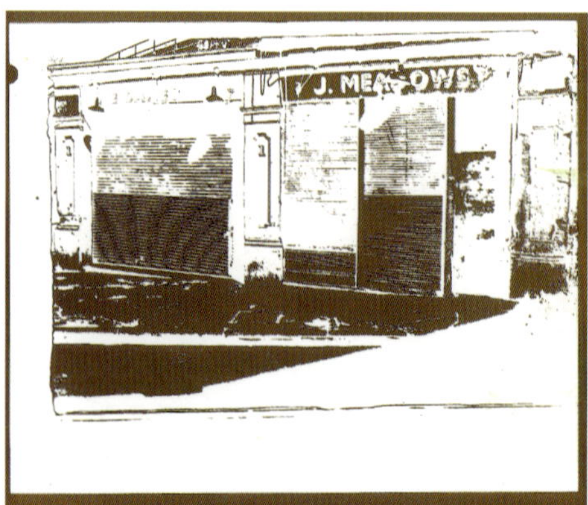

Southwark. Made from manipulated lith film. The colour is a mixture of yellow and blue vegetable dye.

Now enlarge it in the normal way onto the resin-coated paper and develop fully in standard paper developer, (Ilford PQ Universal or similar). Expose it to give a pure black image with no fogging on or around the edges of the whites.

Develop it fully - at least two minutes. It is imperative that the black areas reach right down through the emulsion to the base.

Fix, wash and dry as normal.

Next you bleach the print. Mix up sufficient solution from the two bottles of Kentmere bleach etch bath as per the instructions on the container, or mix your own as:

Solution A

Cupric chloride	15 grams
Acetic acid (concentrated)	40 ml
Water	500 ml

Solution B

Hydrogen peroxide in small (250ml) bottle from chemist. Peroxide goes off quite quickly in the bottle, so don't buy too much at once.

Note. Both peroxide and chloride solutions should be kept in a bottle with the cap **not** screwed down tightly. Pour either your Kentmere solution mixed as instructions or equal amounts of your own mix A and B into a developing dish. Immerse the paper in the liquid. Take a lump of cotton wool, and holding it with a pair of print tongs, or wearing rubber gloves (or both), gently rub the surface of the print under the liquid. Within a minute the black part of the image will lift off the paper, leaving a clear white sheet. Remove it from the dish and wash the paper for a few minutes in running water. What has happened is that the black image has been removed and at the same time the white part has been etched by the cupric chloride, giving it a fine rough surface.

Now we apply the colour. Pour a little of one of your dyes into a saucer, and wearing rubber gloves (to avoid staining your fingers), dip a small lump of cotton wool into it.

Now rub the dye onto the surface of the print. The dye will stick to the rough, etched surface of the paper, but will slide off the shiny surface.

You now have a bleach etch print in white and one colour.

You can vary your colours in two ways. Either mix different colours in the dish, eg blue and yellow to make green, or red and green to make brown etc. or rub another colour onto the first one. This will mix on the surface of the print to make a new colour. Now you can experiment with the dyes to your heart's content. Any dye that remains on the shiny white part of the print can be wiped off with a slightly dampened lump of cotton wool. Paler colours can be obtained by diluting the dyes with clean water. Any white spots can be touched out with a little dye on a fine spotting brush. Leave it to dry for a few hours. That's it.

Solvent Transfer

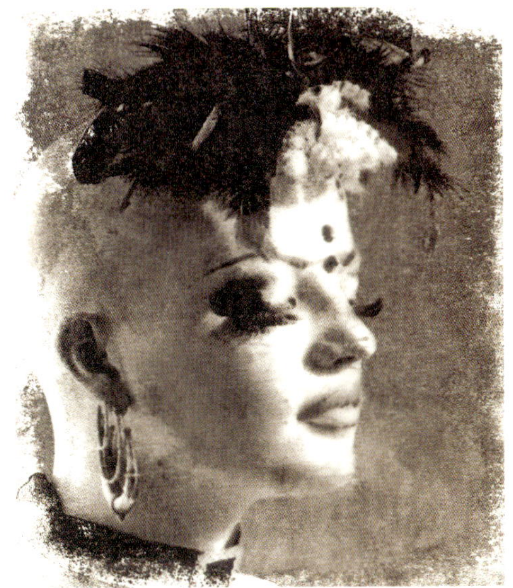

Enlarged photocopy of 10 x 8" print. Transferred onto Cranes smooth paper with cellulose thinners.

Solvent transfer is a very useful mixed media technique, a sort of instant photocopy without the use of a photocopying machine, and has been used successfully in America by artists such as Robert Rauschenberg. It is a quick and easy means of transferring an image from a printed page such as a newspaper or magazine onto paper or fabric. Illustrations from magazines can be overlaid onto prints made in other media, as varied as cyanotypes and etchings.

Advantages

The processes is quick, easy and cheap.
You can do it on your kitchen table.
You don't need elaborate equipment or even a darkroom.

Disadvantages

The solvents give off strong fumes and need to be used in a well ventilated space or outdoors.
As in all transfer processes, lettering in the original will come out back to front on the final print.

Shopping list

Solvent. The two most effective ones are cellulose thinners from a DIY store, or silk screen retarder. The latter is used for thinning silk screen oil based printing inks.
Paper or **cloth** on which to transfer.
A **dessert spoon** or roller **squeegee**.
Cotton wool.
Rubber gloves.
A **face mask** fitted with carbon filter (if you think you may be sensitive to the solvent fumes).

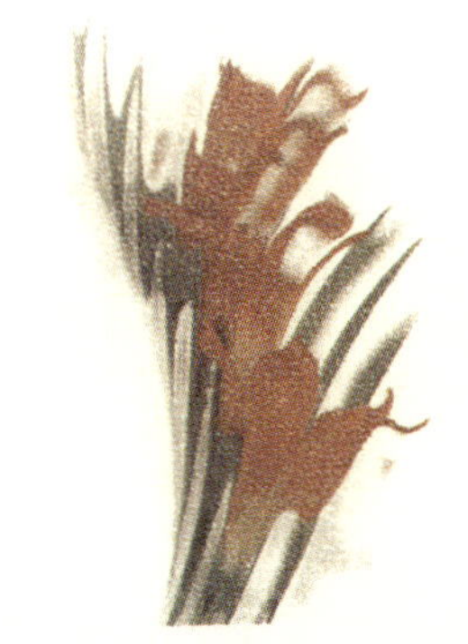

Jocelyn Horsefall

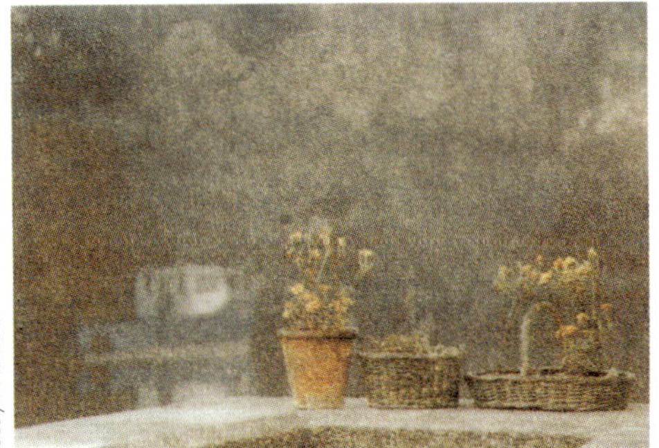

Jocelyn Horsefall

Colour laser photocopies of C41 prints. Transferred onto mould made paper with cellulose thinners.

Method 1

Take an illustration that takes your fancy from a magazine or an expendable book. Not all printed matter is suitable as many publications, especially newspaper supplements are printed using water based inks which do not react to the solvent. **Glossy magazines are preferable.**
Try a variety to find the ones that work best.
Place the magazine page face down on to a sheet of paper or cloth and tape the two together along one edge. Any sort of paper will do.
Now dip a lump of cotton wool into the solvent, (wear rubber gloves), and swab the back of the printed page. If it is printed with the right ink the solvent will soften the ink and allow it to transfer under a little applied pressure.
The solvent will turn the paper translucent as it is applied, letting the picture underneath show through.
Now rub the back of the picture with the back of the bowl of the spoon or with a rubber roller. The pressure of the spoon will transfer the ink

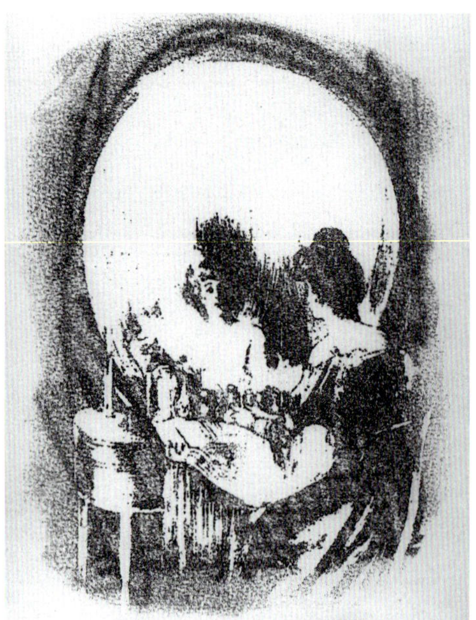

At the dressing table. Half close your eyes. Solvent transfer from a photocopy.

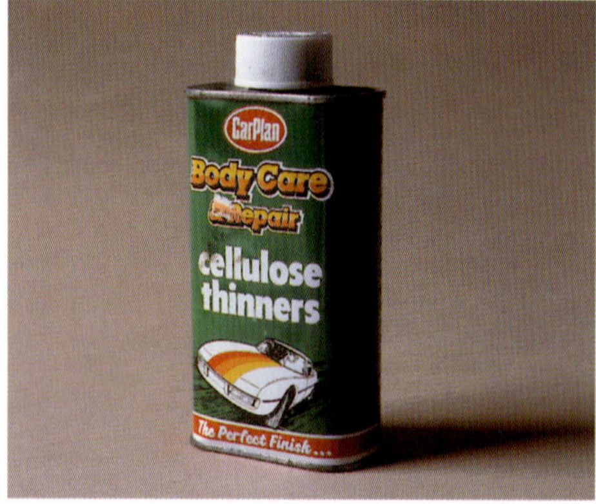

This is one of the most effective solvents available for solvent transfer, with the benefit of being generally available.

from the picture to the transfer paper.
Depending on the type of picture and the paper you use you will arrive at a transfer that should have the look and feel of a pastel drawing.

Method 2

The same as method 1, but with one essential difference.
Instead of a book illustration as your original, use a photocopy.
Photocopy a photograph any size, colour or black and white - family snapshots work well - enlarge it in the machine if necessary.
Now make the transfer as in 1, but this time use a smooth hot pressed paper and rub it with the edge of a piece of board or a ruler. The photocopier ink will run as it transfers and produces a very authentic 'lithographic' look. Cranes paper does a good job on this particular process.
When your transfers are dry you can go completely mad and colour them with pastels, water colours or felt tip pens.

There still ain't no rules.

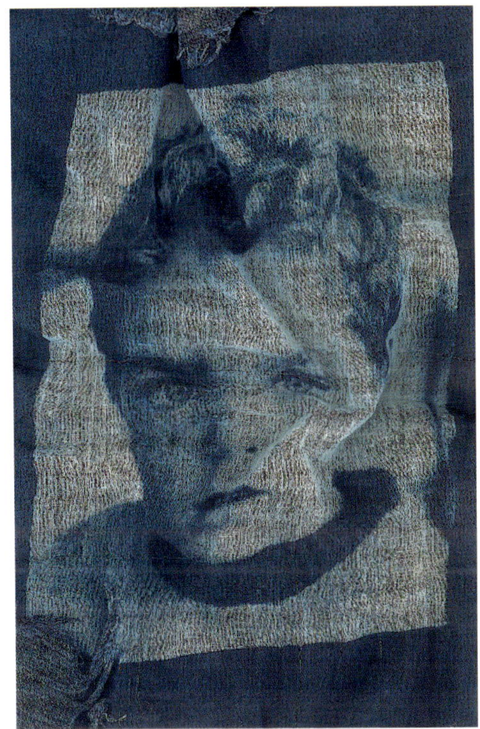

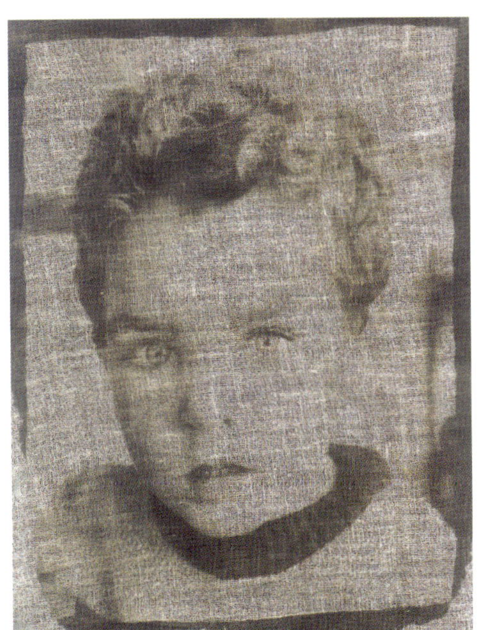

Cyanotype and Van Dyke prints on muslin.

A number of the alternative processes lend themselves very easily to making photographic prints on a range of materials other than paper. The only differences in technique involve some small adjustments in coating and exposure, the use of a flat iron and knowing which process is chemically compatible with which material.

It is important to remember that the best results come from using only 100 per cent vegetable fibres. These include cotton, linen, calico, linen and cotton union, (the base for chintz), muslin, sail cloth, canvas and, of course, pure cotton T- shirts.

Printing on animal or man-made fibres such as polyester and nylon is less easy as the sensitisers cannot soak into the fibres. The same applies to silk.

Traditionally, the easiest processes for printing on fabric are Van Dyke printing and cyanotype.

If you are very affluent you can try platinum printing on large sheets of canvas, but check with your bank first.

Cyanotype and Van Dyke prints on cloth

All the information on cyanotypes and Van Dyke prints on paper holds good for printing on fabric, but these are additional notes.

Cyanotypes are very susceptible to the effect of alkalis. Unfortunately for us, a lot of substances used to finish cloth, as well as many washing powders, and indeed tap-water itself, are alkaline.

So before you start to prepare your cloth for coating wash it thoroughly in mild soap or soap flakes and rinse it very well in plain cold water.

Van Dyke prints do not suffer from this problem. When you have printed your portrait on your T shirt you can put it in the washing machine as often as you like without harming the image.

Coating the sensitiser on the cloth

Take a piece of clean, slightly dampened cloth about 4 inches larger all round than your image and iron it smooth with a flat iron set at the appropriate setting. **Do not** set the iron on steam setting for these procedures.

Stretch the cloth - not too tightly - over a piece of glass, card or hardboard a little larger in size than your image. Fold and tuck the spare edges of the cloth behind the glass and tape them lightly together.

Now brush your sensitiser onto the front of the cloth as you would on paper. It will take more solution to soak into the cloth than it will for the same size of paper. It will also bleed into the cloth around the edges in an irregular shape. Don't worry about that at this stage.

Now, carefully remove the wet cloth and hang it up to dry in the dark or in subdued room lighting. You can speed up the drying with a hair drier at this point. When it is dry, iron it smooth again with a flat iron.

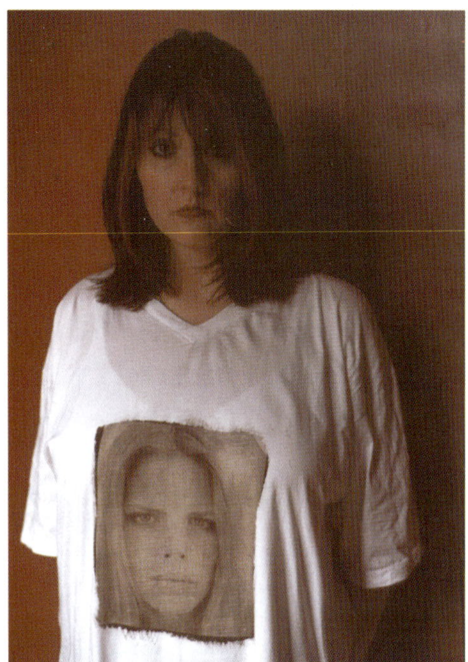

Van Dyke print on pure cotton T shirt, image and modelling by Darlene Honey, Van Dyke print by author.

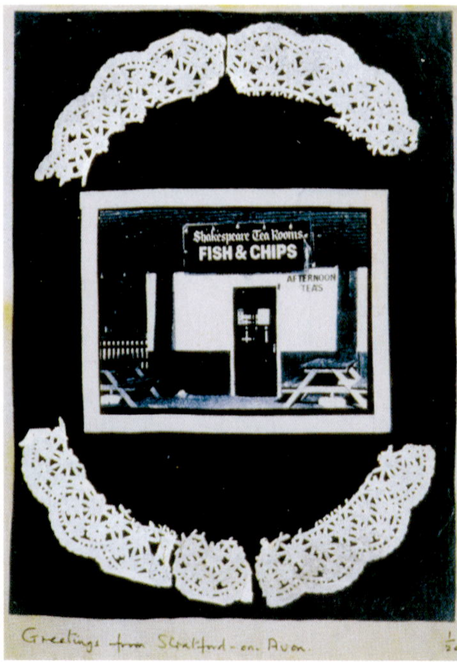

Greetings from Stratford on Avon. Cyanotype on linen. Paper doilies stuck on with glue.

Stretch it over a **clean** piece of glass or card and tape the spare edges at the back. Tape your negative along one edge and place it on the coated part of the cloth. Place another piece of glass over them and clip them altogether with a bulldog clip along each edge.

Expose as you would for paper and process in dishes in the appropriate solutions.

When you wash it finally, treat it as you would any other cloth and finish by wringing it out with your hands. Hang it up to dry and then iron it again until it is flat.

Another way of coating fabrics, especially delicate ones such as muslin, is to dip the whole piece of cloth into the sensitiser solution and wring out the surplus back into the container holding the liquid.

To avoid blue or brown hands please use rubber gloves!

If you want clean white edges round your image you must mask the area around the image with a sheet of black paper or fogged lith film. Cut out a window the size of your image and place it over the negative when you expose. In this way the sensitiser will not be exposed and will be washed out during processing.

There may be some residual staining left even after taking these precautions, but you will have to live with this.

Note on cyanotypes

If the image on your cloth fades at any time, you can revive the colour by rinsing it in a solution of 500 ml water mixed with 10 ml hydrogen peroxide.

Solvent transfer

Make a transfer as in [28.Solvent transfer], but use a photocopy from a basic cheap photocopier which will give a fairly graphic image. Do not expect to get a transfer with a wide range of tones.

Use a fairly densely woven fabric such as an old shirt or pillow case to start with and progress to more exotic materials as you go on.

Mordant prints

This method uses some of the principles of gum printing with the water colour pigment being replaced by organic vegetable dyes. The method, briefly, is this;

A piece of cloth is sensitised with potassium dichromate, exposed under a negative and then washed.

The cloth is then simmered in a bath of organic vegetable dye. The image formed by the dichromate exposed to the light combines with the vegetable dye and holds it in the fabric. The dye in the unexposed parts of the image is then washed away.

Shopping list.

A **negative preferably made on lith film** to give a bold graphic image.

A **length of cotton or linen**.

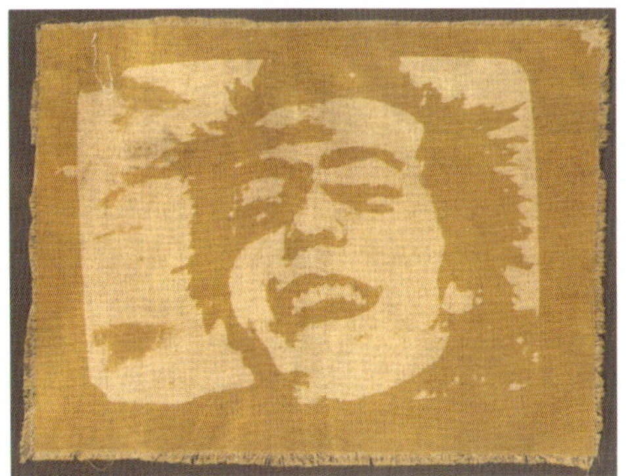

Sex Pistol. Mordant print on cotton using onion skin vegetable dye.

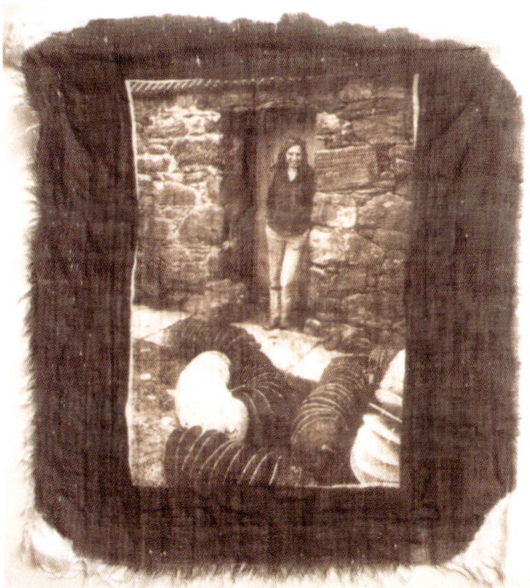

Outside the smokehouse. Van Dyke print on muslin.

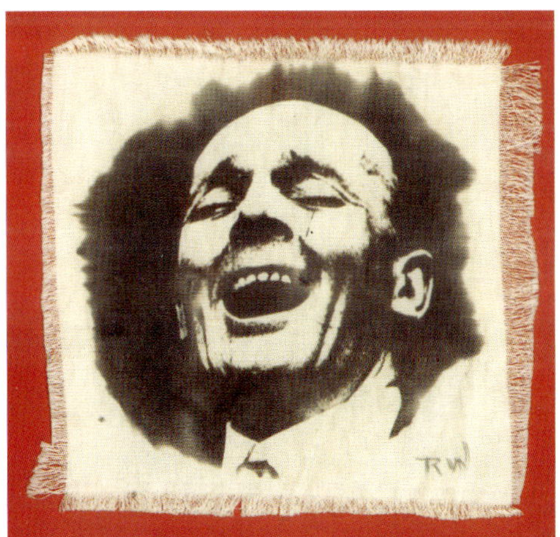

Van Dyke print on cream cotton.

10 g **potassium dichromate**.

A large stainless steel or enamel **saucepan**.

A medium sized **brush for coating**, (2" wide).

A **sheet of card or glass** to hold the cloth when coating and exposing.

Six medium sized **onions.**

Method

The traditional way of starting this process is to use onion skins as the base of our organic dye. There are several other plants that can be used and they are listed at the end of this section.

The day before you make the print you should prepare the dye bath. Take six medium sized onions and remove the brown outer skins. Bruise the skins with a spoon, place them in a dish, cover them with water and leave them to soak overnight. The white inner flesh of the onion you can use in a salad! The following day, place the onion skins in their liquid in a sauce pan and boil them for an hour and a half. The more skins you have in proportion to water, the darker the colour of the dye. Let the mixture cool, strain it through a kitchen strainer and discard the skins.

Mix 10g potassium dichromate in 100 ml of water. Using the same procedure as you did with cyanotype, coat the fabric with the dichromate, dry it and expose it under a negative. (About ten minutes in the sun or a bit more if you use a UV lamp. Use a test strip if you want to be absolutely sure).

Wash the fabric in a dish with cold water running through it until all the unexposed yellow dichromate disappears.

Heat the dye bath in an old saucepan to about 40° C and dip the fabric into it. Stir the fabric with the wooden spoon so that the cloth is evenly distributed in the liquid.

Now raise the temperature of the bath to about 50° C and let it simmer for about an hour and a half, stirring occasionally.

Rinse the fabric in several successive pans of water reducing the temperature for each one. When all the excess dye has been washed out and only the dyed image remains, squeeze the cloth gently to remove the excess water and hang up to dry.

Other sources of vegetable dye;

Plant	Colour of dye
Alder bark	Gold
Aster flowers	Gold
Bracken shoots	Green
Carrot tops	Bronze
Dalia flowers	Orange
Dandelion flowers	Orange
Dock leaves	Red
Floribunda rose leaves	Brown
Loganberry leaves	Deep green

Albumen print on portion of plywood tea chest. In retrospect it appears that the wood should have been more thoroughly sized. Note the stencilled lettering showing through.

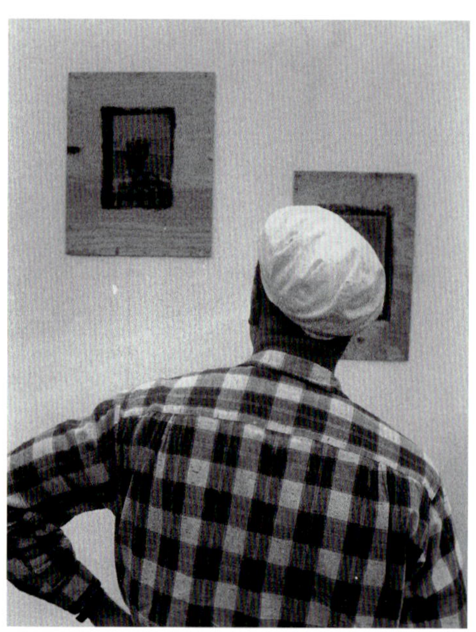

The picture, the model and the shirt.

There are, of course, many other sources of vegetable dye but those listed react best to the light sensitive dichromate mordant.

Financial advice

Wedding photographers may find printing on cloth quite a profitable activity. A cushion cover or a pillow case bearing a Van Dyke print of the loving couple often proves a useful way of relieving the father of the bride of an even larger cheque.

Printing on wood, plywood and hard board

The main thing to bear in mind when using these materials is that the surface must be well sized before you apply the sensitiser. This not only prevents the sensitiser soaking into the wood, but also isolates it from any substances in it which may contaminate it.

Size the wood with several coats of gelatin or egg white, letting each coat dry thoroughly between coatings. If you don't want to print directly onto the wood, paint the surface with two coats of white emulsion paint, lightly sanding each coat when dry with fine sandpaper. Then coat with gelatin or egg white.

Make cyanotypes, gum prints or kallitypes as you would on paper.

When you wash and fix the image, hold the piece of wood on its side over a dish and pour the water and fixer so that they run down the surface of the wood, thus avoiding the problem of immersing the whole piece in the liquids.

The carbon process works well on wood, provided you prepare it with at least four coats of gelatin before you transfer the carbon image.

Printing on ceramic tiles

Decorate your bathroom or kitchen with your own photographic images. The gum process is best for this.

Purchase some unglazed white ceramic tiles from a tile supplier and scrub them with hot water and a brush.

When they are dry make up your gum mixture but substitute the water colour pigment with underglaze pigment. This is used for decorating pottery and can be obtained from a pottery materials supplier or a pottery studio.

Coat the tile with the gum mix, let it dry, expose it under a negative and wash in warm water.

When it is thoroughly dry,.take it to a pottery studio and ask for it to be coated with transparent glaze and fired.

Do enough of these and you can cover a whole wall.

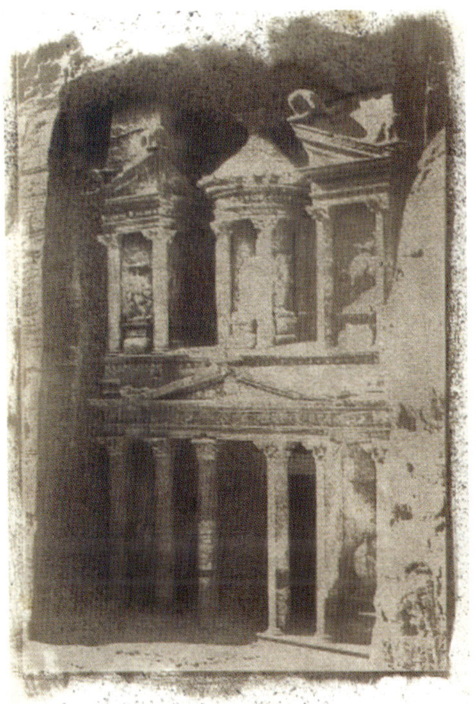

Petra, Jordan. Gum over cyanotype.

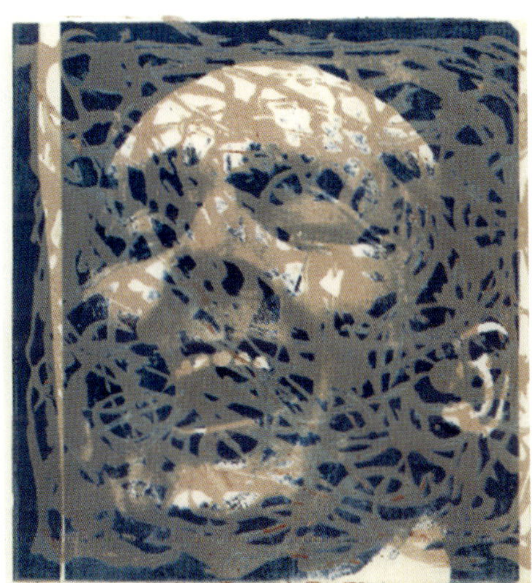

Mixture of gum and bichromate squeegeed through a hand-drawn abstract pattern on a silk screen. Exposed to light and washed, and a cyanotype printed over it. The cyanotype adheres to the paper, but not to the abstract pattern in gum.

There are two ways of approaching the use of old processes. Salt prints, platinum, kallitype and carbon can be used as a straight substitute for modern silver gelatin printing. This is in fact what they were traditionally meant to do and they are still a perfectly valid method. However, for present day workers they may also be employed for more graphic or experimental techniques.

There was a convention at the turn of the century to use gum printing to overlay images on to platinum or cyanotypes. Steichen and Stieglitz, amongst others, would use gum to multiple print a negative onto a platinum image, mainly to reinforce the depth of tone in the shadow areas of the platinum image. Modern taste now tends to regard this as a waste of good platinum.

You must bear in mind that when you print one process over an existing image, the negative must be superimposed exactly on top of the original print when making the second exposure.

Please refer to the section on exposure for details of making proper registration. Here are a few examples of combinations that can be used.

Gum as overlay - gum prints can be overlaid on many of the processes:

Gum over **cyanotype**.
Gum over **salt print**.
Gum over **kallitype**.
Gum over **platinum** or **palladium**.
Gum over **bromoil** (provided the bromoil ink has dried out thoroughly).
Gum over **photo etch**.
Gum over **gravure**.
Gum over **silk screen**.
Gum over **solvent transfer**.
Gum over **bleach etch**.
And of course gum over **silver gelatin,** in the form of **liquid emulsion**.
Gum over carbon is not really practical as the warm water soak may lift off the gelatin carbon image.

Cyanotype as overlay

Cyanotype over **platinum** or **palladium**.
Cyanotype over **gum** is a bit strange as it doesn't always stick to the gum image.
Don't bother with cyanotype over the silver based processes e.g. salt or kallitype as the ferricyanide in the cyanotype will bleach out the silver in the other two.
Cyanotype over **solvent transfer**.
Cyanotype over **carbon** or **bromoil** may work but are less likely to give a pleasing result.

Solvent transfer will work in combination with most processes but this is subject to individual taste.

Photo etch, gravure and silk screen will work on most processes. Photo etch works very well over gum prints.

Bromoil is difficult to print over most processes, as the bromoil bleach adversely affects the original image.

This list of combinations is a bit like the football pools. If you try enough permutations you are bound to get a winner. Eventually. On the other hand the chances are better than in the old joke of the thousand monkeys on a thousand typewriters taking a thousand years in the hope of writing a Shakespeare sonnet.

If any reader comes up with an unusual combination please let us know. Unfortunately there are no prizes for this, just the satisfaction of doing something new!

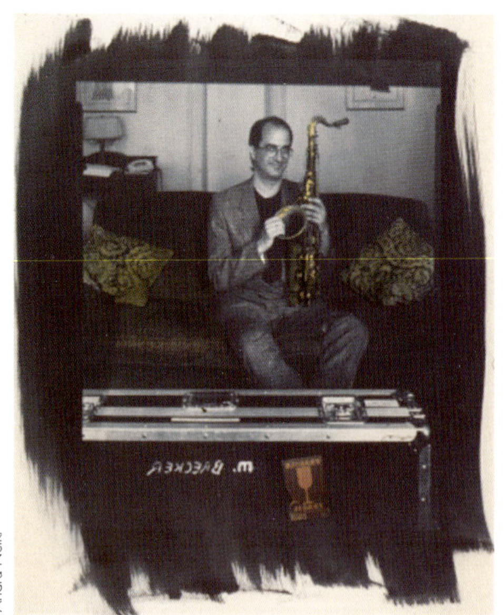

Andra Nelki

Hand colouring over cyanotype.

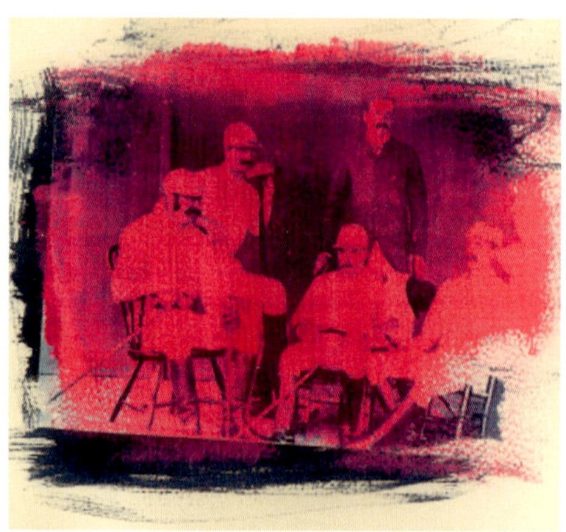

Shocking pink polo players. Pigment and glue brushed on paper and allowed to dry. Cyanotype printed over.

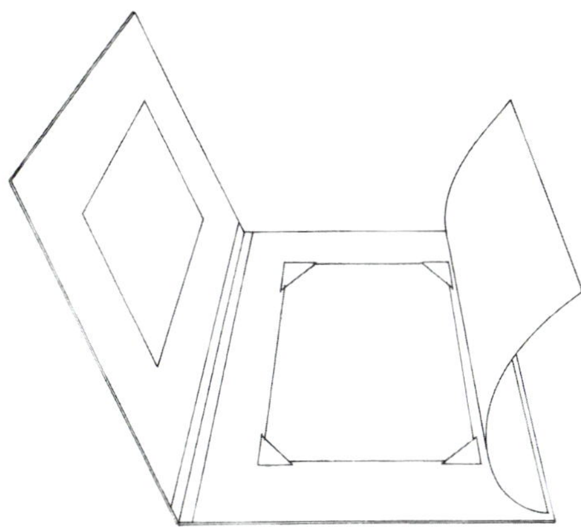

The classic museum mount. Print attached to back board with archival photo corners or hinges. The window matt is attached to the backing board with linen tape hinge. Acid free tissue covers the surface of the print.

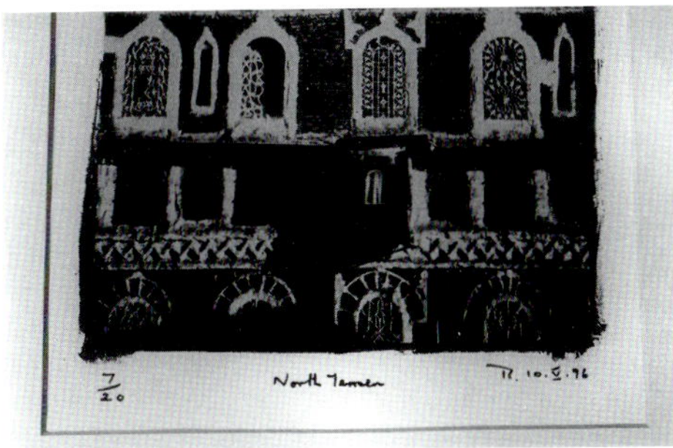

Conventional way of signing and editioning a print.

Using hinges to attach print to mounting board. The minimum amount of adhesion between print and linen tape is achieved with this method.

Having arrived after much effort at what may or not be a masterpiece to grace the walls of the Tate gallery, you will need to find the best way of presenting your print. There is nothing to stop you (except good taste) from mounting it behind a gold and dayglow pink plastic frame. However there are some fairly well established conventions which you should find fairly easy to follow.

Mounting your prints

If you look in most books of photographs and most museums and galleries, the surrounds will usually be white, off-white or cream. Avoid garish colours except for special occasions, and under no circumstances whatsoever use black, which used to be a convention in camera clubs about thirty years ago.

1 Window matts. Cut the hole in the mount so that only the image shows, hiding the brushed edge, **or;**
cut the hole in the mount so that about an eighth of an inch of brushed edge shows as a fine dark border round the image, **or;**
cut a larger hole in the mount so that the image and all the brush marks on the margin show. This will leave your audience in no doubt that it is indeed an old process.

2 Stick it on the surface of the mount. **Do not** in any circumstances dry mount or glue your print to the card. It will be bonded for ever to the same piece of card.

Rather, make two small hinges from archival quality gummed paper tape and use them to lightly stick the print to the mount so that all the print shows, including the brush work and the pretty deckle edges.

3 Use a choice of photo corners as illustrated over the page.

Now put it in a plain wooden frame. The frame can be any colour provided that it is black. In some circumstances plain unpainted wooden frames will do.

One other point. Use acid free mounting board. Your descendants in later years will thank you for expending the extra few pennies on good board.

Limited editions

There is not much point in making limited editions of black and white prints. For one thing negatives are infinitely reproducible in books, magazines etc, and secondly it is just a little pretentious. If you have a few gullible buyers who don't know any better then we suppose it is OK.

When you make prints with old processes you may consider yourself to be approaching the world of the 'art' printer, and it may be useful to know a little about how the system works.

Limited editions signed by the artist protect to some degree the purchasers of printed art works such as etchings, lithographs and more recently, screen prints, from having fakes or reproductions foisted on them by unscrupulous dealers. At the same time they add a little stability to a volatile market.

Using the law of supply and demand, an edition of 10 etchings has a greater rarity value than an edition of 1000. The artist's signature establishes its authenticity. There are artists who sell four colour commercial prints, ie posters, place them in an elaborate frame and sign an edition of 2000 selling at £150 or more each. The frame and the signature are worth £149.50 and the print 50p. As a result art dealers and buyers expect the artist to observe a few ground rules, or at least guidelines.

Here are some of them.

Decide before you start how big the edition will be. It can be as little as 4 or 5 or as big as 500. You don't need to produce all of them at once, but every time you make another one, record in a diary the number of the print, the date you made it, and if applicable who received it. Most important of all record the selling price.

Apart from the price, these details are also written on the lower margin of the print in pencil. Don't sign it with a felt tip pen (the ink fades) and please **don't** sign the mount. If the purchaser of your print decides to have it reframed or remounted, all that information will be lost and the value of the print reduced. (Having said that, there are photographers out there selling black and white prints at inflated prices in beautifully signed mounts. We think they should be told!)

At the lower left hand side write the total edition number below the number of that particular print, eg 6 / 20. This means print no. 6 out of an edition of 20. In the centre the title or the dedication eg 'Misty Morn' or 'For Cynthia'. At the right hand side your signature and the date eg 'Fred 2.VI.96'. If you have an impossibly long name use your initials.

You may have made one or two prints at the beginning of the run which are not quite good enough to sell but too good to throw away. In this case, instead of putting the edition number in the left hand corner, you write A/P, which stands for artist's proof. Don't do more than two or three of these or you will soon be found out.

Don't wrap your print and its mount in miles of wrapping paper and tape. It tends to annoy your purchaser. Instead use a polyester sleeve.

What happens when you sell all of your edition? Well, that's it. You can't make a new edition the same as the first. An etcher or engraver would strike his plate - that is scratch a big cross on it so it can't be used again.

The best you can do is to make a new edition that looks materially different from its predecessor - for instance change the colour combinations.

Once you have reached this point you can safely say you have made it as a print maker.

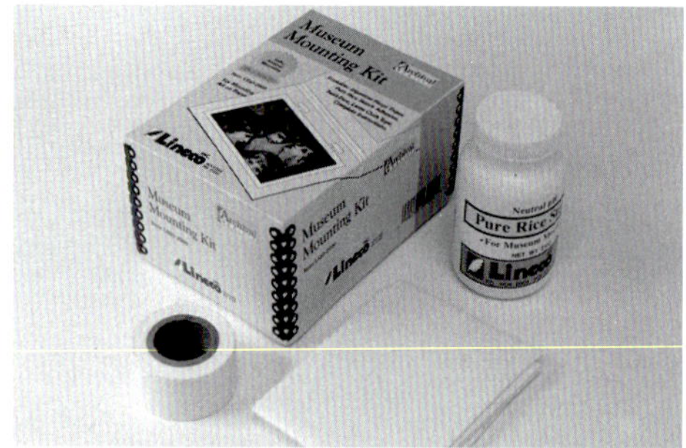

Archival mounting materials, part of the range from the USA archival supplier University Products.

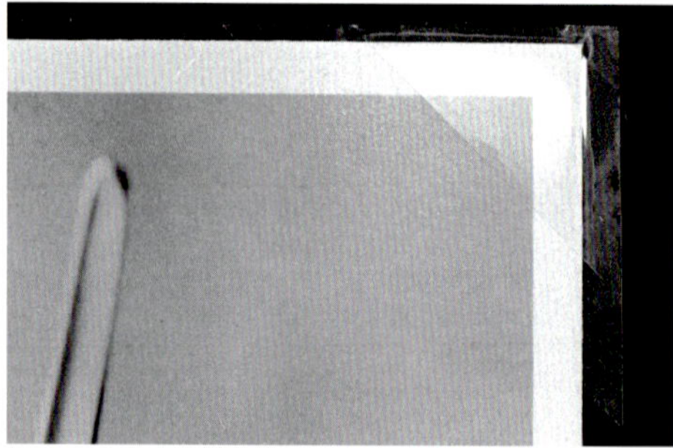

Transparent polyester photo corner. Any method of archival mounting should avoid using adhesive in contact with the artwork.

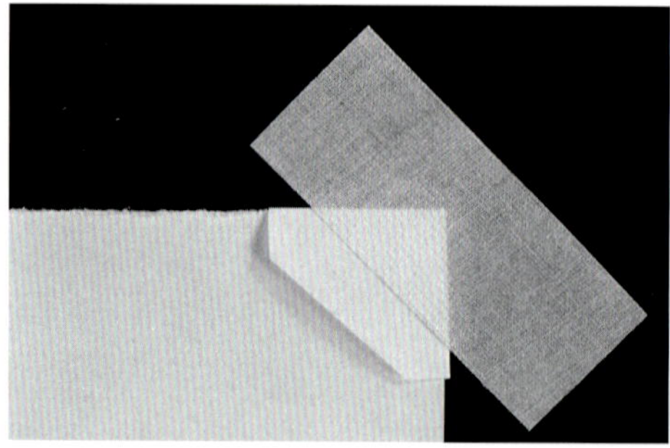

Alternative method, a print held in an archival paper photo corner is attached to the mount with linen tape. This obviously should be covered by the window matt.

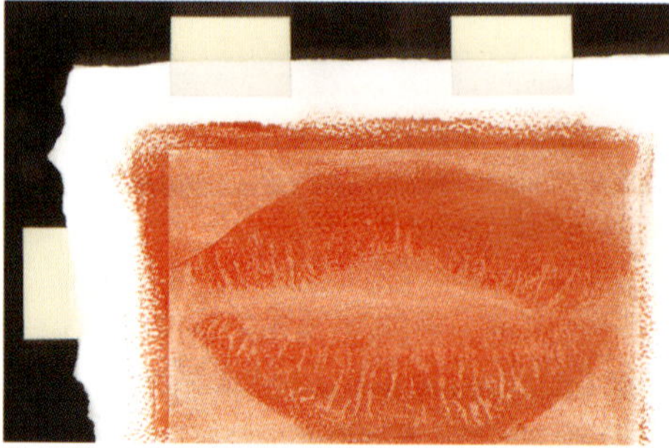

Polyester mounting strips from University Products - useful with large prints, as a number can be positioned around the edges. No adhesive touches the print.

E-Mail Discussion Groups

Sspecialist groups exchange information on topics such as large format photography, photo art and photo history. There are too many e-mail discussion groups to list here, but a list of groups including short descriptions is obtainable at;
www.rit.edu/~andpph/photolists.html

The two groups most relavent to alternative processes are;

Alt-photo-process
The principle discussion group for those interested in alternative processes. Join by posting an E-mail to:
listproc@vast.unsw.edu.au
In the body of the message include:
subscribe alt-photo-process and your name.

A frequently asked question (FAQ) sheet can be found by posting a message to:
listproc@vast.unsw.edu.au
In the body of the message type:
get alt-photo-process faq

All postings to the Alt-Photo-Process group are archived, providing an enormous resource on all aspects of alternative photography. To access an archive post a message to:
listproc@vast.unsw.edu.au
In the body of the message type:
index alt-photo-process
To access a particular archive send a message to:
listproc@vast.unsw.edu.au
In the body of the message type:
get alt-photo-process archive-yymm
where yy is the year and mm is the month you require, eg June 1998 would be 9906.

The Art & Craft of Photography
New group administered by Terry King, aimed at dialogue between experienced practitioners in alternative processes. To subscribe send an e-mail to;
altartcraftphoto-subscribe@listbot.com

To receive images for discussion on the first list, subscribe by sending a blank e-mail to;
altimages100-subscribe@listbot.com

The website for the group is;
www.hands-on-pictures.com
and e-mail address;
takingphotos@hands-on-pictures.com

Websites

Web sites come and go, these addresses were correct at the time of going to press. There is a profusion of photographic sites, USA predominating, and most tend to have good links into other related sites. These, then, are listed just as starting points.

members.aol.com/dcolucci/index.html
Details of the albumen process, and history from Daguerrotype to paper. Good links.

Handmade photo images *www2.ari.net/glsmyth/*
Has links to information on Ziatype, albumen printing and Mike Wares Type 11 Cyanotype.

Artcraft Chemicals *www.nfinity.com/~mdmuir/artcraft.html*
Online catalogue from Artcraft, chemical supplies.

Bostick and Sullivan *www.bostick-sullivan.com/*
Information on Ziatype and platinum/palladium, chemical supplies for these processes.

Daguerrian Society *java.austine.edu/dag/*

Darkroom & technical
www.users.dircon.co.uk/~migol/photo/links.html
Very large site with a lot of information and links to just about everything.

Alternative Process FAQ (frequently asked questions)
duke.usask.ca/%7Eholtsg/photo/faq.html
Information on historic processes, from calotype to platinum.

Fisher Scientific *www.fisher1.com*
Large online catalogue of chemicals & equipment.

Fotospeed *www.Fotospeed.com*
Raw chemicals, kits for cyanotype 2, Argyrotype, bromoil.

Freestyle Sales Co. *www.freestylesalesco.com*
Large format film supplies & paper, related items. Pre-coated cyanotype paper.

Genealogy Reource *genealogy.org/~ajmorris/photo/photo.html*
Genealogical reources site, contains section on photo history, processes, conservation of photographs.

History of photography *www.kbnet.co.uk/rleggat/photo*
Bibliography, Museums, historical processes, styles & movements.

Luminos *www.luminos.com*
USA supplier of Kentmere Document Art, silver/gel emulsion, kits for various alternative processes, inc. bromoil, argyrotype, cyanotype, liquid emulsion.

Luis Nadeau *worldserver.oleane.com/guydr/nadeau.html*
Well known specialist in alternative processes and author of many books.

Mike Ware *www.mikeware.demon.co.uk*
Site provided by the UK-based chemist and photographer, containing full manuals for his processes platinum/palladium, Type 11 Cyanotype, and Argyrotype. Good links.

Photographers Formulary *www.montana.com/formulary/*
Raw chemicals & kits for all processes.

Royal Photographic Society *www.rps.org/*
Good links to other sites concerned with historical photographs.

Silverprint Ltd *www.silverprint.co.uk*
UK based supplier of most materials for alternative processes, as well as conventional photography. The site comprises their catalogue plus changing special features. Down-loadable price list.

Ultrastable *www.ultrastable.com/*
Suppliers of the updated 4-colour carbon printing material.

Bibliography

(books illustrated are in print at time of writing)

Darkroom Dynamics

Ed. Jim Stone, Focal Press 1979, 200 pp.

Although now over 20 years old, this book has a respected place as reference material for creative photo. techniques. Sixteen chapters from guest contributors cover topics as wide ranging as split-toning, photograms, dye transfer and hand colouring.

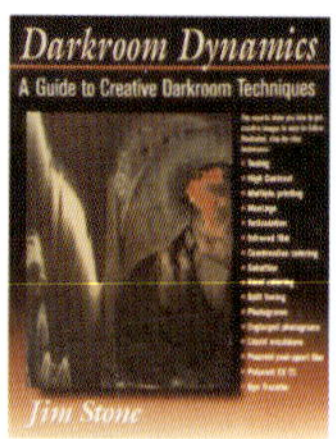

Making Kallitypes - a definitive guide

Dick Stevens, Focal Press 1993, 233 pp.

As the title says, definitive. This looks like a doctoral thesis, is clearly written and stuffed full of information. No colour illustrations, however, so you need to look elsewhere for good examples.

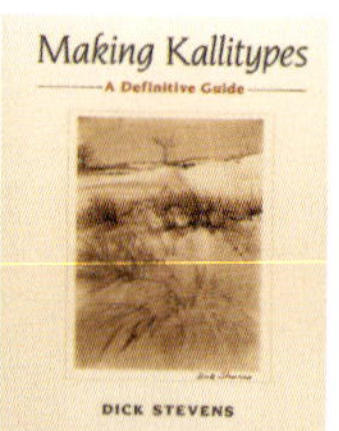

Gumoil Photographic Printing

Karl P. Koenig, Focal Press 1994, 133 pp.

Gumoil was developed from several alternative-processes. Gumoil printing involves contact printing a positive transparency onto gum coated paper. Oil paints are then applied, and with bleach etching mono and polychromatic variations are possible.

The Darkroom Cookbook

Steve Anchell, Focal Press 1994, 206 pp.

You should have this on your bookshelf already. Contains around 140 recipes for working with raw chemicals, covering all areas of conventional silver photography.

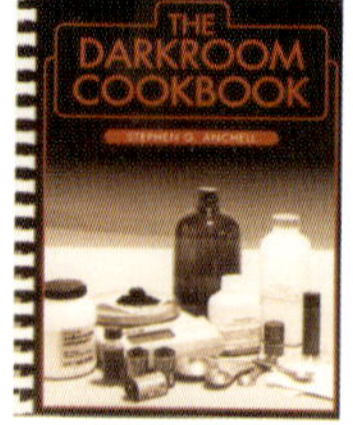

Keepers of Light by William Crawford

William Crawford, Morgan & Morgan 1979, 317 pp.

Nearly 20 years old and still going strong, this is the book that set many people on the old process trail. Only half of the book contains how to do it information, the rest being devoted to a discussion of history and aesthetics.

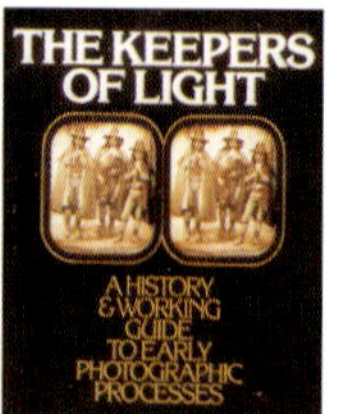

The Gum Bichromate Book

David Scopick, Focal Press 1991, 150 pp.

Impressively complete resource for gum printing. If it isn't here, you probably don't need to know it. Additional chapters cover Kwik Print, sensitometry, contrast control, halftone screens, print editioning.

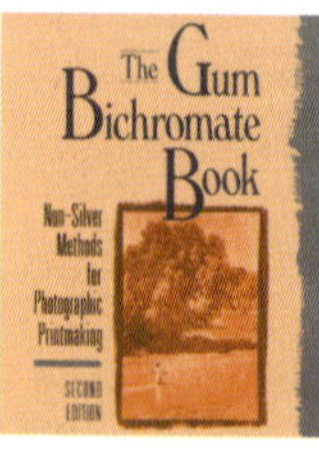

Platinum and Palladium Printing

Dick Arentz, 1991, 54 pp.

Privately published, ringbound, single sided printing. Essential reading for all platinum/palladium printers. Arentz is the best in the business, although the section on sensitometry is pretty heavy going. Not illustrated apart from technical diagrams.

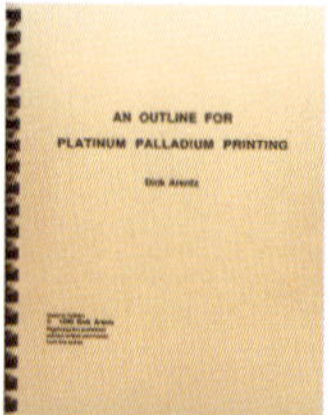

The Negative

Ansel Adams, Little Brown, 1981, 272 pp.

One third of the Ansel Adams New Photography Series, a new edition of his original series, and completed before his death. Concise, wide ranging, well designed and profusely illustrated, it is still one of the best authorities on negative making.

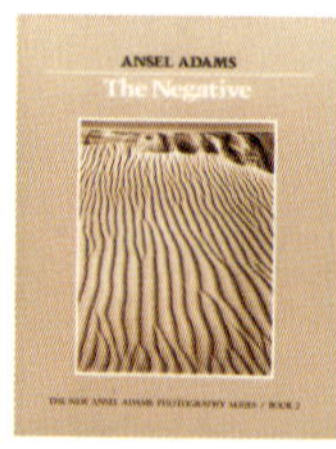

New Dimensions in Photo Imaging

Laura Blacklow, Focal Press 1995, 164 pp.

Thorough working notes for a number of alternative photo. processes, including cyanotype, Van Dyke brown, gum bichromate, casein pigment, platinum / palladium, as well as the proprietary 'Kwikprint' system.

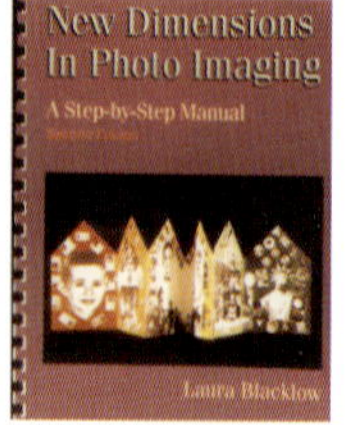

Silver Gelatin

Martin Reed & Sarah Jones

Working Books 1995, 144 pp.

The aim of writing the book was to elevate self-coated emulsion away from the novelty & hobby uses it had been enmired in. Large portfolio section, and very thorough technical chapters.

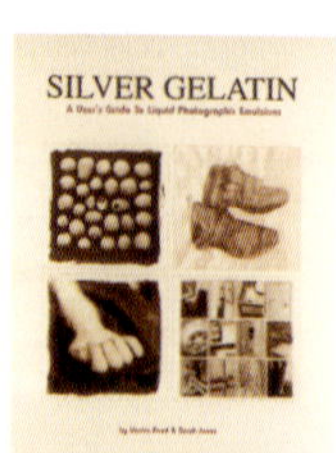

Historic Photographic Processes

Richard Farber, Allworth Press, 1998, 242 pp.

Comprehensive and up-to-date resource covering most alternative processes, with input from a number of individual specialists. Includes salt printing, albumen, cyanotype, kallitype, platinum / palladium, carbon / carbro, gum and bromoil.

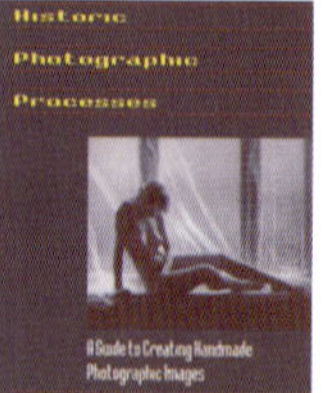

The Art of Bromoil & Transfer

David Lewis, self published, 1995, 117 pp

Nicely produced little casebound manual from the Canadian specialist, well illustrated with many examples in colour.

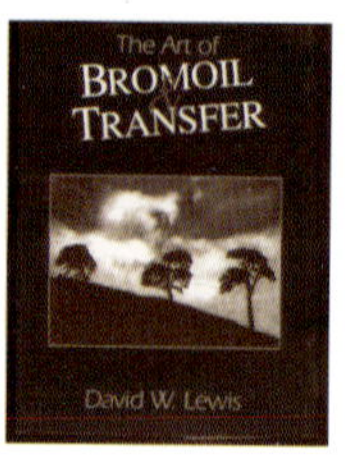

Bibliography [cont]

(some books listed may be out of print, and require access through library sources)

The Albumen and Salted Paper Handbook

James Reilly, Light Impressions, 1980.
A comprehensive account of the subject although a bit repetitive in places.

Alternative Photographic Processes

Kent E. Wade, Morgan and Morgan, 1978.
A useful companion to Keepers of Light.

Before Photography

Peter Galassi, Museum of Modern Art New York, 1981.
A fascinating perspective on the early days of photography.

Bernard Shaw on Photography

Bill Jay and Margaret Moore, Equation Books, 1989.
Opinions on photography by G. B. S. Contains reproductions of many of his platinum prints.

Bromoil Printing and Transfer

G. A. Whally, Fountain Press, 1961.
All you need to know by a disciple of Chris Symes who was one of the great bromoil printers.

Cassell's Cyclopaedia of Photography

Bernard Edward Jones, Cassell, London 1911, 2 volumes. Reprinted by Arno, NY, in one volume in 1974.
Amazing resource for alternative photography, including many obscure processes disused since Victorian times.

Classroom Photography

Ilford, 1984, 176 pp.
No cameras involved, an investigation of image-making using only light, photographic paper, and processing chemicals. Wirebound, profusely illustrated.

Cyanotype - photographic printing in Prussian blue

Mike Ware, Science Museum, 1999, 208 pp.
The first extensive monograph on the cyanotype process.

The Focal Encyclopaedia of Photography

Focal Press. Any edition you can get your hands on. The standard reference book for all photographers.

Fox Talbot - The Invention of Photography

Gail Buckland, Scolar Press London, 1980.
Detailed account of the life and work of the great man. Profusely illustrated with examples of his early salt prints.

'From Today Painting is Dead' - The Beginnings of Photography

The Arts Council of Great Britain, 1972.
Catalogue for an exhibition at the Victoria & Albert Museum in March-May 1972. Includes 914 listings, good notes, 50 pages of images.

A Guide to Early Photographic Processes

Mark Howarth-Booth and Brian Coe, Victoria and Albert Museum, 1983.
Written with all the authority of two experts in their field.

Looking at Photographs - a guide to technical terms

Gordon Baldwin, The J. Paul Getty Museum, 1991, 88 pp.
Written from the point of view of the curator, a concise overview of photographic processes, from the earliest days through to contemporary systems. Illustrated in colour throughout.

Luis Nadeau Books

See his web-site for more details. Nadeau is the expert author of several books, including **Modern Carbon Printing**, **Gum Bichromate and other Direct Carbon Processes**, & **The History & Practice of Platinum Printing**.

The Origins of Photography

Helmut Gernsheim, Thames & Hudson, 1982, 280 pp.
Updated re-issue of the original 'The History of Photography' of 1955. This mighty work is particularly impressive for the standard of reproduction, the Daguerrotypes being reproduced in silver to give a realstic impression of the originals.

Photo Art Processes

Nancy Howell-Koehler, Davis Publications USA, 1980.
The method sections are a bit homespun but the examples illustrated are amazing for their variety.

The Photograph Collectors Guide

Lee D. Whitkin & Barbara London, Secker & Warburg, London.
Essential for anyone interested in collectable historic photography, with details of any photographer who was anybody.

Photography in California 1945 to 1980

Louise Katzman, Hudson Hills Press New York, 1984.
An interesting account of the revival of old processes at the University College of Los Angeles in the 1960's and 70's with some avant garde examples.

Photography in Print Making

Charles Newton, Victoria and Albert Museum London, 1979.
Lucid account of the use of photography in etching, gravure and screen printing. Shows the work of artists such as Joe Tilson, Allen Jones, R. Kitaj, Richard Hamilton, Peter Blake and others who are better known in the art world than to photographers.

Sunday Times Book of Photodiscovery

Bruce Bernard, Thames and Hudson, 1980.
Lavish coffee table book with high quality examples of many of the early processes, many previously unpublished.

Which Paper

Sylvie Turner, Estam - London, 1991.
The most comprehensive coverage of paper in all its aspects. An absolute must for all old process workers.

Where to see examples

The collections in the UK with the most varied selections are:
Bath, Avon: The Royal Photographic Society Museum
Birmingham: The Reference Library
Bradford, Yorkshire: National Museum of Photography, Film and Television
Edinburgh: Scottish National Portrait Gallery
Edinburgh: Public Library
Guildford, Surrey: The Guildford Museum (pictures by Lewis Carroll)
London: The Victoria and Albert Museum
London: The Science Museum
London: MOMI (The Museum of the Moving Image)
London: The Imperial War Museum
London: Kingston-on-Thames Public Library
Manchester: The Northwest Museum of Science and Technology
Oxford: Museum of the History of Science
Lacock, Avon: The Fox Talbot Museum
Edinburgh: The Royal Scottish Museum

Suppliers

Detailed breakdown for UK suppliers, principal suppliers only listed for other territories. All details correct at time of publication.

UK

General

Alternative Photographic Review, 6 Penwith Business Centre, Long Rock, Penzance, TR20 8HL
tel. 01736 330 200
Newletter of alternative photographic techniques.

Historical Impressions, John Benjafield, Old Post Office Cottage, Woodrising, Norwich, NR9 4AH
tel. 01953 850 253
Specialist dealer in 19'th century photographic images and literature.

Chemicals

Aldrich Chemical Co. Ltd, The Old Brickyard,New Road,Gillingham, Dorset, SP8 4JL,
(01747) 822 211

Fotospeed, Jay House Ltd, Fiveways House, Westwells Road, Corsham, Wilts. SN13 9RG
tel. 01225 810596 fax 01225 811801

Johnson Matthey Chemicals Ltd, Orchard Road, Royston, Herts,. SG8 5HE
01763 244 161
Principal supplier of all precious metal salts.

Process Supplies Ltd,19 Mount Pleasant, London WC1
tel. 0207 837 2179 fax 0207 837 8551
General professional photographic supplies, range of raw chemicals.

Rayco, 199 King Street, Hoyland, Barnsley, S74 9LJ
tel/fax 01226 744594
Specialist supplier of wide range of raw chemicals, compounded developers, toners etc.

Silverprint Ltd, 12 Valentine Place, London, SE1 8QH
tel. 0207 620 0844
fax 0207 620 0129
website: http://www.silverprint.co.uk
e-mail: sales@silverprint.co.uk
General professional photographic supplies as well as a good range of materials for alternative processes, inc Bromoil & POP papers. Stocks the 'Gryspeerdt & the Bromoil Process' video. Bergger & Centennial products. Raw chemicals, inc. low price on silver nitrate.

Speedibrews, J. Cottrill Photography, 10 The Triangle, St Johns, Woking, Surrey, GU21 1PP
tel. 01483 772 316
Raw chemicals & chemical products.

Vignette,
tel. 01242 578060
Raw chemicals, kits

Art Papers

Atlantis European Ltd, 146 Brick Lane, London, E1 6RU,
tel 0207 377 8855

R.K. Burt & Co, 57 Union Street, London SE1
tel 0207 407 6474

Falkiner Fine Papers, 76 Southampton Row, London, WC1B 7AR,
tel. 0207 831 1151 fax 0207 430 1248
Retail showroom, wide range of papers.

JvO Paper, 15 Newell Street, Limehouse, London, E14 7HP
tel. 0207 987 7464 fax 0207 987 9307
Specialist and hand made paper.

T.N. Lawrence & Son, 117-119 Clerkenwell Road, London, EC1R 5BY
tel. 0207 242 3534 / 0207 405 4225
fax 0207 430 2234
Art material specialist.

John Purcell Paper, 15 Rumsey Road, London, SW9 0TR, UK
tel. 0207 737 5199 fax 0207 737 6765
Specialist paper wholesaler, very wide range.

Etching Supplies, Inks etc.

Cornellisen, 105 Great Russell St, London WC1
tel. 0207 636 1045
fax 0207 636 3655

Intaglio Printmakers, 62 Southwark Bridge Road, London SE1
tel. 0207 928 2633

Sheet Film & General Photo Supplies

Most cities have at least one large photographic wholesaler, and this is likely to be the best source for run-of-the-mill materials like developer, stop and fixer, and equipment such as thermometers and developing trays

Nova Darkroom Equipment, Unit 1a Harris Road, Wedgenock Industrial Estate, Warwick, CV34 5JU
tel 01926 402090
Specialist supplier of own brand darkroom equipment.

Process Supplies (as above)

Silverprint (as above)

Silkscreen Supplies

Sericol Ltd, Unit C42, Barwell Business Park, Leatherhead Road, Chessington, Surrey, KT9 2NY
tel. 0208 391 5533

Carbon Tissue

Autotype International Ltd, Grove Road, Wantage, Oxon. OX12 7BZ
tel. 01235 771111 fax 01235 771195
Manufacturers of carbon tissue.

Silverprint (as above)

Brushes

Silverprint (as above

Fotospeed (as above)

All art suppliers listed above.

Coating Rods

Silverprint (as above)

Fotospeed (as above)

Chemglass, 1a Cranmer Road, Forest Gate, London, E7 0JW
tel/fax. 0208 534 2262

Printing Frames

Peter Frederick, 34 Trinity Road, Southend-on-Sea, Essex, SS2 4HJ
tel. 01702 308187
Expert in gum and related processes. Produces his own economical design of pin register frame, see p.38.

Gandolfi, Unit 8, Berwick Courtyard, St Leonard, Salisbury, Wilts, SP3 5SN
tel. 01747 820777 fax 01747 820888
As well as the famous large format cameras, the company has recently introduced a high quality hardwood hinged-back printing frame.

Centennial hinged-back frame, stockist Silverprint (as above)

UV Light Sources

Osram PO Box 17, East Lane, Wembley, Middx. HA9 7PG
tel. (0208) 904 4321 fax (0208) 901 1222
Vitalux bulb (via electrical wholesalers)

Starna Ltd, 33 Station Road, Chadwell Heath,
tel. 0208 599 5115

Densitometers

RH Designs, 20 Mark Road, Hemel Hempstead Industrial Estate, Hemel Hempstead, Herts. HP2 7BN
tel. 01442 258111 fax 01442 258112
Inexpensive Heiland densitometer.

Lucht (Europe), 5 Zodiac House, Calleva Park, Aldermaston, Reading, Berkshire, RG7 8HN
tel. 01189 817575 fax 01189 817140
Macbeth & Gretag densitometers.

Europe

Bergger SA, 104 Rue de Turenne, 75003 Paris, France
tel. 33 1 (44) 598 688 fax 33 1 (40) 279 974
Manufacturer of bromoil paper, also supplies Autotype carbon material, POP.

Fine Print Studios, Klaus Pollmeier, Muhleneld 43, D 45470 Mulheim a/d Ruhr, Germany.
tel. 49 (208) 431 051 fax 49 (208) 433 937
100561.2417@compuserve.com
Specialist in supplies for alternative processes, inc. bromoil brushes, chemicals, papers, books.

Hans O. Mahn & Co. PO Box 105202, 20036 Hamburg
tel (040) 23 70 08-88 fax (040) 23 35 77
Supplies sheet film and a wide range of own-brand material for the darkroom user.

Nationaal Fotorestauratie Atelier, Witte de Withstraat 63, 3012 BN Rotterdam, Netherlands
tel. 31 (0) 10 233 16 96 fax 31 (0) 10 233 19 65
www.nfra.v2.nl/
E-mail *nfra@nfra.v2.nl* *sales@nfra.v2.nl*
European distributor of Centennial printing out paper and frames.

North America

Adorama, 42 West Eighteenth Street, New York, NY 10011
tel. (800) 8114004 fax (212) 463 7223

Artcraft Chemicals, PO Box 583, Schenectady, NY 12301, USA
tel. (518) 355 8700 / (800) 682 1730
Photographic chemicals, kits

B&H, 420 Ninth Avenue, New York, NY 1001
tel. (800) 947 9981 fax (800) 947 7008
General purpose paper, chemicals, equipment.

Bostick & Sullivan, PO Box 16639, Santa Fe, NM 87506 6639, USA
tel. (505) 474 0890 fax (505) 474 2857
www.bostick-sullivan.com
richsul@roadrunner.com
Principal source for platinum/palladium supplies, own brand ferric oxalate at good price, bromoil paper & brushes, wide range of chemicals.

Cachet, 3701 West Moore Ave., Santa Ana, CA 92704
tel (714) 432 7070 fax (432) 7102
Agent for MACO products, inc emulsioned linen, graphic arts film.

Chicago Albumen Works, Front Street, Housatonic, MA 01236, USA
tel. (413) 274 6901 fax (413) 274 6934
info@albumenworks.com
Suppliers of own label POP.

Darkroom Innovations Inc, PO Box 19450, Fountain Hills, AZ 85269, USA
tel. (602) 767 7105 fax (602) 767 7106
www.darkroom-innovations.com
73354.2425@compuserve.com
Innovative sheet film developing tubes, specialised sensitometry computer software.

Freestyle Sales Company, 5124 Sunset Boulevard, Los Angeles, CA 90027, USA
tel. (213) 660 3460 fax (213) 660 4885
foto@freestylesalesco.com
Alternative process kits, graphic arts film, wide range of other supplies.

David Lewis, PO Box 254, Callander, Ontario PO14 1HO, Canada
tel. (705) 752 3029
Supplies for bromoil printing, inc. inks & brushes, author of book, p. 156.

Light Impressions Corporation,
PO Box 3012, Rochester, NY 14614 USA
tel. 1(716)-271 8960 (1-800-828 6216)
fax 1(716)-800-5539

Lumino Photo Corp., PO Box 158, Yonkers, NY 10705, USA
tel (914) 965 4800 fax (914) 965 0367
US distributors for Kentmere Document Art, also kits for type 11 cyanotype, precoated cyanotype fabric, argyrotype kits.

The Palladio Company, Inc. 2400, 200 Boston Avenue, Medford, ME 02155, USA
tel. (617) 393 0811 / (800) 628 9618 fax (617) 393 0817
Only manufactuer of coated platinotype paper.

Photographers Formulary, PO Box 950, Condon, MT 59826, USA
tel. 1(406) 754 2891 / 1(800)-922-5255
fax 1(406) 754 2896

Ultrastable Color Systems, 500 Seabright Avenue, Suite 201, Santa Cruz, CA 95062, USA
tel. (408) 427 3000 fax (408) 426 9900
Suppliers of an innovative revision of the carbon process, using polyester base.

Index

Acids & alkalis *30*
Albumen printing
- details & method *57*
- troubleshooting *59*

Argyrotype *68*
Arrowroot paper *59*
Autotype *101*
Bleach etch *143*
Blueprint *71, 76*
Booklist *156*
Bromoil printing
- details & method *89*
- notes on inking *95*
- troubleshooting *96*

Bromoil transfer *97*
Brushes *18*
Brushing techniques *33*
Carbon printing *101*
Carbon tissue, making *103*
Casein printing *115*
Centennial paper *61*
Ceramics, printing on *150*
Chemicals
- listing *31*
- mixing *28*
- terms *30*

Chrysotype *87*
Cliche verre *139*
Cloth, printing on *147*
Coating methods *33*
Collotype *9*
Combination printing *151*
Contact printing frames *16, 37*
Contrast control *40*
Cyanotype printing
- cyanotype *2, 76*
- details & method *71*
- troubleshooting *74*

Densitometry *42*
Density *43*
Dishes *17*
Editions *153*
Emulsion printing *91*
Equipment *15*
Exposure *37*
Fabric prints *147*
Film choice *41*
Fixing *51*
Fox Talbot *47*
Gelabrome *106*
Gold toning *53*
Gold printing *87*
Graduates *17*
Gum printing *109*
Hand made paper *19*
Health & safety *27*
Herschel, Sir John *71*
Hypo clearing *52*
Intaglio printing *118*
Kallitype *63*
Labelling chemicals *28*
Limited editions *153*
Line film *42*
Lith materials *44*
Machine made paper *22*
Measuring solutions *17*
Mixing chemicals *29*
Mordant prints *148*
Mould-made paper *21*
Mounting prints *153*
Negatives, making *39*
Niepce *11*
Oil printing *99*
Palladium printing *81*
Papers
- comparison table *25*
- hand made *19*
- machine made *22*
- mould made *21*

Paper negatives *44*
Paper sizing *23, 52*
Pellet printing *79*
Photo etching *119*
Photographic papers *92*
Photogravure *125*
Planographic printiing *118*
pH *30*
Platinotype *81*
Platinum printing
- details & method *81*
- troubleshooting *87*

POP *61*
Presentation *153*
Printing out paper *61*
Reading list *156*
Registration methods *38*
Relief printing *117*
Resources *155*
Rod coating *34*
Sabattier effect *45*
Salting paper *49*
Salt printing
- details & method *47*
- troubleshooting *54*
- variations *52*

Scales *17*
Selenium toner *52*
Silkscreen printing *133*
Solvent transfer *145*
Sources of supply *158*
Step tablet *42*
Supercoating on paper *92*
Temperaprint *114*
Tone separations *45*
Toning
- gold *52*
- palladium & platinum *62*
- selenium *52*

UV light sources *15*
Van Dyke
- printing *63*
- troubleshooting *67*

Web sites *155*
Wood, printing on *150*